Take Up Your Mission

Mormon Colonizing Along the Little Colorado River 1870-1900

Charles S. Peterson

The University of Arizona Press
Tucson, Arizona

About the Author . . .

CHARLES S. PETERSON, a native of the Little Colorado country, whose forbears participated in the Mormon migration to Arizona, has been privileged as few others in the field to carry out his research directly from tremendously rich primary sources. Among his published works, his biographical sketch "A Mighty Man Was Brother Lot" won the Oscar O. Winther Award for the best article appearing in the *Western Historical Quarterly* for 1970. Associate Professor of History at Utah State University, and Associate Editor of the *Western Historical Quarterly*, he previously served as Dean of Instruction at the College of Eastern Utah, as Professor of History at the University of Utah, and as Assistant Secretary-Treasurer of the Organization of American Historians. Additionally, he served as Director of the Utah Historical Society and as Editor of the *Utah Historical Quarterly* for three years.

THE UNIVERSITY OF ARIZONA PRESS

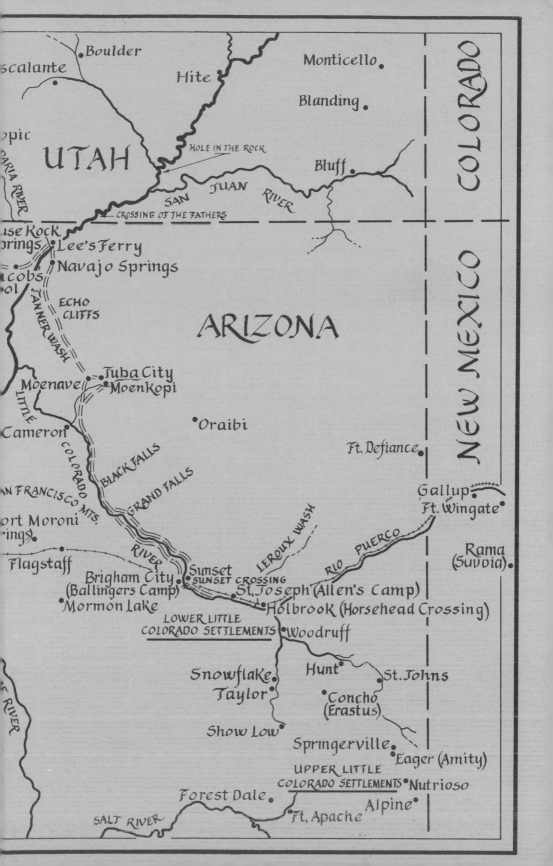

PREFACE

MORMON COLONIZATION in northern Arizona during the last decades of
the nineteenth century constitutes an important episode in the frontier
experience of the Latter-day Saints as well as in the broader fabric of
America's conquest of a continent. In a very real way it was a rerun of a
colonizing drama that had first played at Jamestown and Plymouth Rock
and had appeared previously with an all-Mormon cast in Missouri, in
Illinois, and in the Great Basin. Coming at a relatively late date in the
course of the frontier experience, the colonization of the Little Colorado
River country provides a unique opportunity to study the methods of
Mormon expansion.

In writing this book it has been my primary purpose to portray the
various patterns and processes by which Mormon colonizing progressed.
Because the Saints had already had more than thirty years experience in
the arid West, the goals and techniques of Mormon colonization were
well worked out and thoroughly understood by church leaders and lay
members alike by the 1870s when the colony was established. Yet the
formative years took place before the church had begun to abandon its
most peculiar characteristics, which included polygamy and the practice of
organized expansion. Initially attractive to the Latter-day Saints because
it appeared to be of so little value that others would not want it, northern
Arizona actually proved to be a converging point where Mormons came
face to face with other expansive forces. This confrontation resulted in a
highly organized and prolonged effort on the part of the Mormons to
establish themselves.

Rarely have humans been more preoccupied with recording their
activities than have Latter-day Saints. But Mormons, generally, pale by
comparison to Little Colorado settlers in this respect. They were prodi-

gious diarists whose fine chronicles were fleshed out with official and private correspondence, church records, newspapers, government reports, and non-Mormon sources. The church is front and center — the dominant element in the colonizing process. Spiritual life, education and culture, economic doings, Indian relations, and politics all emerge. Each of these in its own way may be recognized as an element of expansion.

During the period in which the Little Colorado was settled, Mormons were activated by a strong expansionist impulse that was essentially of and for the church. A basic precept of Mormon faith was the speedy advent of Jesus Christ. "Destiny's children," theirs was the obligation to ready the way for His coming. Together with vigorous proselyting and the gathering impulse of the Mormons, this destiny expressed itself in the establishment of a Mormon region — sometimes referred to as the King-dom of God. Paralleling America's manifest destiny impulse in certain of its aspects, Mormon expansiveness reflected a strong southward bent. Arizona, Mexico, and even South America fell within its aspiration. Granting that defensive reaction to the anti-polygamy campaign of these same years, as well as economic pressures growing from large Mormon families, had much to do with the outward push, the movement into Arizona was nevertheless fundamentally the product of the Mormon conviction that colonization was an imperative in the unfolding of God's will. This conviction made haste necessary and sacrifice a duty.

The colony itself — its towns, aspirations, and experiences, and above all, its personalities — appear in the primary records with vivid strength: a cross-section of humanity, grained and textured with man's failings; a cross-section highlighted by soaring ideals, sense of mission, and the heroic.

Without analyzing the relationship of human cost to social achieve-ment, we should note that the Little Colorado frontier was hostile. Over-ruling this fact — perhaps without full realization of the cost of so doing — church leaders drove settlers to a life that was austere if not indeed cruel. The reality of colonization's product — modest homes for a few thousand souls — fell far short of the representation — a teeming unit in an ongoing system that would fill the world. Finally I must cast the Little Colorado of the Mormon pioneer period as a positive experience. It was a success; the patterns and processes on which it developed were inge-nious and effective. To those for whom the colony became home, its life was good, its cost justified, and in the main its prospects sufficient.

C. S. P.

ACKNOWLEDGMENTS

IT IS WITH REAL PLEASURE that I recognize my indebtedness and express thanks for the help given me in the preparation of this book. The materials and research facilities of the University of Arizona Library, the Arizona Historical Society Library, the Arizona Historical Foundation, the Arizona Department of Library and Archives, the Brigham Young University Library, the University of Utah Library, the Utah State Historical Society, and finally and most importantly the Historical Department of the Church of Jesus Christ of Latter-day Saints have been made available to me. For the efficient and gracious help of the personnel of each of these institutions I am indebted and express my gratitude. Also most kind and helpful were the National Archives and the Publicity Division of the Atchison, Topeka, and Santa Fe Railroad at Chicago, who processed numerous inquiries and sent much information by mail.

A Graduate Research Fellowship from the University of Utah and two leaves of absence arranged by John W. Tucker, former director of the College of Eastern Utah, provided funds and time to make the original research possible. I would like to express my esteem and appreciation to the University of Utah history faculty — to David E. Miller, A. Russell Mortensen, and particularly to C. Gregory Crampton, who helped formulate the approach of this study and encouraged and helped me on many occasions. Leonard J. Arrington, Church Historian, and S. George Ellsworth of Utah State University have also been very helpful, particularly during the latter phases of production.

Recognition is given to the Board of Trustees of the Utah State Historical Society, who have encouraged me to complete this undertaking.

A great number of people have helped in various ways during the course of research and writing. To each I express my thanks. Of special helpfulness were George S. Tanner of Salt Lake City and Silas L. Fish of Phoenix, who, because of long-time interest in the history of the Little Colorado, have been able to direct my attention to numerous materials, and possibly more importantly have given me the advantage of their experience and insight.

Robert Russen, who so painstakingly prepared the maps for the book, deserves special mention. In addition, I am appreciative of the work of the University of Arizona Press in bringing out this book under its imprint.

Appreciative mention should be made of my mother Lydia Savage Peterson, whose feeling for the Little Colorado community has in large measure become my own. Of greatest sentimental and practical importance has been the enthusiasm, patience, and support of my family, especially my wife Betty, whose call to the Little Colorado came from my own preoccupation with it.

C. S. P.

CONTENTS

ILLUSTRATIONS

1. OF BEGINNINGS AND FAILURES

> . . . at least while in the circumstances in which we are at present placed, good countries are not for us. The worst places in the land we can probably get, and we must develop them. If we were to find a good country how long would it be before the wicked would want it and seek to strip us of our possessions?
>
> GEORGE Q. CANNON

> . . . I do not know that it makes any difference whether a country is barren or fruitful if the Lord has a work to do in it.
>
> HENRY HOLMES

THE SPRING OF 1876 was a time of colonization along northern Arizona's Little Colorado River. One of the groups that arrived intent on locating on the broken terrain of its wind-seared banks was a party of young Bostonians. They had been recruited by one Samuel W. Cozzens, an author of some reputation who had lectured extensively in New England on the advantages of northern Arizona, with which he presumably was well acquainted. Representing the valley of the Little Colorado as a verdant and beautiful area hidden by its remoteness, Cozzens' glowing words excited so much interest that he at length joined other promoters to organize the American Colonization Company, with the immediate objective of settling on the northern Arizona stream.[1]

---

1 Cozzens also wrote a book in which he imaginatively extols Arizona's virtues. Challenging the reader to "accompany us in our travels," he promises to "convince you that Arizona is the most marvellous portion of this wonderful country — America." Only passing reference is made to the Little Colorado River, which he writes of as the River of Flax, or Rio Chiquito. See *The Marvelous Country or Three Years in Arizona and New Mexico* (Boston: Lee and Shepard Publishers, 1876), p. 45.

About one hundred recruits, most of them unmarried men, joined under Cozzens' banner and lightheartedly set out for the West. Taking only thirty pounds of baggage each, they traveled by train to the end of the track west of Santa Fe. There they purchased six wagons, a few implements, and a string of worn-out mules, and forged on, now forced to make their way on foot. By the time the front ranks reached the Little Colorado about April 15, the glamour that had attached to it in Cozzens' imaginative representation had been seriously tarnished by the difficulties of the desert trail.

Disillusion was sharpened when the Bostonians discovered that a Mormon colony had preceded them into the region by three weeks. Nonplussed and with mounting resentment, they gingerly picked their way through the Mormons, on to a site that later would become Flagstaff, where they established a temporary camp. There they fashioned a flagpole which gave the place its name, explored a little, and considered legal action against the expedition's promoters. In the end they scattered, to be caught up in mining and other activities of the West or to return home. Ill-conceived and naively conducted, the expedition left little mark of its passing, and its very defeat was soon engulfed by time.[2]

The American Colonization Company, however, was not the only organized effort to settle and fail in the valley of the Little Colorado. Three years earlier, a Mormon party of about the same size, after a brief sojourn in northern Arizona, likewise abandoned its plan to colonize. Although its failure was, if anything, more complete than that of the Boston Company, the Mormon expedition of 1873 had not followed will-o'-the-wisp pretenses, nor was its personnel inexperienced or uninformed about the general nature of the country. Long interested in the south as a possible region of expansion, the church had been collecting data on northern Arizona for nearly a generation. Most of it was the product of firsthand exploration and observation.

The earliest Mormon penetration of Arizona from north to south may well have occurred in 1854. During that year a party headed by William Huntington is said to have made a "trip of discovery among the Navajos." Although its doings are almost entirely obscured by time, this party likely cached the supplies retrieved near present Moab by the Elk

---

[2] For accounts of the Boston party, see James H. McClintock, *Morman Settlement in Arizona: A Record of Peaceful Conquest of the Desert* (Phoenix: Manufacturing Stationers, Inc., 1921), pp. 149-50; *Deseret News* (Salt Lake City), June 14, July 19, and September 20, 1876; *Arizona Miner* (Prescott), April 18 and 26, 1876.

Mountain Mission of 1855.[3] If this assumption is correct, the party's quest carried it far into southeastern Utah, and not inconceivably into northern Arizona, as it visited extensive Indian ruins characteristic of that part of the country.

There can be no doubt that during the summer of 1855 Arizona was visited by members of the Elk Mountain Mission. Alfred Billings, who headed that expedition, took a small party of explorers south from their headquarters at present-day Moab, going beyond the San Juan River into Arizona. Fairly bristling with Indian and Anglo place-names, directions, mileages, and other geographic information, Billings' journal traces the course of the southward journey in such detail as to preclude the possibility that his interest in the route was casual or for the limited purpose of one trip. But if he or the church had immediate plans to extend the Mormon frontier into northern Arizona, they were forced to abandon them when the Elk Mountain Mission was driven from Moab by irate Indians before the summer of 1855 was over.[4]

Later, more important explorations were conducted by Indian missionaries from southwestern Utah. Beginning in 1858 and extending until the early 1870s, Jacob Hamblin and a handful of associates made periodic visits to the mesa villages of the Hopis. Opening trails through the canyons from the northeast and around the Grand Canyon from the southwest, they discovered the major crossings of the river and picked out waterholes along which roads south were later developed. They became well acquainted with the northern deserts of Arizona but do not appear to have explored the Little Colorado River except for a few miles immediately above a crossing low on its course.

In addition to having this direct exposure, Mormons had good opportunity to acquire knowledge through close contact with John Wesley Powell and other government explorers. At loggerheads with Congress over the polygamy question, the church, nevertheless, cooperated closely with official surveyors, and a congenial relationship existed in which interchange of information seems likely. Contact was not limited to Jacob Hamblin, who worked extensively with Powell. Others, including Brigham Young and many of the Little Colorado settlers, make reference to meetings with survey parties in Salt Lake City and in the field.

---

[3] Letter of George A. Smith to F. D. Richards, December 1854, quoted in *The Latter-day Saints' Millennial Star* (Liverpool), vol. 17 (1855), p. 253. Also see "Memorandum, Account Book and Diary of Alfred N. Billings, 1855," typescript Brigham Young University Library [hereafter BYU].

[4] "Diary of Alfred N. Billings."

In 1870 the Navajos, who had carried on intermittent raids along Utah's southern frontier since 1865, were pacified, permitting the resumption of a southward movement that had long been an important element of Mormon colonization. With the establishment of settlements at Kanab, Pipe Springs, Paria, and Lee's Ferry between 1870 and 1873, the approach to Arizona was secured. This cautious extension was accompanied by the development of plans for a broad scale and far-reaching movement south.

Truly remarkable in scope, these plans are best understood in light of Mormon attitudes toward expansion. In this respect the practices of polygamy and the gathering were both influential. In the case of the former, it was a matter of space in which to maneuver, with the territorial and even national bounds of Arizona and Mexico being regarded more as assets than barriers. Where the gathering was concerned, space was of course seen in terms of the population's relation to resources and opportunity. But underlying these practical determinants was a profound doctrinal commitment to expansion that ran through the entire rhetoric and conduct of church leaders and Little Colorado pioneers alike.

At an early time Mormons had conceived of a specific gathering place — one especially designated and hallowed, and one they regarded as their own with a fervor that was at once religious and nationalistic. At

— *Utah State Historical Society*
"Windsor Castle," at Pipe Springs, on the Arizona strip.

Cabin at Old Paria in southern Utah.

first this special Zion was small, a clearly defined area in Missouri. Although the concept of Missouri as the geographic center of their system remained, and for that matter has continued to be of peculiar importance, Mormon ideology soon broadened, taking on many of the aspects and aspirations of empire.

This stretch of ideology is especially dependent upon the events of 1844. At an April conference of the church in that year, Joseph Smith dramatically elaborated an "America the promised land" doctrine taken from the Book of Mormon. Couching his remarks in the spirit and imagery of the Manifest Destiny impulse, which was at its height, he conceived of a Mormon destiny no longer limited to a refuge in some narrow Zion but spreading as the Kingdom of God over the two American continents.[5] After Smith's assassination later in 1844, the thinking and policy of nineteenth century Mormons were never free of the obligation implied by this destiny. With Mexico and in due time even South America as goals, the southward bent of their colonization was its reflection.

In its 1873 phase, the plan was the product of Brigham Young and that long-time and visionary friend of the Latter-day Saints, Thomas L.

[5] Joseph Smith, *History of the Church of Jesus Christ of Latter-day Saints* (7 vols., 2 ed. rev., Salt Lake City: *Deseret News,* 1948), vol. 6, pp. 318-22. [Hereafter *Documentary History of the Church.*]

Kane.[6] Spending most of the winter of 1872-73 together at St. George in southern Utah, the two men conceived of a far-flung movement, one that would establish a second great gathering place in Mexico's Sonora Valley. There were, as Kane suggestively put it, "fortified gardens in Mexico: cradles that will expand with the growth of a Nation in them . . . and rich and well watered as any of the historical valleys of the East renowned in past ages as the Seats of Empire."[7] Planning to connect the new empire to Utah by "intermediate piers" after the fashion of the "Mormon Corridor" to California, Young and Kane apparently hoped that it might be served by a seaport at Guaymos and a railroad extending to the projected Southern Pacific line in southern Arizona. Agreeing to a coordinated effort, they separated in the spring of 1873, Kane to initiate a discreet drive to acquire a large Mexican land grant, and Young to launch the physical movement in that direction.[8]

Acting even before Kane departed, Young hastily dispatched what was known as the Arizona Exploring Company in December of 1872 to make one last reconnaissance. Consisting of fourteen men, the party was directed to visit both the Little Colorado River and the Rio Verde country south of the San Francisco Mountains. This group was headed by Lorenzo Roundy, bishop at the southern Utah town of Kanarraville, and included such veterans of the Indian mission as Jacob Hamblin, Ira Hatch, and Andrew Gibbons, all of whom had been to Arizona on previous occasions.[9] Betraying the influence of the scientific methods of the government surveys that were by this time working in southern Utah, the reconnaissance party's instructions included a directive to gather specimens of fossils, rocks, and soil, and to label the same, noting the place and conditions

---

[6] An active and sympathetic friend of the Mormons prior to 1860, Kane had little to do with them during the 1860s. As the antipolygamy campaign increased in tempo at the end of that decade, Brigham Young again sought Kane's aid, and an extensive correspondence was carried on through the mails and by personal visits from Young's sons and other representatives. After repeated invitations, Kane paid a call upon the Mormon prophet in the fall of 1872.

[7] Letter of Thomas L. Kane to Brigham Young, March 2, 1877, Brigham Young Letters, Historical Department of the Church of Jesus Christ of Latter-day Saints, previously known as the Church Historian's Office [hereafter HDC].

[8] Their ideas about railroad connections were vague and speculative. Nevertheless, they did give the matter some thought and carried on correspondence relative to it. See letter of Thomas Wright to Brigham Young, February 15, 1873, and Thomas L. Kane to Brigham Young, December 4, 1873, Brigham Young Letters, HDC.

[9] Hamblin was charged with supervision of the expedition's Indian affairs, as well as with the responsibility of arranging for guides and Indian runners to bear communications between the explorers and Utah. See James G. Bleak, "Annals of the Southern Utah Mission," HDC, Book B, p. 30, and Robert Glass Cleland and Juanita Brooks, eds., *A Mormon Chronicle: The Diaries of John D. Lee, 1848-1876* (2 vols., San Marino, California: The Huntington Library, 1955), vol. 2, p. 226.

of origin. They were also to make note of the topography and drainage of the country through which they passed.[10]

After crossing the Colorado River on February 2, the party proceeded south, separating near Moenkopi, with Hamblin and Ira Hatch going to Oraibi to pick up a guide while the remainder worked out a wagon route down Moenkopi Wash to the Little Colorado River. Reaching the river, Roundy followed up its course, passing both Black and Grand Falls to what he referred to as the "Butterfield mail road."[11] Rejoined at this point by Hamblin and Hatch, the party abandoned its southeast course for a westerly one, exploring the Rio Verde before turning to cross the snow-covered San Francisco Mountains en route to Moenkopi and Lee's Ferry, where it arrived on February 26.

Roundy found the Little Colorado to be an inhospitable and forbidding waste. This much was patent. It was patent as he and his comrades picked their way through the volcanic deposits, the sand drifts, and the painted deserts that flanked the river. It was also patent in his written report of the expedition. Yet Roundy did not condemn the country, nor did he recommend that plans for its colonization be abandoned. A seeming contradiction, this attitude is not surprising — indeed it could hardly be otherwise. Long before Roundy and his chilled band plodded the winter miles of their exploration, the web of Mormon experience had woven itself around church doctrine in such a way as to virtually dictate his response to Arizona.

As indicated previously, the Manifest Destiny impulse of the 1840s had a sequel in the Mormon destiny to spread God's earthly kingdom over the western hemisphere. In part it was religious theory. But it was also a matter and condition of the heart. Stubborn and almost practical in their confidence that Christ's second coming and the literal establishment of God's earthly kingdom was imminent, Mormons regarded themselves as the people of destiny, chosen to foster and hasten the day when Christ should reign over his kingdom in a physical and personal way. In this connection the concept of redemption is central. Man and the world in which he lived were in a wicked and ungodly state. The redemption of the righteous was the first imperative and implied the second, the redemption of the earth. Cosmic in its breadth, this doctrine found practical expression in the Mormon missionary system and in repeated efforts to lay claim to specific sectors of the American frontier. In the early years of the church the redemption of the earthly base for God's kingdom, like

[10] Bleak, "Annals," Book B, p. 30. There is no indication that the directive to collect scientific data was complied with.

[11] *Deseret News,* May 28, 1873.

the redemption of souls, was primarily a social matter — specifically a process of reclaiming regions of Missouri and later Illinois from a worldly society already in possession of the area. This attempt to monopolize entire regions, along with other peculiarities, led to friction and ultimately to the expulsion of the Saints from the Midwest.

Two new and related aspects become apparent in the Mormon destiny as they turn to the Great Basin. In the first place, their tragic experience in the Midwest led them to embrace fully a policy of self-help that had long been implicit in their chosen people concept of themselves. Paralleling the states rights impulse, Mormon self-help in turn resulted in a preemptive expansion — an expansion calculated to establish the first claim to unattractive and little wanted areas. Growing from this was a shift in the nature of that part of the redemptive process pertaining to the land. What in Missouri and Illinois had been a competitive struggle to redeem land from the wicked had now become, in large part, a struggle to redeem land from hostile natural forces. Deeming that God's will and their destiny as His chosen servants gave them the best possible claim to the American continent, Mormons now expanded along the line of least resistance. Unable and unwilling to compete with the flood tide of western movement into attractive areas, they found in the voids of unwanted deserts both the opportunity to "redeem the kingdom" and evidence that God willed their expansion to follow the course it took.

The Mormon concept of God's will was an element of profound importance in this as in other connections. Indeed the mantle of God's will was thrown over the whole of their movement. Found everywhere and in all sorts of promptings, its clearest manifestation in the early years of Arizona colonization was in the person of church President Brigham Young. As prophet, seer, and revelator, his interest in the southward movement was taken by himself and many, if not most, of his followers, to be God's will. Typical was the old Indian missionary Jacob Hamblin who often repeated that he and other early explorers had been told by Brigham Young that since Salt Lake City would one day come under Gentile rule it was God's will that the church "go into Sanora [sic]. . . ."[12]

Nor was Young the only leader who regarded the colonization to the south to be a divine imperative. Perhaps no one expressed the idea that God willed Mormons to take such lands as they were able to claim more cogently than did George Q. Cannon, who was both a general authority in the church and Utah's territorial delegate. Speaking during the summer of 1873 immediately after the initial bid to "lengthen the cords of Zion" into northern Arizona had failed, he assured church members that

---

[12] Minutes of Eastern Arizona Stake Conferences, 1879-1882," HDC, p. 180.

retraction from beyond the Colorado River was only temporary because "the time must come when the Latter-day Saints . . . will extend throughout all North and South America, and we shall establish the rule of righteous and good order throughout all these new countries. . . ." He continued:

If there be deserts in Arizona, thank God for the deserts. If there be wilderness there, thank God for the wilderness. . . . When we go hence to extend our borders we must not expect to find a land of orange or lemon groves, a land where walnut trees and hard timber abound; where bees are wild and turkeys can be had for the shooting. It is vain for us to expect to settle in such a land at the present time. But if we find a little oasis in the desert where a few can settle, thank God for the oasis, and thank him for the almost interminable road that lies between that oasis and so-called civilization.

Further elaborating his point he told his listeners that:

. . . at least while in the circumstances in which we are at present placed, good countries are not for us. The worst places in the land we can probably get, and we must develop them. If we were to find a good country how long would it be before the wicked would want it and seek to strip us of our possessions?[13]

That even the Little Colorado might be too good was the fear of another leader, Brigham Young's counselor Daniel H. Wells, when on the occasion of the first top-level visitation to Arizona he told settlers that he feared "the country was too good and we would not be able to keep it from our enemies."[14]

Lay members were thoroughly conversant with these ideas and in varying degrees gave them credence. Although the mission that followed Lorenzo Roundy's trail to Arizona in 1873 wilted and retreated before the new territory's drought and heat, many of its members thought the question was not whether the country would sustain life but whether or not God willed their presence there. Characteristic were the words of missionary Henry Holmes, who in a long letter written while in the south mused: "I do not know that it makes any difference whether a country is barren or fruitful, if the Lord has a work to do in it."[15] In seeing God's will as a most important norm, Holmes spoke not only for himself but for the Roundy explorers and many a Latter-day Saint who later made his way into Arizona.

With Brigham Young, whose mind was already fixed, the question also had little to do with the nature of the country. To him it was rather a matter of determination or lack thereof on the part of his subordinates. This was clear in 1873 when, hearing that the Arizona mission had failed,

---

[13] *Journal of Discourses* (26 vols., Liverpool, 1854-1886), vol. 16, pp. 143-44.
[14] "Frihoff G. Nielson Diary 1875-1935," typescript, HDC, June 4, 1876.
[15] *Millenial Star*, 35 (1873): 534.

he rose before a Salt Lake City audience and grim with anger thundered that had he himself been in Arizona "there would have been good places found."[16]

Understanding Young's determination and sharing the general Mormon tendency to let the traditional values of the church obscure practical evidence, Lorenzo Roundy had seen the Little Colorado's stark reality but reported it fit for settlement. Ironically but significantly, the less thorough his examination the more hopeful his report. As he approached the southeast limits of his penetration, a country rarely if ever traversed by Mormons before, the valley of the Little Colorado took on increased promise. Finally pausing before turning back, he mounted a lonely eminence and swept the bleak horizon ahead with his field glass. Like Frey Marcos de Niza to whose fevered eye desert distance and deep desire had transformed squalid Zuni villages into the fabled Cities of Cibola, Roundy saw not broken and arid desert but a promising country much like the "Illinois Prairie."[17]

Completing his role in this particular rendezvous with destiny when he wrote his report on March 7, 1873, Roundy had only to wait. With Brigham Young's energy fully behind the project, his wait was short, and by the latter part of April a colonizing mission retraced his trail into Arizona.

Beginning auspiciously enough with numerous advantages that the Boston company of three years later would not be able to boast, the Mormon mission of 1873 was, nevertheless, inadequately prepared for the conditions it was to face. Called about the first of March, two hundred fifty missionaries were directed to take the road south as soon as winter broke. Of this number, only about a hundred men, a few women, and one child appear to have gotten under way before the mission was abandoned.[18] Field management for the entire undertaking fell upon ailing

---

[16] *Journal of Discourses,* vol. 16, pp. 143-44.

[17] Report of Lorenzo Roundy to Brigham Young, Lorenzo Roundy Personal File. Also report of Horton D. Haight to Brigham Young, August 4, 1873, Horton D. Haight Personal File, HDC. Anthony W. Ivins, who visited the area in 1875, recorded the following, which if stated seriously and correctly raises some question as to the Roundy company's powers of observation: "I remembered what Bishop Roundy . . . said about the country at St. George before I left home. He said they found cottonwoods on the Little Colorado but they were stunted and crooked, probably caused by the turkeys roosting in them so much." See "Anthony Woodward Ivins Journal," original, HDC, November 9, 1875, p. 41.

[18] See "Reminiscence by Brigham Young Perkins" written in 1919 that appears under "Arizona Mission" in the "South West Indian Mission History," compiled by Andrew Jensen, HDC. Also see letter of Brigham Young to Joseph W. Young, March 10, 1873, Brigham Young Letters, HDC, in which the latter is informed that, excluding the Cache County conscription, 165 designees met in Salt Lake City and received instructions from Brigham Young personally.

Joseph W. Young, who as stake president at St. George appears to have been second in command in southern Utah to Apostle Erastus Snow. Making hasty preparations, including the designation of Horton D. Haight as president of the mission, Young began meeting the emigrants early in April at Pipe Springs, where he organized them into companies of not over ten wagons and sent them on, guided by various members of the Roundy party. The first of these groups crossed at Lee's Ferry on April 22; others soon followed. Sensing that the groundwork had been hastily laid, or belatedly realizing they were expected to lay it themselves, a few began to find fault with both the management and the objectives of the mission by the time they reached the ferry. Ultimately affecting many of the missionaries, the leaven of discontent was, of course, an important factor in the mission's unsuccessful outcome.

Henry Day, a captain of a company that arrived at Lee's Ferry on May 26, was particularly disgusted with the frustrations of pioneering and wasted no breath in so informing ferryman John D. Lee. Day offended Lee by deriding the Kaibab road and the ferry as well as laying strong criticism at the feet of the church when he called the ferry "a Poor Shitten arrangement" and declared that the "company never Should have been Sent on a Mission until a good Road and Ferry had been Made first &c." Indignant, Lee gave as good as he took, quickly putting Day in his place and finding comfort in the fact "that few if any endorsed his remarks."[19]

South of the river, Haight inched his way, taking no less than twenty-six days to bring the bulk of his party the seventy miles from the ferry to Moenkopi. There missionaries wasted precious time awaiting the arrival of later contingents. A few acres of ground were broken and crops planted, but no explorations were ventured beyond a day's trip from the Moenkopi springs. For the most part, missionaries loafed and played games; some even wrote poetry. Finally on May 21, Haight got them started on toward the Little Colorado, which the first of them reached grimy and dispirited the next day, after a sandy haul down Moenkopi Wash, which was made particularly miserable by one of the region's characteristic spring winds. After eating the sand of those two wind scorched days, one journalist found wry comfort in the fact that "we will hev suffishent gritt to stand a few hardships."[20]

By now thoroughly shaken, the missionaries were not heartened by the river. Indeed it suited them no better than it had Powell's men four years before, who pausing at its confluence with the Colorado before

---

[19] Cleland and Brooks, *Mormon Chronicle,* vol. 2, pp. 240-41.
[20] Andrew Amundsen, "Journal of a Mission to the San Francisko Mountains, Commenced March 26th, 1873," original, HDC, May 23, 1873.

plunging on down the canyon had found it to be "a loathsome little stream
. . . as disgusting a stream as there is on the continent."[21]

Even a loathsome stream would have been welcomed by the missionaries, who found the Little Colorado rapidly drying up. Disconcerted,
Haight called a halt a few miles after striking the river at a spot later known
as Camp Utah. Sending a messenger to the telegraph line in southern
Utah for instruction, he continued on horseback, exploring upstream with
a chosen party. Proceeding some 120 miles, they concluded that the
country was uninhabitable and turned homeward. One member of the
mounted reconnaissance, a Norwegian missionary named Andrew Amundsen, left the following misspelled but vivid appraisal:

From the first we struck the little Collorado . . . , it is the seam thing all the
way, no plase fit for a human being to dwell upon. In case of hie water the
bottoms are all floded, [there is] no please for a dam for if we could get plenty
of water it would back op about 6 or 8 miles op the Rivver and the Cottonwood is so scrubby and crukked so it would only be fit for fierr wood. No
rock for bilding, no pine timber within 50 or 75 miles of her. Wher ever
you may luck the country is all broken op. The moste desert lukking plase
that I ever saw, Amen.[22]

This negative report occasioned a further slip in morale at Camp
Utah, which together with the failing supply of grass and water led Haight
to order the camp to fall back and await further orders from Brigham
Young. Not yet fully aware they were defeated, but bitter in their disappointment, the missionaries sought to allay their chagrin with an unlikely
musical group. Amundsen tells:

We riged op a Band, consisted on one fiddle, one Pickelo, and the rest tin
pans and kittles. We then went out and wellcomed the Captain on his retreat
from Arizona, we had a good time.[23]

Drummed by this makeshift band, the expedition heavily retraced its steps
through blue hummocked badlands to Moenkopi.

While they marked time there, an interesting exchange took place
between anonymous members of the expedition that revealed something of the tension they were under as well as certain deeply ingrained
Mormon values. On Friday, June 13, according to one account, "some
of the boys" raised a rock "in a conspicuous place at the spring" on which
they had inscribed "Arizona Mission Dead — 1873." During the following
night, a writer who used the name "Faith Hope Charity" left a poem

---

21 William Culp Darrah, ed., "George Y. Bradley's Journal" and "J. C. Sumner's Journal," entries for August 10 and 11, 1869, *Utah Historical Quarterly* 15
(1947): 61, 119.

22 Amundsen, "Journal," May 28, 1873.

23 *Ibid.,* June 5, 1873.

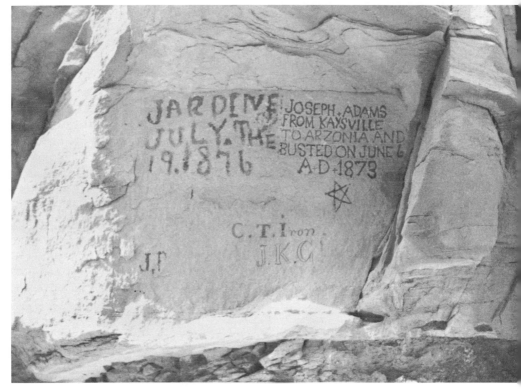

Concise history of the "Mission of '73" at House Rock Springs.

entitled "Arizona Mission Dead Old Doubtful." Beginning "Thou Fool, This Mission is not dead, it only sleeps," the writer invoked such Mormon articles of faith as God's omnipotence, the church's mission to carry "the Gospel" to the Indians, and the fall of "this wicked nation" before he concluded:

> Saints should *not* murmur
> nor this land despise
> Those who do so,
> Certainly are not wise
> Did not God create it?
> Does he not understand?
> What best will suit his purpose?
> A fruitful or baren land.[24]

---

[24] "Journals of John Henry Standifird, 1831-1923," typescript Arizona State Department of Libraries and Archives, Phoenix, Arizona [hereafter ALA], pp. 28-30.

The following night, a writer who signed himself "Hurry Home" came to the defense of the personnel of the mission and advised the writer of the previous night to lay his "perturbed feelings on the shelf . . . nor spend [his] genius, carping at the boys" but to challenge "Doubtful," who was "old Satan's tool."[25]

Having relieved the boredom of their situation and assuaged their consciences, the missionaries made their way on to the river, completely unmoved by the grandeur of the Echo Cliffs lining the Hamblin and Tanner washes through which they toiled. Not having heard to the contrary, they recrossed the Colorado between July 4 and 7. Before belated word to stay in Arizona finally came from Salt Lake City, they had separated with Haight's blessings and were picking their way back into Utah, spreading reports of the country's bad qualities as they went.[26] Although certain members of the mission remained in the south awaiting its revival, the damage had been done, and it remained for another mission in a later year to settle successfully on the Little Colorado.

---

[25] *Ibid.*

[26] One missionary who failed to get under way before the group that had gone to Arizona returned told of meeting "One Stanger of Ogden north of Salt Lake: who had been on the Arizona Mission. Stanger spoke very discouragingly of the country. The whole face of the land is full of mineral. Land and grass are alike full of the *stuff*. Every thing is parched up and the heat is intense during the day — termometer [*sic*] at 136° in the shade — and during the month of June ice froze quite often during the night. . . . When he arrived at the Little Colorado there was quite a stream of brackish and unhealthful water but suddenly dried up. He said however if the whole Seviere was running down there there could not be a settlement made there in consequence of the mineral, heat — frost — the unfertility of the soil — and etc — In relation to what President Young sent by telegraph about the brethren remaining here till fall he said that they would not stay if he should come with Jesus Christ himself (*he* is going to Ogden)." "Diary of Levi Savage, 1873," original owned by Joseph Savage, Chandler, Arizona; typescript in possession of author, pp. 9-10.

2. VILLAGES ALONG THE LITTLE COLORADO

In fact this location lacked but two essentials — climate and market.

EVANS COLEMAN

LIKE THE BOSTON PARTY, the missionaries of 1873 went their diverse ways. But, unlike the Bostonians, their escape to anonymity was not complete and, unlike the American Colonizing Company, the mother institution suffered neither collapse nor loss of resolve. However, the plan to settle the Little Colorado was postponed — postponed for a far longer period than Brigham Young anticipated when he announced in a public meeting in August of 1873 his intent to personally lead a new colony south immediately after October conference. In spite of oft-repeated promises, neither he nor anyone else ventured to the Little Colorado that fall, and it was only after a lapse of nearly three years that colonization was resumed.

Exploration and Settlement of the Lower River, 1875-76

As preliminary measures to this new assault, two exploring parties were sent out late in 1875. One party, under Daniel W. Jones, a Spanish-speaking convert from Mexican War days, was primarily interested in Mexico. Reflecting the influence of Thomas L. Kane's grand scheme to establish a corridor to a Mormon kingdom in Sonora, he sought a route by which not only convenient access to Mexico could be had but which would also sustain a Mormon community along the way. Passing through the Little Colorado country on both his out and return trips, Jones probably came in broader contact with it than any previous Mormon exploration.

His observations bore out those earlier reports that had pictured the region as habitable.[1] Anthony W. Ivins, a member of the Jones party, was much impressed with the country's prospects for grazing and even recorded having seen some promising farm land, but soberly and prophetically reflected as he studied the river that its channel was "wide with quick sand bottom and would probably be difficult to control."[2]

Meanwhile, a more restricted but more thorough exploration was conducted under James S. Brown, missionary to the Indians, who established headquarters at Moenkopi late in 1875. During the next two years, he made northern Arizona, including the Little Colorado, the object of an intensive exploration. Among other things, he located the first area of colonization, opened an alternative, though dry and unattractive, wagon route from Moenkopi to the Little Colorado by way of Oraibi, and became thoroughly acquainted with the Indian country of northern Arizona and northwestern New Mexico.[3]

Finding nothing in the reports submitted by Brown and Jones to deter them, church leaders initiated the settlement of the Little Colorado early in 1876. By March 23, red-bearded and volatile Lot Smith, who is best known in Mormon history for his dramatic attacks upon army supply trains during the Utah War, led the vanguard of settlement on to the alkali bottoms between present-day Holbrook and Winslow. Arriving less than a month before the first of the Boston immigrants appeared, Smith and his colleagues initiated an era of Mormon colonization that extended well into the 1890s. However, the period of most active location was restricted to four years, and by 1880 most of the Little Colorado Basin settlements had been founded and the form of the colony well established.

The pattern of settlement during those four years fell into three rather distinct geographic and chronological phases. The first began and ended in 1876 and was confined to the establishment of four villages about midway along the Little Colorado River's course and to two mission com-

---

[1] Daniel W. Jones, *Forty Years Among the Indians* (Salt Lake City: Juvenile Instructor's Office, 1890), pp. 227-28.

[2] "Anthony Woodward Ivins Journal," pp. 39-42.

[3] It is interesting to note that Brown's tedious probing with its dry marches and physical hardships (Brown had earlier lost a leg and was no longer a young man at this time) was to little avail. His knowledge of the region was personal and beyond a few generalities was never committed to writing, or if it was, was not extensively circulated. The parallel between Mormon exploration as carefully conducted as it was and Cozzens' quick impressions of the Little Colorado is apparent. Unlike the scientific men of the government surveys of the same period, both were subjective, their effectiveness as guides to policy greatly reduced by such variables as weather conditions and the mood of the explorer. James S. Brown, *Life of a Pioneer: Autobiography of James S. Brown* (Salt Lake City: George Q. Cannon & Sons, Co., 1900), pp. 448-77.

munities, one at Moenkopi and one at Savoia, New Mexico, south of Fort Wingate. During 1877 and 1878, a second series of villages were located, this time along the river's major tributary, Silver Creek. The third and final phase took place in 1879 and 1880 along the upper part of the river, thus completing the basic physical outline of the colony. Thereafter occasional mountain villages were established, few of them surviving beyond a year or two.

In 1876 the area of major colonizing effort was focused upon the lower valley of the Little Colorado River. An undesirable region, its choice was the result of several factors. In the first place, its settlers had few alternatives, variables having been fixed in one way or another. The general area had been designated as a place of Mormon settlement by the church leaders who saw advantage even in its high wind, its low rainfall, and its quicksand and alkali.

Another factor that limited selection was the need to break the long journey south into manageable segments. Whether it was viewed as it had been by Brigham Young and Thomas L. Kane as a corridor to an outpost in Mexico or merely as the road to Arizona, prospect of increased migration made the development of a Mormon community on the lower river something of an imperative. Draft animals and other livestock, to say nothing of the pioneers themselves, would have found deeper penetration most difficult if not indeed impossible without a way station at this point. Furthermore, the choice of the lower river, adjacent as it was to several Indian tribes, reflected a long-time preoccupation with Indians as prospective candidates for the gospel's net.

A final limiting consideration was the fact that the lower river was open. Higher up and on Silver Creek, settlers had already claimed the likely agricultural spots and showed no immediate inclination to abandon them. Thus, though not particularly desirable, the lower river area's availability did provide a place of beginning from which it was hoped a community of villages could be extended not only along the entire course of the river but also south to the Salt River Valley and Mexico.

Prompted by these and other factors, the first settlements were established along the lower valley. Arriving on the river, the advance groups met at a rendezvous chosen by James S. Brown near present Joseph City. There they grouped in fifties according to an organization effected earlier in Salt Lake City with Lot Smith, William C. Allen, George Lake, and Jesse O. Ballinger each heading a party, the former asserting general authority over the entire mission. After further exploration, which included plowing occasional furrows in an attempt to determine the mineral content of the soil, Ballinger and Smith retraced their steps westward about twenty-five miles to locate near Sunset Crossing. Allen stayed at or near the rendezvous north of the river, and the Lake company crossed to the south side of the river and located in a low and, as it proved, unhealthy spot about three miles downstream. Thus, within a few days of arrival, four sites were established, with two in close proximity to each other at either end of a twenty-five-mile stretch.[4]

During the earliest months, the camps were known by the names of their respective captains. It was not long, however, until Lake's Camp was renamed Obed or Camp Obed, and Smith's Camp took the name of Sunset from the river crossing near which it was situated. The first attempts to give permanent names to the other camps were less successful, and they were known generally as Ballinger's Camp and Allen's Camp until 1878 when they were renamed Brigham City and St. Joseph.[5]

Townsites selected, settlers wasted no time before beginning to build dams and plant crops. In these endeavors their efforts were joint or communal, with each camp working as a unit.[6] Although they planted fewer acres than they originally hoped, they encountered little difficulty in clearing and breaking ground and putting in crops.

Water constituted a far more difficult problem. Most of the colonists were young men from northern Utah communities with little experience in dealing with the kinds of problems presented by the Little Colorado; nevertheless, they appear to have had some idea as to what needed to be done. Examining the river, they chose the most promising sites, and, while Samuel Ladd, the colony's one trained surveyor, laid out ditches, the others immediately began work on their dams. Constructed with the most limited equipment, these dams were long and low, made primarily of trees, brush, and dirt and rock fill. The dam at Allen's Camp, which was completed on June 6 after two and a half months, stretched 180 feet across the river and was reported to be sixty feet thick and nine feet high.[7] Although

---

[4] See "Joseph City Ward History," compiled by Rulon Porter, HDC, and Kenneth Porter, "Little Colorado River Settlements, Brigham City, Joseph City, Obed, and Sunset" (unpublished master's thesis, Arizona State University, Tempe, 1956). George Tanner of Salt Lake City has given the author much material on the lower river, St. Joseph and the United Order. Tanner is working on a book pertaining to Joseph City and the Little Colorado.

[5] John W. Young, a son and counselor of Brigham Young, gave the camps these names at the time he organized the Little Colorado Stake in 1878. Joseph City's name was later changed to avoid confusion with St. Joseph, Missouri, which also lay along the Santa Fe Railroad. See "Joseph City Ward History," p. 4, and "History of the Little Colorado Stake," compiled by Andrew Jenson, HDC.

[6] Following the direction of church leaders, the settlers lived in the United Order, as Mormon communalism was called. See Chapter 5.

[7] There is some conflict as to the dimensions of this first dam. I have used figures given by Joseph W. McMurrin quoted in the *Deseret News*, June 14, 1876. According to the *Arizona Miner*, June 23, 1876, it was "180 feet long, 40 feet wide, and 18 feet high."

logs had been riprapped in and a great quantity of rock used, the dam held only until July 19 when the first real flood of the year swept it away. At Brigham City the flood cut a new path some 150 feet distant from the dam, leaving it high, dry, and useless.

Thereafter, the toil of construction and the agony of watching the dams go out were oft-repeated experiences on the lower river and, as we shall see, of the entire colony. Church leaders sought to prepare the settlers for such reverses, characteristically admonishing them to persist and learn by failure, and at the same time promising better days. But water development was more than a matter of persistence, it was also a question of sustaining life, and only by the most determined effort and by heavy subsidy were the settlers able to do so.

Unfortunately, farm production tended to vary inversely with the effort to develop water; when the settlers struggled hardest, the season's end often found them with the least to show for it. Dams were gone, ditches out, and little or nothing raised. In 1876 only Sunset produced a crop, and it was said to have been no more than seventy-five bushels of grain and a few melons. Other camps apparently had nothing to show for their efforts. Later they did somewhat better. In 1877 and 1878, for example, St. Joseph harvested 662 and 900 bushels of grain, respectively, and in the latter year produced 1,200 gallons of molasses.[8] Before suffering a sharp decline in productivity, Sunset's farms reached a maximum harvest of 7,000 bushels of grain in 1879, which in the afterglow of the biblically oriented memories of veterans of the Little Colorado resulted in its being referred to as the "Egypt of Arizona" from whose granaries later settlements were succored in their time of need.[9]

Floods which inundated all crops at Sunset and Brigham City in August of 1878 contributed to the failure of an effort to relocate Hopi Indians at those two communities. Never trusting the river, the mesa dwellers had been reluctant to come, but under Mormon importunings sixty of them planted grain and corn during that season. When these crops were destroyed, the Hopis withdrew, refusing to be further enticed.[10]

Generally cautious in its Indian policy, the church was especially anxious to avoid difficulties on this far frontier. Fearing attack and the loss of life, leaders were also apprehensive that discord would invite

---

[8] For production records, see "Joseph City Ward History," pp. 25-35, and "Wilford Woodruff's Journal, January 1st to February 7th, 1880 (A Synopsis of Wilford Woodruff's Travels and Labors taken from His Journal by Himself)," HDC, entry for October 1, 1879.

[9] *Deseret News,* October 30, 1878.

[10] Christian L. Christensen, "Among the Hopis," *Times Independent* (Moab), March 9, 1922.

unfavorable attention to their expansive designs, and they admonished settlers to proceed with the utmost caution, leaving no effort unmade to establish good relations with the Indians. Characteristic of such instructions was a long letter from Brigham Young to Lorenzo Hatch, who had been sent to New Mexico to head up the Indian Mission there. Young wrote:

We desire to impress upon your mind . . . the great necessity of giving no cause of offense to either white or red men. There will no doubt be bad men who will watch for some pretext to get the U. S. officials to interfere with you. To guard as much as possible against these contingencies, be prudent and prayerful. . . .[11]

Church leaders also directed colonists to construct forts as quickly as circumstances would permit. Although there was little fear among the settlers, they complied, building as one of them stated "merely as a precautionary measure."[12] Following similar plans, each camp began construction of hollow, square forts. Varying in size from about 190 feet to 225 feet square, these forts were made of materials available at the various villages — Sunset and Allen's Camp using cottonwood logs in the main, and Brigham City and Obed using red sandstone that abounded in Indian ruins and natural deposits in their neighborhoods. Writing as plans were being laid, young Joseph McMurrin, later a general authority in the church, explained that the Allen's Camp structure would be "built of cottonwood timbers, set firmly in the ground, the walls nine feet high, and of double thickness of logs, surrounded on the inside with houses 12 feet by 26 feet."[13]

Within easy reach of fields, corrals, and stackyards, the forts encompassed wells, shops, and communal mess facilities as well as providing housing for the villagers. Though the settlers anticipated no immediate difficulty, the forts were built with the serious purpose of defense in mind. Elevated guardhouses that extended from the walls were built at two and in some cases four corners, and loopholes constituted the only opening on the outward sides of the homes, which comprised the walls of the fort. Writing in 1878 L. J. Nuttal, a correspondent for the *Deseret News,* described several of the forts. The best of these, his description of the Brigham City fort, follows:

The fort is 200 feet square, a drive way on north and south sides and narrow entrance on east and west. The walls are seven feet high, of rock; there are

---

[11] Letter of September 25, 1876, Brigham Young Letters, HDC.
[12] Letter of Joseph McMurrin, *Deseret News,* July 19, 1876.
[13] *Ibid.*

36 dwelling houses 13 x 15 feet around the inside of the fort, also on the north side, a dining hall 20 x 80 feet. . . . Adjoining the dining hall (on the outside) is a kitchen 20 x 25 feet, also a bakehouse and oven. There are also six dwelling houses adjoining the west side and six partly built on the south side of the fort, a good cellar 18 x 18 feet, and a storehouse built there on; also a good well 25 feet deep, furnishing sufficient water for family and culinary purposes. In side the fort also, another well 24 feet deep near the kitchen. Good corrals and stackyards south of the fort.[14]

At Obed, Brigham City, and Sunset, the forts probably were the only homes ever used, as the villages were deserted before permanent homes were constructed. Even at St. Joseph, the fort was used for many years before private homes fully supplanted it.

Established to support the four villages were a sawmill and several ranches at Pleasant Valley, or Mormon Lake, which lay some forty miles south and west of Sunset on the incline of the Mogollon Rim. Encompassing an oval area about five by six miles in extent, Pleasant Valley was surrounded by splendid stands of yellow pine in which were scatterings of mountain juniper, oak, and other timber. The valley itself was a vast meadow broken only by a lake near its center and amply watered by six springs, all of which rose along its west perimeter. Across to the east was a low volcanic mountain of a reddish color. In this upland paradise game abounded, and wild turkey, antelope, deer, and an occasional bear excited hunters among the early missionaries. Taken all together, it was a most attractive spot — one that the Mormons were anxious to claim but did not regard as a likely site for a permanent village because of its elevation. During the summer of 1876 the area was explored and at least sixteen log cabins were built, each claimed in the name of one of the settlers. Rarely inhabited on a year-round basis, Mormon Lake featured strongly in the lumber and ranching ventures of the lower village United Orders.[15]

Also part of the earliest colonization was the establishment of Indian missions at Moenkopi and at Savoia in western New Mexico. Beginning in 1873, John D. Lee, Jacob Hamblin, John L. Blythe, and a few other missionaries had lived intermittently in the Moenkopi area, but it was not until James S. Brown's arrival there in December of 1875 that a stable village was founded.[16] Building what was called the "old mission house,"

---

[14] See *Deseret News,* October 23, 1878. Also see plans of the Brigham City and Sunset forts in "History of the Little Colorado Stake."

[15] The best account of the establishment of claims to Pleasant Valley is "History of John A. Blythe 1876-77," original, Utah State Historical Society [hereafter USHS], entries for August and September, 1876.

[16] For information on early efforts to claim Moenkopi, see William Henry Solomon, "Diary of the Arizona Mission 1873-74," typescript in possession of Mrs. Mary Elizabeth Shumway, Taylor, Arizona.

Hopi farm in a canyon that once was farmed by Mormon settlers of Tuba City.

Brown and his associates, including Andrew S. Gibbons, Thales Haskell, and M. P. Mortensen, explored and carried on missionary work as well as providing a way station for the migration of 1876 and 1877.

In 1878 Apostle Erastus Snow, field commander for Arizona colonization, laid out the site of Tuba City about two miles north of Moenkopi, which became the main location of Mormon settlement. Brigham Young's wayward and headstrong son John W., who had first visited the country with Jacob Hamblin in 1859, disregarded Snow's counsel and established a trading post and woolen mill at Moenkopi in 1879. His choice of Moenkopi rather than Tuba City may have been predicated upon the greater availability of water to run the two hundred spindles of his mill and upon the thought that the wool trade might be plied more readily at the Indian village. The success of his enterprises seems to have been meager, for Young turned his back upon Moenkopi when opportunities for railroad contracting and cattle ranching developed during the 1880s. Rising to as many as 125 people in the early years of that decade,

Tuba City's population remained small, and the Mormon claims were eventually turned over to the United States after the turn of the century.[17]

Attracted by remarkable success in the first effort to proselyte among the Zuni Indians, Brigham Young dispatched Lorenzo H. Hatch and John Maughan to western New Mexico in the summer of 1876. Settling first at a place they called San Lorenzo, they were joined by William McAllister, E. A. Teitjen, and L. C. Burnham before the year was out. Early in 1877, Hatch and Maughan inspected Savoia Valley some twelve miles distant from their earlier settlement. Pleased, they immediately commenced a village there as well. In 1878 Ammon M. Tenney replaced Hatch as president of the Zuni mission and with his father and several brothers moved into the area. Decimated by a smallpox epidemic and not encouraged by any real success among the Indians, San Lorenzo appears to have been abandoned entirely and Savoia nearly so. Resettled after 1880, the latter was called Navajo for a time and finally given the name of Ramah. By 1884 its population amounted to about a hundred people who maintained themselves by freighting to nearby Fort Wingate, trading with the Indians, and a little farming and livestock-raising.[18]

Settlement on Silver Creek

Although Hatch and Maughan found stable Indian and Mexican communities and even a few white settlers in western New Mexico, the Mormon settlements of 1876 were established at spots previously unclaimed. Most of the later villages, however, rose on sites located by earlier settlers. By 1876 stockmen were beginning to recognize the worth of the country. Boosters stated that outfits boasting no fewer than fifty employees were approaching from New Mexico.[19] Such talk was not entirely empty promotion. Both James Brown and Daniel W. Jones had been spurred on in their explorations by the presence of large herds of sheep. Furthermore, in the short weeks between Brown's exploration of the lower river and

---

[17] "Joseph City Ward History," pp. 38-39. Also see Tuba City Collection, Southwest Museum, Los Angeles, and Shachi Nagata, "Modern Transformations of Moenkopi Pueblo" (unpublished Ph.D. dissertation, University of Indiana, 1968).

[18] For the best account of Ramah's early history, see Irving Teller, "Ramah, New Mexico 1876-1900: An Historical Episode with some Value Analysis," *Utah Historical Quarterly* 21 (April 1953): 117-36. Also see "Joseph City Ward History," p. 41, and Joseph Fish, "History of the Eastern Arizona Stake of Zion and of the Establishment of the Snowflake Stake, 1879-1893," p. 66. [Hereafter "History of the Eastern Arizona Stake"] This manuscript history exists in typed form in several copies — one of these is in the HDC, another in the possession of Silas L. Fish, Phoenix, Arizona.

[19] *Deseret News*, June 7, 1876.

the establishment of villages there, five settlers had taken up one of the sites he had hoped to see the Mormons occupy.[20]

The upper part of the Little Colorado Basin had been settled even earlier. Beginning in 1871, farmers had located at Round Valley in sufficient numbers to attract a New Mexican merchant named Henry Springer, who founded a store and gave his name to the town of Springerville, which was well established by 1876. In 1872 or 1873 Solomon Barth and a handful of Mexican retainers founded St. Johns about twenty-five miles down stream from Round Valley. By the time of the earliest Mormon visits, Barth's town was a squalid village of a dozen or so flat-topped mud houses. During the years immediately before 1876, Silver Creek, too, had been settled by several ranchers. Indian scout and rancher Croydon E. Cooley, whose accommodation to his Apache neighbors is said to have included a bigamous arrangement with two Indian women, lived on the west branch at a fertile spot known as Show Low.[21] About halfway down the creek lived James Stinson, who by 1876 was farming successfully at Silver Creek Valley, later Snowflake, and running stock along the creek north to its juncture with the Little Colorado. Richard Bailey and James Scott claimed Spring Valley and the forks of Silver Creek some miles south of Stinson's.

Although Mormon explorations during the summer of 1876 indicated that the prospects of continued expansion were rather dim, earlier claimants soon began to abandon their claims or sell them to the newcomers. The first break occurred before Christmas of 1876, when Felix Scott gave up a claim to "Black Butte Valley" about twenty-five miles above Allen's Camp near the confluence of Silver Creek and the Little Colorado. Moving quickly, a few men from Allen's Camp occupied the site, spending the winter there working on a ditch. In the spring they were joined by others, including Nathan Tenney and his sons. The following winter Lorenzo H. Hatch was transferred to the new settlement and traded his New Mexico property for the Tenney holdings. Located in a well-grassed but unwatered valley south of a black volcanic butte that dominated the countryside for miles around, the place was soon named

---

[20] No definite word as to where these settlers were located has been found, but the fact that several Mexicans are reported to have been living at Horsehead Crossing, later Holbrook, when Lot Smith and his followers arrived and that no other reference to ranchers on the lower river has been found leads the author to believe that it was to the Horsehead Crossing settlers that Brown referred when he reported: "Between this time and my previous visit five houses had been built there, so our purpose was interfered with a little." Brown, *Life of a Pioneer*, p. 460.

[21] H. B. Wharfield, *Cooley, Army Scout, Arizona Pioneer, Wayside Host, Apache Friend* (privately published, 1968).

Woodruff and embarked on what proved to be a long drawn-out struggle for existence.[22]

During 1878 several other places along Silver Creek became available to Mormon colonization. Visiting the territory in September of that year, Erastus Snow found no fewer than six new settlements on the creek, and one, Forest Dale, located just beyond it on the Salt River side of the Mogollon Rim, which we shall consider as one with the Silver Creek towns. L. John Nuttal, who served as historian on Snow's tour, noted that about 175 colonists were already living on Silver Creek in settlements that varied in number from thirty-five at Forest Dale to twenty-two at Cluff's near Show Low.[23] According to Nuttal's account, none of the Silver Creek villages had been established before 1878 except Cluff's, the site of which had been purchased in January from Heber Dalton, a son-in-law of John D. Lee, who had previously located there.[24]

The experience of the Cluff family was not unusual. Arriving on the west branch of Silver Creek, later called Show Low Creek, they found two Gentile partners, Cooley and Clark, in possession of most of the valley. However, the upper portion, a secluded and timbered canyon about "two and a half miles long and from one quarter to three quarters of a mile wide," was claimed by Dalton. For $200 they bought out his 160-acre claim. During the year they added another 100 acres of tillable land, some by purchase and the rest by clearing timber. Unirrigated crops were thriving at the time of Snow's visit, though the Cluffs rightly feared that they would not do so well other years. Four log houses had been constructed, and Cluff was planning to set up both a sawmill and a gristmill. In addition to the aged Mr. Cluff, who at eighty-four years must have been among the oldest of the Little Colorado immigrants, the community was composed of his son Moses and a Brother Jensen, giving it a total population of "three men, four women, seven boys and eight girls."[25] Similar ranches appeared in descending order at Reidhead, or Lone Pine, about six miles north of Cluff's, at Silver Creek Crossing which later became Solomon, and at two sites in Walter's Valley, or Bagley, near present-day Taylor. Although the Snow party makes no reference to them,

[22] Fish, "History of the Eastern Arizona Stake," pp. 41-45.

[23] *Deseret News,* October 30, 1878.

[24] *Ibid.* Andrew S. Gibbons found the Cluffs and Dalton at Cooley's ranch in August of 1877. According to his report, the Cluffs had located claims in the neighborhood but were renting farm land from Cooley for that season. See "Andrew Smith Gibbons Diary, 1877," original in possession of Francis Gibbons, Salt Lake City, p. 10.

[25] *Deseret News,* October 30, 1878.

a few other families appear to have been established at isolated spots on the Silver Creek drainage by this time as well.

These communities lay between two larger settlements. At the extreme south, eight miles beyond Cluff's, was Forest Dale, a beautiful sheltered spot, as its name implies, which because of its proximity to the White River Apaches had not attracted earlier attention. Located in a timbered valley where the water of seven springs join to form the head of Carrizo Creek, it was discovered by Oscar Cluff in the fall of 1877. After sending his brother Alfred and Joseph H. Frisby to the San Carlos Apache Agency and ascertaining, as they thought, that the site was not on the reservation, Cluff filed claim. This action was taken with the full cognizance of the San Carlos Indian agent, who encouraged the move, as in his judgment the establishment of white settlements in the vicinity would tend to hold the foot-loose Apaches on the reservation. During the spring of 1878, a dozen or so families, including those of Ebenezer Thayne, Llewelyn Harris, and Oscar Mann, moved to the location. By the time of Erastus Snow's visit in September, the colony had erected thirteen houses, dug several wells, and had 180 acres under cultivation. Giving his full approval in spite of discomfitting rumors that the place was on the reservation, Snow helped lay out a townsite and set up a church organization.

Soon after Snow's visit, Thayne and Harris, who were missionaries to the Indians, invited a few Apache families to join the community. Much to the consternation of less altruistically inclined settlers, the Apaches appeared in goodly numbers. By April of 1879, they had pressed their right to the valley as part of the reservation with such effect that all but a few colonists, who lingered as missionaries to the Indians, moved on to the Gila Valley. If the commentary of Ebenezer Thayne, who was sympathetic toward the Indians, can be depended upon, this first transfer of property from the Mormons to the Indians was accomplished with a good deal of grace and did not badly mar relations between them. Writing on April 10, 1879, he explained:

When these Indians first came into this place, they found the land all taken up by the brethren, and very few of the brethren were willing to divide with them, so we were at a loss what to do. Bishop Mann deeming it advisable went and had a conversation with Brother Jesse Smith, he being president of this Stake of Zion. He counseled the brethren to give up the land to the Indians and seek new homes for themselves in some other locality. As soon as this was arranged, Bishop Mann and myself, accompanied by Bro. Llewelyn Harris, the interpreter, went to inform the Indians of the decision that we were going to leave the valley for them. The chief said he was very sorry for this, he said he did not want us all to leave them. . . . We promised him that we would not go more than five or six miles from here, and that we would visit him often, and we would plow and help them plant some corn, but as we thought that this valley was on the reservation, we did not think we could stay here at present.[26]

Soon, however, even the missionary families departed, and Forest Dale was literally left to the Indians, who once their claim was unchallenged lost interest themselves.

In 1881 it was rumored that Forest Dale was after all not on the reservation and thus open to settlement. Losing no time, William Crookston and others from Brigham City, which was failing rapidly, resettled Forest Dale. The following spring after crops were in, the Indians once again asserted their rights. In a futile attempt to placate them, the settlers gave them thirty acres of corn. Unappeased, the Apaches shortly forced the Mormons from Forest Dale, which was finally and definitively decided to be part of the reservation. Thus, the Little Colorado Mormons failed in two efforts to preempt this peripheral bit of land, not because of thin soils, short growing seasons, or even water development, but because of Indian resistance to their approach, and the decision that ultimately placed it within the reservation.[27]

The last of the Silver Creek sites to fall into Mormon hands during 1878 was Stinson's Ranch at Silver Creek Valley. The ranch was located in a well-grassed country of rolling hills and scattered cedar growth, and the new settlers had been favorably impressed with it from the first but had made no serious effort to acquire it until midsummer of 1878. James Stinson, who Jesse N. Smith described as a "jolly Irishman of doubtful morals," but who proved to be one of the most true and steadfast friends of the Mormon colonists, had come to the valley about 1873 and during the interim had developed a prosperous farm and ranching operation.[28] Claiming all the waters of Silver Creek, he had about three hundred acres under irrigation at the time of the purchase. Other improve-

---

[26] *Ibid.,* May 14, 1879.

[27] McClintock's treatment of the Forest Dale story is the best available; see *Mormon Settlement in Arizona,* pp. 170-73. A group of the exiles petitioned for relief through Arizona's Senator Henry Ashurst in 1916; claims varied from $2,000 to $15,000 in amounts. See U. S., *Journal of Senate,* 64 Cong., 1st sess., pp. 80, 118. Some additional information may be found in the *Deseret News,* October 30, 1878, and March 19, April 23, and May 14, 1879.

[28] Jesse N. Smith, *Journal of Jesse N. Smith* (Salt Lake City: Jesse N. Smith Family Association, 1953), p. 224. According to reminiscences of Eugene Flake, a grandson of the first Mormon settler at Snowflake, Stinson stumbled onto "Silver Creek Valley" while on a cattle-buying trip from Colorado. He was so taken by the spot that he returned and established squatter claims to it. This narrative was related to Albert Levine of Snowflake in 1971.

Erastus Snow, Mormon apostle and "Field Marshal"
for colonization in Arizona from 1878 to 1887.

— Historical Department of the Church of Jesus Christ of Latter-day Saints

William J. Flake, Mormon land agent in northern Arizona.

Snowflake in 1884.

ments included several flat Mexican-style houses and farm buildings and a surprising amount of machinery.

Considered in the light of the communitarianism that had character-ized Mormon settlement to this point, the purchase of Stinson's property by William J. Flake was a notable bit of individual action. Called to make Arizona his permanent home, Flake found life at the United Order villages intolerable. In an effort to fulfill the larger measure of his call, he with-drew from the order and after considerable scouting contracted to buy Stinson out for $12,000. Payment of $11,000 in three annual installments was to be made in 550 Utah cattle, which were superior to the native scrubs of the region. The final $1,000 Flake arranged to work out, har-vesting Stinson's crops that fall to complete the deal.

Taken without leave of the local authorities, Flake's action was

— *Albert J. Levine, Snowflake, A Pictorial Review, 1878-1964*

sharply criticized. Disturbed, he set out toward Utah to gain the ear of Apostle Erastus Snow, who was approaching, and easily won his whole-hearted endorsement. Shortly thereafter, Snow found Flake and a handful of settlers located at two different sites in Stinson's valley. Joining these into one community, which in a happy break with the Mormon penchant for tedious place names he called Snowflake, Snow laid out a townsite in characteristic form with large square blocks and wide streets. At his suggestion, the town did not enter the United Order but followed a more limited form of communalism whereby its land was distributed among incoming settlers. Dividing it into city lots and ten-acre field plots of two qualities, a committee valued each city lot at $30 and each "first-class" ten-acre field plot at $110, while the "second-class" plots went for $60. According to the plan each settler was to receive one unit of each category, giving him property valued at $200, or ten head of cattle. Flake was paid for his earlier claim to the land by most, but not by all, of those who moved in as neighbors.[29]

In the actual distribution there was some deviation from the simple formula of one city lot and one farm plot of each grade per settler. Flake, Jesse N. Smith, and a few others took more. Smith, for example, received four city lots.[30] Several years later, his son Joseph W. Smith wrote: "This fall we divided the land and teams. Or, more properly speaking, father gave some to Jesse and me. I received the 'ten' known as the Grassland, five across the creek, and five acres across the wash—twenty acres in all."[31] The elder Smith may have drawn land for those of his sons who were approaching a marriageable age, and as they set up families turned it over to them. Or, more likely, polygamists may have been allowed to draw one land unit for each family, thus permitting Smith, who was wed five times, to take multiple allotments.

Snowflake quickly became a center of Mormon settlement in Arizona. Among the early comers were a number of southern Saints. These people had come empty-handed from Georgia and Arkansas the year before and by the fall of 1878 were reduced to near starvation. Settling first in the United Order villages, they had neither thrived nor been easily assimilated by the Utah immigrants. They came now to Flake, also a southerner, and for months he and Stinson provided foodstuffs for quite a number of families.[32]

St. Johns and the Upper Little Colorado, 1879-80

The third and final area of colonization was the upper Little Colorado River. As indicated previously, a number of Gentile settlers were well established there, and, like Silver Creek, the area did not at first attract Mormon attention although the elders of the Zuni Mission traveled through it and must have been well acquainted with it before the end of 1876.

The earliest real indication that the Mormons intended to extend their colonies in that direction was manifest by Erastus Snow, who planned to include a visit to St. Johns in his tour of the mission in 1878. Frustrated

---

[29] Fish, "History of the Eastern Arizona Stake," p. 48.

[30] Smith, *Journal of Jesse N. Smith,* p. 233.

[31] "Diary of Joseph West Smith, 1859-1936," original in possession of Lenora S. Rogers, Snowflake, Arizona; typescript BYU, p. 54.

[32] "Autobiography and Diary of Lucy Hannah White Flake," original and typescript, BYU, vol. 1, p. 69.

in this design by the pressures of his itinerary, Snow nevertheless instructed local leaders to look into the matter generally and if possible to purchase the town of St. Johns. Complying, L. H. Hatch and Jesse N. Smith made separate trips in January of 1879 with the intention of buying part or all of St. Johns in the interest of the incoming migration. Smith had been instructed to make his home there, but he was so little impressed by its appearances and its settlers, whom he thought to be "low in the scale of intelligence," that he returned to Snowflake without consummating the deal.[33] Later in the same year, Ammon M. Tenney became interested in the prospect of settling there and called the site to the attention of Apostle Wilford Woodruff, who was in exile on the Little Colorado at the time. At Tenney's invitation, Woodruff visited St. Johns, thereafter taking a keen interest in it.

Laying out a plan of colonization which he hoped would quickly dispose of all Gentiles, Woodruff directed Tenney to buy the holdings of Solomon Barth, the town's founder and main figure. Years before, Barth, a Jew of German background, had followed an uncle who had been converted to Mormonism to Salt Lake City. Having no personal connection with the church, young Barth quickly moved on, drifting about the West to finally engage in supplying the army at Fort Apache and to locate along with a group of Mexicans at St. Johns.

Well established by 1879, Barth nevertheless was willing to sell if the price were right, and after some negotiating Tenney effected the purchase, paying 750 Utah cattle for the original and what was understood by the Mormons to be the entire claim. Unfortunately for their aspirations, Barth contrived to hold back an important water right, and it was necessary to make an additional purchase at the heavy price of $7,500, again payable in Utah cows. The total sum paid was subsequently given by Church Historian Andrew Jenson as $19,000, almost all of which was forwarded by the church.[34]

This price seemed far out of line to Mormons of the era, as well it might, for Barth, Stinson, and others had found this new briskness in the market to their liking and played it to the hilt. More than a year after he first evinced interest in St. Johns, and ten months after Smith and Hatch had tried to negotiate its purchase, Erastus Snow wrote the following relative to the increment in price:

In reply to your enquiries about the proposed purchase of the St. Johns property in Arizona and secureing that key to the Little Colorado region . . . I

---

[33] Smith, *Journal of Jesse N. Smith*, p. 232.
[34] McClintock, *Mormon Settlement in Arizona*, p. 179.

beg to recommend that you send men from the North to purchase and settle that place under the Supervision of Elders Woodruff and Jesse N. Smith — I advised this move a year ago as important for that country. But the settlers going to Arizonia seemed either unable or unwilling to do so probably did not then see as they now do the necessity of it. Five thousand Dollares part cash & rest Stock might have secured it then. But double that is doughtless required now to accomplish it; and still more the longer is delayed. Some 30 men with $10,000 surplus propperty could do it by employing wise forerunners to make the purchase. . . .[35]

In keeping with Woodruff's aggressive policy, Tenney was instructed to take up surrounding lands before the St. Johns deal became public and alerted non-Mormons to the church's designs. Men were called from the four towns on the lower Little Colorado and elsewhere in the mission to locate as Tenney directed. In order to accommodate the largest possible number of settlers, sharp limits were placed on the amount of land available to any one man, with the purchase cost being prorated to $8.00 per acre for land and $25.00 for city lots. Adamant in their determination that St. Johns was to be used in behalf of the community, Woodruff and John W. Young addressed the following denunciation of private speculation to all parties involved:

. . . and we wish it distinctly understood, by the Saints who settle there that we do not expect to enter into any speculation in the purchase of this country, for ourselves or our Brethren. Our labors, in these matters are for the building-up of Zion, and the settling of the Saints. We have·figured this matter as closely as we can, and we feel that we cannot put the Land and Lots at any lower price. When the land and lots are sold, and the debts paid, if there is anything left, it will be returned, *pro. rata,* to those who have paid for the land: and if we fall short of the payment, we consider it right and just that those who have purchased the land, shall also pay, *pro. rata.* . . .[36]

By mid-March St. Johns was reported to have a population of 190 Mormons. Small communities had also sprung up at the Meadows and Concho, which were respectively eight and twenty-five miles downstream. Barth and other Gentiles showing no disposition to leave, Woodruff rushed back to Utah in time for April conference and pushed through a call for a hundred families to join those already there. Calls to reinforce St. Johns were also made in 1881 and 1884, but, a rapid growth of population notwithstanding, the plan to make St. Johns a tight Mormon community failed. Moreover, the seeds of discord sown in this bid for monopoly

[35] Letter of Erastus Snow to President John Taylor & Council, November 1879, Erastus Snow Letters, HDC.

[36] Letter "To the Saints at St. Johns," February 19, 1880, Le Sueur Papers, Arizona Historical Society Library, Tucson, Arizona [hereafter AHS]. In the Le Sueur Papers are about two dozen letters from Wilford Woodruff and other prominent church leaders that provide a sketchy view of the land purchase. Also see Evans Coleman, "St. Johns Purchase," Coleman Papers, AHS.

cankered the course of the little town's history throughout the remainder of the century.

Settlements were also established on the headwaters of the Little Colorado River above St. Johns. The first one of these was at Round Valley. Visited early in 1879 by Peter J. Christofferson and others from St. Joseph, the first-Round Valley ranch was purchased during the same spring by William J. Flake. Other ranch property was soon acquired, and a community shortly came into existence. However, the Mormons were unable to acquire any of the large centrally located farms on which to base a village, and until a relatively late date they were forced to content themselves with bits of peripheral land.

In 1882 scattered locations, rather than the number of settlers, required a division of the Round Valley Mormons into two wards — one of which was known as Amity and the other Omer. In 1888 during a drive to bring scattered elements together, a townsite was located two miles south of Springerville. Reflecting this joint action, the new town was called Union, but as the circumstances that led to its establishment paled, the name fell into disuse, and it has subsequently been known as Eagar after prominent residents of that name.

Farther up the river, a number of other small villages were established during these same years. Important among these were Nutrioso, Greer, and Alpine. Located near the New Mexico border at an altitude approximating 8,000 feet, Alpine was first settled by a man named Bush whose rights were purchased in 1879 by William B. Maxwell, an old missionary to the Hopis. Joined by J. C. Owens, E. A. Noble, the Colemans, and Jacob and Frederick Hamblin, Maxwell ran livestock and did some farming. The town they organized was first called Frisco and later Alpine. Plagued by Indian raids and killing frosts during every month of the year, its inhabitants remained poor and few in number. In writing of the town, Evans Coleman, whose parents brought him to Alpine as a child, noted that while it never had "a jail, a saloon or a pool hall," it boasted of the "largest cemetery of any town its size west of the Rio Grande." The course of its history was marked by "sickness, death, heartaches and adversities. No doctor, no medicine — nothing." After observing, in something of a contradiction, that it was an easy place to live as nothing but time could be spent there, Coleman concluded his narrative with wry humor and tempered bitterness: "In about 1886 the people of Alpine made two startling discoveries. One was; that a man would never get wealthy in Alpine; second; fishing bait was plentiful almost any place in the valley."[37]

---

[37] "History of the Coleman Family," Coleman Papers, AHS, pp. 48-49.

Nutrioso, a ranch sixteen miles southeast of Springerville, which had been named in Spanish for the otter and the bear, was first visited by grain-hungry Mormons and then purchased in the spring of 1879. First occupied by Albert Minerly, Adam Greenwood, George Peck, and John Burke, its population grew to 130 by 1884, but like Alpine it never transcended the difficulties of its isolation and has since been almost totally abandoned. Nutrioso's early development was paralleled by that of Greer, which lay in Lee's Valley to the southwest of Springerville. After its beginning in 1879, it soon came under the domination of a southern convert, Thomas Lacy Greer, who made it part of an extensive ranching operation.

Greer and Nutrioso had much in common with the mountain villages on the upper part of Silver Creek. There was a unity in their remoteness which in a day of horse traffic and limited communications effectively barred them from even such modest cultural benefits as St. Johns and Snowflake came to boast. There was also unity in their poverty and in the nature of their financial interests. As the years passed they developed into something of a three-way cross between cattle ranch, lumber camp, and Mormon village. Instead of taking on an air of permanence as did the lower towns, they remained poised in a half-transitory state. Though not beyond the pale of general church interest, they did lie off the beaten path of the periodic church visitations. Even leaders like Brigham Young, Jr., who followed the course of northern Arizona colonization step by step, did not find their way into them with any frequency.

Mountain villages remained small, their poverty even more grinding than that of other Little Colorado towns. Doubtlessly many factors contributed to this, among which might be mentioned the subdivisions made for church administration, geography and situation in relation to the railroad, problems of climate and elevation, proximity of Indians, and, finally but not of least importance, the priority arrangement fixed by the church which enabled the lower Little Colorado villages of Woodruff, Snowflake, Taylor, and St. Johns each in its turn to receive substantial subsidies and the help of the most capable leaders of the church in times of crisis. Nowhere has record been found that the mountain towns enjoyed similar benefits. Simply put, the vaunted communalism of the church fell short of them. In making his choice to establish in one of them, a settler went without expectation of a mission call to build up his community or of other special dispensations in his favor. On the other hand, he was less bound by the Mormon system and made his way into cow camps and onto the freighting roads with less restraint and, one may presume, with easier conscience than did his down-river brother.

By the end of 1880, the process of founding the Mormon colony on the Little Colorado was well under way. Most of its villages had come into being, and most of the relations that subsequently characterized the community had formed. We have seen something of this process and have observed the Mormons moving into the area until by 1880 they had come to constitute its most numerous element. However, colonization was just begun, and most of the next two decades were consumed in the process of consolidating the claim that had been laid.

3. THE MORMON MISSION: AGENCY OF EXPANSION

In the path of duty and counsel.

WILLIAM HENRY SOLOMON

Mission Forms

IMPORTANT AMONG the cooperative forms that featured in the extension of the Mormon frontier into northern Arizona was the mission. By 1870 the mission concept had acquired multiple meanings, all of which were well known to Latter-day Saints and used in their varied applications in promoting and colonizing the Little Colorado River. These may be reduced to four basic forms: (1) the mission as a calling or obligation incumbent upon a chosen people; (2) the mission as specific errand; (3) the mission as a geographic and administrative subdivision; and (4) the mission as means of social mobilization. Although the lines separating these concepts were neither precise nor consistently applied, they all contributed not only to the process of colonization but also to the understanding the Mormon people had of it.

In its broadest context, the mission was the Mormon consciousness of their destiny as a chosen people gathered out of Babylon and charged with a vital role in a divine course of events. To them fell the rare obligation of making temporal preparations for what they regarded to be the most sublime and important event of history — Christ's Second Coming.[1] In this respect life itself was the grand mission and all Mormons were

---

[1] For a characteristic reference see *Documentary History of the Church,* vol. 2, pp. 52-53.

missionaries. Expansive movement including the colonization of the Little Colorado Basin was deeply charged by this quality of mission.

Also recognizable as a mission form were those specific errands by which the kingdom's cause was advanced. The earliest of these had been embassies to gather the elect from a decadent world and reclaim the fallen remnants of Israel from among the Indians, whose forefathers Mormons believed migrated from Jerusalem. But in the Mormon matrix the intimacy of God's relationship to the world and the imminence of Christ's Second Coming tended to obscure distinctions between the temporal and spiritual, and soon an errand, cash in hand to redeem Zion or to wait upon a president with some political appeal, came to be regarded as much an act of mission as the redemption of human souls. Such missions marked the entire course of the church in Utah and continued to characterize its movement into Arizona as individuals and groups were sent to explore, to settle, or to attend the conversion and regeneration of the Indians.

In yet another context, the mission was an administrative subdivision with more or less precise geographic bounds within which an errand of the kingdom was performed. Over the years the term had come to designate not only the confines of a proselyting region where chosen leaders directed a cadre of preaching elders but also the area to which detachments were ordered to colonize a strategic spot or to develop some facet of Mormon economy. In this guise the mission implied some special task or interest that did not fall under the purvey of the ordinary administrative organization of the church. Where the colonizing mission was concerned, the special need arose in no small measure from the total lack of social organization upon the new frontier and from its geographic remoteness. Tightly disciplined task forces were needed to transform the wilderness. It should be noted that in this sense the mission was an agency of transition. By its very success, it diminished and ultimately extinguished its own usefulness as the frontier society took on permanent character and the ordinary institutions of administration began to function.

In the mobilizing of individuals to achieve common ends, a final usage of the mission concept appeared. The church was never hesitant in ordering and directing its members, but within the confines of the established community a certain routineness of activity existed and many functions fell essentially in the private realm. Considerable latitude in the choice of location and profession existed, and people followed their own inclination in many of their daily pursuits. Furthermore, even the harassed circumstances of existence in Utah and the continuing pressure generated by church leaders could not keep members forever poised at the ready, fully geared for action. As an instrument of mobilization, the mission provided

Salt Lake City, April 10th, 1884.

Prest. John Taylor:

Dear Brother.--- Your Committee to whom was referred the subject of making the distribution of families among the various Stakes of this Territory to be called to strengthen the settlement of St. Johns, respectfully submit the following report, and apportionment taken from the statistical report read at our late Conference.

	Stakes.	No. of Families.	Apportionment.
1.	Bear Lake,	730	3
2.	Beaver,	308	2
3.	Box Elder,	1286	5
4.	Cache,	3135	13
5.	Davis,	865	4
6.	Juab,	510	2
7.	Kanab,	244	1
8.	Millard,	261	2
9.	Morgan,	263	2
10.	Panguitch,	305	2
11.	Parowan,	389	2
12.	Salt Lake,	4631	20
13.	Sanpete,	1972	8
14.	St. George,	772	3
15.	Sevier,	867	4
16.	Summit,	569	2
17.	Tooele,	489	2
18.	Utah,	3156	14
19.	Wasatch,	589	3
20.	Weber,	1894	8
		23,555	102

Emery Stake omitted.

W. Woodruff,
Chairman.

The above apportionment has been approved by President Taylor.
W W

Form levying mission quotas to reinforce St. Johns in 1884.

a means of rising above this lassitude of the ordinary. Used to condition and organize society it became the source of an adequate and elastic supply of manpower. Few official undertakings of the church were faced with greater reluctance on the part of lay members than were the ventures of colonization in the deserts of the south. The mission was of notable utility in a number of such situations, including the settlement of northern Arizona. Indeed, in its use as an instrument of expansion, the mission and the call which expedited it became something of a frontier selective service, with local leaders joining the general officers of the church to constitute the conscripting agencies.

The Call

The entire ecclesiastical process of the church moved on the initiative of the call. Emanating from the First Presidency through the priesthood, it was the basis of administration. Colonizing missions were especially dependent upon it since not only did they carry on the ordinary church functions under its auspices but the missionaries themselves were designated as such by call.

After deciding to launch a new colony or to strengthen one previously established, the first step was to fix upon the number of missionaries required. In the original Arizona Mission of 1873, it was felt that over three hundred missionaries would be needed in the vanguard group. In 1876 the number was reduced to two hundred. Thereafter, a more or less constant process of calling small groups and individuals as opportunity permitted was supplemented by the call of at least two groups of one hundred families each.

Where large numbers of missionaries were designated under one call, quotas were distributed throughout the stakes and wards of the church. In the case of the mission of 1876 the levy fell most heavily upon the populous stakes of central and northern Utah. While the strength of these areas and the easy access church leaders had to their manpower likely accounted for this arrangement, proximity to region of colonization was likewise a consideration in some cases. For instance, the primary call to Castle Valley in eastern Utah fell upon the Sanpete settlements, which lay just over the Wasatch Plateau to the west. Iron County's location also figured in the heavy draft made upon it for the San Juan Mission of 1879-80.[2]

---

[2] David E. Miller, *Hole-in-the-Rock: An Epic in the Colonization of the Great American West* (Salt Lake City: University of Utah Press, 1959), pp. 9-10.

However, proximity appears to have been less important in the establishment of quotas than were population and economic considerations. Thus, the Virgin Basin settlements which lay contiguous to northern Arizona were given no quotas in the early calls. Voluntary movement from them, which was not inconsiderable, so depleted their population that Erastus Snow informed President John Taylor that more men could not be spared.[3] In 1884 when the last major Little Colorado call was made, every stake in the church except the one in Castle Valley, which had been organized only a short time previously, was given a quota commensurate with its membership.[4]

Mission calls were extended by the authority of church leaders and received full validity by public announcement and popular ratification. Throughout the entire course of the Little Colorado Mission, the General Authorities of the church exercised the power to set the call in motion; but beyond this control at the center, there was considerable variation in how and by whom the call was made. Frequently it was extended in a personal visit by one of the apostles or by the president of the church himself. This was more true during the days of Brigham Young's intense interest in expansion than later when lines of administration and delegation of responsibility were necessitated by the growth of the church and preoccupation with political problems.

Then, too, the role of the General Authorities in the calling process was altered by the constant shifting in the size and the nature of the mission as progress and events required different functions of missionaries. For example, top-level leaders often chose and called the personnel of exploratory expeditions themselves. George W. Brimhall's call to a lonely and hazardous exploration of the Colorado River in 1864 was characteristic. Approached personally by Apostle George A. Smith, who was in charge of the church's southern frontiers at the time, Brimhall thought the venture was dangerous and foolhardy. Never of a retiring nature, he promptly told Smith so. According to Brimhall's account, Smith had no desire to discuss the matter, making only the laconic comment that "he had done his errand, and I should go and do mine."[5]

---

[3] See letter of L. J. Nuttall to Sixtus E. Johnson, November 22, 1879, L. John Nuttall Letter Press Book #1, BYU, p. 55. The mission as an economic measure has been discussed by Leonard J. Arrington, in *Great Basin Kingdom: An Economic History of the Latter-day Saints, 1830-1900* (Cambridge: Harvard University Press, 1958), pp. 33 & 155.

[4] See form apportioning call of 1884 in letter of Wilford Woodruff to John Taylor, April 10, 1884, Lot Smith Papers, University of Arizona Library, Tucson, Arizona [hereafter UA].

[5] George W. Brimhall, *The Workers of Utah* (Provo, Utah, 1889), p. 41.

In 1875 two years after problems of leadership helped defeat the first attempt of the church to open northern Arizona, Brigham Young sought to avoid another failure by giving close personal attention to the choice of leaders for the preliminary expeditions of a renewed effort. James S. Brown, a veteran of many frontier experiences, including the march of the Mormon Battalion, was called into Young's office and approached directly by the president. Young's response to Brown's immediate and affirmative reply as related by the latter reflects the easy and intimate relation that existed as well as the former's methods:

President Young then said: "Bless your soul, the Spirit does and has dictated to me all the time to send you to take charge of a mission in that country. You are just the man for it, and if I had sent you before we would have had a mission and settlements there now."[6]

As the operation changed from one of exploration to one of settlement, the method of making the call also changed, with more responsibility falling upon local leaders who now nominated most of the prospective missionaries. The General Authorities still formalized the call and on occasion read the lists in conference. They also nominated a few of the mission's leaders; but other leaders as well as the rank and file appear to have been suggested by local officers who were intimately acquainted with the circumstances and abilities of the men involved and proposed them accordingly. Some of the missionaries suggested followings of their own, who were then duly called and ordained for the mission.

Although it is difficult to determine what qualities or circumstances were looked for in placing specific calls, a few general considerations stand out clearly. Unlike the colonists who founded southern Utah's Cotton Mission and other settlements in connection with Brigham Young's industrial self-sufficiency drive of the 1860s, Little Colorado colonists were chosen in most cases for reasons other than specialized skills. Furthermore, the Little Colorado Mission was not used — as were some — to provide publicly generated enterprises at which skilled converts from Europe's workshops could be employed while they became acclimated to western deserts.

However, it should not be assumed that there were no missionaries called on the basis of specialization. Even in a mission of agricultural villages there was need of certain skills — this need was met by call. The United Orders especially placed great stress upon home production. This involved them in enterprises that required knowledge and experience beyond the ordinary frontier skills. Concerning one such situation,

[6] Brown, *Life of a Pioneer*, p. 450.

Erastus Snow wrote that "in obtaining sufficient leather to shoe the men, women and children . . . we deem it expedient that a Tanner and currier should be called and directed to locate under the direction of the Presidency. . . ."[7] Others were called to man the sawmill at Mormon Lake and still others to work in the "Mechanic shops," but it is not clear that these men were called solely upon the basis of experience along these lines.[8]

Over the years, numerous calls were made upon nonindustrial specialists. This was often the case in the Lamanite missions where a facility in the Spanish language was desired. Calls were likewise predicated upon a peculiar knack for Indian languages, with certain individuals finding satisfaction and prestige in the roles they played because of this ability. Others were designated because of qualities of leadership, including stability and sufficient property to hold some of the tiny communities together. Passing reference should also be made to the calling of teachers for the secondary schools or academies that grew up during the last decade of the century. "Professors," as they were locally known, were directed to the Little Colorado communities through and by the recommendation of Mormon educator Karl G. Maeser for missions of two or more years.[9]

Wealth does not seem to have been one of the essential requirements; at least almost no one who could be termed affluent was called to northern Arizona. Missionaries were not unaware that the call rarely uprooted the well-to-do, and they took this knowledge with measured stride. Writing of Arizona's prospects in 1880, D. P. Kimball was content that the wealthy remain in Utah but continued:

. . . should any of those who have small means think this climate and country would increase their financial basket . . . we would like them to join us, as we can provide many with homes and government lands are plentiful. . . . Our millionaires we do not expect, as you need them and a good deal more than you get, to fight the adversary and his lawyers, carpet baggers, etc.[10]

---

[7] See letter of Erastus Snow to John Taylor from Sunset, Arizona Territory, September 24, 1878, Erastus Snow Letters, HDC.

[8] See letter of call to William C. McClellan and others from Brigham Young and John W. Young, May 15, 1877, Erastus Snow Letters, 1881 file, HDC.

[9] The author's father was the recipient of such a call. A graduate of the Brigham Young Academy at Provo, he had been called to the Southern States Mission in 1898; however, as he awaited the date of departure, a change was suggested and he was called to the Snowflake Academy for two years.

[10] *Deseret News,* January 28, 1880. Substitutes were sometimes hired by missionaries. Alma G. Jewkes, an original settler in Utah's Emery County, stated in an interview in 1952 that many of those who were well fixed among the Castle Valley missionaries hired substitutes to take their place and remained in Sanpete. See Elmo G. Geary, "A Study of Dramatics in Castle Valley from 1875-1925" (unpublished Master's thesis, University of Utah, 1953), pp. 29-30.

On the other hand, it was felt that ambition and business acumen were needed in key positions to provide a nucleus around which the community could form. Individuals of "small means," usually rising younger men, seemed especially susceptible to call. One such was William J. Flake, who during the half-dozen years prior to his call had put together substantial holdings at Beaver and Escalante in southern Utah. David K. Udall was another. In 1880 as Apostle Wilford Woodruff made his way north from his exile on the Little Colorado, he met Udall, who was one of several promising young men building homes and businesses for themselves in Kanab. Woodruff was impressed and did not rest until the energies and abilities that had attracted him to the younger man were in St. Johns guiding Mormon interests there.[11] Several others who were of what Erastus Snow termed "easy circumstances" were called and served in northern Arizona.

However, most of those to whom the call came may justly be classified as poor. Yet on the Mormon frontier, as upon others, migration and the process of new establishment implied a certain minimum of property, little though it might be. The communal nature of Mormon society often provided goods in the form of donations to carry the new missionary along. In fact the First Presidency often authorized active solicitation. Characteristic was the 1875 call of the Daniel W. Jones party, which was described by young Anthony W. Ivins of St. George as he made preparation to accompany Jones:

In the meantime I was engaged in making preparations for my mission. My resources were very limited and it was necessary to sell everything I possessed in order to provide an outfit for the journey. Prest. Young had authorized Bro. Jones to solicit subscriptions to aid the expedition and a circular letter was sent to me authorizing me to receive funds that might be subscribed. My friends also contributed to aid me personally.[12]

There follows a list of donations totalling $119.15, and a mule and a horse. This seemed to outfit the missionary adequately, and he soon set out for the south. Although church leaders privately outfitted a few missionaries, and Utah wards sometimes assumed the obligation of equipping migrating members, most emigrants traded and patched and repaired to put together the essential rudiments of colonization.

---

11 See Osmer D. Flake, *William J. Flake, Pioneer-Colonizer* (published privately, 1954), pp. 56-59. Also see David King Udall and Pearl Udall Nelson, *Arizona Pioneer Mormon, David King Udall, History and His Family, 1851-1938* (Tucson: Arizona Silhouettes, 1959), p. 139. Also letter of Wilford Woodruff to Ammon M. Tenney, May 27, 1880, Le Sueur Papers.

12 "Anthony Woodward Ivins Journal," pp. 22-23.

If the call passed over people of wealth, it sought out those who for some reason or other were regarded as surplus. In this respect it appeared as a device by which the community rid itself of useless or bothersome elements and accomplished desired ends at the same stroke. Openly indulged leisure suggested expendability and led directly to mission calls. An interesting example of this sort was reported by Brigham Young's peppery first counselor, Heber C. Kimball:

> There has been Courts in session here for weeks and weeks, and I suppose that one hundred and fifty or two hundred of the brethren have been hanging around, with the Council House filled to the brim. This scenery continuing for a long time, one day brother Brigham sent Thomas Bullock to take their names, for the purpose of giving them missions, if they had anything [nothing] to do of any more importance. . . . These are all good men but they need to learn a lesson.[13]

Soon calls had been made, and the courtroom loiterers presumably found themselves where the demands upon their time were greater.

Evans Coleman, who accompanied his missionary parents into Arizona in the 1880s and spent the rest of his life in the Mormon community there, wrote suggestively in the same vein when he half-facetiously referred to some of the applications of the mission in a polygamous society:

— C. Gregory Crampton

A Christmas Day inscription: John D. Lee enroute to mission at the Ferry, 1871.

Cabin and dugway beside the Colorado River at Lee's Ferry.

In the Church "inspiration" is stressed. Missionaries "called by inspiration." Bishops and other officials appointed or "called by inspiration." But in those early days when polygamy was in full swing there was many a young man who was "called" into the mission field for the usual two year period, and if the case warranted, three years. For if that young man were keeping company with some young lady on whome some married man had designs, but who was for one reason or another, "just waiting" and he had sufficient "standing" in the ward, that Bishop would right now be "inspired" to send that young man's name up to headquarters, and Johnny would mighty soon be packing his war bag and starting out to "spread the gospel among the nations."[14]

This situation would be difficult to document indeed, but there can be no doubt that the call was sometimes applied to individuals whose chief qualification was a superfluity that for some reason embarrassed the church and made removal expedient. A number of interesting cases can be cited. Perhaps the most widely known was the 1871 call to John D. Lee of Mountain Meadow Massacre fame to establish the ferry that later bore his name at the Colorado River crossing which had previously been discovered by Jacob Hamblin. It was a spot ideally remote yet of utmost

13 *Millennial Star* 17 (1855): 477.
14 See "Teachers," Coleman Papers, AHS.

importance to the southern expansion of the Mormon people. Lee was called to this lonely wilderness and placed in a situation where his experience as missionary to the Indians and as a frontiersman could be utilized for the common good, yet he was effectively taken from circulation and sent where his presence at Beaver or other federal outposts could not attract attention.[15]

A less widely known but equally illuminating use of the mission call as a means of easing social and administrative tension arose out of a conflict between three southern Utah men — William H. Dame and the Smith brothers, Jesse N. and Silas S. All were prominent in Iron County ecclesiastical and civic affairs. Dame, bishop of the Parowan Ward, had played key roles in the militia and the John D. Lee trial. Jesse N. Smith had twice been mission president in Denmark as well as an important figure in community life at Parowan. Silas S. Smith was bishop of Paragonah, a high official in the militia, and a member of the territorial legislature. Contemporary accounts shed almost no light on the origins of the controversy, but it had obviously divided the community into opposing factions by 1877 when Brigham Young paused on his last trip north to reorganize the stake presidency. The events of that occasion are best told by Joseph Fish, who attended the meeting of reorganization.

The President . . . asked the people who they would have for their president. Bro. Paul Smith said William H. Dame. . . . The President then nominated Jesse N. Smith, William C. McGregor, objected. He was asked his objections, he said, "Have had some of Jesse's rule while Bro. Dame was in prison and it was tyrinnical." Pres. Wells then put the vote which was about equally divided for and against Jesse N. Smith. . . . The division among the people on electing a president was a great drawback to the place and was the root and foundation of many bitter and lasting feelings.[16]

At length, an organization was effected, complete, significantly, except for the office of president for which a man designated by Brigham was to be sent in from outside. Dame and Smith were to act as counselors. In the months that followed, Brigham Young died. His most important opposition out of the way, Dame soon won the struggle and became stake president.

Unseated, the Smith brothers now cast about for opportunities elsewhere and began to move to a new area farther east on the Sevier River north of Panguitch, but before 1878 had passed both were picked by important church calls and directed to new frontiers — Jesse to the Little Colorado and Silas to the San Juan and ultimately the San Luis Valley

---

[15] For Lee's life at the ferry (December 1871-June 1873), see Cleland and Brooks, *Mormon Chronicle,* vol. 2, pp. 174-246.

[16] "Autobiography of Joseph Fish," original, HDC, p. 145.

of Colorado, where each of them played important roles. One presumes that after riddance of these adversaries, affairs also ran more smoothly for William H. Dame at Parowan.

Erastus Snow's early selection of Jesse N. Smith to accompany him on a tour of the Arizona mission, and the latter's call, while on the journey, to preside over a new Arizona stake are so suggestive that one can hardly forbear the conclusion that Smith's availability and the call that grew out of it were in large part the result of the conflict. If doubt lingers about the immediacy of the Dame controversy as a factor in his call, Erastus Snow wrote plainly enough about Silas' case:

Bishop S. S. Smith of Parrigona . . . who is under the Ban of Prest Dame and has tendered his resignation as Bishop . . . would make a discreet presiding officer to lead settlements on the San Juan or Salt River. He will prefer the former. . . .[17]

Obviously the mission call curtailed the useless luxury of internal conflict and found satisfying outlets for expansive spirits who might otherwise have wasted their energies.

The Call by Association

The call also was issued because of family or other intimate relations. This practice grew quite naturally out of associations and reflected private interests as well as the need of the party issuing the call to receive a positive response. Beginning with the earliest Indian missions, the sons or young acquaintances of the General Authorities were sometimes called to Arizona for short periods. Among these was Erastus B. Snow, the son of the apostle, who filled a wide-ranging Indian mission during 1878. Apostle Snow drew heavily upon the boy's experience and used it in extending his own contact with the far-flung frontiers of the new mission.[18]

More ordinary was the migration of young men whose fathers had been called to Arizona and had severed their economic connections in Utah, thus leaving their sons with greatly diminished economic opportunity in the place of earlier residence. Sometimes these boys were themselves officially called; more often they moved because their fathers were moving but seem nevertheless to have regarded themselves as among the called.

Women, of course, were as important to the development of a mission of expansion as were men, but in the priesthood-oriented Mormon

---

17 Letter to John Taylor, December 29, 1878, Erastus Snow Letters, HDC.

18 Letter from Erastus Snow to John Taylor and the Council, June 11, 1878, Erastus Snow Letters, HDC.

system, they — even more than their sons — were dependent upon their husbands and received their calls through them. The need for family men frequently resulted in last-minute proposals of marriage as young missionaries faced southward. In 1867 Brigham Young had written Franklin D. Richards that a large group of young men from northern Utah were not only to fill missions to the south but were to "marry and take wives with them."[19] In such cases as the record of the movement to Arizona bears in reference to this question, the young man's ordinary difficulties in persuading the young lady and her parents to accept him were further complicated by the frontier mission that lay in the offing. Of the effect of his call upon his courtship, one missionary wrote:

During this season I was contemplating and preparing for two very important events; getting married, and moving to Arizona.

In the former I had thus far met no obstacle, and the stream of a pleasant courtship would probably have never been disturbed by a single ripple if it had not been for the latter. But the thoughts of going away off into wild and lonesome Arizona, was so repulsive to sweetheart and her parents that the charms of an otherwise attractive suitor were almost neutralized.[20]

A most interesting example of the marriage proposal as mission call appears in John Pulsipher's diary. Pulsipher, a missionary to southern Utah, had lost his wife, and after an autumn visit to Salt Lake City in 1871 during which he had met an appealing young widow wrote:

I think much of the short, but happy acquaintance we have formed, and if you would not think me rude or in haste I would like to hear from you soon. As we live in the days of short prayers, short sermons, and short courtships, I would like you to write me a plain, mountain English letter and tell me truly, if you think it would be best and proper for us to be joined in marriage? Do you think enough of me, almost a stranger as I am, to choose me before all other men that Live?

After this abrupt "plain mountain English" proposal, Pulsipher continued, now couching his proposal in the characteristic vernacular of the mission call: "If you was satisfied to say yes how long a time would you want to close up your business and be ready for a mission to the South?" And then, almost as an afterthought, he made a statement of principle to clinch the call: "I believe in free trade and women's rights, without being coaxed, flattered or hired."[21] The lady in question shortly settled up her affairs and took up her "mission to the South."

---

[19] Letter of October 18, 1867, *Millennial Star* 29 (1867): 763.

[20] See "Diary of Joseph West Smith," vol. 1, p. 26.

[21] See letter of October 24, 1871, included in the "Diary of John Pulsipher," typescript Bancroft Library; microfilm University of Utah Library [hereafter UU], vol. 1, p. 176.

Associations other than family also resulted in voluntary joining of the Arizona Mission. The group that followed Jesse N. Smith from Iron County late in 1878 is instructive in this connection. They had been joined for several years in a close-knit cooperative order which hard times and the Dame controversy nearly upset. After abortive efforts to right its tilted affairs, the group concluded to go south with Smith. He regarded its members as volunteers and submitted their names as such to President John Taylor, who gladly issued missionary recommends to them along with Smith's. Numbering about ten families, they left for Arizona as a unit and remained closely associated in business and church affairs during the entire period of colonization.[22]

Promotion and the Mission

As useful as the mission call was in the move to the Little Colorado River, it was not directly responsible for the removal of all those who went south. We have already observed a certain amount of voluntarism in the migration of families and intimates of missionaries. Such voluntary response was a solicited and to some extent controlled factor and represented a substantial part of the total movement. It was encouraged by the church; indeed, the mission was itself a catalytic agent adding energy to the southward flow. Not only was the sense of motion which the mission engendered exploited to create voluntary action, but prospects in the new country were kept before the eyes of Utahns by means of the pulpit and the press. In certain quarters hard times and a hankering to be on the move also provided a fertile soil in which seeds of migration sowed by the mission and other promotion fell and germinated.

The church always stressed good works performed on individual volition; this theme was not ignored in the recruiting of colonists for the south. It should be noted that the response the church hoped to elicit is more rightly termed voluntarism than individualism, as the ends remained communal and the means of accomplishing the ends were regulated for the good of the whole. The volunteer whose decision to migrate rose out of an idealistic and enlightened self-interest was more nearly achieving the ideal of Mormon social and theological relations than he who was called. Writing in 1876 in an open letter to the bishops, Brigham Young stated the feeling of the church on this point:

We are informed that some of the brethren entertain the idea that it is better to be called by the authorities to such missions than to volunteer. To such we

---

22 See Smith, *Journal of Jesse N. Smith,* pp. 230-231. Also see "Autobiography of Joseph Fish," p. 153.

will quote the saying of the Lord to the Prophet Joseph Smith, as contained in the Doctrine and Covenants: "He that waiteth to be commanded in all things is a slothful servant."[23]

The letter from which this extract is drawn suggested one form of promotion — namely the activity of private recruiters called to function both as missionaries and as agents to raise men for the expansion. James S. Brown, referred to previously, was authorized to raise recruits to accompany him on his exploratory expedition. His promotional activities, however, were not limited to recruiting the handful of men that comprised his first company. On his return from Arizona in the winter of 1875-76, he answered questions for "scores of visitors" who sought him out to inquire of his travels. His southward career on the return trip resembled a barnstorming tour as he stumped for Arizona, preached the mission, and raised funds to cover its expenditures. Later he toured northern Utah, lecturing sixty-five times and raising about eighty volunteers.[24]

Brown's commission to recruit read:

Brother Brown is also authorized to receive the names of those who are willing or desirous of helping to build up the Kingdom of God in that region. . . . We desire the active co-operation of our brethren in this important work; and shall be pleased to receive a goodly list of volunteers through Brother Brown, consisting of men who love the Gospel, have faith in the promise of the Father, and have the integrity, determination and zeal of true Latter-day Saints. We have no fear that too many will respond to this invitation, as the rich valleys south and east of the Colorado offer homes for hundreds of those who desire to extend the curtains of Zion in that direction.[25]

Recruiting efforts as well as the more general calls were attended by a large number of Arizona items in the *Deseret News*. The *Arizona Miner,* published in Prescott, was quoted frequently in reference to opportunity in Arizona and the friendly atmosphere that the region promised Utahns.[26] There is an ebb and flow in Arizona propaganda in the *Deseret News* that closely parallels the southward movement. A good deal of information appeared at the time of the call itself, and then, as the missionaries got on the road, their progress was traced in a flurry of emigrant letters and local news items from wayside towns. Thus, the winter and early spring during which the heaviest migration ran was a time of considerable Arizona news. During the summer, letters of reaction to the

23 See Brigham Young Letter Book no. 13, HDC, pp. 502-3. Also see Brown, *Life of a Pioneer,* p. 466.

24 Brown, *Life of a Pioneer,* pp. 464-67.

25 Letter of Brigham Young, September 16, 1876, directed to "the Bishops and all it may concern," Brigham Young Letter Book no. 13, HDC, pp. 502-3.

26 As an example, see *Deseret News,* June 25, 1873.

mission appeared from new and enthusiastic settlers who sought to promote the country in their own right. Those who were negatively impressed undoubtedly had their hearing, but it was not in the pages of the *News*. As the autumn wore on, the low point in volume was reached and Arizona seemed forgotten for the moment, only to be revived and again rendered a promised land as the next call was launched in the winter and early spring. As the period of founding drew to a close and the Little Colorado began to take its place among the established communities of the church, the promotional type of reporting passed and Arizona items became infrequent and routine.[27]

The lure of movement and the adventure of the unknown fortified the appeal for voluntary action made in the public media. Villages and towns that lay along the routes were particularly susceptible to the contagion of people in motion, and the recurrent American theme of a moving frontier generating its own energy played an important part in Mormon expansion as well. The effect of the outbound settler's enthusiasm was given credence by the return to the wayside towns of old-time residents, some of whom had tremendous prestige locally. As they visited, they plied the home folks with stories calculated to sell them on Arizona and draw thither additional population. Doughty Allen Frost of Kanab was much interested by such reports and on August 11, 1878, wrote: "Jacob Hamblin spoke of his travels in Arizona and New Mexico, created quite a furore among those who are unsettled in their minds as regards Kanab."[28]

Continuing poverty and recurrent drought in southern Utah also made for voluntary migration. This was especially so of the dry years of 1878-79 when people throughout southern Utah suffered for want of flour and cattle starved on the ranges. These conditions resulted in the movement of substantial herds of cattle to Arizona, which though not raising much food had not been affected as badly by the drought. Inevitably men followed. In November of 1879, Frost wrote of Kanab that "out of 116 lots, now occupied in this place 32 are offered for sale. The arizona fever prevails." Frost, upon whom the spirit of unrest was never lost, finally succumbed to the urge himself and made preparations to move after an interview with Erastus Snow which he initiated himself in September of 1883.[29] Thus, the forces of nature joined league with promotional activities and the contagion of adventure to supplement and build upon the

---

[27] See "Index for Arizona references in the *Deseret News*" in unclassified papers of Andrew Jenson on the Arizona Mission, HDC.

[28] "Diary of Allen Frost, 1838-1901," original in possession of Augusta Flake, Snowflake, Arizona; typescript, BYU, p. 194.

[29] *Ibid.*, November 19, 1879, pp. 237, 374.

mission call. This was a voluntary response that took as its own much of the obligation of the mission and submitted to much of its discipline.

An interesting variation of the voluntary response was the delayed answer to an earlier call. Such a case was that of Levi M. Savage, originally called to the unsuccessful mission of 1873. When that mission was abandoned, Savage quite naturally assumed that its failure released him from his obligation to go to Arizona, but only temporarily, and at the time wrote that he expected "if the Arizona mission should be again undertaken to accompany it." His frame of mind did not change and in October of 1876 he wrote:

I . . . started on my mission to Arizona, whence I was called three years since. I should have gone ere this, had not our people all left their settlements in that Territory. But another call was made last winter and some of our folks are now settled on the Little Colorado. I think I must go and join them there in order to fill my mission.[30]

Response to Call

Promotion, of course, was not limited to such narrow objectives as the stimulation of voluntary movement to northern Arizona. The mission system, indeed the entire ecclesiastical organization of the church, rested in the final analysis upon voluntary action. The cultivation of a favorable climate of opinion was consequently essential to the church's success. In the case of the Little Colorado Mission, the natural reluctance of church members to embrace the sacrifice which attended colonizing accentuated the necessity of creating an affirmative frame of mind. Appeals to faith and sense of mission, threats — veiled and open — promises of bright prospects, and adroit management of timing and public opinion were all parts of the arsenal brought to bear by the authorities in mustering out the mission.

The call was often made in such a way as to render a negative reply difficult or impossible. We have already seen Brigham Young soft-talking James S. Brown, assuring him that he would preside in the mission that was to be established in the south. Brown rose to the bait and performed superbly for the church president. His eye upon the opportunity for gratifying leadership, Brown found that northern Arizona held great potential for Mormon settlement. Neither its barrenness nor the difficulties of his own partial disablement (he had lost one leg) dampened his enthusiasm.

---

[30] "Journal of Levi Mathers Savage," original and typescript, HDC; typescript edited by Ruth S. Hilton, pp. 9, 22.

Where Brown was concerned, the call had been tailored to the man. In choice of leaders this was frequently possible. To flattery and promises, other means of recruiting were added including appeal to duty and grand tours of the Arizona Mission. Underlying these was the important if implicit opportunity of shared effort with the General Authorities in the direction of the mission. This close cooperation with the officers from Salt Lake City was a factor of real import, and the prospect of membership in this fraternity was one that made a call to lead very enticing.

To the rank and file of the mission, the call was also made in such a fashion as to increase the likelihood of compliance, although numbers obviously rendered impractical the individual attention given to leaders. Ordinarily the call was made publicly, usually in a general or stake conference of the church. Lists of colonizing missionaries were read along with the calls to proselyting missions, and as much importance attached to assent in one case as the other.

At an earlier date the essential oneness of objectives in temporal and spiritual missions had been stressed when the First Presidency refused to honor a petition requesting release from the Iron Mission:

If you were now on a mission to France or England or any other part of the earth, you would not sit down and counsel together about going to get your families, or about going home till your mission was ended. This is of quite as much importance as preaching the Gospel. The time is now come when it is required of us to build up stakes of Zion and fill these mountains with cities and when your mission is ended you are at liberty to go.[31]

Promises of success often attended the public announcement or were made privately or to the collected missionaries. This was particularly true of dangerous missions. In 1866, for example, when the southern Utah militia was sent into the field during the Navajo disorders, a promise of safety was given to all those who were called. One militiaman recounts the promise and finds an easy out for the disaster that befell one of his fellows in the following:

When Erastus Snow spoke to the party as they were about to leave, he promised that every one that had been called on this expedition should return. Everett [Elijah Everett who was killed by the Indians on August 26, 1866] was not called but was hired to go in the place of another man.[32]

In telling of his father's role in the Arizona Exploring Company of 1873, Osmer D. Flake wrote of another such promise:

---

[31] Matthias F. Cowley, ed., *Wilford Woodruff, History of His Life and Labors as Recorded in His Daily Journals* (Salt Lake City: Deseret News Press, 1909), p. 346.

[32] "Autobiography of Joseph Fish," p. 79.

President Young promised them that they would have dry camp grounds and good feed for their horses every night. He said there was lots of game, and if they did not waste any, they would have fresh meat all the way. The promise was fulfilled; they would ride in snow all day and then find an open space on which there was fine grass and dry ground for camping.

Continuing, Flake related that after riding through deep snows in the San Francisco Mountains all one day one of the men said:

"It looks like Brigham's promise would fail this time; there is no bare ground or feed here." The leader said, "No promise of brother Brigham fails." Soon they came upon a small hill and in front of them lay ten or fifteen acres of fine dry ground covered with grass.[33]

Threats and plain talk were also employed to assure positive response to the call. Interestingly, threats did not often appear in any kind of hell-fire sermonizing about the next life but focused upon temporal failure attributable to disobedience to church counsel. By implication and assurance, the solution was simple if not easy — obedience to God's earthly servants. Characteristic of the tremendous importance that was attached to obedience to counsel was the following written by Wilford Woodruff when he heard that one Little Colorado settler had suffered heavy losses: "I was sorry to hear that Brother Johnson had made such a poor out of his settling. I told him to go to St. Johns. Men who take counsel will be blessed. Those who do not will suffer."[34]

As one would expect, reaction to the call varied greatly, even among those who accepted it. Informed that a call was pending, some sensed that they might be involved and looked forward to the official announcement with high anticipation. Young Christian Lingo Christensen of Sanpete county wrote in 1876:

It was announced by bishop Lars Anderson that Some were going to BE called to go to Arizona   the number was five   the intent of the mission was to Establish the united order and form an acquaintance with the Indians and do them good   a quite lengthy and interesting discourse was delivered and then the Call *Who will go   Who will be called to leave fathers mother and all for the gospel sake   all had their ideas about who would be called   I was shure I was one although I had not herd a word til this time.* Finally the Names   all listened with all attention to the following names   Petter Isacson   Burge Hanson   O. C. Overson   Oley Larsen   C. L. Christensen   all were surprised at this selection.[35]

---

[33] Flake, *William J. Flake,* pp. 51-52.

[34] Letter to Ammon M. Tenney, Le Sueur Papers, AHS. Also see "Diary of Allen Frost," p. 374.

[35] "Diary of Christian Lingo Christensen," typescript, BYU, p. 14. Italics the author's.

Others found the call to a new country appealing for various reasons, including the hope that climatic differences would make life more enjoyable. However, the majority of those who took the trouble to record their feelings were surprised, shocked, or thrown into despair, complying only after considerable self-examination and prayer, or not at all. Frequently, vivid descriptions of more attractive alternatives were recorded. Reaction in some simmered and after days of suppression burst forth; others, like the articulate and self-assertive George W. Brimhall, replied at once and in colorful words. Called to take his family and make a solitary exploration through the twisting and arid canyons of the Colorado River to establish the feasibility of general migration along it, Brimhall exploded to George A. Smith: "I would rather go to Trafalgar's Bay, on the Mediterranean sea, among the Mohammedan Moors, and stay seven years than undertake the head waters of that river." But later he wrote:

I had never refused a mission from the committee [the General Authorities] as yet, and did not wish to this time, although I did not like it. Consulting with my wife she consented . . . but felt conscious that my past conduct had secured for me the aid of my Heavenly Father. Again, I sought Him for information, and was told that I might go, but it would be the destruction of about all of my hard earned property. . . I came away dissatisfied. Again, and again I appealed to the Lord, until I became quite well acquainted with Him and told Him I could not decide myself whether to go or not, and if he would be so kind as to create in me a desire to go, I would thank him all the time. He did, and I began to make ready. . . .[36]

However, Brimhall's free spirit had not been entirely vanquished and he continued to writhe. His torment deepening throughout the trip, he submitted a negative report that reflected his frame of mind as certainly as it did the deserts of the Colorado.

Others were staggered by the call but were not gripped by the fierce internal struggle that kept Brimhall in turmoil. One such case arose at the April conference of 1877 which was held at St. George. This was a celebrated moment — the first of Mormondom's western temples was to be dedicated, and the Saints gathered from far and wide for the event. Into the enthusiasm of the dedication, Brigham Young dropped what for some was a bombshell, a call to the Arizona Mission. This call was given a note of finality when the prospective colonists were told to "sell all that you have . . . leave nothing to come back to." William Flake was among the chosen and plodded with a "sad heart and mental suffering" back to his comfortable home in Beaver. Although he wept and declared "he had

---

[36] Brimhall, *Workers of Utah,* p. 41.

rather go to England," Flake sadly submitted, for he "knew President Young was a Prophet and when the Lord speaks man must obey."[37] Impelled by God's will, he turned south finding in his experience there full vindication of Providence's wisdom and goodness.

Many prospective missionaries either refused the call outright or found the obstacles to their departure to be so great that they never got under way. Some of these obstacles were real, and postponement was permitted or changes made in the call. Others procrastinated from lack of commitment, making "but slow headway," as Wilford Woodruff wryly noted when they were opposed to going.[38] Although no specific data exists, some rough estimates as to the percentage of those responding to the call may be advanced. In 1873 some 250 missionaries were called. About 100, or 40 percent, of these made the trek to Arizona, but others would doubtless have followed had the mission been successful. In 1876 a far larger percentage, possibly as high as 80 or 85 percent, answered the call. During subsequent years, the number who acted favorably slumped. Although a majority of them were said to have reached the mission, the record was on occasion sorry indeed, as was demonstrated at Tooele, west of Salt Lake City, where in 1880 ten families were called. Two made a brief trip south. None remained in Arizona.[39]

In the face of such half-hearted support, recurrent calls were necessary. In spite of the promotional efforts and play upon duty that accompanied mission calls, the rolls of the Little Colorado Mission were filled only with difficulty. It was a process in which manpower was raised by close attention and pressure rather than one in which surpluses afforded ready and anxious recruits.

Duration of the Mission

Surplus populations doubtless existed, but the will to colonize in northern Arizona was another question. Not only did its absence result in failure to answer the call, but it also led to early departure from the mission. After arriving in Arizona and surveying the situation, one pioneer of 1876 saw the problem as one of commitment to the cause:

Large towns inhabited by Latter-day Saints will ere long be built upon this soil . . . I intend to stay and do all that I can to build up this place. All that

---

[37] Flake, *William J. Flake*, pp. 54-55. Also see "Diary of Lucy Hannah Flake," pp. 16-17.

[38] Letter of Wilford Woodruff to A. M. Tenney from Salt Lake City, May 25, 1880, Le Sueur Papers, AHS.

[39] Fish, "History of the Eastern Arizona Stake," p. 59, and "Journal of John W. Tate," typescript, USHS.

is wanted here is some good, faithful Saints, that are willing to wait and work in union and put their trust in God. . . . I would not advise anyone to come to this part of the world that had not the spirit and a knowledge of this mission. They are of no use, for they will not stay.[40]

Many did not have a knowledge of the mission and did not stay. The pattern was set by the withdrawal of the ill-starred expedition of 1873. Later, as successful colonization began, the rate of departure remained high. When the initiates of 1876 learned what the future on the Little Colorado held in store, a mass exodus took place. Many went home by official leave; some returned to Arizona — most did not. Others merely packed up and with no apology withdrew. Early in the course of settlement, Lot Smith, who stayed on until his death in 1892, recognized that transcience was a major characteristic of the mission when he wrote that it had had a "strange history, so far most who came having got weak in the back or knees and gone home."[41] According to one report, the homeward flight was so heavy that after five years "scarcely one-tenth of those who had been called . . . could be found at their posts of duty."[42] In the eyes of those who remained, the dissatisfied returned to Utah to circulate "evil and untruthful reports about the country" and as detractors of the mission richly deserved the censure and scorn of the faithful.[43] As reluctant as it was to broadcast adverse propaganda, the church deemed it better to let the disaffected go than to keep them in Arizona. After an official visit in the summer of 1876 during which he observed this restiveness firsthand, Daniel H. Wells of the First Presidency joined Brigham Young to write:

We are reliably informed that there are a few in some of the camps whose mouths are full of murmuring, and some whose hearts incline to apostasy. We want none such to remain with you, lest they poison the camp with the leaven of their hard feeling. . . . The selfishness and individuality that have characterized the labors of some of our brethren should not find a place with those called to this misson.[44]

Even faithful missionaries found it hard to resist the temptation to return to Utah, and often the major difference between them and the "quitters" whom they so roundly castigated was merely a matter of time. Counter-migration began early and continued to take its toll.

---

[40] George Dabling to *Deseret News,* September 20, 1876.
[41] *Deseret News,* March 27, 1878.
[42] "History of the Little Colorado Stake."
[43] *Deseret News,* September 20, 1876.
[44] Letter to "Elders Smith, Lake, Ballinger, Allen and the Brethren camped on the Little Colorado," July 18, 1876, Brigham Young Letters, HDC.

A matter not clearly defined was the question of the mission's duration. Most missionaries came as long-term colonists intending to make the Little Colorado their future home. Subsequent events and desires, however, probably were more important than were the original calls in determining the duration of the mission which was, consequently, characterized by great variation. As we have noted, many calls were terminated by early departure; others lasted for years — some for the working lifetime of the men involved. An example of the latter was Lorenzo H. Hatch who served in the Eastern Arizona Stake Presidency until 1900. His release at that time terminated the mission he had answered in 1876 and permitted him to return to Cache Valley where part of his large polygamous family had resided throughout the entire period.[45]

One mission terminated as late as 1919 and then only by directive of the presidency of the church. Their letter stating the circumstances of the case and suggesting release follows:

We have just received a letter . . . from Parley Savage son of Levi M. Savage of Woodruff, Arizona, stating in effect that his father, who is now nearly seventy years old, is obliged to work for his living, that he is doing days work on the Woodruff Dam, walking six miles to and from the place of his work; that he has been eager for years to leave Woodruff, and has [been] known to remark to his son about five years ago that he thought that after living forty years on the Little Colorado, shoveling sand a great part of that time into it only to see it washed away, was sufficient to bring him a release, but he is willing to stay provided we think it best for him to do so.

Unless there are reasons unknown to us going to show why Bishop Savage should not have been released from the call said to have been made upon him to settle in Woodruff, Arizona, we would like you to inform him, that he may consider himself perfectly free to make his home elsewhere, and that if he decides to move away we desire him to know that he will go with our very best wishes and blessing.[46]

Shortly, Savage took his leave, returning to Salt Lake City.

Thales Haskell, who as a missionary to the Hopis was one of the first Mormons to winter in Arizona, is another example of the tenacity with which some men stood by their mission:

At a conference in Bluff [in Utah's San Juan country] in 1886 at which Erastus Snow was a visitor, he asked Thales where his family was. Thales told him that they had all moved to Manasa, Colorado. Apostle Snow then asked why he was not with them to which Thales answered that until the same authority which had called him into the mission released him, he did not feel at liberty

---

45 "Lorenzo Hill Hatch Journal," original and typescript, HDC; multilith edited by Ruth S. Hilton, p. 252.

46 "Journal of Levi Mathers Savage," pp. 86-88.

— *C. Gregory Crampton*

Inscription left by St. Johns missionary of 1884.

to leave the field. Brother Snow then said "I take it upon myself to release you as of this day and hope that you may soon join your family in Colorado."[47]

This raises the question of the extent and duration of the Little Colorado Mission as an institution of Mormon expansion. It should be borne in mind that in this sense the mission was a pioneering agency and that its success lessened and ultimately extinguished its need. The wilderness of the frontier onto which it moved and the area's lack of other social organization rendered the mission's beginning distinct. With the passing of time, the ordinary paraphernalia of the church supplanted the mission,

---

[47] See "Thales Hastings Haskell, Pioneer, Scout, Explorer, Indian Missionary 1847-1909," ed. Albert E. Smith, multilith BYU, p. 51.

and the use of the term mission to designate a place and a process passed, shading off imperceptibly at first and more rapidly later. Although no official statement was issued ending the mission, it was largely a thing of the past by 1885.

Extraordinary needs arose occasionally that extended the usefulness of the mission, and the fact that numerous crises marked the course of Mormon affairs in Arizona tended to prolong its use. On the other hand, the fact that the region was settled late in the history of the frontier curtailed its longer use. Indian trouble no longer necessitated extraordinary mobilization, and railroads and contact with the Gentile economy likewise lessened the need for the mission's task-force organization. A combination of such factors resulted in an extensive use of the mission during the first decade of settlement and its passing as a useful instrument thereafter.

By the mission, the Little Colorado's earliest administrative organization came to be. By its use, society was mobilized to carry out what to most was an unattractive task. Even the limited success of this colonization could not have been achieved without the mission.

4. TREK OVER THE MORMON WAGON ROAD

The fond old route known as Lee's Ferry by way of upper Kanab.

L. H. HATCH

To describe this country and its sterility for one hundred miles, its gloomy barrenness, would subject the reader's credulity to too high a strain. Not even the caw of a crow, or the bark of a wolf, was there to break the awful monotony . . . here there was nothing but a continual stench of miasma, and hot streaks of poisonous air to breathe. Was this Hades . . . or the place for the condign punishment of the wicked? Or was it the grand sewer for the waste and filth of vast animation? . . . It was a horrible place.

GEORGE W. BRIMHALL

Preparations

IN JANUARY OF 1876 James S. Brown returned to Salt Lake City from his exploratory mission and reported his favorable impression of the Little Colorado region. Fearing that the open conditions necessary to preemptive expansion were passing, the church moved immediately to establish colonies there. Acting with such haste as to suggest that the plan of colonization had been previously laid and was waiting only on Brown's final report for implementation, Brigham Young prodded the first of recurrent groups onto the southward roads within four weeks. During the ensuing months, trails penetrated earlier by only the hardiest scouts became beaten ways known firsthand to hundreds of Mormon emigrants and to thousands more through personal letters and the pages of the *Deseret News*.

[63]

A call for two hundred men and families was hastily circulated. Following its directive, most of the missionaries met in Salt Lake City late in January, where they were organized into companies of fifty according to the locality from which they came.[1] They were also briefed as to what they might expect in the Little Colorado country and given some idea of how to prepare for the trip. Haste, they were told, was an imperative.

As they rushed to put their affairs in order, these first missionaries were confronted with problems that characterized the entire Mormon migration to Arizona. Since most mission calls were for permanent colonization, it was necessary to make extensive and careful preparations. Although there was a sameness about the process, the time allowed varied greatly, according to the needs out of which the different calls grew and the circumstances and energy of the individuals called. The missionaries who left during those short winter days of 1876 took no more than a month to get under way. Inevitably some were unable to settle their affairs and had to return to Utah to finish their preparations. Later, as the nature of the urgency shifted and the costs of the return trip in terms of time and truancy became apparent, it was more customary to give six months or even longer for the missionary to make ready.

One of the first steps in preparing was the disposition of Utah property. Although such was not always the case, prospective emigrants were usually counseled to dispose of their holdings and sever all economic bonds. Therefore the move south generally required that property not only be sold but that it be moved quickly. Characteristic of the first year's experience was that of a central Utah missionary who received his call on January 23. On January 31 he sold his homestead and at the end of another week left for the Little Colorado River.[2] A favored few were helped in the process when the call by which they were directed to Arizona charged other men to purchase their property. Such was the case at Mt. Pleasant in Sanpete County where "persons were designated to buy out the brethren called at fair, just and equitable prices."[3]

Forced as a rule to seek their own markets, missionaries found it extremely difficult to get "equitable prices." Indeed, mission calls appear to have created a buyer's market with land and improvements almost

---

[1] See Frihoff G. Nielson, "The History of the Little Colorado Mission," a fragmentary document included in "Joseph City Ward History."

[2] "John Bushman Diaries, 1871-1923," handwritten original in possession of Martin D. Bushman, Snowflake, Arizona; typescript prepared by George S. Tanner in possession of author.

[3] *Deseret News,* February 9, 1876.

always going for prices far below the value placed upon them by the missionaries. There is no evidence that the tight land situation that is generally said to have prevailed in territorial Utah was sufficiently acute to result in ready sales for those called to Arizona. Although they sometimes resented the dilemma and commented on its irony, most regarded the losses they sustained as part of the sacrifice incident to settling a new country.

Some tried to minimize losses by leaving their property in the hands of friends or family to sell, or they returned themselves and sought to move it at their leisure during subsequent winters. Even when this course was followed, ready markets and satisfactory prices were rare. An instructive case was that of Miles P. Romney, who after a year or two in Arizona returned to St. George to sell his holdings. After reducing the price to one quarter of its "ordinary value" without finding a buyer, he finally boarded up his buildings and held on.[4] Others depending upon the returns from property to outfit themselves for the trip found it necessary to sell at whatever price. Most transactions took place with little or no cash changing hands, the emigrant bartering land and improvements for cattle, horses, or equipment.

In planning for the trip and the new life that lay at its end, missionaries drew from various sources. Although at the time of their call many were not frontiersmen in the ordinary sense, the Mormon experience had been one of pioneering, and in a general way they had a good grasp of what would be expected of them. Many had crossed the continent by wagon or handcart; all knew people who had. The processes of the church, including its expansions, had resulted in a mobile frontier so that the pioneers of the Little Colorado were not novices in the lore of the trail. In addition to this environmental or cultural preparation, many of the early missionaries met for briefing sessions where they were instructed as to the route and needs of the trip. Furthermore, during times of heavy migration, successive rendezvous were established where experienced frontiersmen gave additional instruction and aid to travelers.[5] As the years passed, leaders and personal friends in Arizona wrote detailed letters specifying needs that had become apparent during the process of colonization. These letters, some of which were addressed to the *Deseret*

---

[4] *Ibid.*, November 23, 1881.

[5] In the migration of 1873, for example, Pipe Springs and Moenkopi were designated as such rendezvous. At these two sites, incoming travelers were met by Joseph W. Young and Horton D. Haight. See letter of Brigham Young to Joseph W. Young, March 10, 1873, Brigham Young Letters, HDC, and letter of Henry Holmes to F. D. Richards, June 27, 1873, *Millennial Star* 25 (1863): 552-54.

News, received broad circulation, probably coming to the attention of all prospective emigrants.

Special attention was given to draft stock and wagons. Although what a man had on hand was often the determining factor, considerable pains were taken to secure the best. Teams were trained and animals traded. It was thought by some that brood mares would be of the greatest value. Yet individual preference often dictated in favor of oxen or mules. In any event it was a diverse array that took to the trail at the front of the wagons of the Little Colorado settlers, with teams of horses, oxen, and mules to be seen in virtually every group of emigrants.

Wagons were repaired and when possible new ones purchased. From the very first it was found possible to refit along the way, and references to both buying and selling wagons en route are not infrequent. Within a short time it was apparent that well-made, medium-sized wagons were best. But as in the case of teams, variety was the norm. Many proceeded with only one wagon and a two-horse team, while others equipped themselves more elaborately, taking as many as five or six wagons and draft animals in commensurate numbers. Frequently wagons in tandem drawn by long strings of oxen or mules were used. The characteristic wagon was covered with a tarp which kept the worst of the elements out, though inevitably water and dust reached the precious goods within.

Loads were made with an eye to the long haul south and to the needs of the new life at the end of the trail, with each pioneer seeking some kind of a practical adjustment of the problems raised by the two sets of needs. A rule of thumb sometimes followed was to limit the weight to 2,000 pounds per wagon. A more valuable guide came from a missionary who wrote from Arizona to suggest medium-sized work horses and good wagons not loaded "to exceed six (6) or seven (7) hundred pounds to each animal." [6]

Cargoes were characteristically utilitarian in nature. Grain for draft stock and seed purposes was an ordinary item as were implements for use once the new land had been gained. One bachelor missionary from northern Utah's Hyde Park who accompanied Lot Smith in 1876 stressed the essentials, taking:

$50.00 in cash, 4 oxen, one wagon, one plane, hoe, pitchfork, crow bar, one rifle, two barrels of nails, one bucket, milk pan, and strainer, lantern, bake and camp kettle, a fry pan, two tin plates and cups, knives, forks and spoons, four blankets and a bed, two pair of shoes, and three pair of boots, 4 bu. wheat, 1½ bu. of potatoes, 500 lbs of flour, 40 gal of molasses, 20 lbs of apples, one ham and six lbs of butter, 4 lbs of candles, 9 lbs of soap, 16 boxes of matches and some garden seed. [7]

— Utah State Historical Society
Ready for the road: a Mormon pioneer outfit.

All did not limit themselves to such spartan necessities, and luxuries were taken to brighten new homes, including an occasional piano or organ. Men either found it easier to restrict themselves in what they loaded or were persuaded that the items they selected were necessaries. Women, on the other hand, were often accused of taking things that could be done without. Regardless of where the blame lay, these pioneers like others who had gone before often loaded too heavily and found it necessary to jettison a variety of items en route, including family heirlooms and such necessities of the frontier as flat irons, wood ranges, and sewing machines.

Leaders and experienced travelers worked constantly to limit loads. An interesting story related by Daniel W. Jones, who in 1877 led a party south by way of St. George and Pearce's Crossing below the Grand Can-

---

[6] *Deseret News,* March 24, 1880.

[7] See "Diary of Peter Nielson," translated from Danish by J. F. Nielson, compiled by Frihoff G. Nielson, in possession of Mrs. LaVinta Shiner, Price, Utah.

yon, reveals Brigham Young's ability to deal with this sort of trouble where the best efforts of lesser leaders failed. Jones, who had cut his own load to the bare essentials, had given up in his efforts to get others to do likewise and meeting Young in St. George told him so. To his remark, the president replied:

Get your company in the best shape you can and as soon as possible move out. There is a nice little settlement, Santa Clara, on your road. There is a beautiful piece of sandy road from here to there, just as will help you get the brethren to see the importance of lightening up. When you get there you can set up an auction store. The people are pretty well off and will be able to buy what you have to sell.[8]

Jones complied, and it proved to be substantially as Young had foreseen, with the exception that the emigrants traded with such skill that their new loads of grain and dried fruit were nearly as heavy as the irons and sewing machines swapped off. But as the expedition's wagon master laconically commented, it was better to "roll at a wheel to help get a sack of corn over a hard place" than it was to "strain his back to move an old stove along that was not worth hauling."[9]

In addition to the ordinary physical preparations for the trip and pioneer life, many of those called took advantage of the newly opened temple at St. George or the Endowment House in Salt Lake City to solemnize holy ordinances that could not be performed in the deserts of Arizona. Some were married for the first, second, or third times, and others did temple work for their dead. Church and civic positions were resigned, and the inevitable round of farewell parties and meetings wound up the process of preparation. Send-offs were sometimes elaborate. A crowd of four hundred gathered in one town to see their representatives depart. At Lehi the town square was thronged and the 1876 leave-taking charged with such excitement and sentiment that a least one man, born four years later, caught its spirit and though not there in person seemed to recall the square, crowded and festive for the occasion.[10]

The Trail

Preparations completed, the missionaries took to the trail. The routes south through Utah were well worked out and followed the existing line of settlements. Always important in the West, roads were rarely more

---

8 Jones, *Among the Indians*, p. 290.
9 *Ibid.*, p. 291.
10 Interview with David A. Peterson of Lehi, Utah, July 1963.

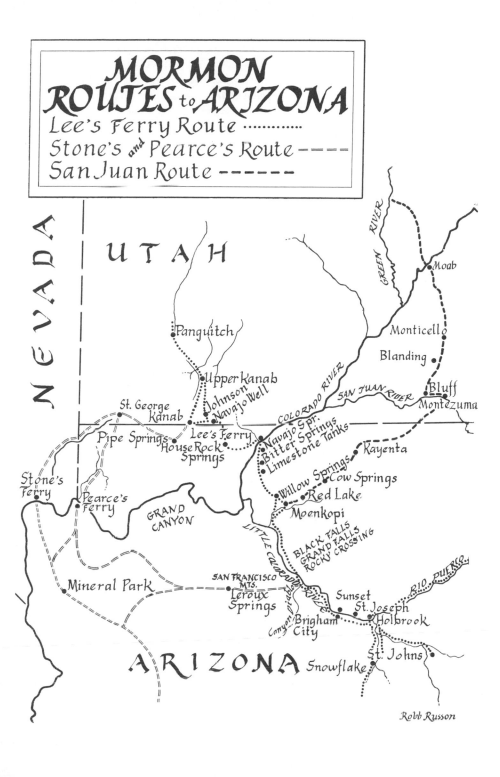

MORMON
ROUTES to ARIZONA
Lee's Ferry Route ·············
Stone's and Pearce's Route − − − −
San Juan Route − − − − − −

NEVADA

UTAH

GREEN RIVER

Moab

Panguitch

Monticello

Blanding

Upper Kanab

Johnson

Navajo Well

COLORADO RIVER

SAN JUAN RIVER

Bluff

Montezuma

St. George

Kanab

Pipe Springs

Lee's Ferry

House Rock
Springs

Navajo Spr.

Bitter Springs

Limestone Tanks

Kayenta

Stone's
Ferry

Pearce's
Ferry

GRAND
CANYON

Willow Springs

Cow Springs

Red Lake

Moenkopi

LITTLE COLORADO

BLACK FALLS
GRAND FALLS
ROCKY CROSSING

Mineral Park

SAN FRANCISCO
MTS.

Leroux
Springs

RIO PUERCO

Sunset

St. Joseph

Holbrook

Canyon Diablo

Brigham
City

ARIZONA

Snowflake

St. Johns

Robb Russon

significant, as the closeness of the religious bond between mother and daughter communities gave a two-way movement that was as necessary to the essential character of the Little Colorado colony as it was constant and continuing. Unlike the great national trails, the Mormon routes bore north and south. Threading through mountain defiles and along desert water courses, they were the product of pioneer use rather than of government or army transportation. Beginning as Indian trails, they became first the path of exploration and later the highroad of Mormon expansion.

By 1880 three routes to the Little Colorado were known. Two little-used passages flanked the canyon lands that lay athwart the borders of Utah and Arizona. The western road, which had been pioneered by Jacob Hamblin, ran south from St. George to cross the Colorado at Pearce's Ferry at the mouth of Grand Wash. An extension crossed the river a few miles downstream near the confluence of the Virgin and the Colorado at Stone's Ferry, or Bonelli's Ferry, as the Mormons knew it. Once over the river, traffic from Stone's Ferry bore a little east of south to about the present site of Kingman, from which it cut east between the headwaters of Bill Williams Fork and the Verde River and then on to the Salt River. Leaving the Colorado River by way of Grapevine Wash, Pearce's Ferry traffic either veered southwest to join the Stone's Ferry road or held nearly due south through Wallapai Valley before turning east by southeast along the Sitgreaves trail which joined the Prescott to Fort Wingate mail road just south of Bill Williams Mountain and thence east to strike the Little Colorado at Canyon Diablo. Little Colorado emigrants who chose the Stone's Ferry route followed it to a few miles south of Mineral Park where they turned sharply east to pick up the Prescott to Fort Wingate road.[11] In addition to these trails there was also some effort to open a more direct route east from Wallapai Valley to strike the Little Colorado north of the San Francisco Mountains.[12] In spite of high hopes among their advocates, these roads did not solve the problems of feed and water and circled far to the west; as a consequence, they did not bear any great portion of the Little Colorado traffic but were important in the movement to southern Arizona.

Another little-used route to northern Arizona went by way of Utah's San Juan country. Taken aback at the rigors of the trip over the Lee's Ferry road, Arizona's first pioneers and church leaders looked to Utah's

---

[11] For a detailed account of a trip by way of Pearce's Ferry, see "Journal of John W. Tate," entries for November and December. Also see Melvin T. Smith, "The Colorado River: Its History in the Lower Canyons Area" (unpublished Ph.D. Dissertation, Brigham Young University, 1972), pp. 374-439.

[12] See letter of Jacob Hamblin to *Deseret News*, February 28, 1877.

southeast for an easier path. Revealing this interest, Brigham Young advised Lot Smith late in the summer of 1876 to counsel missionaries to stay with the known route while the San Juan was further studied. But after William C. Allen, one of the original leaders of fifty, struggled back to Utah through the San Juan during August and September, the route was abandoned temporarily. However, as the movement of the church to the southeast accelerated in the last years of the 1870s, Apostle Erastus Snow continued to feel that this would become a strategic and convenient route. Indeed, the San Juan Mission was to some degree founded to serve in the communications system envisaged.[13] Even after the Hole-in-the-Rock expedition had taken the measure of the area's tangled canyons, Snow persisted in his hope that a Mormon road could be developed, and in the fall of 1880 wrote urging church authorities to settle at Green River Crossing thus securing the route "which is destined to be our nearest and best . . . to . . . Eastern Arizona."[14]

The Main-Traveled Way

The main-traveled way was the most direct, passing between Utah's mountain ranges to cross the Colorado River at Lee's Ferry. It was over this road that the missions of 1873 and 1876 picked their way, and despite persistent effort to flank its canyons it continued to be the most heavily traveled road between Utah and the new colony during the nineteenth century.

The Lee's Ferry road was impressive, among other reasons, for its distances. From northern Utah, it stretched out for seven hundred miles or more. From the southern part of the territory, it was substantially shorter, perhaps a little more than three hundred miles, depending on the points of origin and destination; but these last were the hardest miles and still constituted a long and exhausting trip.

South to the Sevier Valley the route was heavily traveled and ran through a relatively level country. Consequently, pioneers made good time, pausing only to recruit their stock and visit friends in the communities that lay along the way. But as the road wound up the meadowed valley of the Sevier River, conditions worsened, and the cold of the winter

---

[13] Reflecting this hope, Erastus Snow wrote to John Taylor on November 6, 1879: "Silas S. Smith has started for San Juan with forty to fifty men and some boys and quite a few families, with Boats &c intending to hew their way threw the Canyon and open a straight or more direct route to San Juan and as he thinks also to the head of Little Colorado." Erastus Snow Letters, HDC.

[14] See letter of Erastus Snow to John Taylor, September 29, 1880, *ibid.* For the Hole-in-the-Rock company's incredible undertaking, see Miller, *Hole-in-the-Rock.*

travel that characterized most of the Arizona migration was made more extreme by mounting elevations. Forced to cross and recross the stream, winter migrants experienced great difficulty getting in and out of the river by way of partially frozen dugouts. Crossings were further complicated by the necessity of entering freezing water to chop ice not yet thick enough to hold loaded wagons.

Possibly no large group had a better opportunity to test these frosty miles than did the missionaries of 1876. Toiling through snow that lay up to eighteen inches on the level, and in temperatures that froze the feet of both livestock and humans, they were well initiated to the rigors of winter travel by the time they reached Panguitch in the south end of the Sevier Valley. But, as many of them feared, the hardest part of the journey lay in the thirty-five-mile mountain stretch from Panguitch to Orderville. After crossing south of Panguitch, they followed the old road up the west branch of the Sevier, a long day's drive to Hatch Ranch. Here they girded themselves for the push on to the timbered rim of the Great Basin, which they reached near present-day Long Valley Junction. Although there were many outfits on the road, the trace through the snow drifted in almost as it was broken, and each new party was forced to break its own way through drifts three or four feet deep.[15] By pushing far into the night, some who were fortunate in the condition of their animals made it up the divide from Hatch to the rim of the basin in one long day. It took others four days, and one unfortunate party floundered in the snows eighteen days in making the sixty miles from Panguitch to Kanab.

From the summit they continued along the course now followed by Highway 89. Flanked by canyons, whose delicately shaded rock more than hinted at the proximity of the latter-day tourist meccas of Bryce and Zion canyons, the downhill road proved to be nearly as trying as had the drag up. The primary problem of the descent was ice. One man finding that the steepest roads in northern Utah would not compare related that "sometimes three animals were down out of four, and every minute we expected to see an axletree broken."[16]

Although the entire emigration of that winter moved through Long Valley and Kanab (approximately Highway 89's present course), later

---

[15] The following characterizes the accounts of the journey over the rim of the Great Basin: "They were four days on the divide, where the snow was three feet deep, making ten miles a day, working till midnight one night to make that distance. The road had been broken previously, but had filled up again, and was the worst road they had ever seen." *Deseret News,* September 27, 1876.

[16] *Ibid.,* April 5, 1876. The snows of that year were unusually heavy; for one period of over a week it snowed without letup. James T. Woods and three other families who were caught on the divide abandoned all but one wagon in which they escaped, pushing on with their livestock. *Ibid.,* September 27, 1876.

traffic often ran from the rim of the Great Basin east to Upper Kanab, or present-day Alton, and then down a narrow passageway through Johnson Creek past vast cedar forests to the village of Johnson twelve miles east of Kanab. Cutting several miles from the trip, this road avoided a hard pull over the sand hills between Carmel Junction and Kanab. From Johnson migrants passed on east about eight miles to Navajo Wells before leaving Utah and mounting the Kaibab Plateau. The road across the sprawling east bastion of the Kaibab was perhaps the most variable of the journey, changing sharply according to the season. During the winter, it was a frozen waste of juniper and pinon where snows piled axletree deep. In the spring it became a slimy sea of mud and in the summer a searing dust-choked and wagon-wrenching stairway.[17]

From the east foot of the Kaibab, the road dropped through House Rock Valley, which opens out toward the river like a giant cornucopia, to pick up the Vermillion Cliffs which it followed as they looped east and north to Lee's Ferry. Four waterholes — House Rock Springs, Jacob's Pools, Soap Creek, and Badger Creek — provided a scanty and, in the case of the latter two places, a foul-tasting supply of water. Of the four, House Rock Springs, which lay about three-quarters of a mile east of the road at the foot of steep sandstone cliffs, provided not only the best water but good grazing and firewood as well. Consequently, it was a major resting place, and the cliffs and rocks around it became the most complete register of the Arizona migration, as hundreds of travelers took time to chisel their names and the dates of their visits. Some idea of the potable qualities of Soap Creek may be gained from one early diarist's account that it had been named when Jacob Hamblin and other Indian scouts used its water to boil pork and beans and found that the entire concoction turned to soap.[18]

Presaging the future of travel across this section, John D. Lee's experience in opening the road between Johnson and the Colorado River at the mouth of the Paria in 1871 had been almost unbelievably difficult. Like most Mormon colonizing endeavors, the establishment of the ferry

---

[17] "Lorenzo Hill Hatch Journal," p. 87. In May of 1876, James T. Woods, who a few weeks before had suffered from frostbite and fled the drifting snows near the rim of the basin, found the Kaibab stretch to be transformed by unseasonable heat and had his "entire satisfaction of summer." See *Deseret News,* September 23, 1876. Anthony W. Ivins noted that the mountains received their name "Kaibab," or "lying," in Indian from their sprawling nature. "Anthony Woodward Ivins Journal," p. 27.

[18] "Horatio Morrill's Book," typescript USHS, October 8, 1869. I have chosen to refer to most of the springs and wells along the road to Arizona in the plural, because pioneer diaries use the plural. In so doing I have ignored the established nomenclature of modern maps where most are referred to in the singular.

was a cooperative action, and scouts who knew the Kaibab–House Rock Valley trail were directed to guide and help Lee in opening the new road. As it turned out, the entire undertaking was a medley of error, miscalculation, and struggle. Men failed, equipment broke, and cattle and Lee himself went astray. Consequently, it was only after weeks of appalling exertion that Lee succeeded in moving his livestock to the site and working the first wagon trace south to the ferry.[19]

Persistent rumors of hostility on the part of the miners, coupled with the fact that a considerable number of them were crossing the country en route to the San Juan mining field in Colorado, raised fears among the apprehensive Mormons. Their suspicion mounting when certain miners announced their intent to claim key waterholes, Hamblin and Lee moved to acquire clear control of the springs on the House Rock section of the road. Hamblin established a small livestock operation in the House Rock Valley, which according to his son the Indians had ceded to him. Developing the springs somewhat, he built a small cabin at the site.[20] A few miles to the southeast Lee claimed the water at Jacob's Pools and after building a rock hut there ran stock in the area for several years before trading his claim to Hamblin. Lee, whose name was closely linked with the Mountain Meadows Massacre and who was finally tried and executed for his implication in the event, felt his vulnerability. He was therefore anxious to exclude Gentile neighbors. Pushing to secure the water in the interest of the church, he found the "want of a little snap" on the part of his associates to be most galling.[21]

However, the flurry of prospecting interest soon passed and with it the threat of Gentile control. With the exception of Lee's holdings and occasional use by Orderville herds, the ranching operations appear to have lapsed for a time. Nevertheless, the movement of miners over the

---

[19] Cleland and Brooks, *Mormon Chronicle,* vol. 2, pp. 185-86.

[20] *Ibid.* Also see Pearson H. Corbett, *Jacob Hamblin, Peacemaker* (Salt Lake City: Deseret Book Co., 1952), pp. 328, 330, 518.

[21] In company with John Mangram and a Brother Heath, Lee arrived at Jacob's Pools on April 16, 1872, where the following exchange took place which is instructive as to both the plan to control the route by possession of its water and Lee's feelings about it: "Here [Jacob's Pools] Jno. Mangram proposed to return home & at some future time come & secure this & the Ranch at Soapcreek. I felt so indignant at the Idear of Coming some 80 Miles & going back without doeing anything and risking the chance to fall into the hands of our Enemies for the want of a little snap, that [I] spoke a little cross & sharp & said that I had to much reguard for the confidence that leaders reposed in me & too Much interest for this Kingdom than to flat out like that; that he was a conselor & Should be the last man to flat out."

Lee evidently won some concessions from Mangram as they stayed. On the seventh, they staked off the springs and built a "3 feet wall of a House by noon" when a company of miners came along and announced that they had intended to secure "those Springs." But as Lee exultantly notes, "we were ahead of them." See Cleland and Brooks, *Mormon Chronicle,* vol. 2, pp. 185-86.

route in 1872 and the Mormon effort to retain control did much to establish the road. Government surveyors, especially those connected with the Powell Survey, also found frequent cause to use the route during this period; by the time of the Little Colorado migration, its course was well fixed. But for many years the approaches to the ferry remained a challenge and a threat to all who passed that way.

Lee's Ferry

A vital link in the chain of communications was Lee's Ferry. This crossing had been discovered prior to 1860 by Jacob Hamblin, who along with other scouts used it occasionally. As we have observed, John D. Lee was dispatched to the spot late in 1871, establishing a ferry which he operated until he was taken by the federal authorities in Panguitch in 1874.[22] At the time of Lee's arrest, his wife Emma assumed responsibility and with the help of Warren Johnson operated the ferry for the next five years. Before his death in 1877, Brigham Young authorized Ephraim K. Hanks to purchase the ferry in the interest of the church, but the transaction fell through on the passing of the president. Thereafter, Warren M. Johnson made similar overtures, but the ferry remained in Mrs. Lee's hands until the spring of 1879. It being rumored that outsiders were negotiating with Mrs. Lee, President of the Church John Taylor directed John W. Young, who was at Moenkopi during that spring, to buy the place. This Young was able to do for a consideration of $3,000 paid mostly in livestock. The ferry became the property of the church and of the Little Colorado settlements which advanced some of the cattle used in the purchase.[23]

Important Mormon use of the ferry, however, had begun in 1873. The outward-bound missionaries of that year found Lee living in primitive

[22] By 1870 Lee was a source of some embarrassment to the church. Some hint of Brigham's thoughts as to the future was apparent in a conversation between Lee and Young recorded by the former when the president visited Paria in 1870: "Pres. Young . . . Said to Me that he would like to have Me Gather My wives, sons & Daughters around me & setle in any of the Places we should Select & Start the Family order, stating that I had passed through a great deal of Hardship in my life & Now he would like to See me Enjoy peace the balance of my days. I replied that My Mind led further to a country that I had Seen in visions & dreams. He continued, You will see that country; it [is] over the Colorado in the San Francisco Mountain. I intend Bro. L. Stewart to go there & you May go too when the Time comes &c." See Juanita Brooks, "Lee's Ferry at Lonely Dell," *Utah Historical Quarterly* 25, (1957): 284-95.

[23] For reference to the role of Hanks and Johnson, see McClintock, *Mormon Settlement in Arizona*, p. 93. Young's purchase of the ferry is recorded in the "Diary of L. John Nuttall, 1834-1905," original in possession of Mrs. Clara Nuttal Glass, Provo, Utah; typescript BYU, p. 285. For the important role of Warren Johnson at Lee's Ferry, see P. T. Reilly, "Warren Marshall Johnson Forgotten Saint," *Utah Historical Quarterly* 39 (1971): 3-22.

conditions, but their wagons were moved across the river without untoward incident and without delay. Most of them were pleased with the operation and commended Lee for his service. With inimitable spelling, Andrew Amundsen recorded his favorable impressions: ". . . we corsed . . . all over sef and sound. . . . Dea Lee was a verry jocky, an jovele, full of fun." [24] As the spring wore on, some missionaries even found time for pleasure and, much to Lee's satisfaction, joined his family in moonlight boat rides "over the Still waters of the Colorado" complete with "Music by the constantina." [25]

The river's passage was always accompanied by a certain amount of tension and fear. In part, this was a matter of expediting traffic and keeping this potential bottleneck clear. The nature of the desert over which the migration moved required that emigrants be spread out, and delay at the river complicated the trip. An additional factor was the limited feed at Lonely Dell, as Emma Lee had named their home. Large numbers of stock simply could not be fed; consequently, traffic had to be kept moving. This was not easy. The ferry was small and open, and excited cattle crowded onto its unfamiliar deck often quit it singly or en masse and headed back for the north shore. Pioneer accounts indicate that much stock was forced to swim, an expedient that appears to have been more successful with horses than cattle. After 1879, as large herds were driven to Arizona, cattle sometimes milled on the north bank or, if crossed early, strayed unattended from the river while herdsmen struggled at the ferry as long as ten days to get herds across. [26]

At other times, crossing was accomplished much more quickly. On at least one occasion, early in the winter of 1878, the river froze, enabling pioneers to cross on the ice without waiting for the ferry. Children and household belongings were loaded upon upended tables and sledded across while wagons were pushed and cattle were either thrown and dragged or driven after the ice had been sanded. It was an easy crossing but still a slow process and not without its anxieties as the burdened ice groaned and snapped and even parted at one point so that the water could be seen below. Anthony W. Ivins, who crossed the ice thirty-two times in the course of moving one party over, revealed characteristic relief when he wrote that all were "feeling very thankful that we had successfully crossed that horrid river without loss of life or property." [27] Others took

---

24 See Amundsen, "Journal."

25 Cleland and Brooks, *Mormon Chronicle,* vol. 2, p. 238.

26 See Evans Coleman, "Biographical Sketch of William B. Maxwell," Coleman Papers, AHS.

27 "Anthony Woodward Ivins Journal," p. 98.

— *C. Gregory Crampton*

Lee's Backbone, first known as Lee's Hill, a tilted apron of rock on the south side of the Colorado River at Lee's Ferry, as viewed from the north bank.

the ice span which appeared only in the comparatively calm water of the crossing to be a manifestation of the hand of the Lord in answer to their importunings that He "Cast up an highway in the midst of the deep."[28]

Fear grew, of course, from concern for human life. Dry marches, Indians, and bad roads notwithstanding, the river with rapids running only a few hundred yards below the crossing was undoubtedly regarded as the journey's greatest danger. Anxiety was often expressed at the condition of the ferry and other equipment which was of insufficient size and often in a state of disrepair. The ferry operators, on the other hand, inspired confidence and a feeling of well-being. The reaction of travelers to Lee's competence has already been noted. Emma Lee and Warren Johnson were also known as capable and careful operators.[29] But occasionally

---

[28] Logan Brimhall, "Table Sleighs," taken from "Diamond Jubilee Gems, Snowflake Stake of Zion, 1887-1962," compiled by Alice S. Hanson et al., multilithed copy in possession of author.

[29] "Autobiography of Joseph Fish," p. 155. Also see Brooks, "Lee's Ferry," *Utah Historical Quarterly* 25 (1957): 284-90.

mishaps occurred, and in the course of the ferry's history several people drowned. Perhaps the best known of these was explorer Lorenzo Roundy, who lost his life in the spring of 1876 while making a crossing with Daniel H. Wells of the First Presidency, and an official party bound for the new settlements on the Little Colorado.[30]

There was some variation in the fees charged for ferriage. According to Lee's own account, the Haight expedition of 1873 paid $3.00 per wagon and $1.00 extra for horses. By 1876 missionary fees (half-fare) were worked out at $1.00 per wagon and $0.25 for each extra animal. These charges were maintained for several years, but by 1879 there was either considerable inconsistency in their application or the general rate had been altered upward. At that time Silas S. Smith, who was exploring the southern route to the San Juan country, chose to swim his horses rather than pay what he considered the excessive rate of $1.00 per head. However, most missionaries seemed grateful at the nominal prices charged.[31] Some felt that because of the church's obvious interest in the ferry, which included ownership of the ferryboat, missionaries ought to be entitled to free passes, but church leaders instructed Lee to charge "a suitable price" for his labor and stated their own intent to pay on such occasions as they used the ferry.[32]

Before leaving the subject of the crossing, a word should be written about the road out of the river to the south. Hurriedly opened as the migration of 1873 approached, it led up a tilted and precipitate apron of rock since known as Lee's Backbone but called merely "the mountain" or "the Lee Hill" during years prior to 1880.[33] Complicated by the crazy

---

[30] McClintock, *Mormon Settlement in Arizona,* p. 87, gives an account of Roundy's death. For a brief report by an eyewitness, see "Lorenzo Hill Hatch Journal," p. 83. P. T. Reilly considers the entire question of drownings on the Colorado River in "How Deadly is Big Red?," *Utah Historical Quarterly* 37 (Spring 1969): 244-60.

[31] For reactions typical to these two points of view see "Journal of Joseph Fish," original, HDC, December 19, 1878, p. 176. Also see the letter from George Dabling, *Deseret News,* September 20, 1876. For Silas Smith, see Miller, *Hole-in-the-Rock,* pp. 19-149, including "Nielson B. Dalley's Diary," Appendix I.

[32] Letter of Brigham Young to John D. Lee, January 28, 1874, St. George, Brigham Young Letters, HDC. Also see Cleland and Brooks, *Mormon Chronicle,* vol. 2, pp. 327-28.

[33] Joseph Fish notes specifically that it was called "the Lee hill" in 1878, which name he again applied to it in the following year. See "Autobiography of Joseph Fish," p. 156. Jesse N. Smith uses the same name in 1878 and calls it "the Hill" in 1880. See Smith, *Journal of Jesse N. Smith,* pp. 231, 241. Two diaries that refer to it in the 1876 migration both call it simply "the mountain." See "Lorenzo Hill Hatch Journal," p. 87, and "Journal of Daniel H. McAllister, Northern Arizona, 1876-77," typescript BYU; copy in possession of author, p. 4.

After crossing the river at Lee's Ferry, the pioneers faced the difficult climb over Lee's Hill. This original precarious road was constructed from the river, over the hill, toward the south.

pitch of the backbone and its scarred and broken rock surface, the climb was perhaps the worst that the pioneers encountered on the Lee's Ferry route. Teams were doubled and wagons taken singly to the top of the two-mile pull. Slowed by such procedures, parties of any size usually took a half-day or more on the up-grade and a like period dropping off the other side where a steep and contorted terrain required that hind wheels be locked and spring seats and other loose equipment tied to the wagons. When extra teams were not available for doubling, it was necessary, as one pioneer laconically noted, to "unload . . . and pack it up on our backs."[34]

---

[34] "Autobiography of Joseph Fish," p. 163.

The climb over the Lee Hill was regarded with scarcely more enthusiasm than the river crossing itself, and alternate routes were ultimately developed. Even before the work of construction was undertaken, the question of where a road could best be located led to a sharp conflict of opinion between Lee and Jacob Hamblin. Lee had established the ferry at an upper crossing which gained in safety what it sacrificed in ease of leaving the canyon. Hamblin favored a more dangerous crossing somewhat downstream leading to a much easier ascent from the river. After a good deal of consideration, it was concluded that the safety of Lee's upper route merited the added expense of construction and difficulty of travel, and a rudimentary trail was cleared during the late winter of 1873. Thereafter, occasional crews made small improvements, but the road remained substantially as it was left by the original construction mission until 1887 when a way was cleared, circling somewhat to the left of the rock apron but still making the climb over the hill.

Although Lee's judgment had prevailed and the main crossing led out over the backbone, the ferry did use a lower crossing when conditions permitted, thus enabling travelers to avoid the hard climb out of the canyon. Finally, in 1898 a long dugout was constructed from the upper ferry around the edge of the cliff to the lower road which was used until 1928 when Navajo Bridge was completed a few miles downstream, consigning both the ferry and its routes out of the canyon to disuse.[35]

Arizona's Mormon Wagon Road

After crossing the river and struggling up Lee's Backbone, emigrants moved south and east, following the Echo Cliffs on the left and on the right a country of rolling hills fractured by deeply etched washes that fell sharply toward the Grand Canyon. Opened first to wagons by the mission of 1873, this trail became known in Arizona as the Mormon Wagon Road. Proceeding south their course approximated the route along which Highway 89 eventually would be constructed, leading into the Little

---

[35] For a thorough study of Lee's Ferry, including data on the road, see C. Gregory Crampton and W. L. Rusho, "A Report on the History of Lee's Ferry, Arizona," prepared for the National Park Service, mimeographed, 1965. P. T. Reilly of North Hollywood, California, has also provided much information on the ferry from his personal collection. For much of my information about the ferry and the road on both sides I am indebted to Gregory Crampton of the University of Utah. As he has kindly pointed out to me, the wagons of the 1873 mission were the first wheeled vehicles to penetrate this remote quarter of Arizona. For additional information see Dr. Crampton's work written for the National Park Service, "Mormon Colonization in Southern Utah and in Adjacent Parts of Arizona and Nevada, 1851-1900," mimeographed, Salt Lake City, 1965.

— *Lynn Lyman*

Crossing at Lee's Ferry, about 1925.

Colorado River a bit above the present-day bridge at Cameron some eighty-five miles south of the Colorado River.

Passing Navajo Springs eight miles from the ferry, the road ran up what is variously called Tanner Wash and Roundy Creek twelve miles through intermittent rocks and sand patches to Bitter Springs. Nine miles beyond Bitter Springs over a similar road were the Limestone Tanks where rain collected in pockets to afford a scanty supply of water. From the tanks the road continued up a gentle but sandy slope into the cedars of the divide between Roundy Creek and Hamblin Wash, which is part of the Little Colorado drainage. About fifteen miles beyond the divide, the road ran through a litter of weather-sculpted stone monoliths to Willow Springs, which flowed out under the cliffs, providing the best water on the direct route to the Little Colorado. A much-used stopping place, the rocks around it became covered with the graffiti of migration, travelers

chiseling and daubing axle grease to record their passing. Leaving the
main road south of Willow Springs, an alternate route ran several miles
out of the way to the east, passing through Moenave to Moenkopi.
Traveling this way for the first time, one prominent churchman described
the area as:

A strange country of a barren desert of rocks, sand hills, mounds, gravel beds,
and many curious rocks. . . . The hills are of thin slate in a decayed state,
rocks are in every shape of men, women, children, and palaces. The country
is without grass, or soil.[36]

Leaving Moenkopi the road turned west to pick up the main trail again
in Moenkopi Wash. Through-traffic ran from Willow Springs down Moenkopi Wash twenty-five miles to the Little Colorado across what was often
termed the "bad land."

No other part of the road was more barren or dry than this section
between rivers. There was live water at only three places, and at two of
these — Navajo Springs and Bitter Springs — it was often limited in amount
and, as the name implies, was bitter tasting at the latter spot. By timing
their migration to coincide with the cooler and wetter seasons and carrying water for the dry marches, humans and draft stock usually made the
trek without undue suffering; but efforts to trail large herds of livestock
brought heavy losses, and bleaching bones soon laid a melancholy mark
on the road.[37]

From where the road struck the Little Colorado River, it was approximately a hundred miles to the first Mormon settlement. Although the
Mormon Wagon Road along this section was regularly traveled until the
turn of the century, it has since fallen into complete disuse and no modern
traffic follows the river's course except for the last twenty-five miles into
Winslow, which stands near the sites of the defunct villages of Sunset
and Brigham City. Many of the landmarks and names that designated the
route have likewise fallen into disuse. Since this is true, and since the
writer has visited only the more accessible spots along the river, it is
difficult to reconstruct the course of the road with any precision, and yet
some tentative remarks should be made.

After reaching the river, the road evidently followed its sandy bottoms for about four miles to old Camp Utah, as the site of Haight's 1873

---

[36] Cowley, *Wilford Woodruff*, p. 513.

[37] Several herds of over a thousand head of stock were brought over the trail
before 1880. Most of these lost heavily, some well over one-third of the total. According to one pioneer who later became an Arizona cowboy, the loss was in large part
the result of ignorance as "none of them had the remotest idea of handling cattle
or horses on the trail." See Coleman, "Biographical Sketch of William B. Maxwell,"
Coleman Papers, AHS.

Grand Falls of the Little Colorado River in high water.

encampment was known, which because of sheltering cottonwood trees became a primary resting place. About twenty-five miles beyond, through drifts of sand that had been regarded as impassable by the mission of 1873, was the first major landmark, Black Falls, where the river spread over a lava outcropping to form a waterfall of about 125 feet in width and with a fall of twelve or thirteen feet. Unlike most of the country along the lower river course, the rolling hills around Black Falls provided fairly good grazing. From the first, herdsmen, who marveled at the Indian ruins that have since been dignified as the Wupatki National Monument, held stock there that were too weak to make it on to the settlements. About a half-day's trip up the river lay Powder Hill, which became a nooning place between Black Falls and Grand Falls. In the neighborhood of Grand Falls, which took its name from a spectacular drop in the river of about a hundred feet, grazing grounds were also found, and around it were established a number of temporary camps for herders and travelers.

Some six miles beyond was Rocky Ford, where most of the traffic crossed from the north to the south side of the river. Beyond, the road went past Roundy's Point to Canyon Diablo, or San Francisco Wash, as the earliest pioneers knew it, where it joined the Prescott mail road. From there it continued to the Mormon settlements, following the bend of the river up a broad valley, which because of its heavy cottonwood growth was reminiscent of the Platte Valley to a few widely traveled immigrants. Thence it proceeded through a monotonous landscape up the south side of the river to Horsehead Crossing, or Holbrook, where it split into three divisions.

The old mail road followed up the Rio Puerco east by northeast into New Mexico, while another trail crossing to the north side of the river worked its way along cedar ridges to St. Johns and on into beautiful senecas and timber near the New Mexico border. The third branch was itself two separate roads — one crossing the Rio Puerco a mile or so east of Holbrook before turning south through Woodruff to Snowflake along the east side of Silver Creek, while the other, bearing abruptly south at Holbrook went over the cedar hills on the west side of Silver Creek's canyon to Snowflake where the two joined to run on to Fort Apache.

The lower portion of this road was by all odds the more difficult, and unlike the part that lay above Sunset it remained a trail through an uninhabited desert. Although heavy sands and lack of feed complicated its use, water was the major problem. Bad-tasting and dirty at best, it could be so filthy that when left overnight to settle only an inch or two was clear and that had a white or milky appearance. As we have seen elsewhere, the river also was frequently dry. In such event travelers were forced to dig for water or seek it in foul pools and tanks along the way. While water found by digging was of better quality than that of the river, it was both laboriously acquired and not without its hazards, as in the process of digging the unstable sands of the river bed were stirred, and thirsty stock rushing to drink often mired in quicksands.

Summer travel across this desert stretch could be a chancy thing indeed, and, while there is no record of loss of life due to water's lack, seasoned travelers undertook it with some apprehension, and well they might, as is apparent in the following account of a July trip in 1879:

We found but little Grass and no water to speak of, occasionally there was a little in holes along the bed of the river but it was so salty that it could not be used. We dug near the mouth of some of the large washes that came in where we found some water that was a little better. . . . At the crossing of the river we found a little in a hole but it was very salty. On the 30th we found enough at Grand Falls to fill a ten gallon Keg. At Black Falls we found a little but it was not fit to use as the fish had died in it and it smelt very bad, like carrion.[38]

Touring the area in 1900, forester Gifford Pinchot found things substantially unchanged. Running out of water his party could locate only

a stagnant pool of terrible green water. Sticking out of it were the horns of rotting carcasses of cattle that had waded in and drunk till they bogged down and died. . . . We had to drink it or go dry . . . although the water was so rank that in camp at nightfall its taste completely hid the taste of strong tea. Why it wasn't poison I don't know. In the desert such corruption seems to be harmless.[39]

It is not difficult to understand why oldtimers have later said that "you had to bite it off."

Travel over the Mormon Wagon Road was nevertheless comparatively heavy. It was not only the avenue by which most Little Colorado colonists came to Arizona, but the lifeline by which they maintained themselves. During the early years, supply wagons lumbered the three hundred miles from southern Utah to supplement the meager production of Little Colorado farms. Over it came the livestock which served as a medium of exchange in the Mormon land purchases and as foundation herds. Over it, too, moved churchmen, polygamists, wedding entourages, and jaded missionaries returning to Zion. Many settlers made the trip numerous times. Not unusual was William J. Flake, who between 1878 and 1895 came and went between Utah and northern Arizona thirteen times.

---

[38] "Autobiography of Joseph Fish," p. 161.

[39] Gifford Pinchot, *Breaking New Ground* (New York: Harcourt, Brace and Company, 1947), p. 178.

His wife Lucy made the trip nine times.[40] Although traffic diminished somewhat after convenient and reasonable rail connections with Salt Lake City were opened, the peculiarities of Mormon society led to its continued use well into the twentieth century.

Patterns and Experiences of the Trip

Having focused primarily upon the route to this point, we shall now shift our attention to the journey itself and certain patterns and experiences that characterized it. As we have observed, the migration to northern Arizona was rarely made in large companies. The first parties that left Salt Lake City in February of 1876 departed in small groups as they got ready and with whatever company was convenient. Chance meetings sometimes resulted in the joining of as many as twenty-five outfits which split and regrouped as the fortunes of the road dictated. Little concern was manifest for maintaining any group identity other than that growing out of bonds of family and friendship. Lot Smith, who was with the vanguard of the 1876 migration, left word as he rolled out of Kanab that groups of ten wagons should travel on to Lee's Ferry and to the Little Colorado together.[41] Some effort may have been made to follow this directive, but the accounts of the southward trek that year and later leave the impression that people moved along the road pretty much at random. The usual traveling group was probably something less than the recommended ten wagons, and in many cases single teams or lone horsemen made the entire trek by themselves.

Although the trip to the Little Colorado was always long, time spent on the road varied greatly according to the nature of the outfit making the trip and the season of the year. Official church parties with good animals sometimes made summer trips from the southern Utah communities in two weeks or less. However, emigrants burdened with belongings and extra livestock took far longer, particularly those who made the passage during the winter. The first groups of missionaries in both 1873 and 1876 were two or three months on the road. Thereafter, single-wagon outfits made it from Kanab or Johnson or even Panguitch in four or five weeks. Even in the case of those who made good time, the course was marked by innumerable reverses and delays as outfits broke down, animals gave out or slipped away during the night, or delays were necessitated at the ferry or at slow-filling waterholes. Parties that started together often

---

[40] "Diary of Lucy Hannah Flake," June 16, 1895.
[41] *Deseret News,* March 29, 1876.

split, those able going on and those more plagued with hard luck falling back to be picked up by new groups or to labor on by themselves.

Indicative of the frustrations and delays of the trail is the following list of difficulties gathered from the diary of a missionary who with the help of his family took three wagons and a small herd of stock from Kanab to the first Little Colorado settlements during the summer of 1876: between August 8 and 17, they looked for cows, were limited to a six-mile day by rain, waited six hours for water, held up an additional hour for balking horses, looked for horses, attended a council meeting, lost entire string of horses one day out from the river, relayed wagons while other members looked for horses, broke a wagon in a night drive, spent a half-day in travel for tools and repair of wagon and finally spent two entire days finding remaining animals. To moderns used to convenient, undelayed progress, such interruptions would seem interminable, but the party made the drive in quick time, spending only three weeks on the road.[42]

The trek was usually marked by a good deal of individualism. At no point was this more apparent than in the mess practices. There is no evidence of a commissary or chuckwagon which cooked for entire companies. The ordinary procedure was for each family to carry and cook its own food. During the winter months, women with long flowing skirts and poorly made shoes kicked the snow back and, as half-frozen children warmed themselves and played underfoot, pulled heavy grub boxes out and cooked on open fires. Served up on tin plates, the food soon cooled in the near zero weather in which many of them traveled. It must have been a harrowing process — one that could have been materially eased by adopting the characteristic chuckwagon of the cow camp to their own trail or even the "long table" that some of them had seen in Orderville as they came south. Laundry and other chores were also done within each family, with women standing at the scrubbing board for hours in the cold and snow as they tried to maintain some semblance of cleanliness.[43]

Some pioneers sought to prepare to meet the cold of their winter trip. A few fixed special facilities for their women and children. Evans Coleman wrote of the arrangements enjoyed by himself and his mother:

My mother and I together with numerous house-hold goods occupied the trail wagon. It was quite comfortable. The bows were set out from the sides of the wagon bed proper; a heavy carpet was stretched over them and tacked down, then a wagon cover was stretched over the carpet, making a water and wind

[42] See "Lorenzo Hill Hatch Journal," August 8 to 28, 1876, pp. 86-87.
[43] "Diary of Lucy Hannah Flake," vol. 1.

proof room, small wood burning stove and a large lantern, looking glass, comb, towels, wash basin, etc., completed the inside makeup.[44]

There were not many of these. Far from entertaining themselves in the comforts of specially constructed vans, most women and children rolled about on top of household goods or walked to ease the burden upon overloaded animals or to warm themselves. Women as well as older boys and girls teamstered, herded stock, and otherwise made themselves useful.

Sickness and physical hardship often attended the journey. Childbirth was not uncommon. Throwing ideas about protracted nineteenth century confinement into question and reflecting a hardiness foreign to modern women, the courage of expectant mothers who set out for the south knowing they would face delivery by themselves under winter conditions is almost unbelievable. Characteristically such events did not wait for convenient moments. One child's untimely arrival halted a party struggling through the snow in a crossing of the rim of the Great Basin.[45] Another was delivered on the Kaibab but lingered only nine days before finding a lonely grave at House Rock Springs and becoming the only casualty of the 1873 mission.[46] Another was born in November of 1880 in the remote and rugged approach to Pearce's Ferry. Noting the new arrival, one missionary wrote: "A pretty rough country for such an event, and then to travel over a rough road the next day." But indicating that it was to be taken in stride, he continued: "Yet I came into this world under similar circumstances."[47]

During the migration of 1877 an epidemic of diptheria flared late in December as the emigrants who all used the same waterholes approached Lee's Ferry. William J. Flake, whose own daughters "took diptheria" and "had it dredfull bad," came upon a standing wagon at the east foot of the Kaibab Plateau and, as his son Osmer recounts, found a woman

. . . sitting on the seat with a dead babe on her knee. It had died as she drove the team down the mountain. Mother prepared the body for burial. Father got a few short boards from the wagons and made a box, the teamsters dug a hole, and we buried her darling in a lonely grave. It looked as though her life too, would go. Their outfit had gone on for water. We took their wagon with ours and went down the road.[48]

Although there were no doctors, midwives and other lay practitioners did provide minimal medical service. For example a blind mid-

---

44 "Autobiographical Sketch," Coleman Papers, AHS.

45 May N. Christensen, "History of Bendt Nielsen Jr., 1855-1944," mimeographed copy in possession of author.

46 "Journals of John Henry Standifird," July 13, 1873.

47 "Journal of John W. Tate," p. 15.

48 Flake, *William J. Flake,* p. 60.

wife named Abbie Thayne rendered yeoman service during the diptheria outbreak mentioned above and was remembered afterward by grateful pioneers as Dr. Thayne, "a very fine physician."[49] The versatile John W. Young's gifts also extended to healing, as Apostle Wilford Woodruff, whom he nursed through a severe illness at Moenkopi in the spring of 1879, had good cause to appreciate. In December of the same year, Young happened into the Little Colorado communities in time to ply his medicinal skills upon an aging immigrant. After diagnosing his eighty-two-year-old patient's ailment as "Lung Fever," Young "drew his water off with a Cattelan [?] which was a great help to him."[50] The oldtimer was evidently far gone and his relief was temporary, for three days later it was necessary to treat him again.

Interesting and sometimes even bizarre home remedies were practiced among the migrants. Two examples will suffice. One traveler whose son was afflicted with shingles cut the tip from a black cat's tail and rubbed the blood over the shingles. Without attributing the cure specifically to the medication, he noted that the shingles "soon began to disappear." Wilford Woodruff also tried his hand at home remedies, prescribing sagebrush and charcoal poultices for infection. It was, as he said, a "safe medicine and can do no hurt." For cases that did not respond to this treatment, he recommended that the afflicted part of the body be held over a "smoke of woolen rags on wood." Presumably this too did "no hurt."[51]

When such skills as Woodruff and "Dr. Thayne" could boast were either unavailing or unavailable, the stricken traveler had recourse as elsewhere on the Mormon frontier to administration with blessed oil and prayer and often felt himself improved by the power of faith and the priesthood. Nevertheless, a goodly number gave their lives as the price of the exposure and the exertion of the long trek.[52]

This was in substance the experience of the trek to the Little Colorado River. Marked by its length, its isolation, and its barren and drouth-stricken stretches, it constituted a trying trip indeed. It was also one with

---

49 *Ibid.*

50 "Wilford Woodruff's Journal," April 25-May 1879. For the lung fever episode, see December 20-23, 1879.

51 William Henry Solomon, "Diary of the Arizona Mission," p. 31, and letter from Wilford Woodruff to Lot Smith, January 31, 1882, Lot Smith Papers, UA.

52 Characteristic gratitude for divine protection is obvious in the following words from Lucy Hannah Flake's brief account of the Flake family's winter journey: "We traveled very slow we had a very hard trip our two oldest daughters took the diptheria when we had been on the road about two weeks they had it dredfull bad and we never had seen a case of it before we did the best we could and the Lord hered our prairs and spared their lives." See "Diary of Lucy Hannah Flake," vol. 1.

which many Little Coloradans became well acquainted. Some even developed a certain nostalgia as they contemplated its role in their lives. One remembered it as the "honeymoon trail." Another as "the fond old route known as the Lee's Ferry by way of upper Kanab."[53] And in the waning years of the nineteenth century as the colony was stabilized, the entire community came to commemorate the trek, reliving it one day each year as they celebrated Old Folks Day in connection with July 24. Conscious of their past and of their bond with the mother community in Utah, Little Colorado Saints did not forget its miles.

---

[53] See "Joseph City Ward History," p. 27, and "Lorenzo Hill Hatch Journal," p. 181.

5. THE UNITED ORDER

> . . . and I must say that I felt in spirit that these settlements . . .
> were living in the United Order as near as any people could, in
> mortality, until a better way shall be revealed.
>
> WILFORD WOODRUFF

> . . . We consider it the will of the Lord to live in this manner —
> otherwise many would prefer living in the old style, for there is a
> great many trials connected with this style of living not known
> to the other. . . .
>
> LEVI M. SAVAGE

Bond of Peculiarity, Agency of Expansion

MORE IMPORTANT EVEN than the Mormon Wagon Road in forging the
bond that held Little Colorado Mormons to the mother institution were
the cultural and spiritual values common to both. None of these — save
possibly polygamy — was more unique or more consciously cultivated
than the United Order, a communal arrangement under which the first
villages on the Little Colorado were settled. As planned and in effect, the
United Order was a badge of peculiarity. In its Arizona phase it was also
a vehicle for the outward thrust of the Mormon Kingdom.

When the Mormons began their colonization of Arizona, the United
Order movement had been underway in Utah for three years. Reduced
to its simplest terms it was an effort to seek out grass-root social arrangements that would enable the Latter-day Saint society to advance more
quickly in Christ-like attributes, maintain the church's separation from
the world, and solve a variety of economic problems. It implied a unity

of purpose, common effort, and shared returns.[1] But it was also a quest, its emphasis upon experimentation and upon spiritual and social development. God did not vouchsafe the Order's perfect formula. Nor were His people ready for it. The rudiments were given, but the obligation to perfect the system and at the same time grow in righteousness so the system could flourish rested upon the Saints. Several types of Order evolved. Running through four major classifications, these varied from cooperative production projects of sharply limited scope in established and more affluent communities to the austere family-type Orders of peripheral areas where communicants committed all property and time to a common pool and shared equally in the proceeds without regard to quantity or quality of input.

By choice or by the limits of their influence, Mormon leaders did not advocate a lockstep unity, nor were they snared as completely in the web of theoretical systems as were some communal reformers of the nineteenth century. Yet they overran their own will to sustain the Order and the ability of their people to improvise, and the movement soon lost its impetus. Indeed, it had already passed its high noon in Utah when Mormon migration to Arizona was initiated. Nevertheless the history of the Little Colorado colony was deeply influenced by the Order. This, of course, was no accident. Church leaders and, after proper conditioning, the first waves of Arizona settlers hoped that the United Order and the expansionist impulse would prove to be mutually complimentary. Their ideas about the subject were simple. Arizona lay beyond the pale of the administrative and spiritual intimacy of their self-contained empire. Colonists would be exposed to the divisive social and economic influences of the world. Moreover, Arizona's hostile natural character, which had previously defeated the mission of 1873, was recognized as a major obstacle. Such social and natural challenges demanded new means of stirring devotion to the kingdom's objectives. With its emphasis upon unity, equality,

---

[1] For general accounts of the United Order in Utah, see Edward J. Allen, *The Second United Order Among the Mormons* (New York: Columbia University Press, 1936); Joel E. Ricks, *Forms and Methods of Early Mormon Settlement in Utah and the Surrounding Region, 1844-1877* (Monograph Series; vol. 11, no. 2; Logan: Utah State University Press, 1964), pp. 105-114; Nels Anderson, *Desert Saints: The Mormon Frontier in Utah* (Chicago: University Press, 1966), pp. 374-83; Andrew Karl Larson, *"I Was Called to Dixie," The Virgin River Basin: Unique Experiences in Mormon Pioneering* (Salt Lake City: Deseret News Press, 1961), pp. 290-313; Leonard J. Arrington, *Great Basin Kingdom: An Economic History of the Latter-day Saints 1830-1900* (Cambridge: Harvard University Press, 1958), pp. 323-49; Arrington, *Orderville, Utah: A Pioneer Mormon Experiment in Economic Organization* (Monograph Series; vol. 2, no. 2; Logan: Utah State University Press, 1954); and Thomas O'Dea, *The Mormons* (Chicago: University of Chicago Press, 1957), pp. 188-97. The most useful of these is Arrington's *Great Basin Kingdom*.

and compactness, the United Order seemed a godsend, its discipline ready-made for the situation.

Happily the new frontier also bore an opportunity. Brigham Young and the colonists of 1876 saw in Arizona an environment unspoiled by conflicting social patterns, one in which the United Order could prosper and grow. Such opportunity was rare. Even in Utah unseeming worldliness caused the Saints to quail in the face of the Order's equalitarianism. Forms then in vogue could not win full acceptance. By 1876 it was fully apparent that settlers of submarginal outlying regions were more amenable to its discipline than were most Saints. Consequently they were encouraged to regard their communities as laboratories, themselves the guinea pigs of experiment in severe and restrictive versions of union.[2] With little to lose, a few remote colonies gave themselves over to this mission and for a time found meager satisfaction in their efforts to improve the system. The Little Colorado colony was conceived as one of these. Its first missionaries were directed to live in the so-called family associations and work toward the perfection of the United Order. This errand in the wilderness was not expected to be easy, but the stakes were high. From their humble beginnings success would emanate, becoming churchwide and even worldwide.[3]

The Division of a Mission

The United Order villages were the first fruits of Mormon colonization in Arizona. In addition to the original four at Sunset, Brigham City, Obed, and St. Joseph, there were experiments at a fifth village on the lower river called Taylor, as well as at Woodruff and at Snowflake. But this brave beginning notwithstanding, the Arizona Orders enjoyed only the most fleeting success. By 1878 it was obvious that they would not be the only mode of settlement. By 1879 the three newer villages and Obed had collapsed in the face of divisive forces and the physical problems of colonization. At St. Joseph, Sunset, and Brigham City, the Orders' day in the sun was a bit longer, Brigham City surviving until 1881, Sunset and St. Joseph until the mid 1880s. But the experience of each led to the same end — increasing isolation from the mainstream of Mormon settlement and ultimately failure.

A variety of problems contributed to this dilemma. In the first place the close family Orders of northern Arizona were essentially frontier

---

[2] These ideas are most fully articulated in a series of letters from Brigham Young and other church leaders to Lot Smith, George Lake, Jesse O. Ballinger, and Wm. C. Allen [hereafter Lot Smith et al.], Lot Smith Papers, UA.

[3] For numerous statements about what United Order pioneers thought their purpose to be see "Minutes of the Little Colorado Stake Conferences," original, UA.

institutions best adapted to the most primitive unwanted areas. Without recognizing that in its broader implications this fact doomed the Orders to short duration, Mormon leaders had observed the special affinity between the family unions and remote regions. Within a few months of the movement's inception, Apostle Orson Pratt ventured the opinion that it would be necessary to "start a new settlement" to find the United Order's true and practical mode.[4] Later, Brigham Young told Little Colorado pioneers that it was "far better . . . to introduce the principles of the United Order at the beginning of new settlements, than to bring people into them, after their individual interests were more firmly established."[5]

While no early Mormon appears to have been fully aware of the fact, the family Orders were dependent in a peculiar way upon free public lands. Especially apparent in the case of the Arizona Orders, this was due, in large measure, to the fact that they were settled by an impoverished group which because of its general lack of property had few if any alternatives. Most of the Arizona Order colonists were young. Indeed, many were unmarried boys of no more than twenty years in age, their only worldly possessions a team and wagon and the grubstake of provisions donated by their parents or home wards.[6] Few could have purchased land — even at the minimal values of the day. Consequently, they took advantage of their early arrival, claiming such free land as they could find. By 1878, as men of somewhat easier though still limited economic circumstances came, they disdained both the Orders and available unclaimed lands, buying out established ranches as the sites for their new villages.

Furthermore, the communal effort implied by the Order organization was especially adapted to communities which lay exposed to the threats of nature and native population and beyond the normal reach of the country's industrial and commercial system. These frontier conditions existed on the Little Colorado in 1876, but quickly passed. With their passing the strongest practical reasons for the Orders' existence were removed and cohesion became increasingly difficult.

Another matter of basic importance in the failure of the Arizona Orders was the unsureness of the church with regard to the entire United Order movement. This was manifest at every level. Residents of Utah's established communities avoided the Orders or accepted them in a watered-down form. Colonists called to settle new regions were divided

---

[4] *Journal of Discourses,* vol. 16, April 17, 1873, as quoted by Allen, *Second United Order,* p. 44.

[5] Letter to Lot Smith et al., January 10, 1877, Lot Smith Papers, UA.

[6] For insight into the circumstances and age of a characteristic missionary, see "Frihoff G. Nielson Diary," entries for January and February 1876.

in opinion. Church leaders themselves fell far short of full agreement, vacillating as to its advisability and fostering other policies that contradicted or weakened the Order movement. As far as the Little Colorado villages went, the results were progressive: first internal tension and division, then formal separation from other Mormon settlements, and finally, the extinction of the Orders.

Even Brigham Young, who was the surest advocate of the Orders, did not follow a course that steadfastly supported them. He had sent the first missionaries to Arizona to live in the close family-type unions. Then and later he hammered on the themes of unity and strength. But even unity had its divisiveness, and in his call to solidarity Brigham Young directed Order members to brook no dissent. Any whose mouths were "full of murmuring" or whose hearts inclined "to apostasy" were not to remain "lest they poison the camp with the leaven of their ill-feeling."[7] Furthermore, Young simultaneously issued another directive requiring Arizona colonists "to extend continually" until all the suitable spots in the territory were occupied.[8] Coupled with an avid application of his injunction to reject dissenters, Brigham's order to expand resulted in an exodus that soon reduced numbers on the lower Little Colorado below that considered to be consistent with the church's interest. Once again employing the unity theme, Young emphasized the need to maintain the integrity of village life and demanded that the outward movement stop, but the damage suffered by the Order villages was never repaired.[9]

Not surprisingly, local efforts to counter the exodus only deepened the fissure between advocates and detractors. Journals and minutes of church meetings from the period are replete with arguments supporting the Order and with accounts of controversy. Characteristic was a declaration by George Lake, bishop of Brigham City, that anyone who would oppose the Order was apostatizing. Equally reprehensible in his eyes was the prospect of "men dragging their families into the forest and around springs by themselves."[10] A speaker of more liberal inclination admonished his brethren to "let anyone go to any settlement who might desire to do so," but clucked that he pitied "anyone who did not feel to comply with the will of the Lord."[11] Another, counseling patience, thought that any "who would not comply with the order would in due time leave and

---

[7] Letter of Brigham Young to Lot Smith et al., July 14, 1876, Brigham Young Letters, HDC.

[8] Letter of Brigham Young to Lot Smith, July 20, 1876, Brigham Young Letters, HDC.

[9] Letter of Brigham Young to Lot Smith et al., January 10, 1877, Lot Smith Papers, UA.

[10] "Minutes of the Little Colorado Stake Conferences," p. 115.

[11] *Ibid.*, pp. 67-68.

the system would purify itself."[12] Others could not wait for "due time" and applied pressures of various kinds which hastened the outward movement.

In May of 1878, Lot Smith, by this time stake president, forced John Reidhead, who as a volunteer to the mission claimed the right to locate where he chose, from the stake high council because his example in moving "off 100 miles" was having a negative influence.[13] Administrative action and protest doubtlessly shored up confidence and helped maintain unity. They did little, however, to bridge the gulf in opinion, and Silver Creek and other sites were settled in large measure by those who took exception to the Order's mode of life.

But the most important factor in the division of the mission was the compromised position in which church leaders found themselves with reference to the Order's meaning. Brigham Young had thrown the full weight of his prestige and authority behind the movement. Some of his subordinates, including John Taylor, who succeeded him as president of the church, and Apostle Erastus Snow, field commander for the Arizona colony, had been less than enthusiastic about the tendency of the Order to monopolize initiative. With Young's passing in 1877, their opinions bore more weight, yet they could ill afford to repudiate the former prophet's program as unsound. Consequently, they found themselves in the awkward position of sustaining the Orders and even hoping that positive social advance might be salvaged from them, but at the same time encouraging a cooperative program as being better calculated to achieve the church's ends.[14]

The result of this shifting emphasis was the establishment of a second form of union in Arizona, thus following Utah's example. In reality the system that developed was more a cooperative relationship than the one of

---

[12] *Ibid.*, p. 83.

[13] *Ibid.*, pp. 70-72.

[14] A forthcoming biography of John Taylor by his grandsons Sam and Raymond Taylor will fully explore Taylor's position on the United Order. In his "A Study of Joseph Smith's Order of Stewardships, and Brigham Young's United Order," Feramorz Young Fox states that Taylor was at best "only acquiescent about the United Order." See his chapter entitled "Cooperation after the Death of Brigham Young," typescript HDC. Allen, *Second United Order*, p. 144, quotes Angus Woodbury that Erastus Snow said that the Orderville association "was no better than a cooperative concern, that their system of giving an equal amount for unequal production was defective and that the United Order as practiced was not a commandment of God, but a financial experiment initiated by Brigham Young." The *Salt Lake Tribune,* May 9, 1874, termed Snow a "doubting apostle" and continued that he took the Order "quite reluctantly. He had to be labored with long and assiduously in St. George before he would take hold worth a cent. He came to terms finally."

the United Order, and we shall consider it in that context; but during the time of transition, at least, church leaders were at some pains to refer to it as a form of the Order.

The earliest indication that an official shift was in the wind grew out of the location of William J. Flake at Stinson's Ranch on Silver Creek during the summer of 1878. Although Flake was censured by his fellows and the local authorities, it was not long until some of his Order associates, led by John Kartchner, followed him. Arranging to take over one-fourth of his purchase, they proceeded to set up an Order. In September Erastus Snow visited the new community. Supporting the more individualistic group around Flake, he counseled Kartchner to abandon his site and the United Order and to join the former at his settlement.[15] The town of Woodruff also abandoned the United Order shortly after Snow's visit. While it seems unlikely that he was the direct cause of this change, the trend of his policies and appointments was such that it undoubtedly contributed to it.

Among the important measures initiated by Snow on this visit that signify a modified approach was the division of the Little Colorado Stake. Falling hard on the heels of the controversy over Flake's break with the Order, the division severed the Order villages from the rest of the mission.

Of utmost significance in this connection was the attitude of the man Snow nominated for stake president over the newly created Eastern Arizona Stake. This was Jesse N. Smith, who, though devoted to the church, was no friend of the United Order as it was practiced in Orderville and on the Little Colorado.[16] Having passed through both communities with Smith, Erastus Snow could scarcely have been oblivious to this fact. Smith's feelings about the family Orders were reflected in his response to the instructions relative to the United Order contained in his letter of appointment, part of which is included here:

We presume you are well aware that it is the desire of . . . the Apostles that all the settlements . . . in the southern country, should be organized and carried on as near as possible, in the United Order. . . . For the manner of so doing and the details thereof, we refer you to Bro. Erastus Snow who is more intimately acquainted with the necessities of the country than are the rest of the brethren.[17]

---

15 See *Deseret News,* October 30, 1878, p. 615; also Flake, *William J. Flake,* pp. 79-80.

16 Smith, *Journal of Jesse N. Smith,* p. 221.

17 "Journal of Samuel Hollister Rogers," typescript BYU, p. 202. Original in possession of Sarah Rogers Decker of Snowflake, Arizona.

These instructions seem plain enough. Smith, had he been of such a mind, was authorized to establish the Order on Silver Creek and the upper Little Colorado, but he hesitated. Apparently suffering some ambivalence, he sent his letter of appointment to Samuel H. Rogers, a friend in Parowan, inquiring how he would interpret it. Rogers minced no words:

The way that I understand President Taylor, at the onset I should have the sound of union and Order vibrated on the Peoples eares like peals of Thunder bursting right upon their heads thereby if possible to have awakened the People to the importance of the principle and then, for the manner of so doing and the detales thereof we refer you to Brother Erastus Snow, who in all probability would then have acted in the premises, but for the want of this is most likely waiting. . . .[18]

But no peals of thunder emanated from Smith, nor did he take action to initiate the Order. It is hard to avoid the conclusion that he knew the mind of Erastus Snow and therefore gave a loose interpretation to his instructions.

Thus there is good reason to believe that the division of the church relative to the United Order was formalized by the separation of the two stakes. Called into existence by divine fiat yet passed over by events, the Order villages became an anomaly that nearly defied adjustment. Lot Smith was left at his post on the lower river, presiding, in effect, over a protracted wake. Administratively, the church could hardly afford to embarrass him; on the other hand, to demand that the entire area live under the Order would drastically limit the number of people who could be depended upon to develop the mission. Hence, it is probable that Snow recommended a division to inhibit factionalism and broaden the human resource of colonization.

Organization of the Little Colorado Orders

A tight social organization was, of course, one of the distinguishing features of the Order villages. Almost immediately after arriving, Lot Smith and the other missionaries of 1876 had turned their provisions and property into de facto Orders. The activities of that first summer were conducted on the basis of complete communalism. Colonists worked together, ate together, and submitted to common direction. When it became necessary for some to return to Utah, each of the companies met and gave permission for certain members to take temporary leave. How-

---

[18] *Ibid.,* pp. 209-10.

ever, no formal organization was set up during these early months. Indeed, it was only in the following spring when those who did return from Utah began to arrive that formal Orders were established.

The best surviving account of the organizing process is from Allen's Camp, or St. Joseph. A committee of three drafted "Articles of Association" which were unanimously accepted on April 28, 1877. These stated in the briefest terms such things as the nature and purpose of the association, membership qualifications, and the selection and duties of directors. "By-Laws" and "Rules of the United Order" were also adopted. Delineated in the former were the usual matters of timing and frequency of meetings as well as less ordinary patterns for joining or leaving the Order and appraising property. The "Rules of the United Order" constituted the religious and moral code of the community. Identical to rules accepted by Order members throughout Utah, these were somewhat more severe than the general Mormon moral code.[19] Taken together these instruments served as the basis of St. Joseph's government until well into the 1880s. They were general in nature and left much to be worked out in the daily functioning of the Order. Elsewhere in the mission written rules appear to have been even more rudimentary and vague.

At St. Joseph primary authority was vested in the board of directors. This board consisted of a company president, two vice-presidents, a secretary, and a treasurer. The president and vice-presidents were often, but not invariably, the bishopric of the ward. Another important agency to which one or more of the directors belonged was the board of appraisers upon which fell the obligation of evaluating property of incoming and outgoing members. Of less importance were committees of trade which coordinated the external business dealings of the Orders. The St. Joseph Order also boasted a board of school trustees which handled its business in conjunction with the company meetings. In the case of Sunset, where if directors existed at all their position was only nominal, Lot Smith managed most company affairs, and the responsibility for appraising property was placed upon the ward bishopric.

Activities were organized along functional lines. Departments were set up to care for draft animals, range stock, wagons, and equipment as well as such technical activities as carpentering, leather work, blacksmithing, and school teaching. Some degree of specialization was permitted by this arrangement, and skilled workers manned a sawmill, tannery, and mechanic shops. Men with particular abilities were often assigned the

---

[19] "Joseph City Ward History," pp. 11-14.

same duty each year. Inevitably unappealing jobs were permanently wished off along with a few words of praise on defenseless individuals who would have been happier with other assignments.

However, the degree of specialization may be easily overestimated. Most members were general farmers. The problems they faced were the general problems of pioneering. These were facts of reality that the peculiarity of the United Order could not alter. Some individuals were moved from assignment to assignment, first teaching school, then planting crops, and later tending dairy stock or keeping books. While variety may have been the spice of life, the general laborer who was moved from task to task at the whim of the community ofttimes envied the specialist whose job gave him a certain immunity from the constant interference of his peers. One St. Joseph member noted that "when he was away and had a job to do he would work with a zeal, but when he was dictated by everybody he felt a little rebellious."[20]

After the coming of the Atlantic and Pacific Railroad in 1881, Order members at St. Joseph engaged in a unique departmentalization of work. Hoping to extend the brief prosperity they had enjoyed in constructing the road and at the same time keep non-Mormons out by preempting the work themselves, they bargained to "take two sections on the railroad to keep up" and appointed section bosses.[21] This arrangement appears not to have been maintained for long.

The directors, or one of their number, assumed the responsibility of managing the village farms. These were never large. Planting was limited to about 200 to 250 acres in small grains, with possibly half that amount in corn and sorghum and even more restricted acreages in gardens and orchards. Little alfalfa hay was produced and that probably not until late in the history of the Orders.

Confronted with a continuing struggle to control the river, and devoting an increasing amount of time to livestock, the Orders neglected farming. There was also a tendency to regard the farm as the obligation and interest only of the man charged with its management. William C. Allen, manager of the St. Joseph farm, complained that members whose fortunes were as intimately related to its successful operation as were his own would send word that the cows were in "his corn" but not bestir themselves to drive the stock off.[22]

---

[20] "Minute Book of the Allen City United Order" [hereafter "Allen City Minutes"], typescript, BYU and HDC, p. 21.

[21] *Ibid.,* p. 16.

[22] Interview August 18, 1966, with George S. Tanner of Salt Lake City, formerly of St. Joseph, who heard this story from his parents and other village elders.

— Austin Fife

Ripgut fence, widely used by Little Colorado settlers.

This problem was aggravated by the fact that dairy and draft animals were herded in the hills adjacent to the villages. During the lifetime of the United Orders, there seems to have been no fencing, not even the familiar "ripgut," crisscross cedar-post fences of the area. Joseph Fish, who migrated to Arizona in 1879, recorded: "There was not a rod of fence in any place that I was aware of at that time."[23] Others complained that range cattle ran on the fields. As the 1880s progressed and northern Arizona became a great cattle country, the problem became increasingly acute. However, the fields of St. Joseph were not fenced until 1886, and then fencing came only after more personal interests supplanted the United Order. As the only other surviving Order was in total disarray at Sunset, there is reason to believe that fences had never been built there.

The failure of Brigham City and Sunset was laid in part to the rapid depletion of the soil. There can be no doubt that after an initial

---

[23] "Autobiography of Joseph Fish," p. 158.

increase of production, yields fell quickly; however, in the light of the fact that some of the same acres have been farmed for years in modern times without undue exhaustion, we may safely assume that the problem was in some degree the result of the Orders' failure to function successfully. The tendency to shirk farm responsibility and the lack of personal incentives, along with the aggressive thrust into other enterprises, were undoubtedly contributing factors. But it should be borne in mind that the de-emphasis of farming was also a reflection of its cost. The expense of water control, which was always high on the Little Colorado, was almost prohibitively so on the lower river. Consequently, attention was increasingly diverted to other enterprises until cultivation of the village farms became a slipshod and uneconomic sideline.

Life in the Orders

Life in the Arizona Orders was characterized by physical closeness and by the great number of domestic functions conducted on a community basis. After the first months, which were spent camped in wagon boxes, people lived in forts. Occupying apartments that comprised the forts' walls, they had little privacy. At Brigham City and Sunset, the intimacy was made the greater by the practice of eating together. The dining halls, which were the largest rooms in the communities, became the focal point of life, being used for school and church purposes as well as eating. Along with adjoining kitchens, bake-houses, cellars, and storehouses, they comprised the commissary. Working under the direction of a "superintendent of the eating department," women whose children were tended by their sister-wives or neighbors prepared the food while teen-age boys and girls waited table. Meals were served at regular intervals to families who as a rule sat together.

Lot Smith made the "long table" at Sunset something of an institution, and many if not most incoming colonists had the experience of eating there. While most were impressed with the order and discipline of Smith's company, they often commented on its strangeness, and many did not care for it. Smith presided over his table with a stern and parental authoritarianism. Mealtime was often the occasion for impromptu sermons or lectures about morality or economy. Wilford Woodruff, who as a fugitive polygamist spent several months at Sunset, was favorably impressed. Of the long table's advantages and popularity, he wrote:

I conversed with several of the sisters, they preferred it to cooking at home, all fared alike, the president, priest and people. If any were sick they were nourished, if any man was called on a mission he had no anxiety about his family, knowing they would fare as well as the rest. If any died his family would have a support as long as they lived with the people, and I must say that I felt in spirit that these settlements in connection with Orderville were living in the United Order as near as any people could, in mortality, until a better way shall be revealed.[24]

Another man reported that he was "pleased to contemplate hundreds coming together at one table with less noise and confusion than he had seen in private families."[25] Others found the loss of privacy trying and candid accounts confess that they submitted, if at all, because they felt that it was a religious assignment.

An interesting glimpse of life at Smith's big table was reported by A. C. Peterson, who as a boy lived with his widowed mother and small brothers and sisters at Sunset. According to his account, the long table had a definite "pecking order," with Lot and his family sitting at the head, with the community's hierarchy arrayed in descending order. Widow Peterson and her brood sat at the foot of the table. Food was served to the head of the table first. Passed along, it was frequently well picked over. This was bad enough, but frictions with the other unfortunates at the table's end further aggravated the situation. Across from young Peterson sat a boy several years his senior who in the keen rivalry always took most of the butter patty provided for that quarter of the table by holding his knife at the ready and slicing quickly at it as grace was concluded. One day in a burst of resentment, Peterson reversed his knife and as the older boy grabbed the butter rapped his knuckles so forcefully that the latter cried out, attracting the attention of Lot Smith. Peterson was hailed before Smith, who banished him from the table for a week and lectured Widow Peterson on rearing children.[26]

Ranking much higher than the Petersons, L. M. Savage as bishop of Sunset must have sat near the table's head. However, the following from his diary corroborates Peterson's point of view rather than Woodruff's:

July, 1877 . . . we all eat at the same table   one fares as well as the other. We consider it the will of the Lord to live in this manner — otherwise many would prefer living in the old style, for there is a great many trials connected with this style of living not known to the other.

The problem was apparently a continuing source of irritation inasmuch as a year later he returned to the matter, writing: "One of the greatest trials,

[24] *Deseret News,* June 18, 1879.

[25] "Minutes of Little Colorado Stake Conferences," p. 72.

[26] Related by Silas L. Fish, Phoenix, August 1966. Fish had heard the account from young Peterson.

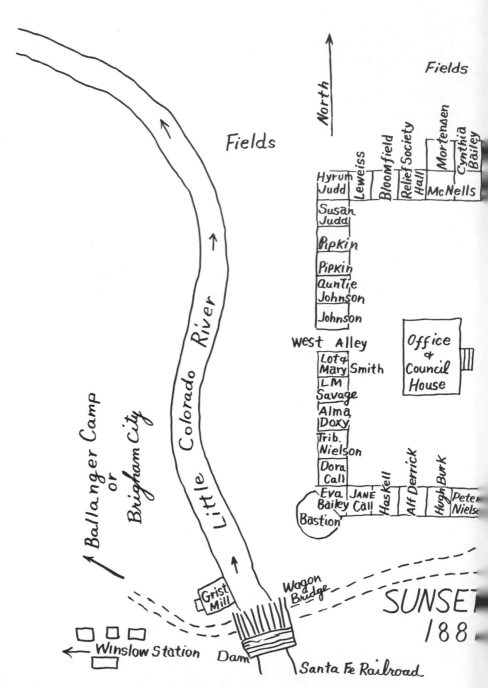

Rendered from an early sketch of the United Order fort at Sunset, with the names of persons who were living there.

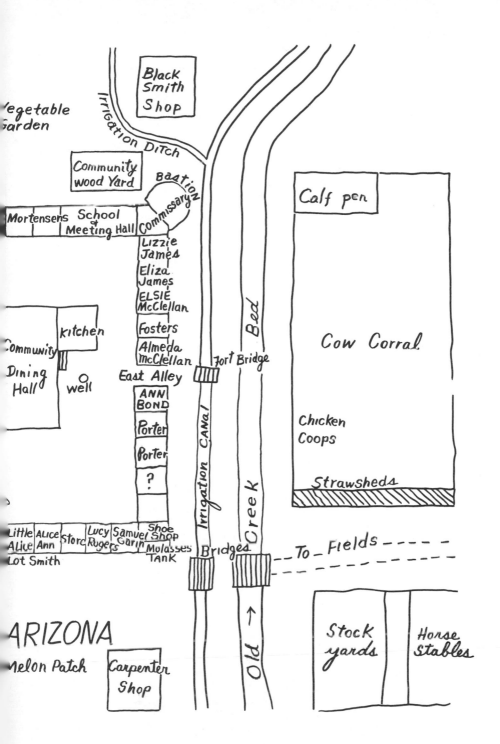

especially to the women in this style of living is the practice of our little settlement all dining on one large table."[27]

That Sunset rigorously adhered to the long table was in large measure the product of Smith's determination to abide by Brigham Young's declaration that greater economy and more complete union would result from it. On the other hand, St. Joseph quickly abandoned communal eating, and each family kept its own board. In part this was a countenancing of Erastus Snow rather than Brigham Young — the former having told members of the St. Joseph Order that eating all at one table had no more to do with the United Order than sleeping all in one bed.[28]

Dress was something of a problem. The stress of the United Order upon equality and uniformity required that the social pretension implicit in variety of style and quality be minimized. Furthermore home production was considered to be imperative. Yet economic reality permitted no waste, and communicants clad in fraying remnants looked anxiously to the day when the supply of clothing brought south would be used up and apparel of uniform lines and local fabrication could become the norm.[29] To facilitate home manufacture, sheep were acquired and simple machinery brought in or made on the spot. From Nephi in Utah came a carding machine — though accounts indicate that most wool was carded by hand comb. Looms too came over the Mormon Wagon Road.[30] At Moenkopi a mill of nearly two hundred spindles was set up which John W. Young, its prime promoter, hoped would contribute to the need of the Orders.

Little success attended these efforts. A mill of sorts actually operated at Sunset, but produced little fabric. Tailors were among those called to the area but appear not to have done much toward meeting the needs of the settlers. Most clothing was made by the women of the individual households. Such diverse materials as homespun wool, wagon tarps, Utah "factory" from the cotton mill near St. George, and cheap commercial calicoes are mentioned. The product was sometimes grotesque, and a few tongue-in-cheek stories about ghostly apparitions have survived. Efforts were also made to set up functioning tanneries. Some leather was produced, and shoes that crippled and deformed were made. Apparently the need for work shoes was pretty well met, as even the leaders of the community report having submitted to this peculiar form of torture.[31]

---

[27] "Journal of Levi Mathers Savage," pp. 25-26, 28.

[28] "Allen City Minutes," p. 38.

[29] "Minutes of Little Colorado Stake Conferences," p. 71.

[30] "Journal of Levi Mathers Savage," p. 28.

[31] Grant Gill Smith, ed., *The Living Words of Alice Ann Richards Smith* (published privately, 1968), p. 47.

From the first, the Orders were sensitive to the needs of their children. As early as January of 1877, a school was established at Sunset.[32] Thereafter, earnest efforts were made to provide schooling; but, as there were few suitable books and almost no facilities, school was at best a hit-and-miss affair.[33] In addition to physical difficulties, conflicting pressures transcended the needs of the children, and schoolmasters frequently were changed to meet the varying demands of water development, farm work, or other pressing business. Often responsibility for instruction devolved entirely upon some older female pupil.

At first schools were staffed in precisely the same fashion as other Order functions, with the master being assigned by the Order and drawing upon it for his needs. Later, schools came under territorial control. After 1880 it was necessary for teachers to qualify under the law, and the Orders received some financial aid. These arrangements cut down the autonomy of the communities but provided better and more stable services. In some instances Orders still managed to staff schools from among their own numbers. In other cases it was necessary to cover the expense of non-Order teachers who came in. Sunset appears to have been fortunate in attracting school teachers to its ranks. St. Joseph frequently had to resort to teachers from other Mormon towns. The latter village had a board of trustees who took the responsibility of hiring teachers, but interestingly the entire company entered into such business as declaring special vacations and establishing dates of opening and closing.[34]

In spite of the opportunity for experimentation, few irregularities marked the care of the young. Indeed, early residents are of the opinion that there was no significant difference between child care in the Orders and elsewhere in the Mormon community. Nevertheless a concern for the young contributed to a loosening of the Orders. This was most obvious in St. Joseph where the more flexible stewardship plan of union was adopted in 1883. Some of the shortcomings members saw in the old system stemmed from the fact that children had little opportunity in the departmentalized Order to work with their parents.[35] It was also significant that many of the St. Joseph men and women had been young at the United Order's inception. During the early years their concern with family dis-

---

[32] "Journal of Levi Mathers Savage," p. 22.

[33] On January 27, 1878, John W. Young told a gathering at Sunset that "teachers should be enlightened by the spirit of revelation. They should read Church Works in school not these common school readers which do not mention the names of the good men of the Kingdom of God. . . ." See "Minutes of the Little Colorado Stake Conferences," p. 55.

[34] "Allen City Minutes," pp. 7, 11.

[35] *Ibid.*, p. 19.

cipline had been minimal, but as their children grew, the need to shift their primary allegiance from joint affairs to family confronted them. Dissatisfaction with the effect of the old Order upon the young contributed to its demise.

Of Property and Labor

More persistent if not more important than family matters were economic considerations. Complicated by the intimacy of the Orders, problems relating to capital and labor invested and to proceeds withdrawn were an abiding and complex aspect of life.

Initially capital investments consisted only of such chattel property as the colonists brought with them. Real estate was not an investment factor. The land they moved onto was unsurveyed public domain. At the time of occupancy their right to it seemed as valid as anyone's. Experience in Utah had underscored the need for legal title, and claims were located for miles along the river bottoms immediately after arriving and allocated to individuals for purpose of legal entry by drawing lots.[36] Somewhat later, as grazing potential became apparent, claims were established at key springs in the mountain country to the south.[37] All early claims, however, were based on squatter's rights and held only by use and improvements, subject to a variety of conflicting claims. At St. Joseph persistent efforts to acquire title were made but were unsuccessful until well into the twentieth century. Elsewhere Orders never established legal right.

Squatters on Uncle Sam's domain, the Orders admitted neophytes to their ranks without requiring any payment in consideration of the real values represented in land. On the other hand, members were expected to pool all of their possessions. Immediately upon arrival each member turned his entire holdings, including his time and talents, to the company. Great or small, this qualified him to draw from the association for his needs.

In most cases capital investment consisted of provisions, livestock and implements. Even private effects necessary to the household appear to have been committed and re-issued. As a rule capital input was of limited value. Fortunately, a list that reflects the restricted means and varying amounts of investment in the St. Joseph Order is at hand. As of December 31, 1881, the town's seventeen families had contributed property totaling $9,098. Individual investments varied from $28 to $1,820

---

36 "History of John A. Blythe," April 16, 1876.
37 *Ibid.,* August, 1876.

and averaged only $535.[38] Not infrequently some Order members had property in Utah, some of it fairly liquid, that could have — and in keeping with their agreements probably should have — been committed to the Orders. It is not known how extensive this practice was or that it created problems.

Communicants also put their labor into the Orders. At Sunset no attempt was made to place value on either quality or quantity of labor. Each member was expected to do "as much as he can reasonably perform of the work."[39] In reference to this situation, Levi Savage wrote on July 4, 1878: "Each performs his portion of labor if he be able; if not able then nothing is said about it." That this arrangement had its disadvantages cannot be doubted. That Order members were not oblivious to them is apparent from Savage's concluding comment that it was "truly a work of love and kindness."[40] Discontent notwithstanding, there was apparently no formal deviation from this procedure at Sunset.

St. Joseph's pioneers established one pay rate for all adult males. It was not a popular ruling. To a strong minority it seemed to discriminate against those with special skills. Despite frequent attempts to tip the scales in favor of classified pay, the single rate prevailed until 1883 when the family Order at St. Joseph gave way to the stewardship plan. Thereafter rated incentives became common. Displaying a good deal of ingenuity, members worked out a variety of wage differentials. Some were given share leases on livestock. Some were assigned specialized tasks for which they were voted appropriate labor wages. Still others tilled farms on the product of which values were placed, fixing their income. Obviously, such practices constituted a great stride away from the previous arrangement.[41]

At St. Joseph there was also some question as to when a boy should receive a man's pay. In the eyes of the majority, twenty-one years demarked sufficient maturity. Others, insisting that full physical strength had developed by eighteen, called for revision. The majority, however, was obdurate, insisting that lack of judgement in the younger boys justified keeping them at a lower rate.[42]

Communicants were urged to abandon all forms of individual trade and barter. But necessity was often in league with temptation, and trade in livestock, guns, and other personal items was common during the

---

[38] "The Life and Labors of John Bushman," rewritten from his original diaries, typescript, BYU, p. 70.

[39] "Journal of Levi Mathers Savage," p. 25.

[40] *Ibid.,* p. 27.

[41] "Allen City Minutes," pp. 28-40.

[42] *Ibid.*

colony's earliest months. In January of 1878, John W. Young reacted to reports of one especially brisk run of trade. Himself a free-booting promoter with trade deals developing throughout northern Arizona, he denounced "the general system of bartering one with another after the business system of the world as being radically wrong." Continuing that it was the "word of the Lord," he directed the Order saints to "cease this selfish trading" and "live more unitedly together."[43]

For a time circumstances permitted little trading with the outside world. But after the advent of the railroad in 1881 the problem was broadened and intensified. In November of that year it merited Lot Smith's attention, and he forcefully reminded the people of their duty to the body of the whole at a stake conference. The gist of his instruction was reduced to one trenchant sentence by the recorder. To wit: "He thought that no member had the right to start a little private fund amounting even to one dime for their individual benefit — no matter how obtained."[44]

Up the river, St. Joseph saints had cause for concern at about the same time, as certain of their numbers began "sending for things on their own account and selling them."[45] Most members feared the practice for what it might lead to and felt it was unfair to the company, but one brother (giving possible clues to the identity of who had entered into this clandestine traffic) "thought every individual had the privilege of taking advantage if they wished to."[46] Despite periodic concern with such trivial waywardness, the "no trade" policy prevailed until the Orders were reconstituted or far decayed.

A unique feature of the Little Colorado Orders was their common or "conjoint" enterprises. These were owned, managed, and operated jointly by the different villages. Although this practice was in complete accord with Mormon cooperative tradition, the combination of factors that permitted it to be tried on the Little Colorado likely did not exist elsewhere. Whereas Orderville and other communal villages in Utah were isolated from others of their kind by a more individualistic Mormon society, the Little Colorado villages had been located as a community. This permitted the extension of the self-contained bond of the Order village to a broader multigroup unit.

As always, rhetoric played an important role in forging this bond, but more important were Brigham Young's steps to unite the Arizona

---

[43] "Minutes of the Little Colorado Stake Conferences," January 27, 1878, p. 55.
[44] *Ibid.,* p. 204.
[45] "Allen City Minutes," p. 15.
[46] *Ibid.*

villages through common economic interests. During the summer of 1876 he sent word that the Mount Trumbull sawmill which had supplied the lumber for the St. George Temple would be turned over to them.[47] By September 1, men and teams from the Little Colorado were at Lee's Ferry to take delivery. Crossing the Colorado River with some difficulty, they dragged the unwieldy machine to Sunset and then into the mountains near Pleasant Valley where it became the second functioning sawmill in Arizona. Warren Tenney, William C. McClellan, and others were called to operate it, which they did with the help of unskilled labor from the various Orders. For a few years, the mill was run jointly by, and in the interest of, the Order towns. However, as markets failed to develop and the need of the Orders was limited, the mill was sold on March 1, 1881, to a Snowflake cooperative headed by William J. Flake for $4,000.[48]

A gristmill was also shipped south. By May of 1878, it was functioning at a site near Brigham City. There the Orders operated it conjointly for a number of years, but their failure to grow and their poor agricultural success resulted in increasingly spasmodic use, and in 1884 it was permanently closed. Two years later it was turned over to a Woodruff company and moved to that town but never assembled.[49]

Livestock operations were also conducted on a conjoint basis. In July of 1876 sheep had been leased and land and water taken up at Pleasant Valley. Mormon Dairy in Pleasant Valley soon became a major outpost for the Orders, and regular summer operations were conducted there. In November of 1878, L. John Nuttall, who was touring the colony with Erastus Snow, found five families there. These had milked 115 cows during the summer and had produced 5,400 pounds of cheese and 442 pounds of butter. There were three good houses at the site as well as a cheese house and other facilities connected with the dairy. According to Nuttall, Sunset and Brigham City claimed the place, but other sources indicate that St. Joseph may have been involved at this time, and it certainly was by 1879.[50] The dairy operation continued to prosper, and by the early 1880s over two hundred head of cows were milked. Other livestock were also handled conjointly, but little information is available.

Ranching operations became increasingly important in the economy of the United Orders as the villages declined. With the passing of Brigham City, Erastus Snow bought its interest in the Pleasant Valley place for

[47] Letter to Lot Smith et al., August 7, 1876, Lot Smith Papers, UA.

[48] Statement defining ownership of the mill in Erastus Snow's handwriting and bill of sale transferring the sawmill, Erastus Snow Letters, HDC.

[49] Letter of Erastus Snow to John Taylor, Snowflake, May 31, 1886, Erastus Snow Letters, HDC. Also see "Autobiography of Joseph Fish," p. 240.

[50] *Deseret News,* December 4, 1878.

$500 and turned it over to Lot Smith on which to keep the Little Colorado Stake Tithing herd.[51] Thereafter, the Sunset Order made frequent overtures to St. Joseph to buy out its interest in the joint property. Finally in 1884, after refusing to consider it seriously on earlier occasions, St. Joseph offered to sell its interest for $2,000 or to buy out the Sunset interest for $4,300.[52] Sunset did not act on either proposition, and St. Joseph continued in its conjoint business until the matter was finally settled in connection with the Sunset investigation of 1886-87.[53]

The experiment with conjoint enterprises appears to have been as successful as any element of the United Order program. The relationship of the various villages was not marked by undue strife, and it did add an economic bond to the ideological commitments that held the Orders together.

St. Joseph and Sunset: A Study in Personalities and Method

Quite obviously the Little Colorado Orders had much in common. But, overriding similarity did not preclude variation. In character and inner working each was different. Life in each had its own recognizable temper. Distinction was especially apparent between St. Joseph and Sunset where variation in personnel and in method made life quite different.

The St. Joseph Order was small. After initial shrinkage had reduced its population to fifteen or twenty families it remained surprisingly constant in the numbers and personnel of its membership. This is not to imply that it was a closed group. Occasionally new members were added, but few wanted to join. Some of its members did withdraw, particularly after 1881. In some cases, however, those who had severed their relationship with the community returned disappointed with life on the outside and were readmitted.

St. Joseph displayed an abiding concern for the individual, which set it apart from the other Orders. Leadership there never rested heavily upon any one man but was spread through the entire association.

Closely related to its concern for the individual was its determination to organize effectively and maintain running accounts of capital investment and labor input on the one hand and company disbursements on the other. Frequent settlements were made, and a just and honest picture of each member's relationship to the Order was at hand. The result was fair play and good feelings. While St. Joseph members were disap-

---

[51] "Joseph City Ward History," p. 8.
[52] "Allen City Minutes," p. 33.
[53] "Frihoff G. Nielson Dairy," July 13, 1887.

pointed in their aspirations to pioneer a new social order, few of them were dissatisfied in their relations one with another.

At no point was the essential democracy of their approach more apparent than in the debates that accompanied the transition from the family-type Order to the stewardship plan in which the common property of the Order was distributed to the various families whose individual management and labor was substituted for the joint effort of the older system. Pursuant to this reorganization, fourteen of the Order's members met on November 7, 1882, and opened the discussion. They were a solemn group of men, anxious to take full advantage of every resource as they considered their future. During the entire discussion, which continued through eight meetings and two months, the initiative was taken by Joseph H. Richards, ward bishop and company president. However, sixteen men, probably the entire adult male population, entered into the debate. The tenor of opinion favored change, but some feared that it would lead to disorder, and all were loath to take the step without careful consideration. At least one man, Samuel G. Ladd, the group's only bachelor, was opposed to the change but did not press his opinion. During one of the November meetings, resolutions stating proposed amendments were agreed upon. These were shown to Lot Smith and sent to Erastus Snow, neither of whom took a positive stand except to indicate that they would go along if the people of St. Joseph wanted change.[54]

On January 5, 1883, Snow's reply was read and full satisfaction was expressed with the new arrangement, yet the brethren of St. Joseph hesitated. Finally, they adjourned their meeting, leaving the matter unresolved but agreeing to return to the task of decision-making the same evening, this time in company with the sisters of the Order. Consequently, the men and women assembled at an evening meeting where the ladies of the town straightway cut the Gordian knot and a vote favoring the change was taken.[55]

Although the St. Joseph association limped along for several years after the shift to stewardships, the trend was increasingly away from the United Order. For a time, a "sinking fund" of surpluses over and above the stewardships was held in reserve as a sort of insurance to help unfortunate members, but even this was shortly discontinued. Finally, in 1886 the Order closed its books. Still showing their characteristic concern for detail, they settled accounts on the basis of the initial capital investment and the subsequent balance of labor valuation and withdrawals charged to the various members. As in earlier transactions, the final dis-

---

[54] "Allen City Minutes," pp. 23, 26.
[55] "Life and Labors of John Bushman," p. 27.

solution was handled with little friction and to the substantial satisfaction of all.[56]

We have learned a good deal about Sunset in the foregoing pages. It has been obvious that its leadership was largely assumed by Lot Smith. Born in 1830, Smith had been a member of the Mormon Battalion and acquired a noted and lasting reputation in the Utah War of 1857 when he burned army supply trains and drove off large herds of government cattle. Determined and able, he was financially far and away the most capable man in the Order villages. According to his own lights he was honest but had no sense whatever for points of view other than his own. He possessed a rare capacity for single-minded commitment and was entirely willing to make great personal sacrifice for a cause. There can be no doubt that the church and the Sunset Order were the great causes of his life. In many ways he was the most forceful character involved in the Mormon colonization of Arizona and must be acknowledged as one of its most colorful and interesting figures. Unfortunately he was also over-bearing, intolerant, and hot-headed in the extreme. Assuming that his call to "general overview" of the Arizona mission and later to the position of stake president gave him total command, he badgered, threatened, and fumed to make his domination a reality in Sunset. As president and busi-ness agent for the Order, he determined its course, riding roughshod over the rights and freedoms of others in the process. A board of directors seems to have existed, but no real authority rested with it except as it related to the person of Smith who sat as one of its members.

Reported by quitters as well as by the complaining voices from among those that stayed, this one-man-show was a matter of grave concern to church authorities. This was particularly true after the passing of Brigham Young, who had felt that Smith's strong hand was needed to make the Arizona mission succeed. But, as we have seen, after Young's death milder men were advanced in the church's hierarchy. Seeing in Smith's conduct the seeds of collapse for Sunset and the entire Arizona colony, Young's successors made frequent and urgent appeals for reform, but they pro-crastinated for years before taking the strong action necessary to rectify the problem. Characteristic was John Taylor's plea of April, 1879: "We wish liberty given to all as far as righteousness will permit, that they may not have cause to complain of undue pressure . . . this law of heaven [the United Order] has to be accepted freely."[57]

It seems probable that Wilford Woodruff's decision to spend his year in exile at Sunset was not unrelated to the problems of Smith's jurisdiction. There can be no doubt that Woodruff presumed himself to be Smith's

---

[56] *Ibid.*, January 28, 1886.
[57] Letter to Lot Smith, April 17, 1878, Lot Smith Papers, UA.

Lot Smith, leader among the Mormon pioneers in northern Arizona.

moral mentor.[58] But discreet suggestions were insufficient. Lot Smith continued on his own course. Probably it was the only one of which he was constitutionally capable.

Complaints about his conduct also continued. Some of these were directed at his tendency to dominate all available natural resources. One resident of Sunset asserted in 1878 that:

... within five miles of Lot's Camp there are choice lands ... with grazing facilities and distant timber to sustain five thousand people and while it is held free to all who join and remain with his company, it is virtually monopolized by it, and all outsiders elbowed off.[59]

This estimate of the carrying capacity of the country is high, but the analysis as to Smith's policy is sound. Competition from Mormon settlers unwilling to enter the Orders was not permitted.

Another cause for complaint was Smith's practice of plowing all dividends back into the company — usually in the form of livestock. Content in his management of Sunset's thriving herds and with few and spartan personal needs, he refused to lay out expenditures on things that many of his subordinates considered absolutely essential. One characteristic indictment of his policy from 1881 read:

Living is unnecessarily poor & niggardly — our houses very uncomfortable with little or no hopes for better — as every energy is bent in gathering around us large herds of horses and cattle but if a Sister wants a little Thread, Sheeting, Buttons & etc to use in her Family She is told there is none or if She get it, it comes frequently with a lecture on economy.[60]

Monopoly and parsimony were rendered more galling by Smith's explosive temper. Few escaped the sting of his tongue, and more than a few were threatened with physical violence.[61] All too often he met problems with anger and overcame opposition by sheer force. Most of his followers were either cowed or deemed it their duty to avoid conflict. Nevertheless some efforts to control him were made from within. Usually dissenters were informed that they could leave if they found "our style of doing things objectionable."[62] Many did. But on one occasion an obdurate group refused to be silenced or driven away by his usual tactics.

---

[58] There are about twenty letters from Woodruff to Smith among the Lot Smith Papers, UA.

[59] Letter of Erastus Snow to John Taylor, December 19, 1878, Erastus Snow Letters, HDC.

[60] Letter of William C. McClellan to Erastus Snow, May 1881, Erastus Snow Letters, HDC.

[61] Letter of J. R. K. Pipkin to William C. McClellan, Sunset United Order Papers, HDC.

[62] Letter of William C. McClellan to Erastus Snow, May 1881, Erastus Snow Letters, HDC.

Finally he rid himself of this opposition by using his authority as stake president to call two of its leaders on an Indian mission to Savoia, New Mexico.[63]

But the most acute problems grew from Smith's failure to set up an adequate system of accounting. When people joined the company their capital stock was usually appraised and recorded. Otherwise, almost no books were kept. No account of labor, rent, foodstuffs, schooling costs, or other family expenditures were maintained. Growth and dividends appear never to have been calculated until after the collapse of the Order. Time spent on records in a system where all things were held in common and all proceeds shared was time wasted to Smith. Others recognized that the practice of doing business without records could only lead to inequity and discord. Seeing to the core of the matter, President John Taylor had written at an early time that "the present system will encourage people to leave with only what they put in — not what has accrued."[64] As it turned out this was precisely what happened. Departing members were told all increment belonged to the church and, with Smith making the decisions as to what represented their original investment, given only what they put in. Erastus Snow briefed the problem as follows:

Those who leave are not allowed anything for the use of their property and means while with them, nor for labour, however, faithfully performed, except what they eat, and if their stock, teams or other property is used up in the company or damaged they lose it, but if their labour helps to make improvement or their stock increases, such improvements or increase accrues to the company — and when parties become dissatisfied, They must take what is left of their effects and go to some other part of the country because . . . these companies wish to monopolize all around them whether they need or can use it or not. . . .[65]

The Sunset question finally broke in 1886. For Arizona Mormons it could hardly have come at a more critical moment, as the territory's politicians were in full hue and cry against them. Blood had been drawn in several polygamy cases, and the Latter-day Saints were in retreat; many of them, including Sunset's most prominent figures, fled to Mexico. Had any of the dissatisfied Orderites decided to ignore the church's teaching that to "law a brother" was wrong or had any chosen to place economic interest or personal animosity above the interest of the church, the entire question might have been aired in court, giving Gentile opponents another weapon against the beleaguered Mormon colony. As it was, loyalty

---

[63] See Erastus Snow's "Statement of Proceedings at the Preliminary Sunset Hearing," July 12, 1886, La Ascencion, Mexico, Erastus Snow Letters, HDC.

[64] Letter to Lot Smith, November 27, 1878, Lot Smith Papers, UA.

[65] Letter of Erastus Snow to John Taylor, December 19, 1878, Erastus Snow Letters, HDC.

held up and moderating machinery within the church proved equal to the task of settlement. Prompted by the need to deal with the matter while it could still be dealt with internally, church leaders, including several apostles who were in Mexico in 1886, could no longer postpone the unpleasant task of confronting Lot Smith. Consequently a preliminary hearing was conducted in July at La Ascension by Apostles Erastus Snow, Brigham Young, Jr., and George Teasdale. Finding evidence of favoritism and irregularity of accounting, they ordered a full-scale investigation and appointed a committee, of which Lot Smith was to be president, to carry it out.[66] David K. Udall was substituted when Smith asked to be excused from serving.

Fortified with a long letter of instruction, the committee began its task immediately. During the fall of 1886, what books the Sunset Company had were consulted, and a subcommittee headed by John Bushman, a member of the St. Joseph Order, rounded up, tallied, and marked the livestock at the Mormon Lake ranches. Animals still held by Lot Smith and bearing his Circle S brand (formerly the Sunset Order brand) numbered at least 1,200 head of cattle, 2,400 sheep, and 175 horses.[67] Real estate at the old townsite as well as in the Mormon Lake area was inventoried. In addition the committee took statements and gathered private accounts from as many former members as could be found. Using this information, it undertook to construct a fiscal history from which to settle the accounts of the various members.

The company's total assets exceeded $85,000.[68] This sum included debts and overdrafts and stock in the Arizona Cooperative Mercantile Institution as well as livestock and ranch properties. Exclusive of the property held by Smith, it was found that at least $9,500 had been overdrawn by eight members, some of whom had been Smith's confidants and supporters. A substantial sum of money was also owed the company, the largest single account being that of John W. Young, who during his Arizona railroading adventures had borrowed $2,821.[69]

The inventory complete, the committee moved to the difficult task of distribution. In studying the records it is impossible to avoid the conclusion that at least two formulas were used — one for the rank and file and one for Lot Smith. Quite naturally the latter had ideas about how the settle-

---

[66] Letter of Snow, Young, and Teasdale to D. K. Udall et al., July 13, 1886, copied in "Minutes of Frihoff Nielson for the Sunset Committee," typescript in possession of author.

[67] "Life and Labors of John Bushman," pp. 108-119, and "Diary of Frihoff G. Nielson," entries of August-December 1886.

[68] This figure is arrived at by totaling settlements received by Smith and all other Sunset members. See Sunset United Order Papers, HDC.

[69] Letter to John W. Young, August 19, 1887, Sunset United Order Papers, HDC.

ment should be made. Ignoring as usual the need for accounts, he proposed that one thousand head of horned stock, twenty horses, all moveable property, and the company's debts be distributed among the members. As his share he proposed to retain the residue of the cattle and horses, all the sheep, and the mountain ranches. Feeling that the proposition was not in keeping with their instructions, the committee refused to consider it.[70] Stymied, Smith stormed and sulked but submitted. His forceful demands, however, resulted in what was essentially a compromise settlement with him receiving some $51,000 in various assets. This sum represented his capital investment, salary for himself and sons for the two and a half years since the Order's dissolution, and dividends on his investment and labor for the eight-year period he was in the Order.[71]

The remaining assets amounting to about $34,000 were distributed to forty-seven families. Unlike Smith, each of these had been given a previous settlement. In spite of earlier statements to the contrary, it was now found that none of them had left the Order with less than his original capital investment. Taking this into consideration, the committee gave each former member a proportionate amount of the company's assets including its debts, many of which were bad. Characteristic of the committee's settlement was the following letter to Levi Savage:

The Sunset U. O. Committee have allotted you $116.10 on W. B. Maxwell; $13.90 on John Bloomfield [each of whom had received substantial overdrafts in earlier settlements] and $750.00 in Stock orders for all which you will find inclosed. If you cannot collect the debts you will be the loser as the Committee have endeavored to apportion the debts and poorer assets proportionally amongst those to whom property is due. The Stock is to be paid at Mormon Ranch between the dates of Aug. 25, 1887 and Oct. 1, 1887. If you are not there by the latter date to receive your stock the committee will not be responsible for them. . . .[72]

Lot Smith and a few others emerged with less than if there had been no settlement. Most members gained substantially.

In terms of the success of the Mormon colonization of Arizona, the Sunset controversy was a heavy blow. It may be asked why church leaders failed to take steps to solve the problem earlier. Any answer will be speculative, but some thoughts relative to the subject must nevertheless be advanced.

In the first place, close personal relations between Smith and numerous general officers of the church led to a reluctance on their part to

---

[70] "John Bushman Diaries" and "Frihoff G. Nielson Diary," entries for August and September 1886.

[71] Letter of Sunset Committee to Erastus Snow et al., March 19, 1888, Sunset United Order Papers, HDC.

[72] Letter of August 6, 1887, Sunset United Order Papers, HDC.

initiate action against him. In addition he was willing to stay on the Little Colorado and fight for a vital interest of the church. During the first years when many (some accounts say as high as ninety percent) of the Arizona missionaries turned tail and ran, Smith remained. He is said to have repeated time and again: "You may all go if you want to and I will stay and keep tavern" here.[73]

But the most important consideration in Smith's retention is the fact that the role he played in Arizona's colonization was by no means as negative as the Sunset settlement made him appear. It should be borne in mind that the only accounts of the settlement are those of the committee and its various members. Most of the latter had been connected with one or another of the United Orders. Some had much to gain from a decision adverse to Smith. One or two were long-time enemies who were at best jealous and at worst vindictive. Financially their settlement was favorable to Smith, but in a personal sense their verdict was tinctured with hostility.

Taken in its Mormon matrix, Sunset can only be viewed as a failure. As a farming village it was a dismal flop — at least after its earliest years. As a movement of social and spiritual union it was a cruel miscarriage. But as a business venture it did not fail. Quite to the contrary it was economically the most notable Mormon success on the Little Colorado. It was never a balanced communal unit, but as a livestock operation it flourished. In this phase of its program, Smith was in his element, his ability and the force of his character providing the only wealth most of his colleagues ever knew. This fact is dramatically apparent in the Little Colorado journals. We may draw briefly from two to emphasize the point.

Locy Rogers, like Smith, hailed from Farmington, Utah. Gentle and filled with good humor, he was altogether one of the most lovable figures in the region. He was loyal and honest but utterly without financial acumen. Indeed Locy Rogers came near being the prototype "Peter Tumble Down" — a quality his contemporaries quickly discerned, and he became known as "Locy who puts his brand on tools with baling wire."[74] (In after years baling wire was known as "Locy" in more than one Little Colorado town.) Rogers left the Sunset Order with considerable property — enough to trade for a home and a farm in a neighboring village and have a substantial herd of livestock left over. Being, as the Sunset United Order Committee delicately put it, "unfortunate in the management of this property," he was soon reduced to the near edge of poverty.[75]

---

[73] "Diary of Andrew L. Rogers, 1882-1902," typescript, USHS, p. 24.

[74] "Life Sketch of Andrew L. Rogers," typescript, BYU, p. 13.

[75] Letter to Erastus Snow et al., March 19, 1888, Sunset United Order Papers, HDC.

Another whose fiscal fortunes reached high tide under Smith's direction at Sunset was Levi Mathers Savage. Stern and inflexible, he was long-time bishop of Sunset and at Woodruff where he was feared and even hated by the boys of his ward, including his own sons, but widely respected by Gentiles and church people alike. Reluctant to discuss the United Order, almost to the point of total silence, he nevertheless dropped an occasional shred of information that casts light upon the relationship of Lot Smith's livestock operation to the general economy of the Mormon community in Arizona. Savage got a settlement of $750.00 in cattle and soon moved to Diaz in Mexico, taking his stock along. For a time the poverty that characterized his pioneering was alleviated. A dairy business was launched. Then problems of management, Mexican relations, and illness rendered the enterprise impossible. By the time Savage returned from Mexico, the grubstake accumulated under Lot Smith's hard hand had been dissipated entirely. In the afterglow of subsequent years, his wife recalled the Diaz days as a golden era, and significantly, as far as the character of Mormon nationalism was concerned, indulged in an abiding expatriation of the soul as she longed for the good life of Mexico.[76]

What Levi Savage and Locy Rogers ever knew of prosperity was in connection with the Sunset United Order. Their cases were not unique. In an area plagued by chronic poverty, Smith's success cannot be ignored.[77]

---

[76] "Journal of Levi Mathers Savage," p. 41. Also interviews with Lydia S. Peterson, daughter of the Savages, Snowflake, Arizona.

[77] During the years after 1887 when the Sunset Order settlement was finished, Smith's Circle S Ranch interests sprawled from Mormon Lake and Fort Moroni on the south and west to Tuba City on the north. His tenacity and toughness were again demonstrated by his ability to hang on in a country that by this time was the preserve of the mammoth Aztec Land and Cattle Company. His final home was at Reservoir Canyon several miles east of Tuba City. Here, near the flowing springs which Mormons had dammed to run a woolen mill and for irrigation purposes, he built a home as well as owning a house in Tuba City. In 1892 he had an altercation with the Navajos whose sheep often ran on his meadow below the Mormon reservoir. Finally, he shot several head of sheep and was shot himself by Navajos hiding on the gray canyon wall that lines the upper end of the meadow on the east. He rode two or three miles home though mortally wounded and died within a few hours. At his own request, he was buried near the Upper Pasture Canyon house but was not permitted to rest. Sentimental oldtimers among Little Colorado's officialdom soon became exercised that their comrade in arms was buried in this lonely canyon. Particularly trying in their eyes was the fact that when the reservoir which was about a mile and a half down canyon was full, the water table rose, inundating the old warrior's body. Finally, after considerable talk, David Brinkerhoff, bishop of Tuba City, was directed to exhume the body and ship it north. Pursuant to these instructions, the bishop made preparations to send the body with a son who was going on a mission. At the disinterment, interested spectators gathered, and one eyewitness account related that water actually poured from the casket, washing whiskers from his long red beard with it. After a period of dehydration in a sand bank, his body was duly shipped to Farmington, Utah, where he was finally permitted to rest. For the details relative to his death and subsequent events, I am indebted to Mrs. Lois Heward Gardner of Woodruff, who lived at Moenave at the time of Smith's death. Personal interview with Mrs. Gardner, Woodruff, Arizona, August 28, 1966.

Other orders starved out or, in the case of St. Joseph, persisted in an impoverished fraternity. As far as the United Order and its thinning rank of supporters went, Lot Smith's success as a stockman may well have been Sunset's great failing.[78] Property rather than union of the Order became the basis of its relationships. Unity and the Mormon destiny gave way before the growing emphasis upon livestock. To idealists who came to Arizona dreaming of startling spiritual strengths, the bonds of its material success were frustrating and devoid of satisfaction.[79]

From the foregoing pages, it is apparent that the Little Colorado United Order began to deteriorate almost before it was formed. In view of the ambivalence of church policy and the ideologic and personal conflicts that characterized its course, the wonder is not that it collapsed in the mid-eighties but that it did not fold completely at an earlier time. Although both the scattering of its leaders by the polygamy scare and the Sunset investigation may have hastened its final demise, the collapse was nearly complete before they struck. Likely the Order had merely outlived its usefulness.

It will be recalled that early in this chapter the United Order was portrayed as an agency of extraordinary control to facilitate the Mormon expansion beyond Utah's territorial bounds. The dependence of the family Orders upon free public lands and other frontier conditions was also pointed out. With the progress of colonization and the closing of the frontier, the special circumstances that at the same time permitted the Order to function and posited a need for it had passed and more ordinary patterns replaced it. Also the idealism of the church had undergone changes by 1886, and the errand in the wilderness concept had overlived its meaning. Little Colorado communicants were tardily forced to acknowledge that their quest for a new way of life had failed and that part of its failure lay in the fact that the body of Mormondom had very little interest in that quest.

---

[78] For more on Lot Smith, see Peterson, " 'A Mighty Man Was Brother Lot': A Portrait of Lot Smith, Mormon Pioneer," *Western Historical Quarterly* 1 (1970): 394-414.

[79] "Diary of Andrew L. Rogers," p. 65.

6. UNION OR DISCORD:
The Problem of "Money Matters"

> ... It is not the privilege of any man or company of men to take advantage of the circumstances of the people and their necessities and farm them out for their private profit. As Latter-day Saints we are all equal, and we should labor for each other's benefit and no man should selfishly build himself up or enrich himself at the expense of his brother or brethren. If he had superior advantages either of his position or of skill, let him have a fair remuneration therefor; but beyond this he should not go. He should labor as we all should for the welfare, advancement and prosperity of the people.
>
> LETTER OF INSTRUCTION

> ... In these parts good health and moderate prosperity prevail — except in money matters.
>
> LEVI MATHERS SAVAGE

Economic Cooperation: A Labored Product

ALTHOUGH THEY REJECTED the United Order, Mormons of the Little Colorado continued to follow communitarian programs that were initiated and coordinated by the church. Falling short of the thorough union required by the Orders, such practices nevertheless extended to most aspects of life. Towns were founded where the Saints could live in close proximity. Self or local employment was encouraged, and occupations that took members from the Mormon community were frowned upon. Emergencies were met by common planning and effort. Centrifugal tendencies were condemned alike by popular opinion and official counsel. And perhaps most importantly, religious and economic programs were

[123]

launched and conducted on the basis of what was essentially voluntary and cooperative action.

Yet Little Colorado cooperation was a labored product. Mormons there never successfully put aside the countering tendencies of personal interest. Their failure to unite appears to have been particularly marked in those activities that impinged most directly upon the general economy. At no point was unity of feeling and action more vital — nor more difficult to achieve. Mormons who labored joyously together on missions or sweat in desperate accord to control the Little Colorado were never more conscious of the peculiarity of their individual interests or of conflicting loyalties than they were in "money matters."

This is not to say that an excess of individualism existed. Indeed, individualism struck only muted tones, but its persistence, along with the prolonged but benevolent determination to repair the holes it occasioned in the communal fabric, affords an unusual opportunity to study the problem of an ideologic voluntarism as a means of social motivation. By no means immune to the forces of individualism themselves, church leaders found it necessary to let the commitments and loyalties of the personnel involved join in shaping communal programs. Thus challenged and limited by personal interests, a restricted cooperation emerged which was consistent with the nature and circumstances of the community. The difficulties encountered in balancing the need for collective action and individual interests were etched with particular sharpness in two developments: the construction of the Atlantic and Pacific Railroad across Arizona and the establishment of a cooperative mercantile institution.

The Board of Trade and Regulation of Railroad Construction

On the Little Colorado as elsewhere in the church during the years following Brigham Young's death in 1877, the United Order was progressively supplanted as the primary agency of communal economic action in the church by the board of trade movement. Hoping to gain the advantages of collective bargaining in the realms of production, merchandising, and labor management, a church-wide system was established with Zion's Central Board of Trade at the top and committees throughout the stakes and wards.[1] In addition to its regular structure, which followed the lines of church organization, the board of trade movement also included certain *ad hoc* committees set up to deal with particular problems. One of the most important of these was the board established in 1880 to control and regulate Mormon labor and contracting on the Denver and Rio Grande

---

[1] For information on the board of trade movement, see Arrington, *Great Basin Kingdom,* pp. 341-49.

and Atlantic and Pacific railways that were building through southeastern Utah and northern New Mexico and Arizona. Manned by prominent colonizers, this effort to provide effective leadership foundered on a division between its members and resulted in contention and exploitation rather than in the benefits of collective action. Although the jurisdiction of this board extended to the construction of both the Denver and Rio Grande and the Atlantic and Pacific, our narrative is primarily concerned with the latter.

Commissioned by Congress in 1866, the Atlantic and Pacific road did not begin laying track over the 35th parallel route through western New Mexico until the spring of 1880.[2] During the next eighteen months, the line was pushed 565 miles from Isleta to the Colorado River, passing through the Mormon colony in the process.

Mormon reaction was varied. Having settled the Little Colorado in some degree because a railroad was scheduled to be built along its course, and not totally devoid of the characteristic promotional impulses of the frontier, the Mormons welcomed its coming. However, its challenge to the isolation of their position stirred profound feelings of unrest. Misgivings were widely voiced in church meetings where a number of solutions were suggested, most of which echoed the themes of Mormon self-sufficiency through home and village manufactury and a self-contained marketing system.[3] As in the more general surges of Mormon self-sufficiency, the need for autonomy was felt to be doubly urgent because they believed the collapse of worldly systems would shortly render Mormon economic independence a necessity. To such cries were added admonitions to erect barriers against the influx of unwholesome populations by preempting the labor of construction. However, plans to monopolize construction reflected deep feelings of relief as well.

Indeed, some regarded the opportunity for work on the railroad as a godsend, for the winter of 1879-80 had been one of extreme shortage, and by early summer colonists were digging for roots and suffering the

---

[2] See U. S., *Congressional Globe,* 39th Cong., 1st sess., pp. 1101-1102, 4182, and *U. S., Statutes at Large,* vol. 14, p. 292, for congressional provisions for the 35th parallel route. The only accounts of the Atlantic and Pacific Railway with which this writer is acquainted leave much to be desired. While L. L. Waters, *Steel Trails to Santa Fe* (Lawrence, Kansas: University of Kansas, 1950) is poor, other general histories of the Santa Fe Railroad are even worse. Sanford Musk, *Land Tenure Problems in the Santa Fe Railroad Grant Area* (Berkeley: University of California Press, 1944) and William S. Greever, *Arid Domain: The Santa Fe Railway and Its Western Land Grant* (Palo Alto: Stanford University Press, 1954) are both short and limited in their scope, but they improve upon the general treatments as far as the early history of the line is concerned. The writer depended upon the latter, especially pp. 10-35. Not much more useful than the early histories is H. Craig Miner's, *The St. Louis–San Francisco Transcontinental Railroad: The Thirty-fifth Parallel Project, 1853-1890* (Lawrence: University Press of Kansas, 1972).

[3] See "Minutes of Eastern Arizona Stake Conferences, 1879-1882," p. 97.

effects of "the flux," a debilitating malady occasioned by a diet heavy on pigweed greens. Despite the relatively good crops of the previous summer, perceptive members of the community had sensed that famine was impending as early as December and made what provisions they could to cope with it. Their efforts failing, the situation soon became critical. In the first place, the migration of that winter was unusually heavy. Apprised of the good harvests, many of the new immigrants brought nonedibles. In addition all surplus cattle had been applied to the St. Johns land purchase, thus limiting the most ready item of barter in the money-short community. Moreover, an extended drought in southern Utah closed this traditional source of relief, and, as a final blow, the winter of 1879-80 surpassed all precedent for severity. Livestock perished, and humans, many of them still camped in wagons or makeshift huts, suffered intensely from long periods of cold and snow.[4]

Contracting I: Frontier Relief Measure

Into this situation stepped John W. Young, bringing with him a plan for relief and the makings of discord and communal breakdown. An enigmatic and controversial figure who rarely did what his more conventional brethren wished, this flamboyant and suave son of Brigham Young had early seen opportunity on Arizona's frontiers. Setting a precedent that was followed by the less fortunate son of Apostle George A. Smith who was killed by the Navajos on a similar junket two years later, he had accompanied Jacob Hamblin south to Arizona on that worthy's second visit to the Hopis in 1859.[5] From that time forward, he was interested in northern Arizona, engaging at various times in the wool trade, railroading, livestock, and land speculation. Sensing the limitations of Mormondom's self-imposed agrarianism, he sought to go beyond it to take control of economic and industrial development in northern Arizona but was frustrated as much by his failure to win other Mormons to his unorthodox approach as he was by outside hostility toward the church, business competition, and chronic lack of capital.

While Young's loyalty to the church has been questioned, an examination of his activities in Arizona and in the East during the 1880s reveals something more than a sharp appetite for wealth. He understood better

---

[4] At a stake conference in June, a survey of grain supplies revealed that the Eastern Arizona Stake members lacked 10,000 pounds of having enough to feed themselves through to harvest. *Ibid.,* p. 109.

[5] James A. Little, *Jacob Hamblin: A Narrative of His Personal Experience, as a Frontiersman, Missionary to the Indians and Explorer.* . . . (Salt Lake City: Juvenile Instructor's Office, 1881), p. 69.

John W. Young, mercurial son of church leader Brigham Young.

than anyone else connected with the Little Colorado colony the power inherent in the economic promotion of the late nineteenth century and hoped by coming to terms with it to exploit it in behalf of the Mormon cause. Other prominent Mormons, including those on the Little Colorado, recoiled from his seeming reconciliation with Babylon and continued to seek the basis of their economic and political strategy in the isolation of a narrowly construed frontier agricultural kingdom. In their company, John W. Young was indeed an enigma, one whose imagination and skill were occasionally sought but whose activities were never understood or condoned. The conflict of forces in his person as well as between him and other leading figures on the Little Colorado was symptomatic and symbolic of the sharp edge of individualism that cut through the very backbone of economic cooperation in the northern Arizona colony.

Arriving at Moenkopi early in 1879, Young established a woolen business that included a factory of some two hundred spindles and a commercial house through which he hoped to corner the growing wool trade of the Navajos. First as counselor to his father and later as a roving ambassador, without portfolio, styled "Counselor to the Apostles," he had shared the top-level leadership of the Arizona Mission with Wilford Woodruff and Erastus Snow. When the news of the Atlantic and Pacific construction broke in the spring of 1880, he was visiting the towns of northern Arizona, preaching the necessity of cooperative mercantile stores — drumming up interest in a movement which, we may be sure, was not unrelated to his own plans to exploit the country's obvious potential for wool trade.

On hearing that construction was to be resumed, Young shifted his attention forthwith from cooperation and wool to railroading and headed east late in May with Jesse N. Smith and Ammon M. Tenney to secure a grading contract. After some delay they located A. A. Palmer, chief engineer, at Pueblo. With him they signed a contract for five miles of grading on a stretch that lay astride the continental divide some 150 miles northeast of Snowflake. Organizing themselves as Young, Smith, and Tenney, they placed orders with Albuquerque houses for food to relieve their hungry towns as well as for the feed and equipment necessary to carry out the contract.

Rushing back to Snowflake in time for stake conference in the latter part of June, they presented their action to the members of the stake who "agreed by vote of the Conference" to take the contract.[6] The assembled members of the priesthood also agreed to take additional contracts and,

---

[6] Smith, *Journal of Jesse N. Smith*, p. 245.

suggesting the course events were to take, organized a board of trade composed of the stake presidency and two prominent bishops to "stand between the contractors and the people."[7] It is significant that this latter measure was undertaken entirely at Smith's instance, Young concerning himself only with the promotion of the grading contract.

By midsummer, the villages of the Eastern Arizona Stake stood half empty with twenty teams and forty men heading east from Snowflake and smaller numbers from the other towns. Arriving at the construction site, they found themselves completely without provisions and equipment. In spite of some tense and hungry days, most of the snarls were soon worked out. By the first week in August, all the men were equipped and working. A makeshift commissary was set up from which the needs of the construction crews and the hungry communities back in Arizona were met.

As the enterprise developed so did questions about the nature of the contracting agency. In the movement's initial stages, Young, Smith, and Tenney had taken the contract as a conventional company and had organized their affairs along characteristic lines. But the immediate objective had clearly been the relief of the food shortage, and all had worked to this end and in what was acknowledged to be a cooperative effort to meet a common threat. By the first of September, it was apparent that John W. Young saw the future of Mormon railroading in a different light than Smith, who conceived of it as a program to bolster the economy of the colony and as a means of keeping Gentile labor out. As far as immediate considerations went, Young regarded it as a promising private opportunity and was determined to run the enterprise so as to develop fully its economic potentials. But at the same time he was anxious to employ Mormons and give them any advantage of the activity generated by his company. Uneasy as the complexion of the situation emerged, Smith temporarily withdrew and returned to Snowflake.

Contracting II: Private Enterprise

As the work of the first contract proceeded, Young moved to get others, forcing Tenney out as he went. In October when F. W. Smith, superintendent of the railroad, visited the head of the line, Young was able to interest him in a personal tour of the work remaining to be done across Arizona. In company with J. M. Latta, a lumberman who had contracted to furnish the road's ties, they dashed off in a spanking new outfit provided by Young, the luxury of which dismayed the thrifty church members who were working for him. But the ostentation paid off, or, for the moment

---

[7] "Minutes of Eastern Arizona Stake Conferences, 1879-1882," p. 110.

at least, seemed to. On their return Young closed deals, contracting with Smith to finish one hundred miles of grading by July of 1881 and sub-contracting a half-million ties from Latta to be filled no later than September.

However, it was necessary to sign on less favorable terms than previously. Rather than reducing the actual rates, the railroad placed Young at a disadvantage by demanding a ten percent rebate on the entire operation and withheld about half of the very liberal freight drawbacks allowed on goods hauled over the road under the terms of the earlier contract.[8] During the autumn, Young worked feverishly to organize this immense new project. Borrowing heavily at high rates from Santa Fe and Albuquerque banks, he built his outfit. The commissary was enlarged. Merchants in New Mexico extended credit for goods to stock new outlets which were established in makeshift tent buildings along the road. To his Fort Moroni ranch at Leroux Springs on the southwest side of the San Francisco Mountains, he added other key spots along the track, buying Thompson Ranch at the fork of Rio Puerco Wash and the Little Colorado and taking over the defunct Mormon forts at Obed and Brigham City. Significantly, he failed in an effort to capture control of important coal deposits that were coming to light in the area of Gallup, New Mexico.[9]

It was also necessary to recruit a large labor force. Young, who thought that no fewer than a thousand men and teams would be required, looked to the church as his primary source. Authorities in Arizona supported him from the first in building his crew. As on earlier occasions, they urged the faithful to take a fair share of the proceeds of this new development and to keep out "the vicious" by doing the work themselves.[10]

Recognizing the impossibility of drawing the entire force from the Arizona communities, Young requested help from Utah. Soon a large number of men headed by Salt Lakers Abraham F. Doremus and Rulon S. Wells, general superintendent and chief bookkeeper, respectively, were

---

[8] Erastus Snow explained this phase of the business in a letter to President Franklin D. Richards of the First Presidency written January 22, 1883, Erastus Snow Letters, HDC. Similar concessions were no doubt made to Mr. Latta. The tie contract was a close proposition, and Young knew it, as he had previously refused to bid on the prime contract on the basis that the going rate was too little to allow a profit. See "Minutes of Eastern Arizona Stake Conferences, 1879-1882," p. 111.

[9] "Autobiography of Joseph Fish," p. 186.

[10] Mormons gathered from far and near to work on Young's undertaking. However the effect was not always what church leaders had hoped. From the outlaw country of northern Utah and southern Wyoming came young Matt Warner. Not content to join his father in grading work he electrified the country by robbing what he called "a sorta store and bank combined" at St. Johns and with a determined posse in hot pursuit fled to Utah's Robbers' Roost. See Matt Warner and Murray E. King, *The Last of the Bandit Riders* (New York: Bonanza Books, n.d.), pp. 65-76.

en route from that quarter. By December, no fewer than five hundred men and teams had assembled. Doremus and Jesse N. Smith, who had been directed by the church to rejoin Young, were swamped as they struggled to let subcontracts and organize the grading work. Although the surveying was not carried out on schedule and much of the earth work was consequently delayed, construction was soon under way along the entire front of Young's contract, which extended west to a few miles beyond Sunset.

Tie-cutting proceeded simultaneously. Timber camps were located at Fort Moroni on the west and near Young's headquarters at Bacon Springs on the continental divide in New Mexico. Elsewhere cooperative groups set up mills and subbed tie contracts.

As the pressures of his tight contracts and unfavorable loans built up, Young drove his subordinates and failed to pay his docile Mormon subcontractors and laborers. Soon he was at sword's point with railroad representatives as well as the banking and mercantile interests of the New Mexican cities. In this condition he limped along harassed by both sides to complete his contracts, with the primary losers being the workers whom he was unable to pay.

Contracting III: Limitations of the Board of Trade

Meantime, the church had begun to take an interest in railroad construction. In part, this was a reflection of the mounting importance of John W. Young's business on the Atlantic and Pacific road, but it was broader than that. Colonists elsewhere, principally in southeastern Utah and southwestern Colorado, were finding relief in construction jobs on the Denver and Rio Grande track that was building into Utah.

The Salt Lake authorities took action late in the summer of 1880. At that time, Erastus Snow and Brigham Young, Jr., toured the entire construction area. After their return to Salt Lake City, the church proposed to stabilize the Mormon labor market and bring all contracting and working members under central supervision. Pursuant to this decision, a central board of trade consisting of Erastus Snow, Brigham Young, Jr., John W. Young, and Jesse N. Smith was set up. Long identical letters of instruction were addressed to each on October 27. Along with a letter from B. Young and Snow advising that additional grading contracts not to exceed twenty-five miles be taken, the instructions were forwarded to Smith and John W. Young on the twenty-eighth, two days after the latter had taken the hundred-mile contract referred to previously.

The major objectives outlined in the instructions were the exclusion of the "unruly and disorderly element" and the monopolization of labor as the lines approached the Mormon settlements. In conjunction with stake and local boards, the committee was directed to so organize the labor force as to achieve these goals without damaging the moral fiber of the community or jeopardizing the physical success of colonization. The instructions elaborated that the committee's duties were to include the estimation of manpower needs and its recruitment. Once raised, the work force was to be organized along church lines with presidencies over the various camps in which the strictest discipline was to be maintained. Breach of the sabbath, profanity, drinking, attendance of meetings, and payment of tithes were each the object of special mention.[11]

Finally, the committee was charged in explicit terms to prohibit exploitation and to engender a feeling for the common interest and goals of all Latter-day Saints. In reference to such matters, the instructions denied:

. . . the privilege of any man or company of men to take advantage of the circumstances of the people and their necessities and farm them out for their private profit. As Latter-day Saints we are all equal, and we should labor for each other's benefit and no man should selfishly build himself up or enrich himself at the expense of his brother or brethren. If he has superior advantages either of his position or of skill, let him have a fair remuneration therefor; but beyond this he should not go. He should labor as we all should for the welfare, advancement and prosperity of the people.[12]

Sensing that it might be difficult to determine what represented a fair remuneration where the time of the committee itself was concerned, the Salt Lake authorities went on "as to yourselves, for the labor which you perform . . . five percent would be a proper amount."[13]

Nor did the letter of instructions limit its directives to the organization and pay of the work force. Merchandizing in connection with the operation was also to be controlled. Specifically:

The supplies should also be provided subject to the action and adjustment of the various Boards, no one man or few men receiving the profits therefrom, but like the labor, it should be performed in the interest of all, that confidence may grow among the people and brotherhood, unity and harmony prevail.[14]

Thus the church sought to maintain cooperation and brotherly concern within its ranks while it simultaneously took a fair profit from railroad

---

[11] Interestingly, it was planned to appoint a "Bishop's Agent" to collect tithing monies in the railroad camps. Letter of instructions from First Presidency to John W. Young, October 27, 1880, John W. Young Papers for 1880-1887, HDC.

[12] *Ibid.*

[13] *Ibid.*

[14] *Ibid.*

construction and barred Gentiles from the region by monopolizing the labor market.

The most questionable element in this entire arrangement was John W. Young. Unsure of this mercurial son of Brigham, other church leaders undertook to bridle and control him by surrounding him with more stable men.

Welcoming the help of his associates of the board, John W. Young at first appeared to submit to the propositions set up by the church. Immediately after receiving the instructions, he wired his brother Brigham, Jr., in Salt Lake City informing him of the new grading and timber contracts. Although it was obvious in the context of the telegram that he intended to work with the others, he did not state explicitly that he would comply with the conditions of the letter. Pressed by his brother, he replied that he was indeed "subject to instructions." [15]

Although all parties, including the two Youngs, took this to be a firm commitment, the nature of John W.'s personality and the extent of his involvement frustrated the attempt to restore the cooperative spirit in which the original contract had been launched. In part this was due to obligations already incurred by John W. Not only were the contracts in his name but he had run up a heavy indebtedness. Confronted by the economic realities of this situation, he was reluctant to yield to the more cautious approach of the other members. They, in turn, were hesitant to have their names drawn too deeply into questionable financial deals, the course of which they were unable to alter. Furthermore, the early flirtation between Young and the representatives of the railroad had soured by early winter; the three associates had no stomach for involving themselves and the church in relations that were already far deteriorated.

Burdened with such liabilities, the cooperative leadership of the four men did not materialize. Soon all pretense was abandoned. Erastus Snow stiffly withdrew, rightly convinced that John W. was determined to retain complete financial control of the operation.[16] Brigham Young, Jr., stayed on for a time, held as much by filial ties as by church association. The final member of the committee, Jesse N. Smith, worked for several months directing the grading and maintaining some semblance of the spiritual order suggested by the instructions. His role, however, was that of a salaried superintendent, not that of a partner or associate. As the troubles with railroad officials and financial pressures multiplied, he was subjected to mounting criticism from Young, whose ebullient optimism and general

---

[15] See telegram of John W. Young to Brigham Young, Jr., November 2, 1880, John W. Young Letters, HDC.

[16] "Minutes of Eastern Arizona Stake Conferences, 1879-1882," p. 153.

kindliness were temporarily soured by the threatened collapse of his enterprise. A proud man, Smith chafed under this relationship and remained only because of church directive and of the stubborn hope that he might represent the loyal Mormons who had followed counsel to take employment with Young.

The subcontractors and workers lost heavily. Young apparently had good intentions but simply felt less pressure to pay his work force than he did to meet other obligations. Repeatedly promising early settlement, he negotiated with the railroad, seeking an upward revision in his contract. The railroaders, however, compounded his difficulty not only by refusing to alter the rates of the contract but by favoring other contractors in the surveying and engineering of the line. As a consequence, Young's schedule was often interrupted and the patience of unpaid workers further tried as they were forced to wait on engineering crews.

Not all workers went unpaid, however. As noted previously, supplies had been advanced to the stricken communities at the time of the early contract. It would appear, in addition, that most of those who had worked on the first contract were paid.[17] During the later contract, too, some were paid for their services but found it necessary to take goods at inflated prices from Young's commissary. Even men in managerial positions did not always find it easy to collect. Brigham Young, Jr., though he had to accept goods, appears to have been the exception and was well compensated for his efforts, receiving, according to Snow, "$1500 to $2000 in teams and family supplies."[18] Snow himself drew only $420 in store items, and Smith was paid $75 per month for his services, all of which was taken in "wares out of the store at very high prices."[19]

The docile nature of Mormon labor is attested by the fact that no evidence has been discovered that those who lost most complained. While they must have objected and objected strenuously, they did not write about it in their journals nor did they give vent to their ire in church meetings where word of their feelings would have been recorded. Perhaps part of their complacency may be traced to the fact that Young continually promised to make his indebtedness good. There is no evidence that anyone questioned that he would ultimately make full restitution. Although he went on to deal in large sums of money in Arizona ranching and in railroading and securities in the East, his promotions demanded that every dollar be turned into his schemes. Yet his conscience did not

---

[17] "Autobiography of Joseph Fish," p. 172.

[18] Letter of Erastus Snow to Franklin D. Richards, January 22, 1883, Erastus Snow Letters, HDC.

[19] Smith, *Journal of Jesse N. Smith,* p. 251.

let him rest and frequent reference is found of his intent to square the matter at some future date. Among those who mention his concern was James N. Le Sueur, whose father had worked for Young and was among the few fortunate enough to be paid in cash. Meeting Young in Brooklyn in 1900, the younger Le Sueur told him his father had worked on the Atlantic and Pacific contracts, whereupon John W. said:

"Oh! you are his son? Well, I am coming to Arizona and pay the brethren what I owe them some day." He had taken the contract too low and met too many difficulties to overcome, to any more than pay other expenses than wages. . . .

Continuing, Le Sueur suggested another reason for the complacency of Young's unpaid workers:

Rulen S. Wells, one of the General Authorities of the Church recently died [it will be recalled that Wells came to Arizona in 1880 to manage Young's accounts], told the writer that Utah and Arizona owed a debt of gratitude to John W. Young rather than their censure. For the railroad . . . through Arizona could not have been built in that early day except by a contract so low that nearly all labor could not be paid for. If the laborers considered their services as donated to enhance by many years the development of Arizona . . . it would be a deserving view of the Sacrifice they made in the interest of Arizona progress.[20]

By the end of 1881 construction had been completed and Young turned his attention to other activities. For several years he continued to hope that he might get an additional settlement from the railroad and gathered depositions and written testimony relative to the terms and conditions of his contract. Finally, his lawyers presented claims totaling nearly $50,000 to the railroad officials who evidently ignored them. There is no indication that the matter ever came before the courts or that it was settled out of court.[21]

Thus division and restrained conflict were integral elements of the railroad contracts. An unplanned mix of personal initiative and Mormon cooperation, they point up both a tardy response to a situation that demanded order from the first and the general ineffectiveness of business by committee. However, it should be borne in mind that the contracts which had been taken initially as a community relief measure made a real contribution to the welfare of the Little Colorado community. People were drawn into the country. Original colonists found more to hope for as employment and prosperity temporarily let them view the country

---

[20] See "Mormon Settlements in Navajo Country," Le Sueur Papers, pp. 2-3.
[21] See sworn statements and claims in John W. Young Railroad File, 1881-1886, HDC.

in a more optimistic light. Nevertheless, the entire undertaking was an exercise in divided loyalty — a division that was the more difficult to cope with because it manifested itself at the top among the leaders of the church. Played upon by varying forces, they found it difficult if not impossible to maintain the lockstep uniformity of interests and methods demanded by the board of trade approach.

The Arizona Cooperative Mercantile Institution

A related development of the early 1880s was the cooperative merchandising movement. Talked of even before the railroad entered the country, the practical organization of cooperative stores coincided in large measure with the completion of the railroad. The mercantile cooperatives thus became one of the first fruits of a modest business growth that followed the railway into northern Arizona.[22]

The Arizona Cooperative Mercantile Institution, as the system was called, was composed of a wholesale outlet and a number of retail branches. With the stated purpose of advancing the self-sufficiency and strength of the colony through unifying Mormon trade, it succeeded in some degree, playing an important economic role throughout the entire period of colonization.

In considering the factors that prompted the ACMI founding, two general influences may be noted — the one primarily external in nature and the other internal. Of the first sort, the most obvious and important was the completion of the railroad. Simultaneously making effective merchandising practicable and opening the country to an invasion of Gentile business interests, the railroad's completion seemed to make prompt action imperative. The general Mormon aversion for outside businessmen having been sharpened, even before the tracks were laid, by conflict with St. Johns merchants, it was hoped that the cooperative's early initiation would tend to limit the growth and influence of this "ungodly" element.

The cooperative movement was also indicated by long-standing Mormon experience, Zion's Cooperative Mercantile Institution and other cooperative enterprises having appeared in Utah as early as the 1860s.[23] Furthermore, that part of the Little Colorado community that had turned its back upon the United Order found cooperative activities to offer a practical substitute for the more complete form of union.

Consequently, Erastus Snow and local leaders organized the ACMI during the early summer of 1881 while crews still rushed to complete

---

22 "Autobiography of Joseph Fish," November 1881, p. 181.
23 For the best treatment of this movement and an excellent bibliography, see Arrington, *Great Basin Kingdom,* pp. 293-322.

grading contracts on the railroad. Pursuant to this organization, a committee composed of Jesse N. Smith, Joseph Fish, and David K. Udall had drawn up a constitution and bylaws which were accepted on June 27 at a stake conference. A board of directors consisting of the two stake presidents and nine bishops of the colony was immediately elected. These in turn chose Jesse N. Smith president and superintendent, and Lot Smith and Joseph Fish, respectively, vice-president and secretary-treasurer. The initial steps of organization were completed by laying plans to establish a parent store at Holbrook and retail outlets in the various settlements.

Lot Smith and the two bishops from the lower river villages represented a minority element in this arrangement. Although certain residents of the United Order towns were active in the cooperative movement, control was decidedly in the hands of the larger and somewhat more affluent Eastern Arizona Stake. Numerical and economic matters doubtlessly curtailed the participation of the "Orderites," but a more important determinant was the fact that they entertained strong doubts as to the religious and social soundness of such conventional methods. Lot Smith's reaction was characteristic. "Debt," he declared, would be the "inevitable outcome of co-op stores." Furthermore, he thought that "true saints" could not "refuse to adopt the commandment to unite . . . and become self sustaining" under the banners of the United Order.[24]

A drive to raise funds to finance the ACMI was launched at the June meeting. Many loyal members rose to the occasion, making immediate subscriptions, but, as one of them wrote in his diary, much of this "was not available at this time as Brother [John W.] Young was not in a position to meet his obligations."[25] However, during the next few months some $5,000 was raised in cash which, with $2,500 worth of property and goods taken over and applied in the interest of John W. Young's creditors, served as the original assets of the ACMI.

Although Young's failure to pay his labor had worked considerable hardship, it now proved to be a real boon. Not only had his contracts provided the colony with a supply of cash, but his failure to fully meet his payrolls had the effect of setting up a forced savings which created an otherwise unlikely surplus from which the cooperative was founded. Joseph Fish, who received the remnants of Young's commissary goods, recognized the effect of the situation. He wrote that the goods:

---

[24] Wilford Woodruff, who was in attendance at the stake conference where Smith took his position, sustained his remarks but added the significant and practical reservation "that we only import what we can't manufacture." See "Minutes of the Little Colorado Stake Conferences," November 29, 1879, p. 159.

[25] "Autobiography of Joseph Fish," p. 179.

. . . were taken for Time Checks that different parties held. . . . This was giving each man his credit on capital stock for his time checks. This was not as good as the cash to be sure but in this way we collected many debts for the men that they probably would never have got if left for them to collect. This seemed about the only way for some of the men to get their pay as Brother Young was not in a position to pay his men, and by taking the goods it gave the store a start as some who turned in these time checks would not have turned in the money had they been paid in cash.[26]

From Young's defunct business the ACMI also acquired several lots at the new town of Holbrook. Complete with a railroad siding, these seemed an ideal place to build the store.

Young, who had been one of the prime movers in the earliest cooperative activities, was not permitted a voice on the ACMI board. At least two factors featured in this. In the first place, there was real reason to fear that he would seize control as he had done the railroad contract. Secondly, to have opened the organization to him would have been to accept his property in exchange for capital stock in his own name and would have deprived a number of church members this opportunity to receive something on his debts to them.[27]

Almost before the busy days of establishment had passed, the ACMI was faced by its first crisis, one of the most serious of its existence. Young, believing that a site two miles east of present-day Holbrook would be the depot, had previously purchased Thompson, as this spot was known. Renaming it after F. A. Holbrook, chief engineer for the railroad, he had promoted it during the construction period and turned part of it over to the cooperative in good faith, still thinking that the depot would be located there.[28] However, about the first of 1882, the railroad moved the stop from the long curve at Young's site, leaving the ACMI isolated without the rail connections that were considered essential to its development. The best efforts of its representatives notwithstanding, the co-op was unable to acquire a building site in the new town, and after some hesitation it was moved thirteen miles up the Little Colorado to Woodruff.[29]

---

26 *Ibid.*, p. 181.

27 Unhappy at his exclusion from the board of directors, Young at first refused to turn his property over to the new enterprise, but as it provided a means of easing his embarrassing situation he soon overcame his ire and made the transfer referred to. See Smith, *Journal of Jesse N. Smith*, p. 254.

28 Harold C. Wayte, Jr., "A History of Holbrook and the Little Colorado Country, 1541-1962" (unpublished Master's thesis, University of Arizona, 1962).

29 The ACMI's primitive condition at the original Holbrook during that first winter is apparent in the following reminiscence of Joseph Fish: "I worked here under several difficulties, there was not a house in the place except the store and we had no stove in it. The weather was getting cold and I remember . . . the ink would freeze on my pen so I had to stick it in the fire occasionally to thaw it out." See "Autobiography of Joseph Fish," p. 181.

— Albert J. Levine, Snowflake, A Pictorial Review, 1878-1964

The Snowflake Co-op, branch of the ACMI
(Arizona Cooperative Mercantile Institution).

During the next eight years, the ACMI remained at Woodruff. For a time it enjoyed a modest growth as local co-ops in Snowflake, Taylor, Eagar, Alpine, and Concho in Arizona, and Pleasanton in New Mexico, were added to one established earlier at St. Johns. Business expanded from the dry goods and groceries of the first year to include furniture, wagons, and various lines of farm machinery.

After a brief interlude of prosperity, the ACMI survived a second crisis when most leading Little Colorado Mormons found it necessary to move to Mexico in 1885 because of polygamy prosecutions. Deprived of its leaders, the community suffered a general economic collapse that was as apparent in the cooperative's business as anywhere. It is indicative of its essential vigor, however, that a "creditable" two-story brick building was erected during this time.[30]

---

[30] Fish, "History of the Eastern Arizona Stake," p. 18.

In June of 1888 most of the business community of Holbrook burned; out of this disaster grew opportunity for the ACMI to return to the railroad. Back in Holbrook, the cooperative remained a Mormon outpost in an otherwise Gentile community until its passing in the twentieth century.

Business Adaptations of the ACMI

Although its early backers envisioned a system that would extend throughout the territory, the ACMI never grew beyond the confines of the Little Colorado. Limited in its geographic area and in the public it served, the volume of its business was always small. Some idea of its size may be formed from the fact that the parent store's assessed valuation in 1884 was only $10,350. As late as 1890, after many of the local stores had been assimilated by the central outlet, its capital stock still amounted to no more than $31,000. Beginning with the impressive turnover of $65,000 in 1881 when it virtually monopolized the business of the region, its sales mounted slowly to $111,000 in 1891, which in spite of drought and growing competition was its best year to that time.[31]

The parent store, or the ACMI proper, was involved in both wholesale and retail trade. Most of the wholesaling was to the other Mormon co-ops. Retail trade, on the other hand, was always dependent upon the business of outsiders. In no small part this business was with cowboys and Mexicans.[32] An increasing portion of the establishment's business was with stockgrowers. Wool especially came to be an important item, and the fortunes of the ACMI corresponded closely with those of the wool industry. Indicative of the intimacy of this relationship was Joseph Fish's notation:

April 29, 1890 . . . Trade this spring was a little slack, the spring being late the sheepmen were later than common in shearing, so the money for wool was not coming in as soon as common. And the wool trade was one of our greatest sources of revenue as this brought in more money than anything else.[33]

Fish is not being redundant in stating that wool brought in more money and was one of the greatest sources of revenue. Much of their business was in kind, or barter; wool, however, not only produced revenue generally but was in most cases a cash business.[34] Since, with certain exceptions, Little Colorado Mormons did not acquire large sheep herds, most

---

31 "Autobiography of Joseph Fish," pp. 265, 302.
32 *Ibid.,* p. 267.
33 *Ibid.,* p. 273.
34 *Ibid.,* pp. 273, 275, 282, 287.

— *Albert J. Levine*

The ACMI headquarters and store at Holbrook.

of the wool trade was with Gentiles.[35] Strong in the late 1880s, wool lost ground relatively as cattle and freighting developed in the 1890s.

The wool business and to a lesser degree a trade in cattle were part of the conventional American economy; the co-op's trade with its Mormon patrons was less characteristic. As a rule the Mormon communities were woefully short of cash. Indicative of the adjustment to this fact was the following from the journal of one Woodruff pioneer just after the easing of a long drought that compounded the distress of the Panic of 1893:

[35] Of this subject Fish wrote in 1889: "The sheep business had been a success, this industry had taken a boom, but unfortunately not very many of our people had much invested. . . ." *Ibid.,* p. 267. However, not all Mormons missed out on this opportunity. According to James Le Sueur, "sheep sold as low as 50¢ to $1.00 a head" during the drought of the early 1890s and "many a Mormon bought sheep and cattle at sacrifice prices." See "Trouble with the Hash Knife Cattle Company," Le Sueur Papers, AHS, p. 7. Le Sueur and his father made a real killing, buying 6,000 sheep for $1.00 a head and eight years later reselling the herd which had meantime increased to 14,000 to Babbitt Bros. of Flagstaff for $6.00 each or $84,000. See James N. Le Sueur, "Autobiographical Notes of My Life," Le Sueur Papers, p. 38.

Freight wagons haul wool to the railroad.

Everybody complains of hard times — all over the country — money scarce — business failures, and a general panic prevails. Summer rains are helping the range in these parts. The stock that survived the dreadful drouth are now doing well. In these parts good health and moderate prosperity prevail — *except in money matters.*[36]

A major challenge to Mormon mercantilism on the Little Colorado was the necessity of developing methods and techniques by which it could stay in business under such conditions. While the procedures which evolved were not always original, the adjustment the ACMI made was both hardheaded and imaginative and certainly deserving of attention here.

Initially, the limited amount of money and total absence of banks in the country made it necessary for the cooperative to conduct its business without the benefits of banking. Other modes were developed. Cash payments were made, sometimes by Wells Fargo and sometimes directly by the store's agents who carried the money on their persons. In 1882, for example, Joseph Fish gingerly made his way to St. Louis carrying $7,000, which must have represented most of the co-op's money. With this sum, he had no trouble placing $12,000 worth of orders with several St. Louis firms.

Of greater importance was the credit business between church members and the cooperative. Never able to effectively turn back the impor-

---

[36] "Journal of Levi Mathers Savage," p. 46. Italics the author's.

tunings of destitute Mormons, the ACMI always had more credit on its books than it could safely carry. Its managers, in most cases prominent church leaders, took advantage of their ecclesiastical positions to caution and admonish against credit's use. At a stake conference in 1884, Jesse N. Smith inveighed against its evils in tones reminiscent of Brigham Young's injunctions in their directness and assertiveness:

We have built up a mercantile house which is successful but a system of credit has been inaugurated that will ruin us unless it is stopped. I have all the time taken a strong ground against crediting. The Kingdom cannot be built upon the credit system. We have to educate the people into a better system of business. I do not blame the brethren, but it is the duty of those on the watchtower to give notice of approaching danger.[37]

In spite of cries from the watchtower, the use of credit persisted, and the better system that evolved was, as we shall see, almost entirely in the form of defensive adaptation on the part of the ACMI.

The problem of credit was no less critical in the wholesaling business than in the retail trade. The hardier local co-ops met their obligations, sometimes even in cash; the smaller ones, which in the words of one pioneer were "weakly and meager," were less sure. Characteristic was the cooperative store at Amity (later Eagar) where A. N. Holden was bishop and general manager. Holden "bought on credit, sold his goods on credit, never got his pay, and so could not pay for them. The store failed in a short time, leaving his creditor, the ACMI, to mourn its loss."[38] The business of these small stores was frequently carried on in kind. For example, every entry in one ACMI account book to the credit of the struggling Taylor co-op between September 1892 and February 1893 was for farm produce.[39]

This barter system was one of the primary characteristics of the ACMI's business. It was conducted in the broadest possible sense with lumber, coal, farm produce, livestock, land, and services being taken in on account. But even the barter system had its limitations. Failing to produce sufficient goods to meet their own needs, the Little Colorado settlers were, of course, curtailed in what they had to enter in trade. In discussing the absence of money and the difficulties of bartering, Joseph Fish noted in 1890:

The farmers raised but little more than they needed and nothing was sent out in this line for sale, but much that we used in the way of provisions was imported . . . as there was not enough raised for home consumption. . . .[40]

---

[37] Smith, *Journal of Jesse N. Smith,* September 14, 1884, p. 292.

[38] Fish, "History of the Eastern Arizona Stake," p. 23.

[39] See "Account Book" kept by John McLaws of St. Joseph, p. 60. The original is in possession of George S. Tanner of Salt Lake City.

[40] "Autobiography of Joseph Fish," p. 273.

Thus limited in more liquid barter items, the ACMI occasionally found it necessary to take land on its debts which it then entered into the local market as circumstances permitted.

Perhaps the most important item in this non-cash business was labor — usually in the form of freighting. The ACMI probably did some freighting from the very first, but from 1888 after it moved back to Holbrook it pursued it vigorously and appears to have been one of the major contracting firms in supplying Fort Apache and other government posts.

As in the case of railroad grading, the co-op's entry into contract freighting came as a relief project. Writing to John Henry Smith of the Twelve Apostles in the spring of 1888, Jesse N. Smith reported a "great lack of bread stuffs" in certain of the Little Colorado towns. Ruefully noting that carrying supplies to Fort Apache promised some hope but that the ACMI could not bid as it had no land to offer as surety on the contract (Little Colorado Mormons had not acquired land title in 1888), he continued:

Last year the contract was let to some parties in California and by them sublet to the Jew firm of Schuster Bros. in Holbrook. . . . The Schusters have been very hard on the brethren not paying them any money and cheating them in the goods they let them have. Now that the wool business is declining the outlook is very gloomy for us unless we can secure this freighting or something of the kind.[41]

He concluded by requesting that someone bid out the contract from Salt Lake City which Brigham Young, Jr., shortly did. His bid was not low, and Adamson and Burbage of Holbrook took the contract.

Events shortly intervened. Holbrook's business community burned, and Adamson and Burbage turned over their entire interests including their freight contract to the Mormon firm. Its stockholders acquiring title to their land, the cooperative soon began to take contracts in its own right and subcontracted others.

That freighting was considered a communal enterprise by some but not all Mormons was apparent in 1890 when, in spite of precautions to avoid such a dilemma, the ACMI found it necessary to rush supplies to the hungry fort during the wettest December that the Mormons had experienced on the Little Colorado. William J. Flake, who hauled during this period, used a twenty-horse team and reported that the roads were so soft his wagon box dragged the ground in many places. Others found

    [41] See letter of March 17, 1888, Papers of Brigham Young, Jr., Activities of the ZCMI folder, HDC. For an intimate and sound account of Little Colorado freighting, see James R. Jennings, *The Freight Rolled* (San Antonio: Naylor Company, 1969).

— Albert J. Levine, Snowflake, A Pictorial Review, 1878-1964
A freight outfit is bound for Fort Apache.

that they could make only a mile or two a day and that a round trip usually made in eight to ten days now required at least twenty. There were few who appeared to haul under these conditions. The ACMI first upped its rate from the regular $1.00 per hundred pounds to $1.50, and when this failed to attract freighters, it issued a church call. Enough men responded to take Christmas supplies to Fort Apache and save the reputation of the store.

It is interesting to note that all of those who are recorded as having helped were older men who had come into the country as pioneers. Younger Mormons, some of whom were regular freighters, had, in Fish's words, "tried to pinch us all they could . . . in trying to block our progress and take advantage of our circumstances."[42] The location of the Silver Creek settlements together with the economic needs and the responsible nature of the Mormon settlers resulted in them moving most of the Fort

[42] "Autobiography of Joseph Fish," pp. 299-300. Also see "The Life and Labors of John Bushman," December 9, 1890, p. 143.

Apache freight whether the ACMI or some Gentile firm took the contract. This dominant role was noted by a correspondent of the *St. Louis Globe-Democrat* who wrote the following as he passed through the country in 1890:

All the freighting to and from Fort Apache is carried on by Mormons the superiority of their teams and their own steady habits having enabled them to fill government contracts so satisfactorily that they have completely supplanted Mexican and Gentile freighters.[43]

Whatever its effect as a relief program, freighting lent itself admirably to the broadening of the ACMI's non-money business. While life on the Little Colorado was filled with toil, time was often more available than farm produce and almost always in better supply than money. A direct traffic in services and time had consequently been a characteristic of their commerce. Indeed, it will be recalled that the very foundations of the ACMI rested upon the barter of time for stock in the institution. The practice had continued, but prior to the taking of freight contracts it had been limited by the very nature of the co-op's business. In freighting was found a means of expanding this traffic, as a substantial number of men and teams now found fairly consistent employment. Freighting provided a means by which the co-op could collect bad debts, and at the same time, as Joseph Fish put it, "accommodated those who had no money as they could get their merchandise by freighting."[44]

Interestingly, the accommodations of the ACMI also extended to an important banking role. Mormon reluctance to fraternize with outsiders, coupled with the fact that during the early years there was no bank nearer than Albuquerque or Prescott, demanded that the store provide certain services for its customers that would ordinarily have been handled by banks.

During the polygamy troubles, the store was used as a place of deposit and source of ready cash. A "defense fund" was established and deposited in its safe. Maintained by contribution and a portion of the yearly dividends from the store, the fund was drawn on by threatened polygamists for travel and legal expenses. Others claimed credit that had built up in their names or even withdrew capital stock which was itself fairly liquid until sometime after 1890 when, to forestall depletion of its stock, the co-op's bylaws were revised, making it less liquid. Joseph Fish, who was forced

---

[43] See *Millennial Star* 52 (1890): 167. According to James R. Jennings, Mormons continued to carry most of the freight well into the first decades of this century, *The Freight Rolled*, pp. 10-11.

[44] "Autobiography of Joseph Fish," p. 282.

to resign as superintendent over a controversy rising from such a situation in 1891, described the problem:

Our by-laws were lame in one particular, the share holders were allowed to draw out their capital stock by giving three months notice. It was a bad clause as a few large holders in the enterprize could swamp the institution when ever they chose to draw out.[45]

In a few critical situations, loans were also extended to hard-pressed polygamists who suddenly found it necessary to leave the country.

In 1888 when Little Colorado Mormons began to acquire legal title to their land, the ACMI was again a prime source of ready cash. Indeed, the land purchase worked considerable hardship upon the cooperative. Fish wrote:

. . . All who had any credit was drawing it out and all who possibly could, were borrowing of the store and other places. The store in this emergency advanced some money . . . and every string was being pulled that would raise a dollar.[46]

The ACMI was also used as a place of deposit for territorial monies that were appropriated to northern Arizona communities. One such instance occurred in 1891 when, after the Woodruff dam washed away for the sixth time, aid in the sum of $1,500 was provided.[47] Territorial warrants to that amount were deposited with the ACMI, and James Deans, construction foreman and engineer at the dam, was appointed administering agent.

The cooperative continued to render occasional services of this type until an informal association known locally as the "Smith Savings Bank" expanded to take over the function about 1907. This so-called savings bank had its modest beginning in 1893 when Jesse N. Smith called on the members of his family to bring their "savings in pennies, nickels, dimes, etc, and build up a savings account."[48] Other members of the community joined in, and by 1900 a substantial number of petty investors had an interest in it. The money so accumulated was lent to the ACMI. Soon people in quest of small loans were turned to the Smith Savings Bank funds rather than to the store. This ultimately led to the formal establishment of the Bank of Northern Arizona.[49]

---

[45] *Ibid.,* p. 288.

[46] *Ibid.,* March 8, 1890, p. 270.

[47] "Lorenzo Hill Hatch Journal," p. 159.

[48] Smith, *Journal of Jesse N. Smith,* p. 398.

[49] *Ibid.* Also see "Lorenzo Hill Hatch Journal," January 8, 1899, p. 223, for his record of investment in the bank.

Nature and Purpose of the ACMI

It now becomes necessary to shift our attention from the business practices of the ACMI to a more direct consideration of its nature. Enjoying a quasi-religious status, the co-op was supported by church officials and in most cases accepted by members. In its original conception, it was at complete harmony with the Mormon objectives of isolation and temporal and spiritual advance through social experimentation. Specifically, as we have seen, it was hoped that the cooperative would raise a barrier against the incursions and greed of Babylon's middlemen and that it would contribute to self-sufficiency, internal unity, and brotherly love in the colony.

Despite the similarity of certain of these objectives to those of the cooperative movement outside the Mormon community, it would appear that at no time after the very earliest years, and possibly not even then, was the ACMI's business conducted by associating capital, management, and the consumer in what would ordinarily be termed a cooperative fashion. Certainly dividends on profits were never distributed according to the amount of business done by consumers. Nor did the customer have any but the most indirect effect upon policy formulation. Yet in the early days cooperatives were discussed in terms that lead one to believe that certain leaders either planned to establish the institution after the Rochdale pattern or wanted the people to believe that they so intended. The latter possibility has a certain plausibility as there was some fear that the cooperatives would introduce class distinction and indebtedness into the colony. To discountenance such apprehensions, the popular and responsive nature of the movement may have been given special emphasis.

Whatever the facts, the first proponents of the movement appear to have been sensitive to the interests of the general membership of the colony. Asked to discuss the matter of cooperation in November of 1879, John W. Young declared that among other things a cooperative was:

. . . an institution where all were interested all having a share in it. It should be an institution where all conducted [their business] on a strictly cash and cooperative basis. The profits should first go to pay the capital invested a reasonable interest, the balance to be refunded to customers in the form of a dividend on their purchases. If possible the small stockholders should be protected against those who hold larger amounts. . . .[50]

Later, at the meeting where the ACMI was organized, Brigham Young, Jr., re-echoed the same sentiment. To all appearances, his were the feelings of the majority when he opined that the cooperative should be owned

---

[50] "Minutes of the Little Colorado Stake," November 29-30, 1879, p. 155.

"by the whole people, not by a part of them only."[51] On the other hand, a little different emphasis, one that in the long run prevailed, was given the theme by President John Taylor, who wrote Lot Smith in the spring of 1880 that cooperatives should be under the direction of the stake presidents and the people who "furnish money."[52]

The problem as it appeared here and later was the question of who the cooperative was to serve and what the nature of its service would be. Not surprisingly, ambivalences existed. Promoted as a communal agency, the ACMI often appeared in practice to be managed by and for the profit of its primary owners who enjoyed immediate and substantial social and pecuniary benefits as the result of their connection with it. On the other hand, as we have seen, it contributed to the well-being of the community at large in numerous ways.

Although the "whole people" were never involved financially, the mercantile system's original ownership and management were broadly based. As observed above, the circumstances of the ACMI's founding tended to spread the investment, many taking stock in it rather than accepting as total loss the money owed by John W. Young. Two other factors tended to broaden the circle of those who were involved. In the first place, the original board of directors was composed of the two stake presidents and nine bishops of northern Arizona's ecclesiastical organization. Some of these board members were substantial shareholders, but most were seated by merit of their church positions. Furthermore, the nature of the local stores' relationship to the parent institution tended to enlarge the number of those participating in the direction and proceeds of the system. Rather than interlocking financially with the ACMI, each of the small stores was originally owned independently by local groups. In some cases these investors were the same men who held stock in the ACMI, but as a rule their interest in the central outlet was only indirect. The practical result was a system that permitted as much local autonomy as church organization was capable of.

This system did not survive for long. Within two years most of the bishops had been dropped from the board, which thereafter took on an increasingly conventional business character. The independent stores, too, soon passed from the scene as the weaker ones collapsed and the more viable ones came under the direct control of the ACMI. By the late 1890s, none of the local co-ops, with the possible exception of the one at St. Johns, remained under independent management.

[51] Smith, *Journal of Jesse N. Smith,* June 24, 1881, p. 253.
[52] Letter of April 21, 1880, Lot Smith Papers.

Paralleling this deterioration of local ownership was, of course, the centralization of economic control. Under the pressure of sustained poverty, the original number of shareholders dwindled rapidly. To financial hard times were added the disorders and difficulties of the polygamy raids, which, as noted previously, forced many small investors to turn their assets to cash or apply them on bills. As this attrition took its toll, larger stockholders moved in, picking up bits of stock as the occasion permitted.

Although transactions of this type have come to have a sinister connotation, in this case many of them were regarded as services rather than as undue or ruthless expansiveness on the part of the big shareholders. An interesting case that deviated from the ordinary only in the amount of money involved was that of Parson G. C. Williams, one-time Baptist preacher who had become a Mormon. Quickly and enthusiastically taking plural wives, Williams had been forced to flee to Mexico in 1885. There he purchased a sizeable tract of land which made heavy and recurring demands upon his financial resources, including his substantial investment in the ACMI. In 1891 he withdrew $3,000; two years later he returned from Mexico, requesting that the remainder of his investment be turned over to him. Although the size of his holdings complicated matters, his demands were met immediately on both occasions. Of the circumstances and effects of the latter occasion, Jesse N. Smith wrote:

Parson G. C. Williams with his son-in-law, Peter Dillman came up from Mexico. He was pushed to raise a money payment for his land in Sonora, so he came to raise money on his shares in the ACMI. I took them to Holbrook with my team. Bro. Hulet went by rail to Albuquerque and borrowed $5000 from the bank, and he and I gave our note for $2000 more payable without interest in one and two years. This closed out the Parson's investment, and he went his way rejoicing.[53]

While all parties were satisfied, the Parson deal did much to concentrate both the ownership and management of the ACMI, as Smith and Hulet appear to have been not only the largest stockholders but by this time were president of the board and superintendent of the business, respectively.

Mormons of the Little Colorado were not oblivious to the power that possession lent the narrowing circle of owners. Joseph Fish, who had been an attendant at the inception of the ACMI and its superintendent for years thereafter, made no pretense that his long experience and intimate association, nor yet his position as an important church leader, gave him the right to challenge men who were heavier investors. Caught

---

[53] Smith, *Journal of Jesse N. Smith,* January 1, 1893, p. 319. For further information relative to the Parson's business, see "Autobiography of Joseph Fish," p. 288.

in a sharp controversy in 1891, he yielded to the opposing faction despite strong feelings of the rightness of his position, because being but "a small shareholder in the business" he "did not feel to oppose the plan."[54] Others had even less say. Ecclesiastical officers, branch stores, and small stockholders had by the mid-nineties all been supplanted by a small number of men whose church positions did little to obscure the fact that the ACMI's cooperative claims were increasingly shallow.

Another indication of the ACMI's nature rested in its treatment of profits. The cooperative system outlined by John W. Young in 1879 had conceived of supplier and consumer as cooperating members of a single system in which each was protected and from which each would take his commensurate share of the proceeds. In practice, however, the consumer was never given a dividend. Proceeds accrued to the customer, if at all, in the form of broadened services and reduced prices. Leaving the matter of services, which was examined earlier, we may note that commodity prices constituted an index to the co-op's practices to which pioneers were not oblivious. Early backers had promised savings up to twenty-five percent on purchases. These simply never materialized. Once in business, the cooperative stores met competition in their pricing but did not undersell even other small frontier concerns. Frustrated at the distinction between prospects and reality, church members occasionally inveighed against high prices but were as a rule remarkably complacent.[55]

On occasion, the deeper question of what represented a just distribution of proceeds was also raised. Although rebellion never ran high, local factions sometimes rose in mild protest at what seemed excessively high dividend payments. One such event occurred in Taylor in 1882 where, with the concurrence of the bishop, a privately managed store opened in competition to the cooperative. Justifying their action on the grounds that the co-op was charging excessive prices and drawing back undue amounts as dividends, the insurgents yielded only after considerable pressure was brought to bear by the stake president (also president of the ACMI board). Of the incident, the latter wrote that he personally "did not wish to be identified with anything that purported to be an institution for the good of the people but was not." Continuing in the same spirit he declared that "the people should have cheap goods," but after this short bow in the direction of service, he concluded with a defense of high prices:

"But these little stores run great risks, principally of fire. It is therefore proper that they should have larger dividends than would be the case where investments were more amply secured."[56]

---

[54] *Ibid.*

[55] "Diary of Allen Frost," January 15, 1891, vol. 6, p. 2.

[56] Smith, *Journal of Jesse N. Smith,* December 30, 1882, p. 267.

High dividends were the norm everywhere among the Little Colorado cooperatives. One of the first things one reads relative to the subject is a report in 1881 that the original store at St. Johns had declared a dividend of twenty-five percent after its first year in operation. With this handsome profit to recommend the system, investors subscribed the more readily to the later cooperatives.

In the case of the wholesale outlet and the Snowflake co-op, at least, shareholders were not disappointed in their expectations of substantial yields. This was especially true of the years before the polygamy disorders. During this time the ACMI with its near monopoly of trade paid as high as thirty-five percent and never lower than thirty percent. Even higher dividends might have been alloted but for the restraining hand of the general church authority, as Apostle Brigham Young, Jr., is reported to have told local businessmen that "40 or 50 percent per anum was extravagant in fact outrageous."[57] While business deteriorated during the polygamy scare, there is no record of the concern paying less than twenty percent until 1891 when it dropped to fifteen. By the early 1890s, competition had increased, which, coupled with the drought and the panic, resulted in additional reductions. Only six percent was paid in 1892 and seven and a half in 1893.[58]

The foregoing discussion of the division of proceeds and indeed the entire study of the ACMI has in some degree been concerned with its relationship to the church. No exhaustive examination of this matter will be attempted here, but events that occasionally brought settlers face to face with the question do merit some attention. Therefore, reference will be made to one illuminating incident that grew out of catering to Gentile customers on Sunday.

This practice became prevalent after the store returned to Holbrook in 1888. Although Sunday business was not openly solicited, it grew quite naturally from the needs of the community and the habits of store personnel. Stubbornly eschewing all non-business associations with the Gentile community, Mormons neither brought their families to Holbrook nor boarded in town, but in most cases camped, summer and winter, in the store itself. Unable to make the long trip to their villages each weekend, they whiled away the burdens of isolated Sundays in tasks about the store. Thus, while the front door was closed, the back door stood open. Quickly learning of this, townspeople, ranchers, and merchants did their trading

---

[57] See "Journals of John Henry Standifird," p. 219.
[58] "Autobiography of Joseph Fish," p. 294, and "Diary of Joseph West Smith," p. 96.

on Sundays in such numbers that despite squeamishness among some of the brethren, the front doors were soon thrown wide.

Although Stake President Jesse N. Smith was president of the board, he took no action to end the practice in this capacity. Stake authorities, however, did take steps to end the Sunday trade. After careful consultation, John Bushman, bishop of the St. Joseph Ward and a director, was dispatched to accomplish this purpose. Appearing one June Sabbath in 1893, he demanded the keys and, over the loud protest of Superintendent John R. Hulet, cleared the place of a few customers and locked the door. Thereafter, an uneasy compromise was worked out, and for years the store opened for a half-day on Sunday.[59] Such direct ecclesiastical interference was rare. For the most part the ACMI found little conflict between its pretenses of official connection with the church and its business needs.

While the ACMI was bound to the church in its personnel and in the popular conception of the community, it was also very much a business and accepted many of the values and motives of business. As the years passed, the emphasis initially given to its public nature was perpetuated, and sufficient real service was rendered to lend credence to the theory. On the other hand, economic exigency and the acquisitive drive of the main stockholders resulted in an increasing departure from the premise on which it had been founded. This change in its nature may have been recognized privately but was not accompanied by any major shift in the public utterances where the original communal stress continued. The ACMI's peculiar confusion of religious commitments on the one hand and its affinity for business practices on the other would thus seem to point to the need of a more careful definition of the relative role of church values and financial considerations in the Mormon cooperative movement than has been developed to this point.

---

[59] For the best account of this event, see "Autobiography of Joseph Fish," p. 300. The question did not end with the compromise, and several years later we find the stake high council in a less belligerent mood, appointing a committee to wait upon "Brother Hulet" to request that he close the store on Sunday. See "Lorenzo Hill Hatch Journal," March 1, 1896, p. 208.

7. OASIS AGRICULTURE

> . . . We need have no fears about the gentiles getting all the best places for location in Arizona. . . . It is a remarkable fact that the first settlers of a new country very often fail to select the most desirable places. . . . If brethren will be content to follow the guidance of the holy spirit they will have the best places.
>
> BRIGHAM YOUNG
>
> . . . When once subdued it is good land. . . .
>
> JOHN W. TATE

LAND LAY AT THE CRUX of life for Little Colorado Mormons. They claimed it, lived on it, made it the basis of their economy, and ultimately came to own a few thousand acres of it. In this continuing preoccupation with the land appear three distinct and dominating themes. The first of these has to do with certain deeply held ideas, the second with the cooperative effort that characterized land practices, and the third with competing claims and land controversy.

Attitudes

Little attention has been given to Mormon assumptions about the land. Largely ignored by theology and history alike, an underlying commitment to what may be termed a modified Jeffersonian agrarianism profoundly influenced the church during its nineteenth-century experience in the West, including its colonization of Arizona.[1] Never consistently

---

[1] Lowry Nelson in his *The Mormon Village: A Pattern and Technique of Land Settlement* (Salt Lake City: University of Utah Press, 1952), pp. 25, 53, gives a brief consideration to the subject of Jeffersonian influences upon the Mormon land system.

worked into Mormon doctrines, this belief bound the church to the land. Without concerning ourselves with its consequences, we may here draw attention to a few aspects of the matter which established the prominent and symbolic position that land held in the minds of Mormons of the generation during which the Little Colorado was settled. The stirrings of this position continue to prompt an otherwise urban church to embrace a welfare program based upon agricultural production.

It should be noted not only that the church grew out of the agricultural mold of the American West and partook of its values but also that it was patterned after Biblical and Book of Mormon peoples among whom pastoral and agricultural systems existed that were easily identified with the conditions of the frontier. More practical reasons for the appeal of agrarian ideas existed as well. Perhaps most important among these was the fact that the land and an ideology based upon it bolstered the prominent Mormon policies of the gathering and isolation.

The gathering to Zion, with its emphasis upon withdrawal from a corrupt world, was in practice antiurban and agrarian. Although both the idea and the fact of a central Mormon city were of utmost importance, the gathering ran counter to the urban movement that characterized the great industrial development of the late nineteenth century. Finding a far-flung refuge in the seclusion of Zion's scattered valleys, Mormon converts left the population centers rather than rushing to them. Not surprisingly the general protest of rural America at its loss of status to the city found a ready place in Mormon propaganda. Vividly portraying the vice and sordidness of city life, missionaries called believers out of Babylon before they were caught up in the destruction that was to be visited upon the ungodly. Appearing in the *Millennial Star,* the church's organ in England, the following indictment was not extraordinary:

Look into the cities of our Christian land, which are flooded with vice. See the thousands of poor despised prostitutes that nightly travel the streets of those cities. Look at the diabolical exhibitions in the domiciles and market-places . . . fighting, swearing, cheating, plundering, drunkenness, indecencies, with a multiplicity of other follies and wickedness. See the multiplied lists of robberies, seductions, infanticides, suicides, and murder continually occurring. Of such soulsickening abominations the newspapers furnish the world with a catalogue weekly. This is Babylon.[2]

Continuing, the same writer extolled rural virtues as he pled with the "ransomed of the Lord" to "turn to the land of" their fathers. Once in the "lofty, pleasant hills" of Zion, they would join in singing to the "good-

---

[2] "Literal Gatherings of the House of Israel," *Millennial Star* 23 (1861): 484.

ness of the Lord, for wheat, and for wine, and for oil, and for the young of the flock and of the herd."[3]

Mormon separatism, the end product of the gathering, was also served by agrarianism. The reluctance of the church to embrace mining or other industrial and commercial enterprises is well known. The renunciation of these pursuits in favor of subsistence agriculture was in large measure a reflection of the church's effort to perpetuate not only its geographic isolation but to hold the world at arm's length economically and socially as well. Agriculture, with the looseness of its social structure and its independent farmers, raised up few countering loyalties.

The thought that a life close to the earth was evocative of the highest human virtues was also important in Latter-day Saint thinking. Joining the idea with a firm conviction that hard work and frugality contributed to spiritual growth, Mormons were confident that the unproductive lands of their desert kingdom could scarcely have been better calculated to foster virtue among the Saints. One writer expressed this widely held sentiment in 1877 when he wrote:

The very nature of the country [Utah] demands that man should exercise his mental and physical strength. . . . True our fields, farms and orchards give forth in rich abundance. . . . But the ground has to be petted coaxed and labored upon to give this pleasing result. . . . The gathering place of the Saints is a school in which the Lord is educating a people whom he intends to redeem and use for building up his kingdom.[4]

In a similar vein, Apostle Erastus Snow thought that harsh frontier conditions were the special prerequisites of a powerful and hardy race. Addressing an audience on the Little Colorado as mounting difficulty beset the colony in 1884, he gave meaning to their efforts and reminded them of their preparation to meet the challenges of their mission when he said:

Our people are an agricultural people and wish to . . . improve and cultivate the land. I believe that the Lord has selected this new land for His Saints to gather to, as in thickly populated places wickedness is more prevalent. Here you are not constantly thrown in contact with crime and sin. . . . A race that grows up under such circumstances . . . are more powerful and vigorous than other people. Here they will learn the art of self preservation and defense. . . .[5]

As they observed the social unrest of the era, other Mormon leaders wrote and sermonized of the independence and security inherent in the land and decried the growing trend away from it. Prominent among these was counselor to the president, Daniel H. Wells, who attributed the labor

---

[3] *Ibid.,* p. 485.
[4] *Ibid.,* 40 (1878): 611-13.
[5] Smith, *Journal of Jesse N. Smith,* p. 293.

discord of 1878 to a growing failure to utilize land in the manner God had intended. With "thousands of broad acres lying uncultivated," he saw no reason for strife. Indeed Wells was optimistic that if everything were regulated "as it would be under the government of God, there would be no hard times, no complaints, no strikes, no warfare." Elaborating that the evils of class conflict were the product of dependence and day work and would cease to exist if men lived close to the soil, Wells told his audience that by taking out a "piece of land," any man could acquire

... the nucleus of his prosperity, wealth, and comparative independence. . . . This position in life is much more self-reliant and independent than employment by the day, week or the month in cities or overcrowded business centres. There, when a day's labor stops the supply stops; but when you have your source of supply, and your labor temporarily fails, you still have plenty of grain, and other produce of the farm by which you can get along.[6]

Making little distinction between the temporal of the present and the spiritual of the hereafter, Mormons sometimes carried agrarian values into their speculations about the life to come. Dwelling on such a theme, the church's leading theologian, Apostle Orson Pratt reasoned:

If one per cent of all this imensity of population shall, through obedience to the Gospel, become lawful heirs to the earth, then there will be over one hundred and fifty acres for every soul. If the new earth contains only the same proportion of land as the old, there would be about forty acres for every redeemed soul. But the new earth is represented by the Apostle John, as being without seas, which increases its capacity for inhabitants above the old fourfold. The farmer who is looking forward to the new earth for his everlasting inheritance, need have no fears of being too much limited in his possessions. There will be ample room for the delightful pursuits of the agriculturist. He can have his pleasure grounds; his orchards of the most delicious fruits; his gardens decorated with the lovliest flowers, and still have land enough for the raising of the more staple articles such as manna to eat, and flax for the making of fine robes, etc.[7]

Containing no happy future for the sea industries, Pratt's millennial formula fit neatly into his own social matrix.

Quite obviously capable of visionary flights, Mormons were more often earthbound in their theorizing. Of primary import in this context is the fact that they deemed agricultural pursuits to be essentially constructive. Sharply aware of the exploitative methods of Gentile mining and commercial interests, though less so of their own increasingly destructive grazing practices, they regarded the former activities as being retrogressive

---

[6] *Journal of Discourses,* vol. 19, p. 369.

[7] *Ibid.,* vol. 1, p. 333.

in nature. Indicative of this frame of mind was Daniel Wells' comment that it was not the industry of outsiders that built up the country but that the material advance of Utah was to be attributed only to:

. . . the labors of the Saints, guided and directed by the almighty. It is they who are to be found in the nooks and corners — in all directions — wherever there is a spring or a bit of land — building up, making the earth bring forth its products, and strengthening and enlarging the borders of Zion.[8]

Wells was confident that when the territory then available to the Latter-day Saints had been fully improved, the inevitable progress of God's kingdom would permit the extension of this work of reclamation to other areas.

Mormons, including those who shoveled sand into the Little Colorado, found a divine meaning in their desert diggings. The reclamation of barren wastes along with the enlargement of Zion were conceived to be complementary elements in the building of God's kingdom. As such, efforts expended in making the desert habitable could expect God's special blessings. Men could anticipate both inspiration to guide their labors and supernatural transformation of the elements. Writing in the *Millennial Star* in 1884, J. H. Ward called attention to the change from dreary and monotonous wastes "to fruitful fields, smiling gardens and happy homes" wrought in the thirty-seven years the Saints had been in the Great Basin. Focusing upon the divine element in this joint accomplishment, he wrote:

The blessings of God have rested upon the efforts of the pioneers in reclaiming the desert. Many streams have been greatly increased in volume, and in some places new springs have burst forth in the desert. In some places where, twenty years ago, there was scarcely water sufficient for the needs of a few families, now there are large streams capable of irrigating thousands of acres. The rainfall has greatly increased in some localities. A few years ago it was considered impossible to raise crops without irrigation; now quite a proportion of the land under cultivation is tilled without artificial irrigation.[9]

Settlers on the Little Colorado looked hopefully for climatic change. Looking, some found it. Declaring that "the rigor of the seasons" had been toned down, Jesse N. Smith wondered "why others could not see . . . anything extraordinary in what to him was so manifestly 'remarkable'."[10] The region's terrible winds were said to be abating and moisture increasing.

---

[8] *Ibid.,* vol. 19, p. 370.

[9] "Utah, Past and Present," *Millennial Star* 46 (1884): 520-22.

[10] Smith, *Journal of Jesse N. Smith,* p. 354. Alteration of the elements in Utah was a frequent topic in Little Colorado meetings. Typical was the report of one pioneer of Toquerville in the Virgin Basin that when George A. Smith promised more water, it came, and where there were only four or five families there sprang up a settlement of seventy families. *Ibid.,* p. 349.

To some, change seemed swift and sure, apparent in every extraordinary meteorologic display. Others, particularly those on the lower river whose lot cast them in a desperate struggle for water, had more difficulty in seeing beneficient changes in nature. Some of these, however, including tough old Lot Smith, did not doubt that God's hand tempered the elements nor that it had transformed Utah's climate. Rather they searched self-consciously for failures of their own that had occasioned what in their eyes was a deviation from the norm.

Although they usually took the fertility of the land for granted, Little Colorado colonists were nevertheless confident that in due time it too would produce more abundantly for the sake of the righteous. It was not anticipated, however, that this regeneration would ensue without honest effort. Reflecting this point of view, the following remarks by Jesse N. Smith were delivered as drought and low yields in 1886 compounded troubles arising from the Arizona polygamy raids:

This is a forbidding land; the indignation of the Lord rests upon lands where He has been forgotten. It becomes our duty to sanctify the places where we dwell. We cannot expect these changes to be made in a moment but if we do our duty there will be a gradual change for the better. Have seen the land in Utah redeemed from its sterility by the labor of godly men and women and we have reason to expect like results here.[11]

Along with such attitudes, the Mormons also entertained certain economic convictions about the land. Perhaps most frequently voiced was the recognition that viable land and manageable water were limited in Utah. New frontiers had to be opened. The logic of the situation was set forth simply and without anxiety by Apostle Joseph F. Smith at a stake conference on the Little Colorado in 1884. Assuring the colonists that their isolation from the larger Mormon community was rapidly passing as the church spread, he continued: "It is better for a man beginning in life to commence in a new place. It is difficult already for a young man to make a new stand in Salt Lake Valley. As we increase we want more land."[12]

This need for land had been among the primary forces that had revived the southward thrust of Mormon colonization after the end of the Navajo wars in 1870, and colonists rarely forgot their role as the architects of new opportunity. After years in Arizona, one early immigrant wrote: "There had to be secure and permanent expansion. They couldn't all live in Utah and those pioneers considered it their mission in life to

---

[11] *Ibid.*, p. 330.
[12] *Ibid.*, p. 295.

develop new country and lay a foundation upon which their children could build."[13]

Perhaps the most ardent of the desires entertained by Little Colorado pioneers was the hope that land would continue to provide the basis of a separatist existence for their children. In its failure to measure up to their aspirations lies an important key to the ultimate collapse of insular Mormondom. Devoted to education they labored to establish schools and sent their young people to study in Utah, but they do not appear to have seen this as a practical matter of preparation for a profession removed from the land. Still guided by dreams of a temporal kingdom whose finite bounds and flourishing oases were raised as an offering by their own labors of reclamation, they had not yet succumbed to the material promise of a better life through practical education but conceived of learning as a matter of character molding that broadened and strengthened the individual whose future, like that of the kingdom, still lay in the land. In the early years, vicissitudes of pioneering were more bearable because moral and economic opportunity for the succeeding generations lay in the new lands that were opened. Later, as the period of pioneering closed and lands free for the taking became harder to find, aging Little Colorado pioneers stressed education but struggled to hold both their children and an essential of their life by arranging for land on which to settle the young.

Inevitably their efforts failed. Land was limited, the elements obdurate, and social conditions frustrated attempts to find new areas of development. Schooled without practical preparation in mind, the young found the landed homes of their elders' conception foreclosing. Their increasing numbers forced them into the broader society of the surrounding community, to which, because of the stress on education, they were not unfitted. Herein, more than in the sundering of the Mormon kingdom before the mounting pressure of the United States, lay an end to Mormon isolation.

However, through the period of this study, the growing kingdom and agrarian isolation joined to make the retention of the Little Colorado lands imperative.

Cooperation, Small Holding, and Villages

In the development of the new country as in the founding of Utah, the village and small-holding patterns were followed. Well suited to the dictates of oasis agriculture, these practices resulted in subsistence as contrasted to speculative agriculture which complimented the Mormon policies of separatism and isolation.

---

[13] Evans Coleman, "Historical Sketch of Dr. W. E. Platt," Coleman Papers, AHS.

Thoroughly conversant with Mormon agricultural modes, Little Colorado pioneers sprinkled their early correspondence with estimates of the population the country would carry that appear at first glimpse to have been fantastically optimistic. Along with a certain amount of promotional license, these estimates were based on two considerations, in light of which their optimism is less marked. One, referred to before, was a determined faith that the elements would moderate, increasing the country's capacity. The other, more practical, was a realistic calculation of the subsistence potential of irrigated land under their small-holding system.

Placing little emphasis upon profit, they expected quite different things from land than did the characteristic settler. The building of the kingdom and more immediately the establishment of a community were the primary objectives. The hunger for Zion that led to the gathering stirred deep yearnings for "the company of the Saints," and the sweetest dream of most immigrants was of an expansion of the kingdom that would, in effect, bring the bosom of the church to them. The distinction between Mormon values in this respect and general frontier attitudes was patent in an exchange said to have taken place between William J. Flake and James Stinson when the latter's consternation erupted as a string of improvident Mormons straggled onto the property he had just sold Flake:

"Now Mr. Flake, there is just enough water here for this small farm. If you will keep the place for your family alone, you will have a fine place, but if you let anyone else in, you will all starve." Flake said, "You could not give me the place, if I had to live here that way. I am going to have a town and farm all of the land."[14]

In this frame of mind, Little Colorado colonists submitted to sharp restriction in the acreages they held. Whether they squatted on the railroad grant, homesteaded, or bought out prior claims, it was expected they would be joined by others. Claims were usually established by trusted men who were warned to eschew all private speculation. Occasionally they broke ranks, but to a surprising degree they preferred the interest of the church and the company of an enlarged Mormon community to profits that might accrue from large personal holdings.[15]

---

[14] Flake, *William J. Flake*, p. 74.

[15] The Arizona colony apparently submitted tamely to this situation, and very few cases of internal strife rising from land disputes are found in the history of the mission. Elsewhere, on the southern frontier there was pressure to break step and take larger unauthorized claims. Such was the case in Kanab where Stake President L. John Nuttall, after outlining a new development in Kanab Canyon, deemed it necessary to caution: "Those who shall take an opposite course than this, must be looked upon as apostates, disreputable, dishonest people, living outside for the purpose of living on the property of others, and cannot be held in fellowship with the Saints." See letter of February 22, 1880, L. John Nuttall Letter Press Book no. 1, BYU, pp. 146-48.

Most settlers held only 20 or 30 acres of ground. The Order villages rarely farmed more than 350 acres and in some cases less. Prorated this may have amounted to 20 acres per family. Elsewhere, holdings varied up to forty acres. In Snowflake, for example, each family was limited to a town lot and 20 acres in two 10-acre plots of varying value. Later, the tight land situation may have loosened somewhat as improvements and the government surveys opened more ground, but the advantage so gained was largely offset by growing families and continued immigration.

The original cost of the land varied from nothing at the United Order settlements to substantial prices in other key places. The earliest settlers either squatted or purchased claims from established ranchers. In the case of the latter, small out-of-the-way claims with few improvements and little water were to be had at moderate costs — perhaps a cow or two or a span of mules and an old harness with total value not exceeding $100. Under such circumstances, land with the rudimentary improvements of the day likely cost no more than $1.50 an acre. Larger strategically located spots were at a premium, and prices ranged up to what seemed like staggering sums of $11,000 and $15,000 for the Snowflake and St. Johns claims. Under the original terms, the average price per acre for farming land at these two places came to $8.50 and $8.00, respectively, but amounted to much more before clear titles were obtained.

A seller's market prevailed. The Mormons endeavored to minimize the disadvantages of this situation by buying most of their land through agents, of whom the most important was William J. Flake. Born in Mississippi on July 3, 1839, Flake was stubbornly self-confident and undoubtedly one of the most determined men who came to Arizona. Avoiding important church offices, he came, after the successful Stinson purchase in 1878, to regard it his special province to arrange land purchases.

Interestingly, Flake felt that he had been called to this capacity in a dream in which he had been visited by Brigham Young, deceased at the time for over a year.[16] This dream had taken place during the period of social ostracism rising out of Flake's breach with the United Order to buy the Stinson land. Comforted and sustained by Erastus Snow, he thereafter made it his business to trade for likely claims as they were available, making most of the important land trades between the time of his original deal and 1903 when he bought the last of the large ranches on Silver Creek.

Flake was particularly active in the years before 1881 when, with the exception of the St. Johns purchase, he traded for all the Silver Creek

---

[16] Flake, *William J. Flake,* pp. 77-78.

and upper Little Colorado sites that became towns. These included part or all of the land on which Snowflake, Taylor, Shumway, Concho, Nutrioso, Eagar, and Show Low were established. He apparently made each of these deals in the interest of the community, dividing the holdings at Snowflake with fifty-four other settlers and turning over the other places outright to new colonists. According to contemporary reports, his $11,000 outlay on the Stinson purchase was prorated in $200 assessments as the land itself was parceled out. Most of his other purchases are also said to have been resold at cost. As circumstances often resulted in his being paid in "chips and whetstones," his services to the community were tendered at something of a personal loss.

Flake's reputation as a colonist, rather too fervently promoted by some of his descendants, was acknowledged throughout the Mormon community on the Little Colorado. Writing late in his life, one admiring reporter concluded with characteristic deference, "When he does go, do not place any patent epitaph over his grave but say: 'He bought ranches; he made towns'."[17]

Regular church officers also served in this capacity. In addition to buying land, they acted as clearing agents controlling distribution and directing would-be purchasers to acceptable lands. One correspondent clearly indicated the role played for St. Johns by Bishop D. K. Udall when he wrote the *Deseret News* in 1881:

Plenty of land for all who are called, but none should come expecting to get land without paying for it, as the land has been purchased and is held in trust by the bishop for those who come to purchase at the rates stated in my last letter (The five acre lots near town rate at $11 per acre. The farming land from $6 to $9 per acre according to location.) There are also four or five good stock ranches for sale at reasonable rates within 25 miles of this place. They can be had on application to Bishop D. K. Udall.[18]

The towns that replaced the ranches were another essential element in the development of the colony. Among the first missionaries sent to the country was a steadfast but introverted English bachelor, Samuel G. Ladd, who as a surveyor laid out most of the area's townsites. Situated within easy access of water, these were subdivided into characteristic "City of Zion" grids with wide streets and ample building lots. Fields lay adjacent, open or under common fences.

Some caution, however, should be exerted not to exaggerate the anchoring capacities of land and other real properties under the small holding and village system. Although land comprised an important element

---

[17] George H. Crosby, Jr., in the *Snowflake Herald* as quoted by Flake, p. 120.
[18] *Deseret News,* June 29, 1881.

in the Mormon value system and was the basis of a colony's existence, its hold upon individuals was generally not great. In fact by comparison to the values in modern high-cost property situations, most Little Colorado settlers displayed a remarkable casualness toward specific parcels of land. As newcomers to the region their sentimental attachments were not yet deeply seated, and allegiance could be, and was, shifted with surprising frequency. Vast areas of open lands, tentative claims, poor quality, polygamy problems, and poverty each tended to offset the normal stabilizing effect of land properties. Unfettered by large investment or success, it was easy to look beyond the next hill, and the record is replete with accounts of families — including those most loyal to the church — pulling up stakes again and again, with scarcely a glance behind, and moving to new premises.

Hanging On

But problems of internal movement never assumed unmanageable proportions. External challenges sometimes did. This was particularly so after 1880 when other claimants — in the main large companies — pressed their own interests with increasing vigor. Less sensational and less bitter than the controversy rising out of polygamy, the collision over land nevertheless held in it the seeds of defeat. Had this problem not been successfully resolved, it seems certain it would have resulted in the dissolution of the colony.

In some measure, the history of this conflict was that of the general western land controversy. Armed with early grants, good lawyers, and other advantages of their corporate size, including when necessary a certain amount of coercion, big companies were pitted against the ubiquitous squatter in whose interest a latent sympathy was beginning to assert itself in government circles and elsewhere. But unlike other squatters, Little Colorado Mormons found order and strength in the church. Adamant in its determination to maintain its interests, the church, because of its size and resources, was able to offset somewhat the advantages held by the companies. Its means, including the mission call, legal and financial aid, and a consistent and centrally located policy, were employed in behalf of Mormon claims.

A word about the nature of these claims should be interjected here. Early locations were based on squatter's rights. Prior to 1879 none of the land had been surveyed or opened to homesteading. Consequently, most Mormon claims, both those they took up themselves and those they purchased, were tentative. Furthermore, since legal routine lagged behind the advance of the frontier, a good deal of informality characterized the earliest practice. In this situation, possession was nine points of the law.

Settlements, with their village and field pattern, left little question as to possession and withstood invasion from all but the most formidable opponents. When permanent occupation proved impossible, indications of intent were of primary importance. To seasonally occupied ranches and herdgrounds, rights were asserted by controlling the water and building cabins and sheep troughs or other signs of occupancy. Most of the ordinary subterfuges of land entry were employed. Of early practice in the locality of Alpine, one pioneer wrote:

It was customary at that time if a man wanted to settle in what he considered a desirable spot for him to express the same by cutting four logs as if he were going to build a house, lay those logs as if they were the foundation for a house, cut a hole at one end of the enclosure for a door, and his claim stood. Everybody considered that any man who would jump that claim was not a good citizen. . . . Others in '79 went up in what was called Williams Valley and put up a notice reading: "We claim this valley for dairy purposes." That constituted a bona fide claim.[19]

Such practices were likely inevitable under conditions of the era. When it was necessary to buy established ranches, a primary consideration was the nature of the claim held by the previous owner. In most cases these claims were of recent origin. Too often they were vague and unreliable. About the best that could be hoped for was that the previous claimant would leave the country, enabling the new owner to make the most of his purchase.

Resting thus on tenuous claims, Mormon land rights were subject to contest from the first. Indeed the conflict began before the Mormons arrived when five Gentiles located on one of the spots staked out by explorer James S. Brown to receive the first colonists. Thereafter there was hardly a time when some part of the colony was not involved in land controversy. Not unusual was the promising claim purchased by John W. Young in 1878 at Leroux Springs on the southwest face of the San Francisco Mountains. Visiting the place the following year, Young found his cabin occupied by two men who stoutly maintained they had bought the entire spread from a Dr. Vail. Ignoring the possibility that they may have been telling the truth, Young took direct action by unceremoniously dumping them and their belongings outside the property line.[20]

Later, interest in the lands adjacent to the San Francisco Peaks was sharpened by the coming of the railroad. Competition became so keen during the spring of 1881 that a number of men were killed, and others,

---

19 Evans Coleman, "Land Transactions in the Eighties," Coleman Papers, AHS, p. 1.

20 "Wilford Woodruff's Journal," HDC, entry for April 22, 1879.

including several Mormon squatters, were threatened. In May, Jesse N. Smith wrote Young that some of his springs and his ranch (probably the one at Leroux Springs) had been jumped. Concluding that there existed "a reign of terror throughout the mountains," he advised Young to reinforce the men holding his claims, as the lives of those then on duty were "in great danger."[21] Young hung on — at least for the time being, and according to Earle Forrest, historian of Arizona range wars, later based Arizona's first big cattle company on the Leroux Springs ranch.[22]

The most long-lived and bitter disputes occurred at St. Johns. In part this was the result of the fact that the Solomon Barth claims, upon which Mormon rights rested, were open to grave question. With most non-Mormon squatters convinced that Barth had transferred something he did not own, the matter festered, a trouble spot from the time of the Mormon purchase in 1879. Finally confronted by an armed effort to expel them from St. Johns during the summer of 1884, the Mormons with Bishop D. K. Udall at their head seemed ready to meet violence with violence. Cooler heads prevailed, and after a period of bristling, they resorted to more characteristic expedients. Prayer circles convened, and a quick call for an additional hundred settlers was circulated throughout Utah.[23]

This menace and others emanating from squatters and small ranchers were effectively dealt with. Indeed, by persistent encroachment the Latter-day Saints took over most of the squatters' claims that were suited to their needs until by the century's end only St. Johns and Round Valley had Gentile farming communities. In each of these a *modus vivendi* had been worked out whereby Mormons and Gentiles shared the land. Other claims, better founded legally and pressed by large organizations, proved to be more resistant to the Mormon advance.

Most important in the latter context were the claims rising out of the Atlantic and Pacific railroad grant. Claiming the odd-numbered sections of a hundred-mile checkerboard, the railroad lands struck straight through the heart of the Mormon settlements. Inevitably conflict arose.[24]

In the act of 1866 which authorized the 35th parallel railroad, Congress offered as an incentive twenty alternate odd-numbered sections per mile on either side of the track in the states and forty in the terri-

---

21 Letter of May 2, 1881, John W. Young Railroad File 1881-1886, HDC.

22 Earle R. Forrest, *Arizona's Dark and Bloody Ground* (Caldwell, Idaho: Caxton Printers Ltd., 1952), p. 326.

23 "Autobiography of Joseph Fish," p. 204.

24 For maps showing the land grant areas, see Greever, *Arid Domain,* pp. 30-31.

tories.[25] However, prior grants, reservations, and squatter claims within the railroad's place limits were not extinguished. To compensate the company for these losses, Congress also designated ten-mile indemnity areas on either side of the grant from which lieu lands could be chosen. To encourage speedy completion of work, Congress stipulated:

That each and every grant, right and privilege herein are . . . subject to the following conditions, namely: That the said company shall commence the work on said road within two years from the approval of this act by the President, and shall complete not less than fifty miles per year after the second year, and shall construct, equip, furnish and complete the main line of the whole road by the fourth day of July, anno Domini 1878.[26]

While it fell years behind schedule, the Atlantic and Pacific lost little grant land. In large measure this was due to the fact that, following a practice dating back to the first railroad land grant in 1823, Congress had omitted provisions for making final adjustments of the grant.[27] Since none of the many land grants made during the interim had been officially terminated, the Atlantic and Pacific had little trouble resisting efforts to foreclose its grant and took title to most of it when the track was ultimately completed. As the completion date came and went with the road unfinished, the company argued that an 1871 act of Congress approving a plan to mortgage the railroad was tantamount to an extension of time for completing construction. Although this strained view was denied by the Supreme Court in the 1887 case of the *A & P* v. *Mingus,* most of the grant survived all challenges.[28]

The question of when the grant became valid was an important point because the rights of the railroad and contesting claims both turned upon it. The original act specified that the grant did not attach until a plat showing "the line of said road" was filed in the Office of the Commissioner of the General Land Office.[29] In practice, prior to the year 1883, the time of the field survey had been regarded as the date of definite location, after which the company's rights obtained. However, in the case of *Van Wyck* v. *Knevals* of that year, the Supreme Court held that the date of definite location was when a map approved by the Secretary of the Interior was

---

[25] U. S., *Congressional Globe,* 39th Cong., 1st sess., pp. 1100-1102, 4182. Also see U. S., *Statutes at Large,* vol. 14, p. 292.

[26] *Ibid.*

[27] U. S., *House Executive Document no. 246,* 50th Cong. 1st sess., p. 4.

[28] *Atlantic and Pacific* v. *Mingus,* 165 U. S. 413 (1887).

[29] U. S., *Statutes at Large,* vol. 14, p. 292.

actually filed with him.[30] Rights of settlers and other claimants were not cut off until that time. Thus, a map received by the Secretary of Interior on March 12, 1872, was considered to mark the attachment of grant lands, including those on the Little Colorado, to the Atlantic and Pacific Company. This date preceded all Mormon claims except those at St. Johns and Round Valley, where rights established prior to 1872 were purchased.

To manage the complexities of its vast landed empire, the railroad hired former U. S. Land Commissioner James A. Williamson in 1881 shortly after he left his federal post. Thereafter all land questions moved through him. As land agent he followed a policy consistently hostile to farmers and other small holders.[31] Little Colorado settlers, from their first correspondence with him, were given little sympathy. From his point of view, they were entitled to none. Theirs had not been a blind entry into the country. Aware of the Atlantic and Pacific grant, Brigham Young had directed colonists to the Little Colorado River knowing that their claims would be subject to challenge. Bespeaking confidence that some sort of adjustment permitting them to remain in the country could be worked out regardless of where legal rights lay, Young's action and the subsequent course of Mormon colonization was notably lacking in any sense of the railroad's point of view.

Initially colonists had seemed to be almost oblivious to the railroad as they rushed to take physical possession of the land. However, as problems incident to moving in were solved, they became increasingly aware of the role the railroad played in their lives. After 1881 frequent inquiries were addressed to Williamson. Almost all were answered negatively. At St. Joseph, for example, repeated applications, in the words of one interested party, had "the squelcher effectually put upon" them. Replying to one of these inquiries, Williamson's assistant Thomas S. Sedgewick loftily informed St. Joseph colonists, who quailed before the financial prospect of buying even one section, "that the company will for the present consider only the sale of tracts of 100,000 acres."[32]

At Snowflake Jesse N. Smith was able to extract a grudging promise from Williamson that citizens there would have first chance to buy the land on which they lived. Hoping that this represented a shift in the company's attitude, Smith and his associates sought other means of bolstering their claims. Among the expedients employed were efforts to enter the Mormon claims at various local land offices under homestead,

---

[30] *Van Wyck* v. *Knevals,* 106 U. S. 369 (1883).

[31] Greever, *Arid Domain,* p. 49.

[32] See letter to John W. Young from John McLaws et al., under date of May 31, 1884, and letter of T. S. Sedgewick to J. H. Richards, August 16, John W. Young Personal File 1880-87, HDC.

— *Photo by F. A. Ames, Courtesy National Archives*
Cowboys, employed by the Aztec Land and Cattle Company, in the late 1880s.

pre-emption or townsite provisions. However, these hopes were futile; no land agent proved unwary enough to file claims for them.

The history of Little Colorado land relations entered a new phase in 1884. During that year, the giant and freebooting Aztec Land and Cattle Company bought over 100,000 acres of the Atlantic and Pacific land grant.[33] The purchase gave control to most of the railroad's holdings south of the track along the ninety miles between Silver Creek on the east and Flagstaff on the west. Paying fifty cents an acre, the Hashknife, as the Aztec Company was locally known, trailed in 17,000 head of Texas cattle and shipped in an additional 23,000. Soon vast herds were ranging throughout the entire region with no concern for section numbers or place

---

[33] Of the Aztec Company, William S. Greever writes: "The capital stock of the Aztec, originally set at $963,100, was owned as follows: Atchison, $215,500; certain members of the Atchison Board of Directors, $200.00; J. & W. Seligman and Company, $241,000; [the latter was a law firm which handled much legal business for both the Atlantic and Pacific and the Aztec Company] some people in connection with the Seligman firm, $4,000; and others (in large part Texas ranchers), $502,400." *Arid Domain*, p. 46.

limits. Following the herds came Texas cowboys, behind whom the Aztec Company soon took over virtual control of northern Arizona grazing.

As it related to the Mormons, the Aztec reign may be divided into two parts. The first phase was one of intimidation and strong-arm tactics. The second was less belligerent though still inimical, as the company first threatened legal action to force Mormon evacuation and then demanded that they purchase any odd sections used by them at inflated prices.

Coinciding with the polygamy scare of 1884 and 1885, the advent of the Hashknife found the Mormons particularly vulnerable. Launching an immediate campaign to force them out of the country together with all smaller outfits and sheep men, the company loosed a set of hoodlums upon the settlers. Running wild, badmen rustled thousands of animals, including so many of the company's that it was ultimately forced to make land and not cattle its primary business.[34] In the face of this general assault, which soon became connected with the Pleasant Valley War between contending groups of cowboys and sheepmen, outlying Mormons were forced to abandon their claims and fall back into stronger communities.

Early in 1887 settlers of two mountain towns, Wilford and Heber, which had been located five years before on railroad lieu lands, were given ten days to evacuate. Numbers depleted by polygamy problems, they complied. Heber was subsequently reclaimed; Wilford's abandonment was permanent.[35] Elsewhere during the hectic spring and winter of 1887, claim jumpers ran ranchers off, beating and abusing them. James Pearce, who had recently selected land with intention to preempt, was forced at gun point from his claim which lay over fifty miles from the railroad beyond both the place limits and the indemnity lands of its grant. Another settler was forcibly evicted from his home of nearly a decade by an especially notorious outlaw named John Payne, who told him:

... that he would scalp me, and that he would kill me if I offered to come upon said land, or even if I should touch a thing upon said premises, and also said he would kill me if I attemped to take the improvements. . . . I had not harvested my potatoes, and he said he would kill me if I undertook to dig them. Said land is upon an odd section, and being in the lieu land was not subject to entry, and I am a poor man, and this was my only home.[36]

In May of the same year, Neils Petersen, who persisted in trying to gather his stock from the range where Payne headed a gang of horse thieves, was snake-whipped by the latter. Together with Pearce, he is said to

---

[34] According to one account, rustlers branded 52,000 calves on the Hashknife lands one year. See Le Sueur, "Trouble with the Hash Knife Cattle Company," Le Sueur Papers, AHS, p. 5.

[35] U. S., *House Executive Document no. 232*, 50th Cong., 1st sess., p. 16.

[36] *Ibid*. Letter of John Oscar Reidhead to L. W. C. Lamar, March 29, 1887.

have asked Stake President Jesse N. Smith "if it would be right to kill him." Smith advised them to wait, and within a few days Payne lost his life in one of the skirmishes of the Pleasant Valley War.[37]

During the next few months, the nature of the assault on Mormon claims changed materially. Unable to find redress in the court at St. Johns, the Mormons found an official ally in Special Agent S. B. Bevans of the General Land Office. Apprised of the problem Bevans took a firm stand against the bully tactics and the permissiveness of Aztec officials which fostered them.[38] About the same time northern Arizona cracked down on lawlessness with dramatic force. Vigilantes hanged three alleged horse thieves. Four other notorious outlaws — Payne and his comrades — sensing an unwholesome change in public opinion, hurriedly crossed over the Mogollon Rim to meet their deaths in the Pleasant Valley War. And in Holbrook, a flaxen-haired, Winchester-wielding lawman named Commodore Owens killed four more badmen in one of frontier Arizona's goriest encounters.[39]

Claim jumping and bully tactics were ended, but the Aztec officials joined by Williamson and General E. A. Carr, president of the Cebolla Cattle Company which had purchased railroad lands in western New Mexico, called for a settlement of the Mormon claims. Silver Creek communities were first ordered to buy sections from the Hashknife and then ordered off the same lands. At Ramah, New Mexico, the Cebolla Company took even more straightforward action. With some show of force, it ordered settlers to vacate railroad lands they had occupied since the mid-seventies. Improvements were to be left, and at some future date the company would determine "how much would be required for the use of the land for the time they had occupied it."[40]

Meantime, the Mormons redoubled their efforts to secure legal title and other land. Organizing a land committee consisting of Smith, one-time lawyer Joseph Fish, and D. K. Udall, they secured assurance of the church's full support, including, if necessary, loans and other financial aids. Of immediate concern was the question of the Aztec Company's position. The committee appears to have hoped for a time that the company's land purchase had not been consumated. However, at a session of the district court in St. Johns in April of 1887, such hopeful misapprehensions were dispelled. The report of a "Mr. Donnelly of the land depart-

[37] Le Sueur, "Trouble with the Hash Knife Cattle Company," p. 10.

[38] U. S., *House Executive Document no. 232*, p. 21-22.

[39] Forrest, *Arizona's Dark and Bloody Ground*, gives a good account of these events, chapters 7 and 15. See also Wayte, "A History of Holbrook and the Little Colorado Country," pp. 153-76.

[40] Smith, *Journal of Jesse N. Smith*, p. 358.

ment of the A. & P. Railway" that the land had indeed changed hands was quickly verified in the records of the county recorder's office.[41] Disappointing for the moment, this transfer later proved to be most advantageous as the Aztec people ultimately demanded only about half as much per acre for land under their title as did the railroad.

Local Hashknife officials were again approached. Altering position, they assured the committee that they were now quite willing to negotiate. However, preliminary discussions revealed that they were "after all the money that they could get" and were at the moment not ready to sell.[42] As negotiations continued, a firm offer was made of $2.50 per acre, which was rejected.

Meantime the entire matter, including land claims at Woodruff, Snowflake, Taylor, and St. Johns in Arizona, and Ramah in New Mexico, was laid before Land Commissioner William Sparks. Arguing that the settlers had not known they were locating on railroad sections, the committee requested that lieu lands be given the railroad or some "other equitable turn made by which our rights can be preserved."[43] Verifying the 1872 date at which the land had legally attached to the railroad, Sparks sympathetically promised to "request the railroad company to relinquish its rights thereto, and allow it to select other lands in lieu there of."[44] Subsequent correspondence made it clear, however, that legal action to force such an exchange was out of the question.

During the following months, other expedients were tried. St. Johns, whose position was less precarious because its claim rested upon Barth's early rights, apparently solved its problem during 1888 by incorporating under the federal and territorial townsite laws. The matter was called to the attention of Territorial Delegate Marcus Aurelius Smith, who agreed to present a bill to Congress for the relief of the Little Colorado squatters. The bill evidently did not gain the floor of the House of Representatives.[45]

All other recourse unavailing, the committee concluded early in 1889 to place a formal request that railroad grant rights be relinquished before the boards of the various companies. Failing in this, as seemed certain, it was planned to purchase the land, whatever the price, as to withdraw seemed an intolerable alternative to both the settlers and church leaders. Salt Lake City authorities agreed to provide funds to cover the down payments. An appropriation of $500 also was made to pay the

---

[41] *Ibid.,* p. 348.

[42] "Autobiography of Joseph Fish," p. 256.

[43] See letter of Jesse N. Smith to William Sparks, July 14, 1887, National Archives.

[44] Letter of William Sparks to Jesse N. Smith, July 30, 1887, National Archives.

[45] See Letters of Jesse N. Smith to Wilford Woodruff, February 20, 1888, HDC.

expenses of a trip to Washington, D.C., and New York for Brigham Young, Jr., and Jesse N. Smith, who were to act as agents along with John W. Young, already in the East and by now probably the church's best access to financial and political power.[46]

When the companies refused to drop their grant rights, negotiations to buy were at once initiated, first with the Aztec officials and later the railroad and the Cebolla Cattle Company. In the case of the former, Smith and the Young brothers were happily surprised to discover that the asking price was $4.50 per acre. There was less cause for pleasure at the railroad land office where Williamson opened the discussion with a demand of $10.00 an acre for the land they wanted at Woodruff. Before their first visit was over, he dropped the price to $8.00, which they eventually paid. This was the highest figure the railroad commanded for any non-urban lands. When compared to the fifty cents per acre for which the Aztec and other large tracts went, it seemed a heavy tax indeed.[47]

By secret telegraph code, the Young brothers kept church President Wilford Woodruff informed. They also arranged for funds to be sent on request to make the first payment to the Aztec Company. Taking the position that the Little Colorado settlements had in reality been of material value to Aztec operations, the agents pushed for a reduction to $4.00. However, Wilford Woodruff sent the down payment calculated on the $4.50 cost directly to the Aztec people, thus closing the deal. Irate at this seeming disregard, Brigham Young, Jr., fired a warm letter to Woodruff. The agents, he wrote, had represented the church as "at the end of its ability financially." The board's response that "the church was wealthy" and would not "let the people suffer" had been met by repeated and emphatic assertations that it simply could not meet the high figure asked. Young, who was certain that this line of reasoning could have commanded better terms, regarded Woodruff's action as precipitate and financially unwise as well as extremely embarrassing.[48] On April 2, 1889, the Aztec Company and Smith executed the papers which ultimately transferred seven odd-numbered sections along Silver Creek between Snowflake and Shumway to the Mormons. Final title was to be acquired after the last of four annual payments had been made. One month later at the A & P

---

[46] For the most complete but not always accurate account of John W. Young's role, see "Daily Journal of John M. Whitaker," typescript, UU, vol. 1, March and April 1889. Whitaker was Young's private secretary and confidant during this period, and Young's activities in behalf of the church appear in a day-to-day chronicle in Whitaker's journal.

[47] Greever, *Arid Domain,* p. 51.

[48] Brigham Young, Jr., to President Wilford Woodruff, March 28, 1889, Brigham Young, Jr., Papers, HDC.

western headquarters in Albuquerque, papers were drawn up and the first payments made for the railroad lands at Woodruff.

Returning to Snowflake, Smith convened a public meeting where the particulars of the land purchase were laid before the people. Arrangements were made to spread the cost to the entire community, with holders of government lands assuming half as much of the burden as those on railroad lands. Smith's own account is to the point and conveys the spirit in which the action was taken. It is therefore quoted in full:

Upon the seven sections purchased only about 1000 acres were under cultivation, and valuable, which would bring the price of such cultivated portion up to something over $20 per acre. In view of the fact that we were all equally interested in the irrigation works and water supply for all our lands, both governments and railroad, and owing to the additional fact that holders of the government land could not sustain themselves in the country without the assistance of those on the railroad lands, it was moved and carried that owners of government land joining the purchase should pay half as much towards the purchase as those whose lands were on the purchase, placing the valuation upon the lands actually under cultivation and use, dividing same into four classes according to the quality and desirability of the land and appointing a committee of three from each ward to make the classification of the land. From Snowflake, W. J. Flake, Smith D. Rogers and John H. Willis; from Taylor, James H. Lewis, Sanford A. Angell and Cyrus M. Jennings. I was to be an honorary member of the committee. The whole proceedings were unanimous and harmonious.[49]

The land was soon surveyed, platted, and classified, and accounts were opened with each land holder. Finding a few who were both able and anxious to pay the full amount outright but were reluctant to do so because they could not acquire title to their lands until the final payment was made, Smith inquired if another advance to cover the entire purchase could be made by the church. Encouraged to believe that it could, his plans were given a temporary check when the Aztec people indicated that they would accept payment early but would not discount the interest accordingly. In spite of this setback, the church made the final payment to both the Aztec and railroad companies on April 4, 1891, almost exactly two years after the contract had been signed with the former company. Thereafter, the church held title to the land.

After meeting with initial success, the church's policy of deeding the land to its actual occupants as quickly as payment was received foundered on the hard times of the early 1890s. Pressed by the Salt Lake City authorities, local leaders tried every expedient to procure the money, including an announcement that the matter was one for which members

---

[49] Smith, *Journal of Jesse N. Smith,* p. 367.

were "accountable to Church law" and those who failed "should be cut off if they did not . . . pay. . . ."[50] Even threat of excommunication did not solve the problem, and the church at last wrote the debt off, allowing the individual burdens to be applied on irrigation company and school assessments which delinquent settlers could work out. The entire balance of $19,065 due the church thus served as a subsidy to the continued development of the colony.[51]

By 1896 most Little Colorado settlers had acquired clear titles to their land.[52] In a restricted sense, this represented the successful conclusion to the expansion on to the Little Colorado. Mormons had won a minimum base for their communities. But in the larger sense the achievement was illusory, its implications for the future sharply circumscribed. As we shall see in a subsequent chapter, the isolationist agrarianism of Little Colorado Mormons proved unequal to capturing the essential economic and political control required by their separatism. Furthermore, changing times tended to rob of its meaning the struggle to secure the land. The Little Colorado and the clutch of other colonies that pushed onto the Colorado Plateau and into southern Arizona during the late 1870s and 1880s represented, for all practical purposes, the last physical frontier of the Mormon kingdom. Thereafter the conditions of isolation and opportunity for prior occupation essential to its success were no longer to be found. Without them, the frontier of the kingdom was pinned against the banks of the Little Colorado and other barriers like it to be confronted sooner or later with the necessity of reconciliation with the world.

While land in minimum measure had been won, the vital factor in staying the day of reckoning was that of water development. With the horizons of their external frontiers contracting, the ever-present problems of water became even more critical as it grew increasingly apparent that the primary hope of extending the kingdom lay in developing water for areas then under varying degrees of Mormon control.

---

[50] "Lorenzo Hill Hatch Journal," p. 163.

[51] Smith, *Journal of Jesse N. Smith,* p. 399.

[52] The one major exception to this generalization was at St. Joseph, where as it turned out they had settled upon Section 16 — a school section. It was only after Arizona acquired statehood in 1912 that St. Joseph was able to clear its title. This time, as before, it was accomplished by church-oriented community action.

8. THE COSTS OF WATER

> With a cloudburst of rain, it becomes a raging torrent, rampaging along, sweeping everything in its path. It is dirty, muddy, gurgling, seething, belching, vicious, demon-like, bringing havoc, destruction and death. . . . Yet with all its dangers it was a lifesaver. In the early days, man and beast survived only because of its life-saving power. It was the only water for miles around so it was "that or nothing" and without it that part of Arizona could not have been settled.
>
> ELLEN GREER REES

THE WATERS OF THE LITTLE COLORADO were judged by some early Mormons to be so limited, hard to control, or "mineral" as to render the country unfit for human habitation. Others more optimistic visualized the day when the stream would support a community numbering into the tens of thousands. All, however, acknowledged that water was the key to successful colonization. On its development hinged the prospects of the future. In seeking to escape the strictures laid upon them by the limited water and the capricious nature of the country's streams, colonists struggled for decades to establish effective control, but in the long run found that the costs of all but the most primary developments were beyond their abilities.

Their experience, except perhaps in its extremes, was not unique. As a matter of fact, it was a replica with variation of a drama that unfolded over the entire Colorado Plateau. Settlers in southwestern Utah's Virgin River Basin, in eastern Utah's Castle Valley, and farther east into Colorado and New Mexico encountered similar problems. The name of the river varied and the detail was not identical, but water development on the Price, the San Juan, or the Mancos had much in common with water development on the Little Colorado. The process of taming these desert streams dominated the lives of those who stayed as it dictated the departure of many who left. Certainly, the Little Colorado River left an indelible mark upon the colony that depended upon it.

Although its watershed, which spreads over 25,900 square miles, must be reckoned among the larger areas drained by Colorado Plateau rivers, the Little Colorado is relatively unimportant in terms of the water it carries. Measured by the U.S. Geological Survey at Holbrook, below which the river is fed only by intermittent flooding, its average annual discharge during the early years of this century was less than 200,000 acre-feet — statistics which may be taken as somewhat characteristic of the period of colonization. Comparatively, a section of the Virgin River, which empties only a little more than a thousand square miles, boasted a flow similar in volume during the same years. The San Juan River, whose flow approached ten times that of the Arizona stream, runs from a region somewhat smaller in size. According to estimates made in 1905, the Little Colorado's maximum annual runoff likely never exceeded 300,000 acre-feet. Not only was its discharge small, but its water volumes varied widely during the year, running as high as 69,000 acre-feet in flood months and dropping to little more than a trickle in the dry months of June and July when its flow was only 244 acre-feet.[1]

Rising in the White Mountains near New Mexico's border, the Little Colorado flows northwest, flanked variously by mountain meadows, rolling hills, wide sandy bottoms, and by rugged but comparatively modest canyons. Farther back from the river the country also varies greatly. In the main, however, it can only be termed a desert possessing the thin soils, sands, clays, rocks, and minerals that generally characterize such regions. Whatever prospect such a country held for agriculture obviously lay in the utilization of the river. A moody and fitful stream virtually lost in its vast arid drainage, it was nevertheless the country's primary asset.

Water Development

Early-day water development was of three sorts: diversion, impounding, and conveyance. The first and basic measure was diverting the water from stream beds. In a few cases this was relatively simple. Rock walls

---

[1] The variations would have been even more pronounced had measurement been taken below Sunset where the stream drew additional flood waters from numerous washes in wet periods and dried up completely in the early summer months of dry years. The data presented above was taken from E. C. LeRue, *Colorado River and Its Utilization,* United States Geological Survey Water Supply Paper 395 (Washington, D.C.: Government Printing Office, 1910), pp. 109-120.

into which headgates were built were located at strategic spots, usually at a bend or "at the top of the water" where the flow could easily be drawn off into some earlier course which was near stream level. More often it was a matter of lifting the water and "taking it out" by means of diversion dams. Like the rock walls, these were located according to footing conditions and convenience of diversion. The first dams were not large works, rising no more than twelve feet. As a lift of more than a few feet was usually avoided, it was hoped that such modest barriers would be adequate. Hard experience soon proved that the happy combination of conditions under which the small dam sufficed was limited indeed. Larger works or continuing reconstruction were consequently required.

All of the earliest dams were constructed of dirt-fill, bound and stabilized by rock, cedar brush, and logs. In time settlers learned to lay them with the side fronting the water rising at a gentle pitch so that floods swept up and over, leaving the dam intact. Before the turn of the century, more impressive works had been made on the Little Colorado, but Silver Creek was still controlled by a series of these earthen and rubble diversion dams. For decades it proved necessary to replace them with

— *Albert J. Levine, Snowflake, A Pictorial Review, 1878-1964*

Silver Creek diversion dam near Snowflake.

Mormon reservoir near Tuba City.

heartbreaking regularity. Later a degree of permanence was achieved by pouring concrete shells over the dams and laying aprons downstream onto which flooding waters fell as they came over the dam.

After the earliest years, efforts were made to impound unused water in reservoirs to supplement the natural flow of the streams during periods of heavy irrigation.[2] Between Snowflake and Taylor, for example, three such reservoirs had been constructed by the early 1890s. Dams or levees ten or twelve feet in height and perhaps two hundred yards in length were built, generally at sites removed from the direct path of the river. One of these was said to have "about 4,550 yards of earth work in the bank besides rock and brush." Its capacity was estimated at "enough water to irrigate 1,000 acres over once."[3]

Perhaps the largest and most effective reservoirs were built at St. Johns. Beginning with two in the immediate vicinity of town in the early 1880s, development progressed until before 1915 the Lyman Dam backed up a substantial amount of water. While the utility of St. Johns' dams was great, they frequently broke, precipitating a chain reaction that swept dams away at Woodruff and St. Joseph that might otherwise have held.

---

[2] See "Minutes of the Woodruff Irrigation Company, 1895-1906," pp. 154, 161, 166. The original minutes are in possession of Earl Crofford at Woodruff, Arizona. He has been kind enough to furnish the writer with a copy.

[3] Fish, "History of the Eastern Arizona Stake," p. 22.

The third aspect of water development was ditching. Because of the modest size of Little Colorado irrigation projects, ditches were not of great capacity, rarely being more than six feet wide or of greater depth than two or three feet. On the other hand, they often ran long distances and involved great expense and continuing labor. In the fall of 1876, touring territorial officials noted that the colonists on the lower river had already dug "many miles of large irrigating ditches . . . often for long distances through solid rock."[4] The experience of that first summer was duplicated with variations almost annually throughout the colony during the next decade and a half and occasionally thereafter. With notable exceptions, the terrain through which Little Colorado ditches ran was not unduly rough, but the lower country was covered with sandstone upcroppings and the higher elevations with volcanic malapai formations that complicated ditching. On the lower river, the soil was "sugary" in character and frequently cut out or merely absorbed the entire stream. At the higher elevations, porous volcanic deposits also drained water out of ditches, constituting a technical difficulty that was never solved.

Ditch networks, of course, were subject to constant revision as reservoirs, new lands, and natural factors altered the water situation. Even after primary construction was completed costs remained high. Windstorms and gully-washing rains filled and refilled ditches with sand and debris. Dependent on Silver Creek and the river itself, ditches never escaped the fury of floods and even when left intact regularly filled with sediment. Consequently, ditch-cleaning was a job that settlers knew well, returning to it in a dogged annual rhythm punctuated by periodic repairs necessitated by floods and washouts. Water assessments and work schedules announced from church pulpits were frequent ceremonials as the cycle of maintenance went on. While they bore the expense, colonists often felt oppressed by it. Characteristic of their feelings was the following expression:

Labor on ditches in this stake has been enormous, at Snowflake this year [1889] the tax was a trifle over $3.00 per acre. Paying out this amount every year per acre . . . tells upon the people and they begin to think it is too much of a burden to carry. Other places have paid about as much as this.[5]

Nevertheless, ditch work was a norm of agriculture on the Little Colorado.

---

[4] See Territorial Governor A. P. K. Safford's report of the visit in the *Deseret News,* December 20, 1876.

[5] "Minutes of the Woodruff Irrigation Company," p. 92.

Organization and Leadership

Organization to meet the continuing problems of irrigation was inevitable. Its first manifestations came with an immediacy that indicated that the lessons of Utah's experience had not been lost upon the earliest colonists. The day after the vanguard of settlement arrived on the lower river in 1876, the Allen's Company contingent met to consider "the best way to secure" their "water right by cooperating together." The following day after limited discussion, they accepted an "agreement for an irrigation company" and "commenced work on the Ditch." [6]

Though one of their purposes was to form an association under territorial law, it is unlikely that either this company or others were incorporated in the early years. As a matter of fact, in the years before the mid-1890s some of them appear to have lost their identity as independent agencies entirely. For example, the March association of the Allen's Company water users was soon supplanted as the effective administrative unit by the St. Joseph United Order. As long as the Order remained intact, St. Joseph residents apparently handled all irrigation matters within its jurisdiction. [7] Elsewhere, arrangements corresponding more or less to the church organizations assumed the primary obligations of water development.

Informal associations persisted as the primary form of irrigation organization until the 1890s when they were supplanted by irrigation companies incorporated under Arizona law. Among the early incorporated companies was the one at Woodruff. Although stock in the Woodruff water system had long been divided according to the amount of land held, there is no reference to any formal organization prior to 1895. During later years, Woodruff users reasserted rights to waters that had fallen into disuse, and in the process ascertained that their water right, which was not filed officially until 1898, is anterior to any other on Silver Creek. In view of this fact, it would not seem that Woodruff turned to incorporation primarily because of economic factors or matters of internal regulation. These had been effectively provided by the earlier church-oriented association and were still being adequately dealt with at the time of incorporation. It consequently appears that when incorporation came, it came in large measure as a necessary prelude to the securing of legal title to the water. [8]

---

[6] See "Joseph City Ward History," pp. 10-11.

[7] See George S. Tanner, "Henry Martin Tanner, Joseph City Arizona Pioneer" (multilithed, 1964), p. 59.

[8] "Minutes of the Woodruff Irrigation Company," pp. 24-25.

The shadow of the church loomed large in both the associations of the early years and the chartered companies of the later era. Stake presidencies and bishops played vital roles. They became involved in water development when they entered the country and remained at its forefront until they were removed from office or died. In many cases their successors inherited this obligation, carrying the tradition into the twentieth century.

L. H. Hatch, who served in the stake presidency from its inception in 1878 until 1901, spent the entire period in a struggle to solve Woodruff's water problems. Tending to pessimism and self-recrimination, he was nevertheless the figure around which Woodruff's shifting population formed as he helped build twelve dams and weathered the destruction of eleven of them. His voice on the stake presidency and access to the General Authorities, most of whom he knew well, won concessions far beyond what the size and prospects of the community might otherwise have merited. Driven by despair as dams continued to fail, he carried his requests for aid beyond the confines of the Mormon community, securing funds from public sources as early as 1890. He sulked, preached, threatened, and prophesied to focus the elements of continued effort on the "famous Woodruff dam."[9]

According to a son living in 1966, the old gentleman's determination was in part the result of a personal pact with Brigham Young to locate the "worst place on the Little Colorado" and develop its water as evidence of success to other less determined missionaries.[10] Whatever the facts, L. H. Hatch's leadership was an important, if not the paramount, factor in the course taken by Woodruff's long fight to tame the Little Colorado River.

Less a joust with fate and more a matter of positive leadership was the role of D. K. Udall, who first as bishop of St. Johns and later as president of a stake by the same name also spent the better part of a lifetime in water development. Between 1880 and 1915 he was intimately associated with the promotion and construction of seven reservoirs some of which were immense projects requiring effective cooperation between Mormons and outside financiers and engineers. At Round Valley where he lived for a time, he put "a portion of each year" into "building and rebuilding" a "cluster of small lakes." At Hunt, about halfway between St. Johns and Holbrook, he also participated in successive construction of the "Udall Reservoir" or, as it was called locally, "Zion's Lake."[11]

In company with visiting General Authorities, Jesse N. Smith, president of the Eastern Arizona and Snowflake stakes, provided much of the

---

[9] "Lorenzo Hill Hatch Journal," p. 157.

[10] From a personal interview with Wilford L. Hatch of Franklin, Idaho, August 20, 1966.

[11] Udall and Nelson, *David King Udall,* pp. 184-85.

initiative for water development. His counsel was often sought though less frequently taken, and upon him rested responsibility for a surprising amount of technical decision for which only good judgment and practical experience had prepared him. Local leaders often required him to take a position on controversial issues in order to buttress their own positions or to unify public opinion. As water matters came to take a large part of his time, stake gatherings increasingly assumed the character of staff meetings from which water policy and administration issued. One Danish settler uttered a truism when he remarked from the pulpit that all that was talked about in worship meeting was "Vater Ditch! Vater Ditch! Vater Ditch!"[12] Indicative of Smith's participation in water affairs and their invasion of church meetings is this curt notation from his own journal:

Attended meeting at Woodruff. I spoke of the break in the dam; did not see but what the men who put in the portion that remained could put in more of the same kind. Counseled the brethren not to be discouraged, neither by the reports of what the railroad company was going to do about the land, nor about the damage the water had done to the dam. Know of no better place to make a living by farming in Arizona, any place occupied by Latter-day Saints, than here in Woodruff.[13]

Continuing to give close attention to water development, he broadened his horizons in the last years of the century to become an important figure in the national irrigation congresses of the time.

As noted before, bishops too were in the forefront of water affairs. At St. Joseph, John Bushman manifested a contagious optimism that accounts in some degree for that town's resilience. This spirit was much in evidence when following the loss of a dam in 1890 Bushman wrote: "Our people are not discouraged." Twelve months later when another dam, the product of much toil, went down the river, he noted with equal complacency: "No one seems discouraged. Probably because it is so common."[14] Personal attributes and perhaps other economic opportunity rather than familiarity with disaster appear to have been the basis of St. Joseph's optimism since repetition did nothing to assuage the bitterness of disappointment at the loss of dams in Woodruff. There washouts plunged the populace into such gloom that even ardent supporters rallied their spirits only by leaving town for awhile. Seeing divine rebuke in its repeated reverses, Woodruff tended to self-remorse. More pliant, St. Joseph

---

12 From a personal letter to the writer from Lenora Hansen of Snowflake, Arizona, February 15, 1966.

13 Smith, *Journal of Jesse N. Smith,* pp. 274-75.

14 "The Life and Labors of John Bushman," February 20, 1890, and February 20, 1891.

Jesse N. Smith, president of Eastern Arizona and Snowflake Stakes.

with Bushman and others like him at its head also saw God's hand in the course of events but was less frustrated and guilt ridden by it.

With an eye to temporal means, leadership, and tenacity, the church successively called three bishops to Woodruff. The primary obligation of each was to hold the community together in its effort to build the dam. During the forty years before this objective was successfully accomplished, each of the three succumbed to social discord, depression, or sheer weariness, leaving the village with bitterness and relief. But before each took his leave he had turned again and again to lead a fight in which there was a minimum of personal economic interest and a maximum of commitment to the basic objective.

The Famous Woodruff Dam

Other general aspects of water development may be viewed through the experience at Woodruff. Founded in 1877, the community fought a stubborn battle with the river; the battle, though it may have ended in nominal victory in 1919 when a staying dam was finally erected, was in reality something of a study in postponed defeat, as no really satisfactory solution was ever achieved. Located four miles below the junction of the Little Colorado and Silver Creek, Woodruff lies east of the river where it flows through a rock cut some thirty-five feet in depth. Varying around thirty families, the town's population formed and reformed following each washout. In all they built thirteen dams, eleven of which were lost to the flooding river, one cut voluntarily, and one which was still surviving in the early 1970s.

The pattern began in 1878 when, after months of labor, high water cut around both ends of the first dam. A flurry of construction during the early 1880s was hammered by incessant reverse as dams number two, three, four, five, six, seven, and likely eight were swept away. Brief respite was experienced between 1886 and 1890 as meteorological changes led people to hope they had conquered the river. In the latter year, however, floods of unprecedented proportions again did their "awful work." The construction of dam number ten was immediately launched, bringing the water out again before the summer's end; however, in a wet November that hampered life throughout the colony, it too was lost. Finished again the next year as engineering skills increased and the weather moderated, the eleventh dam, now flagged by stone slabs, held until 1904 when Zion's Dam at Hunt gave way before large storms, releasing a torrent that again left Woodruff's settlers high and dry. Built with much assistance from the church and the Little Colorado stakes, the twelfth and last dam on the river — a masonry structure, remnants of which still were standing in the early 1970s as stark sentinels of the Little Colorado's prowess — was lost

Remnant of the "famous Woodruff Dam."

as the Lyman Dam above St. Johns collapsed in 1915, adding the waters it had impounded to an already swollen stream.

Weary, but this time with substantial state and church aid, Woodruff turned to dam number thirteen. Engineers now determined that ditches could be chiseled along the canyon side making feasible the construction of a dam on Silver Creek just above its confluence with the river. Escaping the silts and minerals of the Little Colorado as well as its fierce floods, a permanent diversion dam was completed in 1919. Mormons in quest of a happy ending for Woodruff's long struggle have tended to regard this as a successful conclusion, ignoring the fact that the technical difficulties of ditching along the canyon walls proved to be virtually beyond the exhausted town's ability to overcome.[15]

Certain characteristics of the entire colony are seen in sharp relief on this troubled background. Keeping in mind that Woodruff's struggle

---

[15] Recent decades have witnessed an almost complete abandonment of irrigated farming under the dam. A move to restore the ditch and once again "bring the water out" is presently afoot. The pace of changing times is apparent in the ironic fact that impetus this time comes not from the church nor even the village natives but to all appearances from an "outsider" who purchased the old home of a long-time bishop and in the process of its restoration has been caught up in the broader course of Woodruff's ongoing struggle for existence.

and its precarious hold on life were in a sense symbolic of the Little Colorado's general experience, we may now turn to a consideration of the village's marginal existence, certain communal elements in its history, its dependence, and the failure of Mormon means to solve any but the most superficial water problems.

Apparent in the foregoing narrative is the fineness of the balance in which Woodruff's existence hung. Closely circumscribed by natural conditions, it barely escaped joining the Little Colorado's roster of ghost towns. From the first, settlers appear to have vacillated about the desirability of staying. After the loss of dam number one in 1878, only three families remained — those of L. H. Hatch, James Dean, and Hans Guldbransen. Interestingly, these, along with the families of James C. Owens, who came in 1879, L. M. Savage, and one or two other latecomers, became the stable element in the town's population. It became the role of these people to recruit others. Time and again the initial phase of construction was building population. Church counsel was used unstintingly in the process, as was any promotional talk the people could muster.[16]

With the town built to a peak population of about thirty families during periods of construction and successful diversion, failure of a dam usually resulted in a general exodus. Most merely left. Occasionally there were those who justified or attempted to justify their departure. At least one, a Brother Dexter, reported that "the spirit had directed him to move his family to Utah."[17] In 1891 even L. H. Hatch became discouraged. Being "very much exercised" about the village's destitute condition, he stated in strong terms, "if we were going to defer longer the building of a dam, I would move and advise the people of Woodruff to scatter out where they could make a living."[18]

In 1905 after receiving a lamenting report of the loss of dam number eleven, Salt Lake authorities, whose willingness to subsidize Woodruff had been unflagging, proposed that the community be abandoned. In reply to a request for help from Jesse N. Smith, they suggested that the village could be moved as a unit to southern Nevada's Muddy River. Smith quickly backed off, responding that he considered it "better for Woodruff and cheaper to the church" to build another dam. Ignoring the facts of the

---

[16] Typical of their overtures were those made to Allen Frost in April of 1889. After conferring with Jesse N. Smith at Snowflake, Frost visited Woodruff in company with its bishop. On April 15 he wrote: "Looked around Woodruff, and visited a little. Received a pressing invitation to locate here." With the laconic but accurate notation of "Poor Water," he declined the invitation and established his home in Snowflake. See "Diary of Allen Frost," p. 550.

[17] "Lorenzo Hill Hatch Journal," p. 170.

[18] *Ibid.*, p. 157.

town's long history of subsidy and help, he rested the crux of his argument on the embarrassment Woodruff's citizens would feel "if they had to take charity." Given such an alternative, he thought "the value of the poor homes they had left would be enhanced a thousand fold in their eyes, and they would long for Woodruff if they went to paradise." Concluding that the distance to the Muddy by rail was six hundred miles and the "wagon road the worst in the country," he turned again to plans of construction and soon won cash grants totaling at least $1,500 from the church as well as the right to apply local tithing receipts to the project.[19]

That Woodruff escaped the tragedy of extinction was due in part to the fact that its citizens were not unduly sensitive about accepting aid. Indeed, their tolerance to "charity" was pronounced, and after the very earliest attempts Woodruff was given help on most if not all its dams. Aid came from various sources. Individuals who saw fit to make the town their permanent home were often helped by family members in Utah. While their strong sense of mission relieved this practice of some of its onus, settlers appear to have chafed under the relationships so imposed. The church, which apparently recognized a broader significance in the town's success than the handful of homes thus provided, advanced aid in various guises. Outright cash grants were infrequent but with the passing of time became increasingly important. According to one account, the church "contributed twenty-two thousand five hundred" of the total cost of $85,000 that the last dam cost.[20] More common were tithe reliefs which were generally gathered in labor and kind from about the Little Colorado community. Also important were opportunities to work out debts contracted to the church for water development, land purchase, and other undertakings.

In addition to grants requiring action of the General Authorities, labor was donated by the surrounding towns on at least three occasions — once in 1884, once in 1890-91, and again in 1905. With tongue in cheek but nevertheless with real insight, Evans Coleman wrote the following relative to this practice:

The Church authorities were practical and philosophical. For example: The people on the Little Colorado were having a hard time, especially at Woodruff and Joseph City. They just couldn't keep those dams in, and a couple of the Apostles came down to look things over and give encouragement and aid to those people.

---

[19] See letters of Jesse N. Smith to Joseph F. Smith under dates of June 6 and December 5, 1905, Jesse N. Smith Personal File, HDC.

[20] See "Our Town and People, A Brief History of Woodruff," (multilithed), compiled by Sara E. Brinkerhoff and Nina B. Brewer, p. 7.

Those Apostles came on up into the more prosperous communities and at meetings asked us to donate. Quote: "Brothers and Sisters: You know the extreme difficulties our people are having along the Little Colorado. We must not let those settlements be broken up. You more prosperous people must help them. Donate of your cattle, horses, grain, wagons — anything you can spare that they can use. . . . Listen, (and the speaker lowered his voice) If we can just keep those old people there till they die off and the young ones grow up, it will be home to those young people. They will know no other home nor want any other home. And when the dam goes out they will be just like a bunch of beavers. They won't know anything else but to go and put it in again. They will be permanently located — rooted into the soil." unquote. Good philosophy, no? Who else would have thought of that but a Mormon colonization promotor? And, the people of the more prosperous communities contributed liberally.[21]

Though inconvenient and at times even oppressive, local contributions generally seem to have been regarded as part of the community responsibility of colonists whose lot was somewhat less austere.

Woodruff's residents were not without their own sense of communal obligation. Indeed, on one or two occasions their willingness to jeopardize their own welfare for the broader weal was heroic. In May of 1880 as their second dam impounded the entire flow of the Little Colorado, it had adverse effects on the lower river villages. Woodruff's response to the dilemma is perhaps best expressed in the words of L. H. Hatch:

Next day I received a letter from St. Joseph about the water affairs. We were damming the water at Woodruff so that it did not flow on to St. Joseph. Our dam had been closed up for eight days and the people at St. Joseph were all out of sorts waiting for the water to flow over our headgates. It would have to fill up two and a half more feet before it would pass over and that was too long to wait. We cut our dam and let the water through. It was a sorry time for those who had worked so hard to put in this immense dam.[22]

The following year, St. Joseph representatives again appeared in May to request that Woodruff turn water down to relieve their critical need. Although "some murmured," the headgates were opened leaving crops dependent upon natural moisture which soon came in good amounts despite the fact that the rainy season generally did not start until much later.[23]

---

21 Coleman, "Historical Sketch of Dr. W. E. Platt," p. 12.

22 "Lorenzo Hill Hatch Journal," May 16, 1880, p. 115. Of the same event, Joseph Fish wrote: "A few days after this Major Ladd came up on behalf of the people of St. Joseph and claimed that there was a great scarcity of water with them, and if the water was not turned down they would lose their crops. A meeting was called and it was decided to cut a hole in the dam and turn the water down. This was a damage to the dam of about $500.00 and blasted their hopes of a crop for that season." See "History of the Eastern Arizona Stake," p. 35.

23 "Lorenzo Hill Hatch Journal," p. 121.

Not surprisingly, Woodruff citizens gained much support from non-Mormon sources. From the beginning, outside work was characteristic of life. With the railroad near at hand, freighting became a major source of income. Sons were hired out to cow outfits. Men scattered as far afield as the mines in central and southern Arizona. Entirely typical was the condition in 1905 when a count made pursuant to commencing a new dam revealed that the community consisted of thirty-three families, ten of which were headed by widows or aged men. The men of twenty families were working at various jobs away from home and could return to the dam only if support could be found for them. Of the total, only three could sustain themselves on their Woodruff holdings for any length of time.[24]

Pressed repeatedly by such need but determined to maintain the principle if not the essence of nonfraternization, Woodruff men and boys, and (over the loud protest of church authorities) occasionally its women, became something of a service community. Honest and steady, they left home for long periods of time to carry on the necessary functions of many businesses without actually becoming part of them. Reflecting a characteristic aloofness, one settler wrote in 1883: "I spent nearly two months among the Gentiles laboring for wages, at Flagstaff. . . . Their company is not pleasant for me."[25] Reserved and closemouthed, particularly after the polygamy raids gathered impetus in the middle 1880s, Woodruff settlers found it to their interest to perform their duties with little protest or agitation. Combined with their impecunious financial conditions, their separatism placed sharp limits upon the nature of their business participation. Few of them acquired stock in or joined the management of outside companies.

Woodruff also sought outright relief from Gentile sources. In 1890 petitions were addressed to the Atlantic and Pacific Railroad requesting that land debts be written off or at least temporarily waived. During the same crisis, the territorial legislature appropriated $1,500 for their relief. In 1915 Arizona, by now a state, advanced $10,000 to rebuild the dam. Before the complex system of flumes and siphons by which the ditch was worked down the canyon from the new dam was completed, the community had also received $26,000 under the Federal Emergency Relief Act of the 1930s.[26]

Conditioned by the climate of crisis in which they lived, Woodruff citizens and to a lesser degree Little Coloradans generally were thus any-

---

[24] See letter to the First Presidency, May 13, 1905, Jesse N. Smith Name File Box, HDC.

[25] "Journal of Levi Mathers Savage," p. 37.

[26] "Our Town and People," p. 6.

thing but independent. The effects of this conditioning were diverse. On the one hand bonds between colony and mother institution were enhanced. On the other was a strong centrifugal force that led colonists into reciprocal relations with the secular world.

Other Little Colorado reclamation projects that sought to control floods or to develop any but the most accessible waters met with a fate not unlike Woodruff's. At St. Joseph where quicksand and shifting river-beds combined with floods, the problems of building a dam that could both survive the river's moods and divert irrigation streams at low water was not permanently solved until 1923.[27] As we have seen, relatively large projects at Hunt and St. Johns either failed totally or succeeded only upon repeated efforts and after large-scale outside help was secured.

Guided by their ecclesiastical leaders and functioning from the basis of informal water boards, Little Colorado pioneers undertook to subdue their stream. This they were able to do only in the most limited sense and then only by dint of lasting sacrifice and effort. The repeated crisis of water development strengthened both the communal bonds within the church and cooperative relationships with the Gentile community with Mormons appearing as trusted employees and as recipients of territorial aids. Closely related was the fact that crisis produced a highly dependent society. Consequently a major factor in molding the size and character of the Little Colorado community was its inability to exploit fully even the modest drainage of the river's vast watershed.

---

[27] See "The Life and Labors of John Bushman," p. 86. For a good short treatment of St. Joseph's experience see Tanner, "Henry Martin Tanner," pp. 57-64.

9. ON THE BORDERS
OF THE LAMANITES: Indian Relations

The President [Brigham Young] . . . declared his intention of building forts on the East side of the Colorado, and place sufficient missionary force there to protect Lamanite industry, should they see proper to be gathered under the wings of Israel's Eagles.

GEORGE A. SMITH

Jacob Hamblin . . . informed me that he had a Telegram from Prest. B. Young instructing him to take as Many of the prestant co. & explore . . . the head waters of the Little Colerado & report, also to locate Said co. on some of the best territory that he could find, then direct his labours to the House of Iseral & turn the Indians into line & let them help the Brethren build up cities, Heard, & Farm. Thus we see the Key of Salvation is about to be turned to the House of Iseral, as the gentiles reJect it. . . .

JOHN D. LEE

Hopis

INDIAN RELATIONS were an important factor in the Mormon expansion to the Valley of the Little Colorado. Founded at a time when major Indian wars still lay fresh in Arizona memory, the colony was nearly surrounded. The Hopis — Moquis, or Moquich, as they were then called — were on the north, the Navajos on the north and northeast, the Zuñis to the east, and the Apaches to the south. Throughout the region of colonization, extensive ruins bore testimony of dense native populations in bygone ages, but at the time of settlement the Little Colorado Basin was itself uninhabited except around its peripheries which extended into Indian territory. While it overlapped tribal grounds at only a few points, the area into which the

Mormons moved was virtually isolated from other whites by Indians. Inevitably there was considerable interaction between the two races — a contact that was not without its rewards to the Mormon colonists.

In addition to the physical fact of proximity, settlers were drawn to the Indians by the general Mormon affinity for the Lamanites, as the Book of Mormon calls all Indians. Believing that the red man had descended from a branch of Israel divinely led to the western hemisphere, Latter-day Saints accepted as part of their mission the obligation of restoring the Indian to his former position of favor in God's eyes and believed that he had a special claim to the American continents. Moved by such ideas, the entire course of the church's history had been marked by a preoccupation with Indians.[1] As early as 1831 a pattern was established when the church followed its first Indian missionaries onto the "borders of the Lamanites" in Missouri. Thereafter, numerous frontiers, including the one on the Little Colorado, were first opened by missionaries to the Indians.

The effective approach to northern Arizona grew out of missionary work in southwestern Utah. From the time of that region's earliest settlement, church officials had devoted a good deal of time and effort to the Paiutes, Shivwits, and other primitive tribes. Moving in among the Indians, whites easily established control and with confident altruism sought to usher them into the white man's world. A few Paiutes were located on small patches of land; others were taken into private homes as wives or adopted children. Individual and mass baptisms were performed, and missionary groups worked to convert and control outlying groups.[2]

However, southwestern Utah's Indians did not dominate the evangelizing impulse of the Mormons for long. Based upon prophetic assurance that a transformation of the Lamanites was both imminent and requisite, Mormon altruism tended to be restless and searching. Needing remarkable and speedy manifestations, it found the dull submission of the Paiutes to be less than satisfactory. A perfunctory if not grudging paternalism supplanted enthusiasm and expectation which were refocused upon untried and more promising targets.[3]

---

[1] This interest still persists. Proselyting is currently carried on among many tribes, including those covered in this study.

[2] For accounts of southwestern Utah Indian relations see Angus M. Woodbury, *The History of Southern Utah and Its National Parks* (Salt Lake City: Utah State Historical Society, 1950), and Juanita Brooks, "Indian Relations on the Mormon Frontier," *Utah Historical Quarterly* 12 (January-April, 1944): 1-48.

[3] According to Mormon belief, Indians had descended from Israelite families led to the Americas about 600 B.C. and thus merited both the name of Israel and the blessings promised to Israel in the Old Testament. See Doctrine and Covenants 19:21.

Then, too, the Mountain Meadows Massacre of 1857, in which Mormons had joined southern Utah's Indians in a sordid and savage business, must have adversely affected the protestations of commitment to brotherhood and the effort to teach the Paiutes. The massacre had a direct influence upon the southward shift of the proselyting impulse. Checking rumors that one of the surviving children was in the hands of Indians southeast of the Colorado River, Jacob Hamblin, Indian missionary and explorer, found opportunity to fulfill a cherished desire of long standing to visit "the nobler branches of the race."[4] Crossing the Colorado during the autumn of 1858, he initiated the long Mormon flirtation with the Hopi Indians. Making fifteen separate winter expeditions spread over as many years, Hamblin led a total of no fewer than 125 white missionaries into the Hopi pueblos.

A word should be interjected about Mormon nomenclature. In the earliest years the Hopis were invariably called the Moquich Indians, and the proselyting operation was referred to as the Moquich Mission. The word Moqui, which was originally used only in reference to one of the Second Mesa villages, gradually supplanted the word Moquich until by 1870 it had become the general designation. The term Hopi was never used by the Mormons, as far as this writer can determine, until after 1880.

With their sedentary agriculture, textile skills, respect for their women, and kiva rituals suggestive of Mormon temple ceremonies, the mesa dwellers captivated Hamblin and his followers. To some, scriptural promises appeared to be partially fulfilled in the Hopis. The interest of others was titillated by the thought that these light-skinned Indians might be the elusive Welch Indians of the old myth that had attracted attention to the Mandan tribe in times past. Welch converts, however, listened in vain for words of Gaelic derivation in the Hopi language.[5]

More important to an understanding of the hold the Hopis laid on Mormon interest was the fact that the missionaries found an isolated people unspoiled by contact with other Americans and as separatist in their own right as the Latter-day Saints themselves. Until 1870 the Hopis lay for all practical purposes beyond the official pale of the United States military and Indian Service.[6] The scholarly and humanitarian interest

---

[4] Juanita Brooks, *Mountain Meadows Massacre* (new ed.; Norman: University of Oklahoma Press, 1962), pp. 102-103. Mrs. Brooks writes that "although Jacob Hamblin knew well that no child had ever been in the hands of Indians," the search gave him "opportunity to do something he had long wanted to do and at government expense." He received $318 in compensation for his trip, according to Office of Indian Affairs records.

[5] Little, *Jacob Hamblin*, p. 63.

[6] For early references to the Hopis see U. S., *Senate Executive Document,* 36th Cong., 1st sess., Lt. Joseph C. Ives, *Report upon the Colorado River of the West* (Washington: Government Printing Office, 1861), and John G. Bourke, *On the Border with Crook* (New York: Charles Scribner's Sons, 1891), pp. 230-31.

Hopi petroglyphs at Willow Springs.

that characterizes the twentieth century's relations with the Hopis had not yet attracted America generally. Furthermore, the Hopis were quite content in their native state, as such contact with the army and Indian Service as they had experienced did not beget confidence.

As significant as the absence of interference from other whites in attracting the Mormons, was their own waning enthusiasm for Utah's Indians. A number of factors had tended to reduce the glamour of tribes closer to home. Included among these were the frictions of close living, the nonsedentary life style of most Utah Indians, and an Indian policy controlled by federal appointees whose conduct was often influenced by the polygamy conflict. Consequently, the Hopis, insulated and aloof, stirred deep feelings of affinity and seemed to promise an opportunity for evangelizing that could scarcely be resisted. From this grew a preoccupation that in its proselyting and colonizing phases lasted from Hamblin's first visit in 1858 to the departure of the Mormons from Tuba City in 1902.

Quickly recognizing the difficulties of carrying on an effective program across Arizona's far frontier and, no doubt, sensing that it would curtail Hopi contact with non-Mormon whites, the early missionaries soon adopted what may be called a relocation policy. At the instance of Brigham Young, Hamblin repeatedly invited the Hopis to cross to the north side of the Colorado River where it was hoped they would "settle in different places under the south rim of the basin in communities of about twenty white men to every ten Indians."[7] Unfazed, the Hopis countered that prophets of their own had warned against crossing the river, and they remained in their tribal homes.[8] Without abandoning the relocation policy, plans were made to spend a year among the mesa dwellers in 1860. The projected mission, however, came to grief and was given up when one of its members, George A. Smith, Jr., son of a prominent church leader, was killed by hostile Navajos.

Not easily dissuaded, Brigham Young continued to push the Moquich Mission. Exchanging deputations with the Oraibis in 1863 — actually the Mormon elders left in the mesa village while four Indians visited Utah came nearer being hostages than being agents — Young satisfied himself that reports of their reluctance to relocate north of the Colorado were true and fell even more fully under the Hopi contagion. Content by this time that the southward bent of Mormon expansion tended to Arizona, Young laid preliminary plans to establish a permanent mission of no fewer than one hundred men southeast of the river. Relocation was still part of the scheme, it being Young's hope that the natives could be lured from their villages to superior sites where they could be instructed in the way of the gospel and Mormon industry.[9] Again temporarily forestalled by Navajo hostility after 1865, the Hopi mission was picked up in the last years of the decade, playing an important part in the decision to send out the colonizing missions of the 1870s.

From 1873 the center of pioneer Mormon activity among the Hopis was Moenkopi. On the main route to Arizona, it served both as a way station and a headquarters for missionary activity. The Hopis had established a temporary village at the site prior to the beginning of Mormon colonization. Members of the Arizona mission of 1873 found them there, and John D. Lee, who spent the last half of that year at neighboring Moe-

---

[7] Quoted in Brooks, "Indian Relations on the Mormon Frontier," p. 24.

[8] With reference to the Hopis' reluctance to cross the river see Ira Hatch, "The Moquis Indians," as narrated to James A. Little, *Millennial Star* 32 (April 1870): 242.

[9] See George A. Smith to Erastus Snow and to Jacob Hamblin, respectively, February 15 and 16, 1863, Jacob Hamblin Letters, HDC. For a more thorough treatment of the early Mormon missions to the Hopis, see the author's "The Hopis and the Mormons — 1858-1873," *Utah Historical Quarterly* 39 (1971): 179-194.

— *Smithsonian Office of Anthropology*

This Hopi delegation from Oraibi visited Salt Lake City in 1863, at the desire of Brigham Young, for the purpose of discussing trade with the Mormons. The man in the center is thought to be Tuba.

nave, wrote of frequent visits to "the Farm of the Native" where he was received with great hospitality by a friendly Indian named Tuba and a few other Oraibis. Lee's journal indicates that the place was well established, having cultivated plots laid out with "Judgment & taste in Terresses" as well as flat-roofed stone houses and prospering herds of sheep and goats.[10] Yet all evidence attests that it was not yet a place of permanent residence. Culturally attached to Oraibi, it was frequently vacated, its people retiring to the older village. In the years before 1876 most if not all of its inhabitants left during the winter.[11]

---

[10] Cleland and Brooks, *Mormon Chronicle*, vol. 2, p. 271.

[11] Hamblin found it empty in January of 1874, its people having "gone to a big dance at the Oriba villages." See letter of J. E. Smith quoted in Little, *Jacob Hamblin*, pp. 131-32. In 1875, Anthony W. Ivins found that it was not inhabited at the time of a November visit. See "Anthony Woodward Ivins Journal," pp. 33-34.

Tuba clearly regarded himself to be the proprietor of the area. Paying Lee a call shortly after the latter arrived at Moenave, the Indian informed him that he was welcome "to setle with him & said that Jacob & I might have those 2 springs & make us a home & bring our Familys."[12] Later Lee was given a pressing invitation to move to Moenkopi and make his home with Tuba and his followers.

Tuba proved to be the most constant friend the Mormons found among the Hopis. More willing than most to accept change, he was one of the few Hopis to visit in Utah and was always a source of support to Mormon missionaries while they were in the villages. Having conceived a vague but, as it proved, abiding vision of a Hopi people liberated from much of life's drudgery, as he had seen the marvels of a cotton mill in southwestern Utah, Tuba stood at the head of a small group which encouraged the Mormons to settle among them. His progressive posture in this respect may have been the result of adverse clan status which in turn forced him to accept economic solutions not attractive to those placed better in the social structure at Oraibi. My thinking on this matter rests upon the fact that Thales Haskell and Marion Sheldon, who undertook to spend the entire year of 1859-60 at Oraibi, found that every parcel of farm land was claimed and jealously guarded but were informed that less firmly held land at Moenkopi might be utilized by them. Since Tuba led the Hopi move to Moenkopi and claimed its adjacent lands, it is reasonable to assume that his clan holdings included Moenkopi and were perhaps limited to it and other peripheral and consequently little-valued lands.[13]

The Hopi mission never really developed. As bright as prospects appeared, few Hopis became members of the church, and, with the possible exception of Tuba and his wife, there were only nominal converts. As elsewhere in the Little Colorado Basin, colonizing proved to be so arduous at Moenkopi that Mormon settlers were never able to devote any real effort to the instruction of the Indians. Thus, while the entire Mormon population at Tuba City was Indian oriented, only a few actually served as Indian missionaries, and these only spasmodically. Under the pressures of pioneer life the idealism of earlier years suffered a progressive erosion until by the early 1890s it appears to have been entirely forgotten. Thereafter, Mormon relations with the Hopis were little more than a matter of coexistence with both peoples adhering to their pacific traditions.

If the promise of Mormon idealism failed, so did the prospect of a Hopi break with the past. Even Tuba was unable to transcend permanently

---

[12] Cleland and Brooks, *Mormon Chronicle,* vol. 2, p. 266.
[13] Juanita Brooks, ed., "Journal of Thales H. Haskell," *Utah Historical Quarterly* 12 (January-April, 1944): 92-94.

the Hopi antipathy for the white man's ways. Familiarity worked its flux upon him, and the promise of relief he had seen for his people when he visited the Washington cotton factory was soon engulfed in the problems of life in close proximity with the Mormons.

However, Tuba's friendship and restraint had more than a little to do with the fact that the Hopis were not moved to really hostile action by anti-Mormon stirrings which cropped up from time to time. As early as 1873, a report came to John D. Lee that "the officer in command of Wheeler's outfit . . . persuaded the Indians to drive off the Mormons."[14] Imagined or real, this threat frightened Lee. Later reports of anti-Mormon agitation arising from more valid sources produced continuing tensions.

Tension was especially high during the polygamy scare in 1885-86. At that time "Speigel Berg Bros from Albuquerque," a Gentile firm which had taken over the old Moenkopi mission house, rallied wool buyers and other businessmen in the country against polygamists. In the general excitement, Gentiles appear to have believed that Mormons "were trying to Unite all the Tribes to . . . Wipe out Gentiles." Fearing the Gentiles in turn, the Mormons carried their guns for the first time in a decade.[15] Considering the isolation of Tuba City and the scattered white population of the northern deserts around it, the polygamy question appears to have generated a debate of surprising warmth. One reason for this was the fact that a number of key inhabitants were missionaries from other churches. But talk was not limited to them, and a trip to the Keams Canyon Indian Agency, to Fort Defiance, or merely to Polacca House at the foot of First Mesa, usually led to hot discussions and sometimes threats and anger.

Indians also became somewhat involved in the polygamy question. While not stirred to militancy by it, the Hopis, who despite early reports to the contrary were monogamous, looked in disfavor on the practice and are said to have suffered considerable loss of confidence in the Mormons on discovering that they had multiple wives. The Navajos, on the other hand, were unabashed polygamists. Urged by federal officers "to put away their Plural Wifes," they told at least one Mormon that they had no intention of doing so.[16]

Final collapse of the Hopi experiment grew from problems rising out of the Tuba City area's sharply limited supply of water. Efforts on the part of the settlers during the 1890s to establish legal claim to the water were met by passive but determined Indian opposition. Less passive

---

[14] Cleland and Brooks, *Mormon Chronicle*, vol. 2, p. 299.
[15] See "Diary of Christian Lingo Christensen," pp. 66-72, for a firsthand account of the general discord generated by the polygamy excitement.
[16] *Ibid.*

were the Indian agents and agency farmers who threw their full support behind Indian claims. Unwilling to let the controversy rest upon its legal merit, the Indian service sought and found evidence of all sorts of moral wrongs among the Mormons — including polygamy. Indicative was the following from a letter written by Samuel E. Shoemaker in 1895:

> . . . I believe it can be proven that Tuba the old Oribe whose name was given to this *doomed* city — was pounded by one of the Mormons to such a degree that he died from the effects. You see by keeping quiet, I am getting to see the inside of many of their acts, dark villanious acts, and they begin to wish me out of this. If I were capable I could accumulate enough *data* to write a most readable novel, and one founded on facts. It would make history, but not favorable to either the Mormons or their allies the Pah Utes, who are the most worthless mischief making scamps in this part of the country, and I wish they could be moved back to Utah where they belong.[17]

In 1902 the campaign to expell the Tuba City Mormons succeeded, and the long mission to the Hopis came to an end. It left little other than its tradition to mark its passing.

Navajos

Nor were Mormons oblivious to the Navajos. In part this was a matter of fear, but it was also something more. Indian missionaries had long been intrigued by this large nomadic tribe. In fact, Latter-day Saints had become cognizant of them as early as 1831 when Oliver Cowdery, then a close associate of Joseph Smith's, made what may well have been the first Mormon reference to any western tribe, as he wrote from Kaw Township, Missouri:

> I am lately informed of another tribe of Lamanites, who had abundance of flocks of the best kinds of sheep and cattle; and they manufacture blankets of a superior quality. The tribe, is very numerous; they live three hundred miles west of Santa Fe, and are called *Navashoes*.[18]

After the move West, the church's interest in the "Navashoes" was soon translated into action. In 1854 William Huntington conducted a mission of "discovery" to their country. Preceding the Elk Mountain Mission by nearly a year and Jacob Hamblin's first mission to the Hopis by four years, Huntington's expedition was perhaps the earliest to outlying tribes.[19] The following year, Alfred Billings and other members of

---

[17] Samuel E. Shoemaker to Major Constant Williams, February 24, 1895, Tuba City Collection, Southwest Museum, Los Angeles.

[18] *Documentary History of the Church*, vol. 1, p. 182. Cowdery, along with a few other Latter-day Saint elders, was on the first of the church's many Lamanite missions when the above was written.

[19] *Millennial Star* 17: (1885): 253.

the Elk Mountain Mission made a tour south of the San Juan River by a route which they recorded with painstaking but misspelled detail. One account of the trip, that of William B. Pace, indicated that it was made as a result of an invitation to visit and teach the Navajos.[20] Spending only a short time in northern Arizona, the elders abandoned further designs, whatever they may have been, when the Indians of southeastern Utah forced them to withdraw.

Thereafter, no contact appears to have been made with the Navajos until the unfortunate meeting of the Hopi mission of 1860 with far-ranging Navajos heralded the first clash of two extending frontiers. Following their defeat by Kit Carson in 1863-64, substantial numbers of Navajos took refuge in the broken canyon lands south and east of the San Juan and Colorado rivers.[21] Smarting from their encounter with Carson, and in dire need, they would have found the approaching Mormon frontier tempting under any condition; given the Indian unrest in Utah incident to the Black Hawk War, the invitation was too much to resist. Fording the river in large parties at the Crossing of the Fathers, they split into smaller bands, plundering first the outlying ranches and, as they grew bolder, even the more populous communities. Their incursions continued until 1870 when Jacob Hamblin and John Wesley Powell made a peace treaty with them at Fort Defiance.

Encouraged by this turn of events, Brigham Young renewed the southward march of the Mormon frontier. Amicable relations, however, came breathlessly near collapse when three young tribesmen were murdered while trading in the Sevier River country late in 1873. Peace was soon patched up by Hamblin, who in a daring bit of Indian diplomacy eased the fury of Navajo anger during January of 1874.[22]

Their early contacts marred by hostility and tension, Mormon colonists approached the Navajo frontier with understandable trepidation.

---

[20] See "William B. Pace Diary of the Elk Mountain Mission 1855-1856," type-script BYU, p. 17.

[21] For a general account of the Navajos in which Carson's role is treated, see Ruth M. Underhill, *The Navajos* (Norman: University of Oklahoma Press, 1956), particularly chapters 10-14.

[22] Little, *Jacob Hamblin,* pp. 124-35. According to Hamblin's account as well as that of the two prospectors who were his comrades in the tense hours of the initial negotiations, Hamblin's diplomacy was daring and effective and his personal conduct without blemish. Some of Hamblin's Mormon contemporaries, however, did not share this point of view. John D. Lee, who it must be admitted was quick to believe the worst of the Indian scout, was convinced that Hamblin lied to save his own life at the time of the peace conference and that his subsequent failure to honor his commitments jeopardized the entire southward movement of the church. In Lee's opinion the favorable eyewitness account of the two prospectors was pure fabrication calculated to "Puff up old Hamblin & thereby get him to show them a rich Ledge. . . ." Others, including John L. Blythe, head of the Moenkopi Mission in 1874, also had serious reservations about Hamblin's role.

Descriptive of this frame of mind were the words of Indian missionary Christian Lingo Christensen:

When we first came into this country we had to stand guard nights to protect our animals and this was all done to make and preserve Peace and good order. Haveing no acquaintance with the Navejoes that was very confidencial we were verry suppicious of them. [They] Haveing commited maney Depridations on the Frontiers of Utah.[23]

While this feeling was general, it was not directed alike toward all Navajos. Some, such as Hamblin's old friend Spaneshanks, whose daughter had married Ira Hatch, a noted Indian scout, were recognized as friends. Enemies, too, were well known, and a surprising amount of detail had been gleaned as to what subtribes and bands had been involved in the raids of the past decade. Ammon M. Tenney, for example, professed to know that a certain renegade Ute called Pahtnish and his band of malcontent Navajos had killed two Utahns at Pipe Springs in 1866.

James S. Brown, explorer and founder of the mission at Moenkopi, was frequently greeted by heckling and other annoying acts when he pressed himself upon the Navajos during a series of missionary trips in 1876 and 1877. Beneath such manifestations of hostility was a growing fear that the Mormon invasion would extend into Navajo lands. Although Brown and other missionaries tried to reassure the Indians, even taking two deputations to Salt Lake City for consultation with Brigham Young, warning signals continued to appear. Even the more friendly and responsible leaders joined in the protest. Brown tells of a meeting with "Totoso-ne-Huste, the head chief of the Navajo nation," who on being informed of Mormon colonization plans requested that he be taken to Utah to discuss the question with church leaders. If Brown's account may be trusted, the old chief expressed the Navajo point of view with restraint and kindness but also with clarity and firmness when he said:

We are glad that you come among us as friends, that you are making a road through our country, and that you have built houses at Moencoppy. We want to live with you in peace and let your animals eat grass in peace. But water is scarce in this country, there is barely enough for our numerous flocks and increasing people, and our good old men do not want your people to build any more houses by the springs; nor do we want you to bring flocks to eat the grass about the springs.[24]

Two years later when Silas S. Smith and the explorers of the San Juan expedition made their way from Moenkopi to the San Juan River,

---

23 "Diary of Christian Lingo Christensen," pp. 19-20.
24 Brown, *Life of a Pioneer,* p. 491.

they were given a similar message but with much less restraint. Their livestock and lives threatened, the explorers averted disaster by capable diplomacy and by digging wells in the neighborhood of waterholes which not only supplied their own animals but permanently enlarged the meager springs whose limited waters were the primary cause of most of the hostility.[25] Later, Navajos in the Moenkopi area levied something of an unstated tribute on the livestock of settlers. Usually this was a matter of butchering single animals or stealing calves to be raised with sheep and goat herds. A late outburst of Navajo hostility resulted in the already mentioned death of Lot Smith in 1892.

But in the main the Navajos were remarkably complacent. As far as this writer has been able to learn, the actual movement of Mormons into Arizona was conducted with no loss of life to the Navajos. Settlers on the Little Colorado appear to have been quickly accepted. During the first hard days of 1876, one of them wrote:

Our relations with natives . . . have been of the most friendly nature. One of them said he had been told we were coming and had little children and thought they might be hungry. . . . The Navajo chief Comah said he was pleased to have us come and live here. They . . . went away well pleased.[26]

By 1878 missionaries in New Mexico lived in small groups or by themselves scattered among the Navajos, whom they found to be receptive to their message and of a generous make-up. As the years passed, substantial numbers of Navajos, some of them prominent, joined the church in New Mexico and elsewhere. Without really understanding what church membership implied, they were most friendly to the Mormons. This was particularly so of two local chieftains of the Ramah area named Jose Pino and Jose Cojo. According to the later account of a man who grew up at Ramah, a thorough social integration had taken place by the 1880s.[27]

A notable evangelizing success was achieved among the Navajos of the Cottonwood Wash area north of St. Joseph during 1883 and 1884. At that time, upward of a hundred were baptized by C. L. Christensen, John McLaws, and one or two other missionaries. Along with graphic preachings about the evils of "adultry, Whiskey drinking and Card Playing," the Indians may have been influenced in their conversion by a recent visit of one of their numbers to Washington, D.C. The visitor, an aged man, "said the americans Were innumerable, He Said it made Him Sick

---

[25] "History of the San Juan Stake," compiled by Andrew Jenson, HDC. Also see Miller, *Hole-in-the-Rock*, pp. 20-34.

[26] Letter of Lot Smith to the *Deseret News* from Sunset, April 28, 1876, quoted in "History of the Little Colorado Stake."

[27] Paris Ira Ashcroft, "Life Sketch," mimeographed copy in the possession of Ida Galagher, Salt Lake City, p. 6.

to See the Sight and He Wished He Was Home." Dismayed at his report, the tribal fathers agreed that they "Would not go to War" in spite of the fact that four Navajos had recently been murdered by whites.[28]

Almost no effort was made to tutor the Navajos in the skills of industry and agriculture. This may have been due in part to the nomadic patterns of Navajo life; it may also have been a reflection of changing times and a shift in emphasis from the spiritual duty of proselytizing to the temporal necessities of colonization.

Zuñis

Missionary work among the Zuñis was a direct outgrowth of Daniel W. Jones's expedition to Mexico in 1875-76. Two of his party — Ammon M. Tenney, who had been called late in 1874 to assist Jacob Hamblin in his work "across the river among the Navajoe nations," and Robert H. Smith — chose not to accompany Jones into Mexico and were "given the privilege of laboring in New Mexico among the Pueblos and Zuñis."[29] Tenney and Smith arrived at the pueblo of Zuñi on April 2, 1876. The Indians, though initially somewhat reticent, soon warmed, gathering in large numbers to hear the missionaries preach. Smith recounted the exciting events of their first day at Zuñi:

We held meeting after meeting with them and explained to them the principles of the gospel, and also told them that the *Book of Mormon* was a history of their forefathers, which greatly pleased them, as they said it was in fulfillment of what had been promised them by their forefathers. Many of the leading men said they believed all we told them, and that their fathers had often told them that at some time in the future a class of intelligent people would come among them, and bring them a knowledge of whom they were and where they came from.[30]

After spending several weeks and performing 111 baptisms, Tenney and Smith returned to Utah where they reported their success to Brigham Young. Wasting no time, the latter called Lorenzo H. Hatch and John

---

[28] See "Diary of Christian Lingo Christensen," pp. 49-51. Also see "Diary of John McLaws, Jr.," original in possession of John W. McLaws of Holbrook, Arizona, typescript BYU, pp. 150-72. Among those baptized was an old man who claimed to have been in the 1877 Navajo deputation that visited Salt Lake City. It is said the he was the last man to shake the hand of Brigham Young, who, as James S. Brown verifies, passed away the same day as the Indians visited him. See Brown, *Life of a Pioneer*, p. 493.

[29] Tenney's letter of appointment is among the James W. Le Sueur Papers, AHS. For the decision to send Tenney and Smith to New Mexico, see Jones, *Among the Indians*, pp. 219-60.

[30] See "Robert H. Smith, Among the Zunis," *The Juvenile Instructor* 11 (1876): 224.

Maughan to take their families and locate among the Pueblos. On their arrival in September, Maughan and Hatch worked diligently but enjoyed no repetition of the earlier success. Long exposed to whites and very much under the influence of their own spiritual advisers, the Zuñis were now unmoved by the Mormon story.

Nevertheless, Mormon excitement over their associations with the Zuñis did not subside for several years. The high anticipation stirred by the experience of Smith and Tenney was fortified by two subsequent events. The first of these involved the remarkable and rather thoroughly documented faith healing of about four hundred Zuñis, many of whom had smallpox. Arriving at their village on January 20, 1878, Indian missionary Llewelyn Harris put up at a home where three children lay ill with the disease. During the night, he blessed the children, one of whom according to his own account had stopped breathing.[31] All three made sudden and complete recoveries. This word soon passed around the village and during the next few days Harris made his way from home to home, leaving relief in his wake. The disease, however, continued to spread, and on a final day he began his ministry in a large room to which the stricken and the threatened came. Working from eight in the morning until sundown, he was told by a Mexican interpreter who accompanied him that he had blessed no fewer than 406 people, many of whom were healed.[32]

As diverse accounts of these extraordinary proceedings worked their way back to Utah, they stirred such interest and controversy that Church Historian Orson Pratt ultimately investigated them. In addition to Harris's own account, Pratt took statements from A. M. Tenney and L. H. Hatch, respectively president and outgoing-president of the Zuñi mission. Their conversations with Zuñis who were healed, or present when others were, substantiated the general truthfulness of the story, though no more specific estimate of the number involved could be had than vague statements that there were "lots of them."[33] Receiving wide coverage by word of mouth and in the Mormon press, this story is interesting in its own right, but it is summarized here primarily as an explanation for the persistence of great interest in the Zuñi mission.

Another factor in the sustained enthusiasm for New Mexico's Pueblo Indians was a visit Apostle Wilford Woodruff paid them in 1879. The sedentary qualities that had attracted Spanish attention centuries before now wrought their influence upon him. Taking note of the Zuñis, Lagunas, and Isletas, he estimated that they numbered some thirty-two thousand

---

[31] *Millennial Star* 41 (June 1879): 337.
[32] *Ibid.,* p. 338.
[33] See letter of A. M. Tenney to L. H. Hatch, February 20, 1879, *ibid.*

in forty villages, some of which were almost opulent by comparison with the destitute Indians he had seen elsewhere. Conducted by Ammon M. Tenney, whose easy confidence and promoter's instinct captivated him, Woodruff's visit was highlighted by a rich experience among the "Lagoonie" Indians. After a powerful sermon by Woodruff, the elders were informed that their message of the Book of Mormon was the first word the Zuñis had heard of Christ as he should be taught. The impact of this experience upon Woodruff is clear in the following from his journal:

This speech brought me to my feet. . . . The spirit of God rested upon me and I taught them in great plainness. . . . I felt as though we could soon baptize them all. . . . While I was speaking the oldest woman of the tribe over 80 years old arose and commenced talking. . . . She said that when she was a girl her Grand Father told her that when she became old, she would see men come from the west, who would teach them the gospel and work out salvation, redemption and deliverance to the Indian race and she says the men are here before us tonight.[34]

Woodruff left New Mexico convinced that the Pueblos were no mere Lamanites cursed and benighted but actually "Nephites," a more righteous but generally extinct Book-of-Mormon people. The Zuñis, he felt, were "in advance . . . of other Lamanites," the Lagunas "much above the Zuñis, and the Isletas . . . far above them all." In correspondence with church President John Taylor and the Council of the Twelve, he wrote freely of his impressions:

Their bearing and dignity in their intercourse with strangers, and, above all else, the expansion of their minds and their capacity to receive any principle of the Gospel, such as endowments or sealing powers, fully equal the minds of any of the Anglo Saxon race. While I have been standing in the midst of that noble-minded people, teaching them the gospel, I could not make myself believe I was standing in the presence of American Indians or Lamanites, neither was I.[35]

The invitation to bring lost Israel to the fold seemed only too patent to Wilford Woodruff, and he concluded his letter:

Thus, dear brethren, I have given you an outline, merely, of the field of labor which I consider the God of Israel has opened unto us, and which I consider the revelations of God require us to perform. I think there is element sufficient for forty good, faithful elders.[36]

----

[34] Woodruff felt that he was divinely directed in his visit to the Pueblos and that they had premonitions of his coming. He wrote: "In what way, I do not know, but in almost every village I visited, they were looking for me." See "Wilford Woodruff's Journal," August 18, 1879.

[35] Letter of September 15, 1879, as quoted in Cowley, *Wilford Woodruff*, p. 522.

[36] *Ibid.*, p. 527.

Other problems demanded Woodruff's attention, and the build-up of elders that he had visualized never occurred.[37] Those that did come found none of the enthusiasm that the apostle had stirred in the Pueblos during his brief sojourn. For all the marvelous works of conversion and healing and for all of Woodruff's enthusiasm, the apathy of the natives and the pressures of colonization quickly brought the Zuñi mission to naught.

It seems likely, however, that New Mexico's Pueblo Indians were indebted to the Mormons for one thing — the smallpox. Brought into the region by migrating southern Saints who had been exposed en route during the late autumn of 1877, the disease affected most of the Mormon communities, but, through good fortune and quarantine practices, which included posting guards around Indian villages to keep the natives home, the whites survived without heavy mortality. Living in villages, the Pueblos were easy prey to the disease. In spite of the blessings of Llewelyn Harris and all other precautions and aids, they died in large numbers. Missionaries who passed through Zuñi as the virulence of the disease abated in mid-February of 1878 "learned there had been from 150 to 200 deaths."[38] In all fairness, it should be noted that the disease might have ravaged the Pueblos had the Mormons never been heard of, as the Mormon migration was not the only movement on the frontier that year. However, without exception, Mormon accounts attribute incidents of the disease among their own people to contact with the southern Saints.

Apaches

During its earliest years as a territory, Arizona had been, in the words of Senator Benjamin Wade "just like hell" lacking only "water and good society."[39] The absence of good society was in no small part due to Apache hostilities which in the 1860s and the early 1870s had come near to being a way of life with whites as well as natives. Observing the situation, General E. O. C. Ord wrote in 1879 that "hostilities in Arizona are kept up with a view of protecting the inhabitants, most of whom are supported by the hostilities."[40] Beleaguered by Apaches, Arizona was thus something of a garrison state. This fact was not lost upon the first Mormon immigrants to whom the conduct of the Apaches was not without its reward. Prolonged hostilities contributed not only to the isolation essential to

---

[37] Woodruff's unflagging determination to build up St. Johns, which lay closer to the Zuñi villages than other Mormon towns of any size, may have been related to the intrigue this tribe held for him.

[38] *Millennial Star* 41 (June 1879): 341.

[39] Quoted by Howard Roberts Lamar, *The Far Southwest 1846-1912: A Territorial History* (New Haven: Yale University Press, 1966), p. 415.

[40] *Ibid.*, p. 432.

Mormon expansion but initially at least, resulted in a warm reception from Arizona's limited white population. According to Prescott's *Arizona Miner,* the "long tusseles with the Apaches had knocked all nonsense" from Arizonans with regard to any peculiarities in the character of prospective reinforcements.[41] Neither was the potential of the Latter-day Saint as shock trooper lost on observers elsewhere. Writing in this vein as the Mormon mission of 1873 approached Apache country, one New York correspondent noted:

> The true Apaches are the most intractable Indians in the world . . . and it would be the most wonderful metamorphosis in all history if Brigham Young could bring these human tigers into the snug and comfortable sheepfold of his Church, and they remain there peaceable and good and not devour the lambs. Doubting whether he has that regenerating power at his command, we shall not be surprised if he does not soon substitute trusty rifles for the sermons he is preparing to preach at the Apaches, and find the best use for those powerful compositions in gun-wadding. In other words, we expect that the Mormons will clean out the Apaches. If they do not, they will themselves be cleaned out. So large a Mormon population as will be transplanted to Arizona will, however, be more than a match for the dwindled Apache tribe. The proposed movement, regarded in any light, is a most important and interesting one; and whatever Young's secret motive may be, it will have the effect of preparing the way for the settlement and development of all of Arizona that is fit to inhabit.[42]

However, the first Mormon colonists were as awed by the Apache reputation as anyone and certainly entertained no idea of subduing them by force of arms. Charged not to penetrate too deeply into Apache land, the mission of 1873 had stalled on the desert some two hundred miles short of it and seemed only too glad to turn from the country without checking its prospects more closely. By 1876 this reticence had been somewhat overcome. Early that spring, the Daniel W. Jones expedition made its way safely through several tribes of Apaches and found Croydon E. Cooley living with his two Apache wives within a few miles of the main camps of the White River tribe. Jones's impression that the Camp Apache military attachment was competent to maintain tranquility was fortified during the summer as officers visited the encamped Mormons on the lower river and offered help in case of Indian unrest. By 1877, as we have seen in an earlier chapter, Mormon settlers were moving freely through Apache country and even going so far as to establish two settlements, Cluff's and Forest Dale, closer to the Indians than Cooley himself. Others located at the head of the Little Colorado on Show Low Creek, and other remote

---

[41] *Deseret News,* June 25, 1873.
[42] *Journal of Commerce,* quoted in *Millennial Star* 25 (August 1873): 543.

spots with a casualness that resulted in sharp sermons of protest from their leaders. In the main, however, the settlers' confidence was ratified by experience, as even during the periods of Apache unrest few lives were lost.

Not surprisingly, the Mormon approach to his Apache neighbors differed substantially from the pattern followed in relation to the other tribes. There appears to have been little hope of converting them. With the exception of a brief upsurge in Wilford Woodruff's interest when he accompanied the Apache war chief Pelone on a remarkable hunting trip and of the dogged determination of two Indian missionaries, Ebenezer Thayne and Llewelyn Harris, the tide of idealism that drew Mormons to the Hopis and the Zuñis was notably lacking.[43]

Another factor in the altered approach to the Apaches was that there was less need for missionary diplomacy to control them. The burden of defense was generally acknowledged to lie with the army detachment at Fort Apache. The "peacemaker" role played earlier by Jacob Hamblin and to a degree by Indian missionaries among Arizona's other tribes was consequently less necessary.

There was, however, some occasion for Mormon diplomacy. Beginning with the daring raids of Victorio in the summer of 1880, Apache disorders became general by the next summer, finally reaching a climax and settlement in 1882. Having little recourse, the Mormon settlers of Alpine and other villages on the headwaters of the Little Colorado met Victorio with a policy of appeasement and retraction. By respecting life and limb above property, they were able to avert bloodshed, though nearly every horse in the entire region was sooner or later taken.[44] The only armed brush with Victorio occurred when a group of the Mormons resisted turning over twelve horses the Indians wanted. Fighting a careful action as they retreated to "the little Mexican fort of Rita Camada" in New Mexico, they escaped without injury, though one horse was killed.[45]

In the tense months that followed, the Apaches, including a number of Indian scouts who were nominally in the service of the U. S. Army, were rallied by an Indian prophet. Failing to effect his capture until the summer of 1881, the army then bungled so badly that the scouts mutinied

---

[43] An avid but not overly successful sportsman himself, Woodruff was enchanted and intrigued by a very successful hunting trip he made with Pelone. For a vivid account of the same, see "Wilford Woodruff's Journal," August 1, 1879.

[44] According to Evans Coleman, 125 horses were taken in one raid, most of them belonging to William Maxwell. Operating in large bands, the Indians became so brazen that horse herds were taken from the herders, who were motioned out of the way by the well-armed Indians. See "History of the Coleman Family," Coleman Papers, AHS, pp. 12-13.

[45] *Ibid.*

and attempted his rescue. In the ensuing melee, the prophet was killed along with several soldiers. The mutinied scouts then retired to the mountains where they remained at large until the entire incident was forgotten. Scattered Mormon ranchers were advised to move in and fort up. Erastus Snow, who "had lately come from Utah," advised that the "best way to preserve peace is to be prepared for war."[46] Half-hearted attempts were made to build forts on the upper river and to organize militia companies. Likely the most impressive result was Fort Moroni, which John W. Young built to house and defend his tie-cutting crews at Leroux Springs. Meantime, messengers maintained contact with more pacifically inclined Indians, and Mormon leaders joined C. E. Cooley and army officers in an effort to bring an end to hostilities.

The final phase of this period of disorder came early in June of 1882. Reflecting the passing nature of the tension, Mormons had reoccupied Forest Dale late in 1881. Their return triggered a new, although fairly limited outburst which in this particular phase appears to have been aimed primarily at the Mormon settlers. Rightly convinced that Forest Dale lay on the reservation, White River Apaches pushed to rid themselves of the interlopers. When the settlers offered a cash settlement for the use of the land but resisted eviction, renegade bands swung north through the scattered ranches of Show Low Creek and west along the Mogollon Rim, killing and stealing livestock. Warned, most of the settlers left their ranches and belongings, pausing only to bring such things as were immediately at hand.[47]

Some settlers, either unwarned or ignoring the warning, did not flee quickly enough. Merlin Plumb, meeting a small band of renegades at Silver Creek Crossing above Shumway, did not stay to contest when fired upon. His horse grazed by a bullet, he raced for the settlements and arrived, foam-and-blood-flecked, about an hour later at Taylor where he caused further excitement and anxiety. Nathan Robinson was not so lucky. Happening upon a band as they butchered his cows, he was killed and his body unceremoniously dumped in Show Low Creek, where it was found the following day. Taking what half-dried jerky they could carry with them and driving a few head of stock, the Apaches disappeared into the mountains to the south.

By now thoroughly alarmed, the Mormons worked quickly but with a good deal of haggling to arm themselves. At Taylor, St. Johns, and

---

[46] Smith, *Journal of Jesse N. Smith,* p. 254.

[47] One woman is said to have fled leaving $1,200 in gold coin at Reidhead, which was duly retrieved by a posse sent out to get it. See "Incident in Jane Hatch's Youth," as narrated by Ann Hatch Lewis in "Diamond Jubilee Gems, Snowflake Stake of Zion."

St. Joseph, militia groups were hastily organized and, as it became apparent that the scare was over, fell to pieces almost as quickly. Elsewhere guard was kept at night for a week or so, but by mid-June ranchers began to return home and soon things resumed their normal course — or they did everywhere except at Forest Dale. There the unwilling settlers were counseled that "it was better to leave the place than to bring on an Indian war by staying."[48] Though a few warm spirits threatened to contest the appeasement policy, the reasons for yielding were overwhelming; soon Forest Dale assumed its normal character, and nearly a century later still stood a pretty forest glade, stirring vague memories among Arizona Mormons of their most serious brush with the Apaches.

The Organization and Role of the Indian Mission

The Little Colorado colony was frequently referred to as an Indian mission. Colonists were told at the time of their call and frequently reminded that they were sent to "help carry the Gospel" to the Indians. Moreover, the colonist was charged to be circumspect in his treatment of the red men and was apt to face punitive action in church courts if he abused them. In part this was doubtless a matter of maintaining tranquil relations, but it was also hoped that the existence of a well-ordered and kindly Mormon community among the Indians would make patent the distinction between Mormons and Gentiles, thus drawing the red men to the church.

In spite of the emphasis upon the mission to the Lamanites, Mormon-Indian fraternization was relatively limited. In a few cases Indians were instructed in the techniques of farming and water development. In others they were taken into homes, either as children or by marriage.[49] As elsewhere on the Mormon frontier, it was deemed cheaper to feed than to fight the Indians, and they were repeatedly given modest handouts in the form of food and clothing. For most Little Coloradans, however, association with the Lamanites was much more a matter of talk than it was of practice. In practical terms the colony was an Indian mission only in the most general sense. However, it helped support active missionaries through donations and by means of "missionary farms" which were worked in behalf of or reserved for the use of the preaching elders.

The primary obligation for carrying the gospel to the Indians fell upon a small group of men. Rarely numbering more than a dozen or two

---

48 Smith, *Journal of Jesse N. Smith,* p. 261.

49 In the case of the latter, the alliance always appears to have been between white men and Indian women rather than the other way around.

and dwindling in size as sagging morale and poverty took their toll, they were confronted by almost insurmountable odds. During the first years, they were headed by presidents whose relationship to the stake organization was generally conceded to be subordinate. First L. H. Hatch and then Ammon M. Tenney presided over the mission. Both were men of some stature, but both tired rather quickly. Thereafter, the mission limped along under the direction of the stake president, who was able to give it only sporadic attention. Missionaries were ordained as such and apparently had no other church obligations. With the exception of such limited help as came from the sources mentioned, they were self-sustaining. Under these conditions their mission work was occasional and varied greatly in extent and effectiveness. Llewelyn Harris and Ebenezer Thayne were either the most faithful missionaries of the earlier years or wrote more about their activities. Their perambulations carried them repeatedly from one end of the colony to the other, with Harris, at least, ranging as far south as the San Carlos Apache Reservation.

The general direction of the Lamanite mission lay somewhat more in the hands of visiting authorities from Salt Lake City than did other church matters. Of the many apostles who traveled in Arizona before 1890, Wilford Woodruff and Brigham Young, Jr., took the most active interest in the Indians. Woodruff's influence was great but short lived. Brigham Young, Jr., who by 1882 had replaced aging Erastus Snow as the primary agent of colonization on the Colorado Plateau, probably had the most lasting effect upon the work among the Lamanites. For several years after 1883, as polygamy charges forced the Mormon apostles to leave Salt Lake City, the church sought to capitalize upon their exile by revitalizing the various Indian missions. Giving Young and his companion in exile, generally Heber J. Grant, something to do, the renewed emphasis also served to bring the Indians into closer contact with the Mormons, enabling the latter to counter adverse influences during this threatening time. Assuming the Hispanicized alias of B. Joven, Young spent much of his time on the Colorado Plateau during the next four or five years.[50] Reminding settlers that "every man and woman in this country . . . are called to assist in this labor of civilizing the Lamanites," he stirred the mission into activity again.[51] Little permanent spiritual gain appears to have been made.

---

[50] According to one oral report, Young made his headquarters in the rough country northwest of Bluff in southeastern Utah. While there he is said to have found time among his missionary activities to take two additional wives from among local Mormon girls. From a personal interview with Judge Fred W. Keller of Price, Utah, February 2, 1967. Judge Keller spent many years in the early part of the century in the San Juan area where he became thoroughly conversant with the folklore of the region.

[51] "Minutes of Eastern Arizona Stake Conferences, 1883-1885," p. 25.

As indicated in the foregoing paragraph, missionaries served as diplomats and agents of control. Jacob Hamblin, who, incidentally, was entirely superceded as missionary and explorer within a year or so of his migration to Arizona in 1879, had served as an emissary of peace and a goodwill ambassador during all his long activity on the Utah frontier. By merit of their greater intimacy with the Indians, missionaries continued to play this role. During the tense times at Forest Dale, for example, Harris and Thayne not only stood between less altruistically inclined Mormons and the aggrieved Indians but also negotiated with the army and Indian agent at Fort Apache.

Far across the Little Colorado Basin at Moenkopi, Christian Lingo Christensen was also a frequent intermediary. Arriving home in May of 1885 after a period of exile in Mexico, Christensen was greeted by a delegation of his townsmen demanding that he sign a petition requesting the removal of the Indians. Refusing, he soon placed himself in touch with Tuba, who thought that the roots of discord lay in the fact that there had been no interpreter during Christensen's absence. The friction continuing, Christensen repeatedly sought out the old chief and, after negotiations that proceeded intermittently for the better part of a year, was finally able to restore mutual good feeling and cooperation.[52] Heeded and trusted, such men made a vital contribution to what James H. McClintock has called a "Peaceful Conquest" as the Mormons settled in Arizona.[53]

Mormons were prone to attribute the general peace that followed their arrival in Arizona Territory to their constraining influence and diplomacy. Perhaps the most assertive claim of this kind was made by Erastus Snow at a Salt Lake City conference in 1882, a few months after he had observed the Apache "prophet uprising." He declared:

To-day the American nation is indebted for the spirit of "Mormonism" that has been diffused through this mountainous country in the maintenance of peace, and the saving to the nation of millions of treasure as well as thousands of lives. . . . The wars that have troubled the country during the last five years . . . have been, to my certain knowledge, greatly mitigated by the presence of our colonies on their borders, and by the labors of our missionaries among the Indians. . . . And I am a witness to the fact, that in every instance where the influence of our missionaries and our colonies has been exerted upon these fallen people, their chiefs have been imbued with the spirit of peace, and they in turn have exerted their influence on the side of peace. . . . And when they . . . have come to us to know our views and to seek our counsel, our advice has always been in the interest of peace, in the spirit of kindness; we have always taught them to restrain their hostile feelings, and have portrayed to them the benefits of peace, forbearance and long-suffering,

---

52 "Diary of Christian Lingo Christensen," p. 70-85.
53 See title page of McClintock, *Mormon Settlement in Arizona*.

and advised them to endure what they considered wrong rather than to attempt to redress their wrongs in their feeble, helpless condition, by taking up arms against the strong and powerful government of the United States; and besides, that it was displeasing to God.[54]

While it is difficult if not impossible to assess the real influence of Mormon missionaries and colonization upon Indian belligerence, there is no question that such influence as they did possess was exerted in behalf of peace. In spite of occasional concern on the part of the country's Gentiles that the missionaries were masterminding some kind of a diabolic Indian uprising reminiscent of the Mountain Meadows Massacre, there can be no question of the sincerity of their interest in a general and lasting tranquility.

Snow's proclamation that Mormon diplomacy was responsible for the general decline of Indian hostilities raises the broader question of the relationship between Mormon altruism and the expansion of the church. Certainly missionary activity was used as a pacifying agent, thus helping to render habitable, country in which hostile tribes made their homes. Moreover, the coincidence of Mormon expansion and of resurgent concern for the soul of the Lamanite suggests that Mormons found the salvation of the Indian to be more urgent when they had designs upon his lands.

Never entirely forgotten, the reclamation of lost Israel was of more importance at some times than others. Mission interest mounted as coloni- zation was pushed into northern Arizona. Remaining high as long as the future of the colony was insecure, the proselyting subsided as Mormon claims to the country were established only to revive briefly, as we have seen, when the polygamy raids again jeopardized the community. The sermons of the period during which colonization was initiated often related outward movement to the Indian mission. Perhaps no one sounded the theme more clearly than did Apostle Orson Pratt. Speaking in Salt Lake City in 1875, he called upon Latter-day Saints to redouble their efforts to redeem the Lamanites. Making the red man's conversion one of the prerequisites to the cherished Mormon dream of returning to Jackson County, Missouri, he declared:

This people — the Latter-day Saints, before they can ever return to build up the waste places of Zion and receive their inheritances in Jackson County, Missouri, have got to exert themselves to bring the remnants of Joseph to a knowledge of the truth. We have not made any very great exertions in this direction unto the present time. The Lord has given us time since he brought the fulness of the gospel from among the Gentiles to lay a foundation so that

---

[54] *Journal of Discourses*, vol. 23, pp. 8-10.

we could commence this missionary work in behalf of and among the remnants of Joseph. We have got the foundation laid . . . we have begun to prosper in the land, so that now I think, is the time for us to wake up our minds in relation to the scattered remnants.[55]

Not surprisingly, the consciousness of obligation to the Indians appears to have been sharpest in those areas where contact with them was most frequent. Among those who noticed this was Mrs. Thomas L. Kane. Making a trip through southern Utah's Indian country in 1873, she wrote of the fervency with which some Saints petitioned for the Indians, praying that they "might see visions and dream dreams that would lead them to embrace the truth."[56]

If altruistic feeling grew from association with the Indians, it was also the product of the emphasis placed upon the matter by church leaders. In addition to constant verbal exhortation, the Salt Lake authorities bombarded the Little Colorado settlers with directives relative to the subject. Typical was Brigham Young's letter of July 15, 1876, from which these lines have been excerpted:

We desire that the settlements in the Little Colorado be built up to the Lord in righteousness, wherein an example will be set to the surrounding tribes of Lamanites. . . . Treat them with kindness . . . set a proper example. . . . Instruct them in the Gospel. . . . Teach them to live in peace, become free from native vices and become useful citizens in the Kingdom.[57]

And again:

Your present position is an important one, surrounded as you are by the Lamanites. The influence of your settlements will spread. . . . It is desireable, yes it is indispensably necessary that influence be of the proper character. The Lamanites may receive an immense amount of wickedness from the so-called christians but from us they are to receive the gospel of the Son of God.[58]

It is significant that the major revival of mission impulse coincided with the polygamy raids. One important development that grew from the crisis was the renewed effort to carry the Mormon frontier on into Mexico. With an eye on what Albert K. Weinberg has termed "the land dowry of Mexico," the church's interest in missionary work among Mexican Indians,

---

55 *Deseret News,* March 3, 1875.

56 Elizabeth D. Kane, *Pandemonium or Arcadia: Which? Twelve Mormon Homes Visited in Succession on a Journey Through Utah to Arizona* (Philadelphia: privately published, 1874), p. 149.

57 Letter to Lot Smith et al., Lot Smith Papers, UA.

58 *Ibid.,* January 10, 1877.

at low ebb for several years, once again flourished.[59] Reflecting a new awareness of duty, Brigham Young, Jr., told Little Coloradans in 1883 that:

... the time is now come to preach to the Lamanites. The leaders of the Church have in view the 5,000,000 of Lamanites located in Mexico. [We] Never before knew how dark were the minds of those people.[60]

But the revival which led to the establishment of a permanent Mexican mission was a passing thing in northern Arizona. Soon more immediate and urgent challenges demanded the attention of settlers there, and as in the earlier case brave designs were forgotten and "Joseph's remnants" remained unregenerate.

In summary it may be noted that Mormon missionary work among northern Arizona's Indians produced little spiritual change in the Lamanites. Although it was a much-talked theme and psychologically important, more practical and self-oriented pursuits occupied most of the settler's time. As a result, only a few hundred Indians were baptized. A handful of these remained in contact with the church. None really became part of the Mormon community and none escaped the heritage of his past.

However, when considered as an agency of control on an expanding frontier, the Indian mission was more effective. As observers and diplomats, missionaries greatly facilitated colonization. Furthermore, the prospect of bringing about the regeneration and civilization of lost Israel helped justify the drudgery and sacrifice of pioneering and tended to obscure moral questions relative to the takeover of areas previously held by the Indians. Completely sincere in its professions of pacificism, the mission impulse also helped make the occupation of the Little Colorado frontier remarkably free of violence and bloodshed. Thus, in its major stated purpose of regeneration, the mission fell short. As an agency of expansion, it was of real utility.

---

[59] See Albert K. Weinberg, *Manifest Destiny: A Study of Nationalist Expansionism in American History* (Baltimore: Johns Hopkins Press, 1935). Of American attitudes during the Mexican War, Weinberg wrote: ". . . as the land dowry of the Mexican people came to appear more attractive, the mission of regeneration became more widely and impressively manifest." See p. 175.

[60] "Minutes of Eastern Arizona Stake Conferences, 1883-1885," March 25, 1883. It is interesting to note that at the same meeting where he expressed the above sentiments, Young told Mormon listeners who were having some difficulty with their Mexican neighbors at Concho: "If you are faithful and true to your religion the native Mexicans will not trouble you, but will sluff off and leave you." See Smith, *Journal of Jesse N. Smith*, p. 268.

10. THE POLITICS OF EXPANSION

How did Missouri and Illinois get rid of the Mormons? By the use of the shot gun and rope. Apache county can rid herself of them also. In a year from now the Mormons will have the power here and Gentiles had better leave. Don't let them get it. Desperate diseases need desperate remedies. The Mormon disease is a desperate one and the rope and shot gun is the only cure. The government refuses to do anything, and the people of Apache County must do something or the Mormons will soon drive them out. Take the needed steps while it is yet time. . . . No Mormon should be allowed to cast a vote. He has no rights and should be allowed none. Down with them. Grind out their very existence.

U. S. COURT COMMISSIONER GEORGE MCCARTER

. . . During the progress of these trials, hell appeared on every corner.

JOSEPH FISH

Mormon Values and the Forces of Arizona Politics

MORMON EXPANSION to the Little Colorado was vigorously and bitterly contested in local politics. Pursued with a boisterous disregard for fine points of the law by the Gentiles and an infuriating defensive unity by the Mormons, it was one of the most bitterly fought engagements of the long crusade against Mormon nonconformity. It erupted in 1879 and 1880 following the purchase of St. Johns. Rising with a noisy pitch to 1885, its passions quickly spent themselves, opening the path for adjustment by the early 1890s.

In order to understand the contending politics of Little Colorado expansion, it is necessary to line up certain values and commitments that influenced Mormon settlers as well as call attention to the established economic and political forces with which they had to deal. The political values and commitments of Little Colorado Saints were those of Mormondom generally. Polygamy proved to be of major significance. Other matters of importance included: the separatism of oasis agriculture, autonomy and self-rule; preemptive expansion with its special claims to such uninviting areas as northern Arizona; and an inability to understand and accept the American party system of leadership — a system whose basic premise of loyal opposition posed a fundamental contradiction to the Mormon doctrine of leadership by divine revelation.

Although much of Arizona lay beyond the pale of effective government in 1876, it was not a political void in which the life style implied by the values sketched above could be peaceably practiced. Instead it was a community in which Indian affairs, mining, frontier merchandising, transportation, agriculture, and livestock had, or soon established, vested interests in the territory and its various counties.[1] Breaking with the economic orientation that all of these held in common, the Mormons found no easy path into cooperating relationships. Pinning political hopes to the idea that in numerical superiority lay the basis of self-rule and security, they pursued a nonaggressive policy, sometimes seeming to seek peace by sinking beneath the political current and again trying to meet minimum needs through cooperative action with varying factions. This policy was less successful on the Little Colorado than elsewhere in the territory. The explanation for the force of the Mormon-Gentile collision there lies in the fact that in the early years Apache County was by far the area of heaviest Mormon population. Uneasy in the face of the challenge posed by the rapid influx of Mormons, Little Colorado politicians tended to let the Mormon question override all other issues.

Another factor that contributed to the controversy was the general moral laxity of Arizona politics. Law and order were under constant attack as opportunism and personal interest exceeded the bounds of propriety for even that permissive age. A raw mixture of fortune-hunting and quest for office affected political events at every level of government. Governors — John C. Frémont and A. P. K. Safford, to name two — were unblushing in the use of office to advance the financial cause of themselves and their friends.[2] The territorial legislature was sometimes afflicted

---

[1] For recent analyses of Arizona territorial politics, see Lamar, *The Far Southwest,* and Jay J. Wagoner, *Arizona Territory 1863-1912: A Political History* (Tucson: University of Arizona Press, 1970).

[2] See Lamar, *The Far Southwest,* pp. 469-70; Allan Nevins, *Frémont Pathmarker of the West* (New York: Appleton-Century Co., 1939), pp. 603-604; and E. E. Williams, "Anson Peacely-Killen Safford," *Arizona Historical Review* 7 (1936): 81.

with the same propensity — especially the Thirteenth Legislature, which in 1885 left such a trail of reckless extravagance and downright misuse of public funds as to give itself lasting notoriety.[3]

On the Little Colorado the time of greatest Mormon-Gentile discord was also a time of general lawlessness. In part this was the product of the controversy itself, law and principle being sacrificed to the intensity of feeling. But tension was fanned by a general permissiveness as the railroad and livestock frontier converged, bringing land-jumping, cattle-theft, robbery, beating, and murder in their wake. At the center of this surging violence was the Pleasant Valley War in which cattlemen and sheepmen struggled to dominate the Tonto Basin. Somewhat removed from the storm's vortex, the Little Colorado was nevertheless the scene of much bloodshed. Joseph Fish, Arizona's Mormon historian, chronicled some fifty violent killings in the neighborhood of Holbrook alone during the decade after the railroad was built.[4] Urged on by vigilante action (enthusiastically supported by the Mormons), the government brought the worst of this under control by 1887, the date again corresponding with a marked change in the course of the Mormon conflict — this time for the better.[5]

Propelled in large measure by factors not of their own making, Little Colorado Mormons were carried along by both the lawlessness of the early and middle 1880s and the process of adjustment that was emerging by the decade's end.

Apache County Politics: The Early Phase

Its development lagging, Arizona initially welcomed colonization by the Mormons. The immigrants were encouraged by their first contacts with Arizona officials. In addition to business with various county functionaries, they soon met Governor A. P. K. Safford, who passed through their camps during the fall of 1876. Safford found them to be an "energetic, industrious, economical," and "self-relying people." They were, he thought, just the sort needed to "use the vast unproductive lands of Arizona." While with them, he listened to their protest against the high land tax imposed by a territorial legislature, which up to that time had no real farming interest to consider in its deliberations. Without espousing their low-tax cause, he won their good will by proposing that "the toil

---

[3] George H. Kelly, *Legislative History, Arizona 1864-1912* (Phoenix: Manufacturing Stationers, 1926), p. 176.

[4] Fish, "History of the Eastern Arizona Stake," pp. 71-75.

[5] Forrest, *Arizona's Dark and Bloody Ground*, pp. 193-219.

worn immigrant who had come there with his wife and little ones to make a new home" to be temporarily exempted, "from the burthen of taxation."[6]

The scattered population of eastern Arizona was already developing vague political lines when the Little Colorado colony was founded. Within two years, these stirrings took definite form. Dominated by mining interests, Clifton in the far southeast of sprawling Yavapai County (which covered nearly half of the territory) and Globe at the east end of neighboring Maricopa County were maneuvering for political advantage. At St. Johns, which was still no more than a few sunbaked Mexican houses at a remote crossing of the Little Colorado, an ambitious merchant group headed by Solomon Barth and the Hubbell family was emerging. At Springerville and elsewhere about the region, a low-tax agricultural faction was awakening to the fact of its distinct identity.

These diverse elements shared one common aspiration — the creation of a new county which would bring the locus of government and its control more within their reach. Agreeing to name the new subdivision Apache County, they split sharply over the location of its seat. By election time in 1878, this issue had become a matter of heated contention everywhere on the east side of Yavapai County except among the Mormons. Busy with problems of colonization and admonished by church leaders to avoid "party conflict" even if it meant sacrificing their right to vote, they took little interest in the county-seat quarrel or in politics generally.[7] Running no candidates of their own, they were not only uncommitted but comprised the largest and most united group of voters in the eastern part of the county. As such, they were not permitted the luxury of total nonparticipation. Courted by each of the factions, they apparently followed economic dictates, giving their votes to the low-tax or Springerville candidates.[8] Among the latter was their friend James Stinson, who was elected to the territorial assembly.

---

6 See Safford to the *Arizona Citizen* quoted in the *Deseret News,* December 20, 1876. Writing in November of 1876, Brigham Young had advised Little Colorado settlers to "draft a memorial to the Governor and Legislative Assembly praying for present exemption from taxation on ground of being newly arrived settlers . . . asking as infant colonies, at least immunity from Territorial and County taxation until you become productive." Accustomed to property tax ranging from one-fourth to three-fourths of one percent in Utah, settlers found Arizona taxes which ran from 3 to 4 percent "perfectly startling." See letter of Brigham Young to Lot Smith, November 25, 1876, Lot Smith Papers, UA.

7 "Autobiography of Joseph Fish," p. 160.

8 Apostle Erastus Snow, who was in the area at the time, met several electioneering parties, all of whom were "very anxious to obtain the votes of our people for, as they say, 'your people generally vote one way, and whoever is successful in obtaining their votes must certainly be elected.' They are very friendly, and give assurances of their good will towards our settlers on this river and its tributaries." *Deseret News,* October 23, 1878.

— *James H. McClintock, Arizona*

Solomon Barth,
prominent merchant and
member of the St. Johns Ring.

— *Museum of New Mexico*

Lorenzo Hubbell, Indian trader and
merchant who was politically
active in Apache County.

At the legislature Stinson pushed through a bill creating Apache County, which included all the Mormon settlements of northern Arizona except Moenkopi. He also staved off determined attempts by the mining and merchant interests to capture its seat. He permanently foiled Globe's aspirations by leaving it under the jurisdiction of Maricopa County. Solomon Barth and his friends from St. Johns were not so easily frustrated, but Stinson was able to give them temporary check by locating the county seat at Snowflake until a special election could determine its permanent site and select its officers. Taking the important interim appointment of probate judge for himself, Stinson threw a number of significant if temporary offices to the Mormons, including several justices of the peace, the county recorder, and one seat on the powerful board of supervisors.[9]

At first glance Stinson's action appears to indicate both his closeness to the Mormons and their power in the county. Close examination, however, reveals that it was more likely the result of their neutrality and general political impotence. Stymied in his efforts to make Springerville the county seat and capture most of the offices for his low-tax colleagues, Stinson, it seems certain, had been forced to work out a modus vivendi with the Barth forces, giving the county seat to the Mormons and hoping that by so doing he could win their support for a future test of strength.

This test came in the special election of June 1879. The Mormons continued to play a cautious and passive role. Submitting tamely to the loss of the county seat, they satisfied no one when, seeking to avoid a head-on collision, they refused to take an official stand supporting either Springerville or St. Johns. Voting individually, they backed Springerville, giving it a clear victory, which was negated, according to Mormon sources, by ballot box stuffing and fraudulent counting by the St. Johns forces. Protests were ultimately appealed to Prescott, where the county seat was awarded to Springerville and the county offices to Barth and his candidates — an arrangement permitting the latter to control the next election and lay permanent claim to the county seat for St. Johns.

During the months that followed, the Springerville element lost much of its identity, merging with the Barth interests or throwing in with the Mormons, who, supplemented in numbers by continuing immigration, became increasingly important. Still hoping to avoid an open political rupture, the Mormons bought Barth's St. Johns holdings, by this means seeking to acquire control of the Little Colorado. Encouraged by the precedent set by Stinson and other landholders who had moved away after selling to them, Mormons hoped that Barth likewise would depart and that with him gone, the rest of the St. Johns Ring, as Mormons were now

---

[9] Fish, "History of the Eastern Arizona Stake," p. 30.

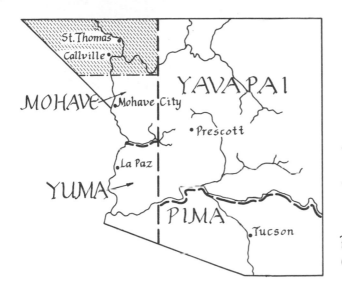

1864
SHOWING
ARIZONA'S
ORIGINAL
COUNTIES

1865
PA-UTE
COUNTY

TERRITORY OF ARIZONA

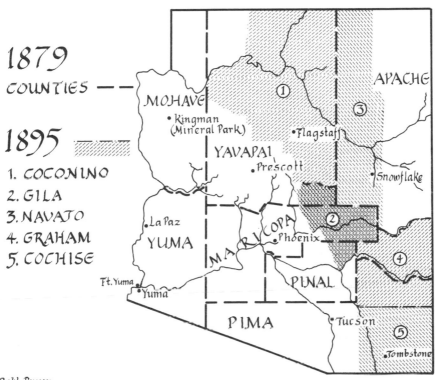

1879
COUNTIES ---

1895 ▨

1. COCONINO
2. GILA
3. NAVAJO
4. GRAHAM
5. COCHISE

Robb Russon

calling the merchant faction, would follow suit, leaving no effective opposition in the county. But Barth did not abandon the field. Retaining his commercial enterprises as well as connections with the region's Mexican people upon whom his political power rested, he continued to assert great influence upon the course of Apache County politics for many years.

Finding some sentiment for conciliation as the election of 1880 approached, the Latter-day Saints scheduled an autumn nominating convention at Snowflake to which they planned to invite Barth. The primary responsibility for bringing him along was placed upon Ammon Tenney, who had successfully negotiated the land purchase with him the previous fall. Busy with the railroad grading contracts of that summer, Tenney failed to make contact with either Barth or his own colleagues. Not hearing from him, the latter presumed that the hoped-for accord had fallen through, and proceeded independently to make up their own ticket. Uninformed of this action, Tenney belatedly met with J. L. Hubbell representing Barth and the St. Johns faction; breaking with the policy of caution, he pledged the Mormon vote to "the compromise ticket" which he and Hubbell "slated out" at that time.[10]

Learning of the Snowflake ticket, Barth and Hubbell took it as an act of bad faith, and ignoring all attempts at explanation turned completely against the Mormons. Resorting again to fraud at the polls, the St. Johns Ring easily retained political power. Although internal fissures occasionally resulted in friendly overtures from individual members, the Ring as a whole showed no further inclination to cooperate with the Mormons until late in the decade when time had swept away many of the earlier issues and personalities.

Until 1884 the Mormons continued to follow a submissive political policy. At the same time they carried on an aggressive colonizing program — especially at St. Johns — which negated much of the advantage of their political self-restraint. The issues that divided Mormons and Gentiles in Apache County during these years were almost entirely local. Originally more the means of the controversy than its cause, the polygamy question became increasingly important until by late 1884 it dominated the scene. In the early stages of the conflict, neither faction appears to have had outside affiliation except the relationship of the Mormons to the church. However, as the fight drew on, the Ring found it could rely upon the sympathy of powerful forces in the territory, including the executive and judicial officers. Yet there was little party politics in the ordinary sense, with neither side claiming any lasting bond with major parties until the election of 1886.

---

[10] "Autobiography of Joseph Fish," pp. 173-74.

Ammon Tenny, selected by the Mormons to effect
a conciliation with St. Johns Ring politicians.

A primary matter of contention was the control of county government. As noted, the Mormons staked their political hopes on numerical build-up. On the other hand, if Mormon accounts may be trusted, the Ring, which even with Mexican support was in the minority, maintained itself by open manipulation of the electoral processes. The Ring's system was not complex, but it appears to have involved a rather thorough-going perversion of certain American ideals. Ballot boxes were stuffed and vote-counting was doubly rigged, with the Ring appointing election officials and dominating the county supervisors to whom contested counts were appealed.[11]

Not content with such sure-fire methods, the Ring harassed Mormon voters, who found it necessary to vote in predominantly Gentile precincts. The dilemma confronting such individuals was manifest in Joseph Fish's words written after the election of 1882:

On November 7th I went down to Holbrook to attend the election there and watch and see if I could prevent any of the frauds that were being perpetrated at the elections by the ring. I soon found that I could do but little. A man stood in front of the polls armed as if for war and I was not allowed to come nearer than fifty feet of the polls and was threatened with arrest even before I had spoken a word to any one. I went up to vote and was marched back by the constable John Conley who again threatened me with arrest. In the meantime others who belonged to the party in power went up and voted without being molested. . . . I returned to Woodruff in the evening having accomplished but little only to find out how they ran things.[12]

Control of electoral affairs was completed by influencing the judicial system of the county. In addition to holding all law enforcement offices, the Ring dominated both grand and petit juries. Through the compliance of federal prosecuting attorneys, Barth managed to have himself appointed as a member and foreman of the first half-dozen grand juries that were empaneled. Barring Mormons entirely from jury service, the rosters were filled with members of the Ring and Barth's people. Judges and other court officials are also said to have connived in the electoral frauds by which the Mormon vote was subverted.[13]

Another point of friction was education. Determined that their children should be educated according to their own lights, Little Colorado Mormons had been hesitant to set up public schools. But hard pressed

---

11 *Ibid.*, pp. 175, 190.

12 In 1882 Barth, who had temporarily fallen out with the Ring, sought Mormon help. Deprived of the support of the county officers, even the resourceful Barth was unsuccessful. Joseph Fish explained this by noting, "no people in the world could beat the St. Johns ring in perpetrating frauds in election matters." *Ibid.*, p. 190, also Fish, "History of the Eastern Arizona Stake," p. 31.

13 Fish, "History of the Eastern Arizona Stake," p. 31.

economically and wanting something in return for the heavy property tax, they soon overcame their scruples and took advantage of the territorial public education provisions which had been a matter of pride to Arizona's citizens since the administration of Governor Richard C. McCormick in the late 1860s. The territory's school system was not only relatively effective but had already proven its worth as an agency of conformity. Arguing that the Mormons were mixing church and state in their public schools, as no doubt they were, the Ring, which had captured the county school superintendency along with all other offices, made it nearly impossible for them to pass the qualifying examinations to teach.[14]

Quite naturally the school board sought to exact a degree of conformity from the Mormon schools through its control of appropriations. Circumvented in most places by the Mormon willingness to lose funds rather than submit, it struck hard in St. Johns. Abolishing the Mormon district there, it consolidated their school with that of the Mexicans. Refusing, in their own words, "to associate their children with those of low filthy habits," the St. Johns Saints made private provisions for their youngsters.[15] There the issue might have rested had the Mormons been content to drop it, but they initiated legal proceedings to reclaim their school district along with the accompanying right to territorial school monies. This case, like others they brought before the courts at this time, was soon bogged down in a legal quagmire and nothing came of it. However, one court action carried. Antagonized, the school board brought an injunction ordering the St. Johns Mormons to assist in the construction of a new school house to meet the increase of enrollment anticipated from merging the two districts. Regarding this a rank injustice, Mormons resisted but eventually paid about $900 on the new school, to which, for a time at least, they did not send their children.[16]

The Polygamy Issue

Aggressive action on the part of the school board was only one manifestation of a general intensification of opposition during 1883 and 1884. Having seized control of county government and fended off challenges in the courts, the St. Johns Ring now gave notice that Apache

---

[14] For an example of Mormon experience in this respect see "Diary of Allen Frost," pp. 90-97.

[15] Fish, "History of the Eastern Arizona Stake," p. 63. Although most Mormon communities maintained independent schools during the early years and some, mainly by merit of their isolation, for decades thereafter, they objected less strenuously to public control of the schools after the general accommodation of the late 1880s. During the 1890s, schools at Springerville and elsewhere among the small mountain towns were "integrated."

[16] *Ibid.*

County was not big enough for themselves and the Mormons and broadened their attack. Establishing "anti-Mormon" newspapers, they made polygamy the focus of their new offensive and moved beyond the county limits, carrying the issue into the territorial courts and into the legislature.

The first move toward an Apache County press was made in 1882 when C. A. Franklin, a violent anti-Mormon, began publishing the *Arizona Pioneer* at St. Johns. Quickly failing, the *Pioneer* was sold to the Mormons and under the editorship of Miles K. Romney published as the *Orion Era*. Unwisely assuming an aggressively polemic tack, Romney printed as regular features strong indictments of the Ring and exposés of its members. At the beginning of 1884, the opposition founded its second paper — the *Apache Chief* — the editorial policy of which was even more extreme.

Published by George McCarter, a Mormon-baiting U. S. Court commissioner, the *Chief* flayed the church mercilessly from all angles but made a number of issues the special object of its vituperation. Prominent among these were colonization and the self-bolstering talk that resulted from it among the Latter-day Saints. Predictions of inevitable and total Mormon domination of the Little Colorado — frequently couched in what struck non-Mormons as an overweening and self-righteous confidence — were picked up by the *Chief* and anxiously waved as examples of the subversive designs of the Utah invasion. Characteristic was a report that church members were exulting in a period of slow business because "the Mormons can live, anyway, and hard times may drive out the Gentiles."[17]

Sermons in which church leaders hopefully looked for the downfall of the United States and the rise of the Mormon kingdom also made good grist for the *Chief's* mill. Reacting to one such speech, one St. Johns brother announced that "inside of fifty years the government will be controlled by Mormons" and that through the assistance of foreign nations and Providence the entire world would be under their rule in a century.[18] To emphasize that such sentiments were not idle talk and that they held direct and immediate implications for Apache County, the *Chief* reported late in the year that "800 wagons entered Arizona Territory" by way of Lee's Ferry in 1884.[19] If Mormons continued to come at this rate for two years, the editor worried, they would outnumber Gentiles in Arizona.

---

[17] *Apache Chief,* June 18, 1884 (to be found in ALA).

[18] *Ibid.,* June 25, 1884. There is no question that Wilford Woodruff, Erastus Snow, and others preached such doctrines from northern Arizona pulpits. For examples, see "Minutes of Eastern Arizona Stake Conferences, 1879-82," June 28, 1879, p. 87, where the former is quoted as saying: "There will be no United States in the Year 1890." Joseph Fish recounts a speech in which Snow predicted that "in fifty years hence . . . the sandy beach would mark the places . . . of Washington and New York." See "Autobiography of Joseph Fish," p. 236.

[19] *Apache Chief,* December 5, 1884.

One of the most unrestrained expressions of fear that the Mormon menace would overwhelm Arizona to appear in the *Chief* was a copy of a speech given on the Fourth of July 1884 at Prescott by Judge Sumner Howard, formerly prosecuting attorney at the John D. Lee trials. Howard had been appointed chief justice of the territorial courts of Arizona, and much to the dismay of the Little Coloradans presided over the district court that met at St. Johns and Prescott during 1884 and 1885. With little show of judicial restraint, he awakened Arizonans to the threat:

There is no danger which menaces this beautiful Territory equal to that black cloud that follows the blasting approach to a polygamous priesthood, and which has already cast its withering influence over the most beautiful portion of your Territory. . . . I say to you, fellow citizens that it is not only the design of the foul and unscrupulous priesthood to seize upon this Territory and those adjoining it but that it will be an accomplished fact unless there is a rising of the people of this Territory . . . to free themselves from the impending danger. . . .[20]

Reporting the trial of certain Mormon squatters, the *Arizona Weekly Journal* took a similar theme:

We hail with pleasure the dawn of the day when honest individual settlement of our productive valleys shall be protected by the law against the intrigues and grasping designs of the polygamous hordes of Mormonism, sent out from Utah to occupy, control and contaminate our beautiful territory. All honor to Arizona juries, they will do their duty and receive their reward in contemplating the grand picture of a settlement of Arizona by a free, honest, and virtuous people who owe no allegiance to treasonable, lecherous, bigoted priesthood.[21]

But the *Chief* needed neither the *Journal* nor Sumner Howard to call its attention to the threat of the Mormon invasion, nor did it yield to either in expressing anti-Mormon sentiments. Writing in May of 1884, over a month before Howard's Fourth of July oration, Editor McCarter fumed:

How did Missouri and Illinois get rid of the Mormons? By the use of the shot gun and rope. Apache county can rid herself of them also. In a year from now the Mormons will have the power here and Gentiles had better leave. Don't let them get it. Desperate diseases need desperate remedies. The Mormon disease is a desperate one and the rope and shot gun is the only cure. The government refuses to do anything, and the "people" of Apache County must do something or the Mormons will soon drive them out. Take the needed steps while it is yet time. Don't let them settle on any more of our lands; don't let them stop in Apache County. Hang a few of their polygamous leaders, such as Jesse N. Smith, Udall, Romney, Hunt and others of this nature and

---

[20] *Ibid.*, July 18, 1884.
[21] *Arizona Weekly Journal*, August 12, 1885, quoted in Udall and Nelson, *Arizona Pioneer Mormon*, pp. 122-23.

a stop will be put to it. . . . The good of the country demands this, and we expect every Gentile to see that it is carried out. No Mormon should be allowed to cast a vote. He has no rights and should be allowed none. Down with them. Grind out their very existence.[22]

The danger of a "treasonable, lecherous, bigoted priesthood" head-quartered in a distant place taking over and quashing all vestiges of "home rule" was also held before the readers of the *Apache Chief.* Judge Howard warned against government by a "supreme authority outside the Territory," declaring that it was better to "bear, invoke and implore the political power of the general government in Washington than the vicious influence of a political polygamous priesthood at Salt Lake City."[23]

Although converts of foreign birth came to the Little Colorado, as they did to other Mormon frontiers, their numbers seem to have been small. Yet the *Chief* picked up the foreign menace theme, writing as Mormons worked to secure a change in the county seat that the legislature would not "deliver American citizens to foreign domination."[24]

But the major emphasis of the *Apache Chief's* attack, as well as of the mounting tide of opposition, generally was directed against polygamy. Although Arizona Gentiles had been conscious of it at least since the time of Governor Safford's 1876 visit to the lower river villages, they appear as a rule to have winked at Mormon marital peculiarities during the early period of settlement. While the Mormons, who had assured Safford that no polygamists would migrate to Arizona, used the new colony from the first as a refuge for wanted bigamists, they also used a good deal of discretion, keeping signs of plural marriage below the surface. Aliases were given to prominent exiles such as Wilford Woodruff, who was known as Lewis Allen during his year in Arizona. Separatist tendencies also enabled them to avoid observation. Women, whether of monogamous or multiple families, rarely found their way from the Mormon towns into Gentile communities. The irregularities of polygamy were somewhat more difficult to conceal at St. Johns where bigamists lived in close proximity to the opposition, but even there it was so well hidden that court cases against St. Johns polygamists were prosecuted on the skimpiest evidence.

Not only did Utah bigamists come to Arizona, but many Mormons took additional wives after arriving. The secret rites of temple marriage had a special utility in such instances. Usually taking the Lee's Ferry route, prospective couples made their way as inconspicuously as possible over

---

[22] *Apache Chief,* May 30, 1884.

[23] *Ibid.,* July 18, 1884.

[24] *Ibid.,* July 11, 1884.

what came to be called the "honeymoon trail" to the St. George Temple, returning as man and wife but leaving little or no public evidence of the act to indict themselves.

In spite of secretiveness and the dearth of legal evidence, it was common knowledge that polygamy was practiced, and for half a decade between 1882 and 1887 Arizona Gentiles, particularly those in Apache County, departed their wonted permissiveness and made it the center of their attack upon the Mormons.

A number of factors may be cited as influencing the shift of Apache County's conflict from specific local issues to the broader one of polygamy. Personalities appear to have been important. George A. McCarter, for example, played a primary role in the changing climate of opinion. Arriving in St. Johns in 1882, he turned both his editorial pen and his position as court commissioner against polygamy with such an impassioned fury that he quickly eclipsed Barth and other old warriors of the anti-Mormon campaign. Of even greater importance was Sumner Howard. Appointed chief justice of the territorial courts in 1884, he threw himself into the fray with full energy, a fact which doubtless encouraged the flurry of polygamy cases that came before the district court at Prescott late that year; but his ardor quickly cooled, again helping to mold the course of Arizona's polygamy fight as his court became less congenial to crusaders.

The quickening tempo of the national attack upon polygamy also emboldened Apache County's anti-Mormons to increase their pressure. Such figures as Senators George F. Edmunds and Luke P. Poland were demanding and getting national attention and were heard even on Arizona's frontier. Editor McCarter regularly printed the following one-line item: "The *Chief* is for George F. Edmunds for President."[25] From Idaho came suggestive word of "test oath" legislation. And, of course, the rising clamor of the attack in Utah heralded a day of reckoning. Furthermore, the general atmosphere of excess and moral laxity which spawned the violence that characterized old Tombstone and the Pleasant Valley War also contributed to the mounting furor.

But the rush to impose political and moral restraints upon Apache County polygamists was in large measure homemade. As chronicled in the foregoing pages, local relations had become increasingly tense in the years prior to 1884. The election of that year in which Mormons and Holbrook politicians united in an effort to take the county seat from St. Johns fed the fires of controversy, giving uneasy Ring members reason to

---

[25] See for example, *Apache Chief,* April 11, 1884.

believe that immediate action to obstruct more successful future alliances was imperative. Allowing tempers no time to cool after the elections, the Apache County polygamy raid was initiated at the fall term of the district court in Prescott.

The proceedings of the raid, which members of the St. Johns Ring admitted were "instituted through malice and for political purposes," fell into two parts — one concerned with charges of polygamy and unlawful cohabitation, the other with perjury in a land case.[26] In the latter Commissioner McCarter carried his editorial feud with Miles K. Romney into the courts, charging him along with David Udall and Joseph Crosby, his witnesses, with swearing falsely that Romney had lived continuously for the requisite two years on a piece of land he was preempting. Doggedly pursuing the case, McCarter overcame several reverses to secure Udall's imprisonment in the Detroit House of Correction in August of 1885. Crosby was acquitted, and Romney, convinced that he had no chance for a fair trial, jumped bond and fled to Mexico.

Seven prominent Mormons, including Udall, Ammon M. Tenney, and William J. Flake, were indicted on the charge of polygamy and unlawful cohabitation by the August session of the grand jury at Prescott.[27] Of these, six were arrested and taken to Prescott where they were placed under bond in September. Long under the impression that bigamists married in Utah could not be prosecuted in Arizona, and assured by legal council that they would be further protected by an Arizona statute of limitations which required that such crimes be tried within three years of the time of commission, church leaders advised the accused to stand trial, hoping for a court victory that would enhance the territory as a place of refuge.[28] Hopeful of victory and willing to endure the risks involved because their trial now appeared to be a test case, all six of the accused appeared at the November term of court over which Sumner Howard presided.

The trial did not go as they had anticipated. Proceedings against Udall were dropped for lack of evidence, but the other five soon found that the place of marriage and the statute of limitations were no defense at all. Pleading not guilty, the first three were convicted, not under the Edmunds Act as they had expected but under a territorial bigamy law, and sentenced to fines of $500 and four years imprisonment at the Detroit House of Correction. The last two, seeing the course the trial was taking

---

[26] See letter of D. K. Udall to John Taylor, August 26, 1884, David K. Udall Personal File, HDC.

[27] Others were C. I. Kempe, P. J. Christofferson, J. N. Skousen, and B. H. Wilhelm.

[28] Smith, *Journal of Jesse N. Smith,* p. 294, and Fish, "History of the Eastern Arizona Stake," p. 36.

and assured of leniency if they pled guilty, did so, receiving $500 fines and six months in the territorial penitentiary at Yuma.[29]

To Mormons, the trials and the harshness of the penalties were harrowing experiences. Polygamist Joseph Fish, who wrote that "during the progress of these trials hell appeared on every corner," likely expressed the feelings of most.[30] There was, however, some variation of response. Even the principles reacted quite differently. Well treated during the trial and at the territorial penitentiary, William J. Flake found repeated opportunities to advance himself and the church and later recounted the incidents of this eventful period with such relish as to indicate that it was in the main a satisfying experience.

On the other hand, D. K. Udall, who kept a day-by-day record of his trial and imprisonment, felt that his dignity as a human being was debased at every turn. Nothing in either the proceedings or his surroundings comforted him. Officials were hostile, he was imprisoned in an oppressive subterranean jail, food was intolerable, and people from the community, a few of whom he engaged for sundry services, were undependable and dishonest. But such things could have been borne; the blow to Udall's pride and self-respect, on the other hand, seemed nearly intolerable. Reflecting an attitude that goes far in explaining the widespread reluctance of other Mormons to stand trial, he wrote while still in Prescott: "God only knows the misery of soul I endured in coming in here." And again he yearned: "Oh God, deliver me from Hell and give me my liberty."[31] Thus tormented, he found the months of his imprisonment to be a great ordeal.

The Little Colorado community was thrown into complete disarray by the trials. Their normal flow of life interrupted, many stake and ward authorities fled to Salt Lake City in December. Returning shortly with important church officials, including President John Taylor, they led a more general exodus to Mexico.[32]

While good accounts of the Mexican dispersion exist, it is difficult to determine how many persons fled, but it seems unlikely that more than

---

[29] Two others were indicted by the November term of the grand jury. One of these fled; the other stood trial, pleading guilty, and was sentenced to three months at the territorial penitentiary.

[30] See Fish, "History of the Eastern Arizona Stake," p. 36.

[31] Flake, *William J. Flake,* p. 102, and Udall and Nelson, *Arizona Pioneer Mormon,* pp. 126-27.

[32] The fears of the retreating Arizonans, who traveling incognito made a winter trip through the waist deep snow of the Kaibab Mountains, were greeted in Utah with tolerant skepticism. Even President Taylor at first counseled them not to be too sensitive, but word from Arizona soon altered his appraisal of the situation. Deeply concerned, he returned with them and helped plan the withdrawal of polygamists to Mexico. The best accounts of the Utah trip as well as the subsequent flight to Mexico is found in Smith, *Journal of Jesse N. Smith,* pp. 296-321.

ten percent of the colony's men made the trip with a somewhat lower proportion of women and children. Not even all polygamists took to the underground. Quite as prominent in some cases as those who left, the stay-at-homes were not disturbed and appear to have gone quietly about their ordinary pursuits. However, the polygamy scare did result in a loss of population and nearly stopped the Mormon migration to Arizona.

Sundering the colony physically, the raid resulted in a renewal of political and spiritual union. All pretense of cooperation with the Gentiles was temporarily dropped. For the moment the Mormon plan appears to have been to remove themselves as completely as possible from the public eye.

As polygamists hurried from the country during the early winter of 1885, another blow fell that seemed to justify their fears. Following the lead taken in the Idaho legislature that same year, prominent Republicans, including Governor F. A. Tritle, moved to disfranchise not only the polygamists but anyone believing in the doctrine. Chosen to introduce the bill was Apache County's E. S. Stover, long an advocate of barring Mormons from the polls and one of the group which had effectively interfered with their franchise by extralegal methods during the previous years. Easily passing both houses, the Stover bill was signed into law and seemed to insure the defeat of the Mormons. With their financial resources depleted by court cases and dispersion, they made no plans to fight the law.

Accommodation

It was just as well the Mormons did not fight the law advocated by Stover. In the first place, the "test oath" was upheld in the Idaho courts and ultimately by the Supreme Court in the case of the *People* v. *Davis*.[33] But more important was the fact that the forces that had spawned the anti-Mormon movement began to dissipate. Continuing over the next decade, this relaxation allowed a progressive accommodation between Apache County's Gentiles and Mormons.

One promising change, the election of Grover Cleveland, coincided with the polygamy trials of 1884. Soon hailed by Little Colorado Saints as the "first president of the U. S., from Van Buren down, who dared do justice for a Mormon," Democrat Cleveland broke the post-Civil War chain of Republican Presidents. Although his administration was not a time of tranquility for the church generally, his appointment of Conrad Meyer Zulick as governor interjected a new element into Arizona politics that bettered the lot of Apache County Mormons. Immediately following his appointment, Zulick began to build the Democratic party. In

---

[33] See Orson F. Whitney, *History of Utah* (Salt Lake City: Cannon and Sons, Co., 1893), vol. 3, pp. 725-29.

the process, he did not eschew controversial issues. Perhaps the most explosive stand he took was one favoring the Mormons. His first step was to pardon the polygamists serving terms in the territorial penitentiary. Next he used his influence to make the Stover bill's repeal an issue in the election of 1886. Although the matter threatened to create a fissure in his party, he overrode the opposition, binding the Mormons to his cause by promising to wipe the offensive legislation from the books. Following his lead, the Democratic legislature of 1887 restored the franchise by large majorities of both houses.

These developments were paralleled by change on the judicial front. Obvious in a sharp decline of interest in prosecuting polygamists, shifting attitudes are perhaps best traced in the events that led to Udall's pardon by President Cleveland before the end of 1885. It will be recalled that Udall had been indicted for perjury after swearing that Miles Romney had fulfilled the "continuous residence" requirement for proving up on land he had entered under the preemption law. Given to understand by the court clerk before whom oath was taken that "continuous residence" was more a matter of intent and improvement of the land than actual occupation, he had willingly attested that his colleague qualified. Claiming that Udall, who knew that Romney lived in town most of the time, had knowingly deceived the government, Commissioner McCarter was able to attract the full support of U. S. Attorney J. A. Zabriskie, who prosecuted the case. The court gave Udall no chance to testify or bring witnesses in reference to the mitigating circumstances under which the oath was taken, and the prosecution easily secured a verdict of guilty. Although the public at Prescott and the court seemed determined to convict Udall, there were uneasy stirrings even among avid anti-Mormons during the course of the trial. Noting that Joseph Crosby, Udall's non-polygamous co-witness, had been acquitted, the *Albuquerque Morning Journal* decried what seemed to be a tendency not "to strike straight from the shoulder" in an editorial entitled "Was It Mormonism or Perjury?" from which the following has been taken:

Joe Crosby was tried at the same term of court for the same offense on precisely the same state of facts and acquitted. Udall is a bishop in the Mormon Church, and Crosby is a lay member of the same Church. . . . It is a good thing to nab a Mormon bishop when he is guilty of practicing his polygamous doctrines and "cinch him" until he is perfectly cured of his lawless indulgences, but it is a very bad thing, indeed to convict such an individual of the grave crime of perjury and acquit another man of the same offense on the same state of facts.[34]

---

[34] Quoted from the *Albuquerque Morning Journal*, August 27, 1885, in Udall and Nelson, *Arizona Pioneer Mormon*, pp. 124-25.

Conrad Meyer Zulick, governor of Arizona Territory from 1885 to 1889, vastly improved the political position of the Little Colorado Mormons.

Almost immediately after the Udall trial there was a general effort to undo its work. The broadness of this reaction was such that plans to appeal the case were soon abandoned and the primary emphasis placed upon securing Udall's pardon. Surprisingly, even the officials of Apache County, all of whom were members of the Ring and some of whom had testified against him, now came to his aid. Declaring that his "conduct was such as to create for him an unblemished reputation," they petitioned the President "in the interest of justice to grant an unconditional pardon."[35] Even Judge Howard and U. S. Attorney Zabriskie sought his release, the latter stiffly confessing that a careful re-examination of the case had "raised reasonable doubt of . . . guilt" in his mind.[36]

As in the repeal of the Stover bill, the territorial executive also played an important role. Governor Zulick's young private secretary, Thomas E. Farish, was attracted to the case by Hiram B. Clawson, a Mormon pioneer in party politics who had come to Arizona as a liaison man between the church and Zulick's Democrats. Advised of the facts in the Udall case, Farish secured the help of an "assistant United States attorney for the Interior Department," who being close to the president conveyed the desires of the governor and his secretary directly to Cleveland.[37] Mormon petitions were also dispatched. Perhaps the most telling of these were made by John W. Young, who now in the East was on friendly terms with Grover Cleveland. Yielding to this solid show of sympathy, the president pardoned Udall on December 12, 1885.

Encouraged, Little Colorado exiles, most of whom had found only trouble and suffering south of the border, began to drift back from Mexico. The conditions they returned to soon led to a weakening of their isolationist and self-determinist policies. Immediately and in the long run, the result was an increasing role in the politics of Apache County.

A major feature in this accommodation was the progressive development of partisan politics. As noted earlier, the latter part of the 1880s was characterized by an accelerating movement away from the politics of narrow territorial interests. None of the traditional political elements ceased to exist, but a new contact with national parties removed the accent from intraterritorial conflict, including the Mormon controversy.

No force was more important in the development of party politics than the election of Grover Cleveland and his appointment of Democrats,

---

35 *Ibid.,* pp. 131-32.

36 *Ibid.,* p. 121.

37 Farish, noted primarily for his *History of Arizona* (8 vols.; San Francisco: The Filmer Brother Electrotype Co., 1915-18), remained on friendly relations with the church. Later, when he was doing research in the HDC, he wrote the article from which the above was extracted for the *Deseret News,* August 31, 1918.

especially Governor Zulick, to the territory's offices. With no real base of power in the Republican dominated post-Civil War period, Arizona Democrats had neither rallied as a party nor been of sufficient opposition to force much discipline or party loyalty upon the Republicans.[38] With important territorial offices in their hands and with Zulick's effective leadership, the three years of his incumbency enabled the Democrats to develop considerable cohesiveness. Seriously challenged, the Republicans too were forced to tighten party lines. As a consequence, issues that had existed previously in their own right were increasingly drawn into the spectrum of party competition.

For the Mormons of Apache County, the rise of two-party politics had a number of important implications. Among the first to become obvious was the fact that under party alignments the responsibility of county government fell less directly upon local factions. Bound to territorial and national seats of power, the parties easily controlled issues that had ruptured relations when county groups were left to contend by themselves. Even in 1885 when Zulick's hand behind the Democratic party first hinted at a new era, the party's impact upon the course of Apache County affairs was remarkable. With the tacit support of the loose congeries of interests that constituted the pre-Zulick Republican party, the St. Johns Ring had manipulated earlier elections to insure its continued control of public office and the effective decision-making processes of the county. The election of 1886, which was not only the first election in which the Democrats had emerged but ironically the only one in which Mormons were legally barred from the polls, was the first election since they became politically active in 1878 that the dominant clique had not seriously interfered with their voting. Insulated by their union with a major party, Little Colorado Mormons voted freely for the first time in nearly a decade in spite of the fact that they were technically disenfranchised by the Stover Act which was still on the books.

Between 1886 and 1890, Mormon political participation was limited almost entirely to the Democratic party. The Republican press charged Zulick with surrender to the church and feared that the Mormon-Democrats would place the balance of power in Mormon hands. On the other hand both the Mormons and the Democrats recognized the union to be of great utility.[39] Comprising one-fifth of the territory's non-Indian population and over half of Apache County's whites, the ostracized Saints seemed made to order to power-hungry Democrats. To the Mormons, Zulick's overtures were a godsend. During the first months of his administration, preliminary arrangements were worked out between himself and

---

38 Lamar, *The Far Southwest*, pp. 458-85.
39 Wagoner, *Arizona Territory*, pp. 242-43.

Hiram B. Clawson representing the church.[40] The way cleared, Jesse N. Smith was directed in October of 1886 by President John Taylor to "get the Saints in the various Arizona Stakes in line to sustain the Democratic nominees" as therein lay the church's only safety.[41] The Mormons voted overwhelmingly Democratic, helping to give the party a substantial victory. Thus bolstered, the Democrats also ran well in the elections of 1888 and 1890, although their successes were less marked than in the earlier year.

Meantime, Republicans continued to make anti-Mormon activity part of their program. Contending that the influx of Mormons jeopardized the political and economic rights of loyal citizens, they called unsuccessfully for legislation to restrict further immigration. They also sought to remove those already in the territory from effective political participation by reviving the Stover bill or raising other devices to disfranchise them. Desultory effort was made to reinstate the polygamy prosecutions, but for the most part the citizenry had lost interest, and few were found who were willing to stand the expense of travel and living away from home that was involved in grand jury and court duty.[42] A brief revival of the anti-Mormon press also failed to attract much enthusiasm.[43]

At the local level, Republican hostility began to erode soon after the election of 1886. Initially its crumbling was little more than a matter of votes and represented a victory of a kind for the Mormon policy of building population through colonization. Beginning in 1888 political necessity led Apache County Republicans to Mormon voters time and again.[44] A situation illustrative of this point developed in Apache County during the campaign of 1890. Determined to move the county seat to Holbrook, which was the region's rail outlet and commercial capital, Republicans on the west side of the county repudiated the anti-Mormon plank of the St. Johns-dominated platform, thinking thereby to win Mormon support for the proposed change. The St. Johns faction, which had just established the *Apache Review* expressly as an agent of its opposition to the Mormons and pledged itself to work for their expulsion, reversed its position as the prospect of a successful raid on the county seat loomed. Scuttling the *Review,* they too sought Mormon votes.[45]

---

[40] Clawson's role is frequently but vaguely referred to in Little Colorado sources. No reference to his Arizona activities is to be found in his own journals which are in the HDC. There is, however, some reference to meetings with Clawson in Zulick's papers at the AHS.

[41] Smith, *Journal of Jesse N. Smith,* p. 331.

[42] "Autobiography of Joseph Fish," p. 285.

[43] *Ibid.,* p. 259.

[44] *Ibid.,* p. 266.

[45] *Ibid.,* p. 277.

At the territorial level Republican leaders did not abandon their fight against the Mormons until 1892. Even then conciliatory action was based more on the church's surrender on the polygamy question and the subsequent relaxation of the raid in Utah than upon local issues. Touring the territory previous to the election of 1892, Governor Oakes Murphy told Mormons that immigration and the franchise would no longer be issues, and invited them to enter fully into Arizona politics.[46]

About the same time, Republican clubs were established throughout Apache County and other Mormon areas. Despite strong loyalty to the Democratic party, many Mormons joined the Republicans. Their division into two political factions marked not only their growing confidence but the consummation of an official policy of the church encouraging bipartisan activity.

Churchwide by 1892, the policy of dividing along party lines had its Arizona inception in the 1886 alliance with the Democrats. Fearing to surrender their maneuverability by committing themselves to permanent alliances, church leaders at first skirted both political division and binding commitments. However, by 1889 halting permission to let Arizona Saints follow their own inclinations in choice of party was forthcoming. Instructing leaders to "let the people divide on Republican and Democratic lines if they felt to do so," Salt Lake City authorities nevertheless cautioned that it was best to vote for men and measures rather than parties.[47]

About a year later, church officials from Colorado and New Mexico as well as Arizona met at Albuquerque, where more definite but still tentative directions were given them by the First Presidency. Recommending that the "Saints in Arizona . . . affiliate with the Republican party" as "far as practicable," Wilford Woodruff was apparently careful not to couch his directions in imperative terms and excused Jesse N. Smith and others from compliance on the "ground of intimate relations with the Democratic leaders and benefits received from them."[48] At a stake conference in Snowflake about a year later, Apostle John Henry Smith again "advocated the Republican course" showing that "we might make friends by voting that ticket." But he was also reported to have modified his remarks by adding that only "part" should support the Republicans as Mormons "ought to divide on politics."[49]

---

[46] *Ibid.*, p. 293.
[47] Smith, *Journal of Jesse N. Smith,* p. 373.
[48] *Ibid.*, p. 379.
[49] "Autobiography of Joseph Fish," p. 289.

Conclusion

During the years immediately after 1890, the pioneer period of Mormon political relations on the Little Colorado came to an end. The aspirations of setting up an adjunct of an independent Mormon kingdom in which substantial self-rule was to be achieved through prior occupation and the isolationism of oasis agriculture had given way to a limited political accommodation in which peace was achieved at the expense of the comprehensiveness of Mormon unity and the nonconforming practices of polygamy.

During the same period, territorial politics had also passed through a transition. Disparate economic interests with little more in common than their conviction that the government should serve their needs had yielded to a system that conformed in most respects with national patterns and in which national interests cut across and muted the violent interchange that characterized the relations of local interests of an earlier day. In the process of this transition, Little Colorado Mormons had become embroiled in a sharp controversy with the ruling clique in Apache County. The excesses that might have grown from their collision were happily averted by the broadening of the political base providing a field in which an adjustment could develop between a chastened Mormon community and their Gentile neighbors. Little Colorado Saints experimented with party alignment at a time somewhat before the church adopted an official policy encouraging it. While the fracture of Mormon-Gentile relations in Apache County had been more severe than elsewhere, the simultaneous development of party politics in the territory and division of church members between the two major parties created cross-currents of interests and political need which overrode the Mormon-Gentile cleavage, thus permitting an effective association of the two groups.

But in the Arizona of the 1890s, the forces of individualism and group interest had not joined completely. The Mormon colonists of the Little Colorado retained a distinct self-image in which most of their earlier values could still be found. Accepting a position somewhat removed from the real source of political power, they avoided the sharp light of controversy and in the resultant obscurity found at least minimal satisfaction of their need to be self-governing. Perhaps it was the best they could have hoped for.

11. SOCIAL AND CULTURAL GLIMPSES

> . . . this ends the month and I dont beleave there has been one
> day that the wind did not blow. It has damaged the crops and
> covered them with sand, filled up the ditches and made it very
> unpleasant, but our Hevenly Father knows what this wind is for.

> . . . I have had much pleasure with my Sisters in meetings and
> invited parties and have had the privelage of visiting my children
> and Grand children but next month we must move to the Farm
> then these nice times will end. . . .
>
> LUCY HANNAH WHITE FLAKE

The Church

RARELY HAVE HUMAN LIVES been more engulfed by a single institution.
At birth, at death, on each special occasion, in the routine of Sabbath
days, and in the rhythm of daily life the church stood predominant. It was
foremost in the fact of the Little Colorado as it was in its rhetoric. Its
force drew eyes across the territorial border to Salt Lake City. It made the
primary decisions of life. It provided hope in the future and lent meaning
to the present. It buoyed heavy hearts, and its failure to fill the full measure
of expectation brought despair. It contested the elements and challenged
other social forces. It built dams, laid railroads, founded villages, and
established schools. Clearly the first decades of Little Colorado Mormon
history belong to the church. In the practical sense it came near being all
things to all men — it was the colony's alpha and omega in affairs of
the heart and soul.

The church's ordinary organization prevailed. The General Authorities, consisting of the First Presidency, the Twelve Apostles, and an

increasing number of auxiliary leaders, interpreted the meaning of the doctrine of the church and applied its patterns. In the colony authority was divided between itinerant members of the General Authorities, whose restless energy brought them often to the Little Colorado, and the stake presidencies. Assisted by twelve-man councils and the leaders of such supporting organizations as the Relief Society (the major women's organization of the church), Sunday School, and the Mutual Improvement Association (for young men and women), stake presidents constituted the chief resident authority. Dominating subordinates in fact and theory, the presidents exercised a good deal of discretion, but submissive in turn, did so with an eye directed toward the Salt Lake City authorities. Completing the structural organization were the ward officers headed by a bishop whose tremendous local influence was reflected in the thankful and repetitious utterance of his name in the prayers of the faithful from the earliest lisping appeals of the very young to the tedious supplications of the very old.

Beginning as a colonizing mission, the Little Colorado community was regularized in terms of church administration by the organization of stakes, three of which were ultimately established. Stakes were in turn subdivided into wards, which varied in number and size according to the fortunes of colonization. Founded first, the Little Colorado Stake never flourished. Headed by Lot Smith it had little chance to escape the rawness of the frontier before division over the United Order and the decline of the lower river villages combined with Smith's shortcomings as an administrator to sap its vitality. Nevertheless, the Little Colorado Stake kept the lines of communication open and provided a minimum of organization until 1887 when it ceased to exist. At the suggestion of Apostle Erastus Snow, it was divided in November of 1878. The new Eastern Arizona Stake encompassed all Mormon settlement east of Silver Creek. In 1887 the Eastern Arizona Stake itself was split, forming the St. Johns and Snowflake stakes. Jesse N. Smith, who had headed the earlier unit, was carried over as president of the Snowflake Stake, and D. K. Udall, bishop of St. Johns since 1880, presided over the new St. Johns Stake.

Deeply interested in the colony, Salt Lake City leaders not only laid out its settlement but superintended its growth through frequent inspections. Upon Apostle Erastus Snow and, with Snow's aging and death, upon Brigham Young, Jr., fell the major responsibility for the colonization of the entire Colorado Plateau including the Little Colorado.[1] Joined by

---

[1] For a more complete treatment of Apostle Erastus Snow's role in northern Arizona, see Andrew Karl Larson, *Erastus Snow, The Life of a Missionary and Pioneer for the Early Mormon Church* (Salt Lake City: University of Utah Press, 1971), pp. 629-705.

Apostles Francis M. Lyman, Heber J. Grant, John Henry Smith, and less frequently by others of the Twelve, Snow and Young traveled extensively in the colony. Of equal significance, they represented it in the general councils of the church, winning repeated aid when conditions might have suggested the withdrawal of support.

With the intensification of the polygamy raids during the 1880s, Salt Lake City authorities made the Little Colorado an important sanctuary. Among those who took refuge there were John W. and Brigham Young, Jr., Heber J. Grant, F. M. Lyman, Moses Thatcher, George W. Teasdale, Erastus Snow, and Wilford Woodruff. Involving themselves in its affairs, these fugitives not only influenced the course of the colony's development while they were on the underground but acquired a personal interest in its success. Some who likely would not have visited the area otherwise thus came to be its advocates.

The impact of visiting General Authorities may be traced in the place names the country bears. The church's practice of naming towns after revered men is much in evidence, and a chronological listing of settlement would be a relatively accurate index of the leaders active in the country or prominent in its promotion.[2] John W. Young, who had a special and, one suspects, obsequious passion for naming villages after well-placed individuals, overrode established usage and local initiative when he named Brigham City, St. Joseph, old Taylor, and Woodruff for top figures in the Mormon pantheon of Saints. As Erastus Snow's important role emerged, Snowflake and Erastus, as Concho was known for a few years, were named after him. Old Taylor failing, President John Taylor was honored a second time when a town on Silver Creek was renamed Taylor. To the west on the Mogollon Rim, the names of Wilford and Heber reflected the sojourn of Wilford Woodruff at sheep camps in the area and Heber J. Grant's frequent visits to the colony. Francis M. Lyman left his brand upon the country at the Lyman Reservoir near St. Johns. These names forfeited much in color to more colloquial nomenclature, such as Belly Button, Bull Holler, Lone Pine Crossing, and Nutrioso, but they made up in appreciation and reverence what they lacked in originality and imagination.

The perambulations of church leaders were also marked in the given names of the community's young. While the region's George Washingtons and Benjamin Franklins were not a few, its Brighams, Josephs, Hebers, and Taylors were legion. And the prodigious crop of Wilfords that corresponded with Wilford Woodruff's year-long exile in 1879-80 caused

---

[2] The practice of naming towns for church leaders is far less pronounced in other areas of the south and southeast that were colonized about the same time.

that worthy to note with pride that "I find quite a large number of fine children among the saints in Arizona named Wilford." Stiffly disowning direct responsibility for them, he continued: "But I am not the father of any of them but am what may be called the God Father of some of them if blessing them would make me so. And today I was called upon to Bless the son of Lot and Allice Ann Richards Smith and he was named Wilford Woodruff Smith."[3]

The colony's close-knit society was in a special way the product of the personal acquaintance between its people and its leaders. Most colonists appear to have known at least one of the traveling authorities intimately, and many knew all of them. The result was an informal but most cohesive web of relationships. Many settlers were veterans of the church's hard experience in Missouri and Illinois and had shared its vicissitudes with apostles, presidents of the church, and other leaders. Typical was tough old Charles Shumway. Reputedly the first man to cross the Mississippi when the Saints fled Nauvoo in the winter of 1846, he was listed as one of Brigham Young's adopted sons and was a member of the pioneer party on its entry to Salt Lake Valley in 1847.[4] His life in Utah continued to be rich in its experience and associations. In 1880 he moved to Arizona, with his place in the community assured. Men like Shumway were called because they were known to church leaders, and their conduct under the pressures of pioneering was more predictable. Once in Arizona, such associations were retained and colonists otherwise unmarked by prestige or position were favored with visits and attention from General Authorities. The lines of communication were remarkably open, with lay members going again and again to visiting officials with their problems, or, on the other hand, being sought out by the latter who asked for information or an opinion relative to some matter of moment.

Polygamy was another important bonding agent. Symbolizing the distinctiveness of the Saints, it was more prevalent among leaders than other classes in the church. On the Little Colorado, it came near being the badge of authority and an appointment of importance was often followed by an admonition to take additional wives. According to family tradition, Levi M. Savage, who was made bishop at Sunset in 1878, was taken aside the following year by Wilford Woodruff and shown scriptural

---

[3] "Wilford Woodruff's Journal," January 3, 1880. A latter-day manifestation of this same practice may be observed among the Indian converts of the Southwest Indian Mission. Called on to christen the young, successful missionaries have sprinkled the desert with children bearing their own names.

[4] Juanita Brooks, ed., *On the Mormon Frontier: The Diary of Hosea Stout, 1844-1861* (Salt Lake City: University of Utah Press and Utah State Historical Society, 1964), vol. 1, p. 242.

evidence leading him to believe that plural marriage was a commandment that pertained to him personally. Obediently, he sought out Lenora Hatch, daughter of L. H. Hatch, made her his second wife in December of 1879, and subsequently married her sister Adeline.[5] Late in 1880 Jesse N. Smith, who unlike Savage already had several wives, was summoned to St. Johns by Erastus Snow and Brigham Young, Jr., who there gave him a "recommend to receive Sister Emma Larson as a member of" his family.[6]

Whatever its moral implications, polygamy drew the most devoted men on the Little Colorado into an intertwined marital alliance in which filial bonds and an emotion-packed and highly personal mark reinforced the ties of organizational structure and common faith. Once committed, the recourse of polygamists was limited indeed. With the national campaign to eradicate plural marriage mounting around them, their only options were to repudiate family ties and responsibility or to accept their slot in Mormon society.

Stake leaders, like those in Salt Lake City, traveled extensively, making annual and sometimes more frequent visits throughout the colony. The burdens of these trips fell heavily upon the presidency of the Eastern Arizona Stake as its jurisdiction extended at one time or another from Moenkopi on the northwest to Smithville (later called Pima) on the Gila River, encompassing a misshapen rectangle over 250 miles long and 150 miles wide. The routine of early visits was often interrupted, but as time passed frontier conditions and anti-Mormon sentiment yielded to more amenable circumstances and trips were made regularly and in full regalia with auxiliary leaders joining the stake presidency in leisurely junkets. Pausing in the communities along the way and reminiscing of early days as they camped at familiar sites, they were often on the road for several weeks at a time. Stake officers were involved in every aspect of life, counseling church members on such diverse matters as Indian affairs, dam building, Gentile relations, and various religious questions. In addition to general preaching, local frictions were worked out, cases appealed from bishop's courts, ward organizations reconstituted, and a broad spectrum of temporal problems dealt with.

To the traveling leaders tithing irregularities were all too often a matter of special concern. Indeed the record indicates an amazing casual-

---

[5] "Journal of Levi Mathers Savage," pp. 30, 37.

[6] In Utah John Taylor and his counselors openly directed "the Elders of Israel to take more wives," saying on at least one occasion that "there was no exaltation without it." So that none should misunderstand the meaning of the term, George Q. Cannon spelled it out, declaring that "what was called consecutive Polygamy, that is, having a wife who had died, and then marrying another . . . did not fill the bill, neither [did] having dead women sealed to them." See "Diary of Charles Smith," typescript BYU, p. 259.

ness with church funds on the part of some bishops who were the primary fiscal agents for the church. Taking most collections in kind, bishops often kept inadequate accounts and during times of duress, especially, some let their own affairs become hopelessly entangled with those of the church. Although some church donations were permanently lost, stake authorities were tolerant and forebearing. Regarding losses as the product of mismanagement, they worked with delinquent bishops to adjust accounts rather than charging malfeasance. Of one muddling bishop who in the process of fleeing from bigamy charges had completely lost sight of distinctions between what was his and what belonged to the church, the stake clerk charitably wrote:

> The Bishop was in a very cramped condition and the handling of the tithing as private property was the result of a very large deficiency in his accounts, much of this shortage was probably on account of his being away as well as his own and others mismanagement. The accounts had not been entered as they should have been and I was of the opinion that much was taken in and used without an account of that which was used, loaned, or given to poor, etc. He was owing some $3,000 which was never paid, or at least a great portion of it had to be allowed to him as he had not means to meet this shortage and I suppose that a large share of it was a shortage that he should have been called on to settle.[7]

Revered and influential, stake leaders were not universally liked or accepted. Indeed, they were frequently rejected. Writing of conditions in southern Arizona's St. Thomas Stake in 1895, Joseph Fish noted:

> Things in the stake spiritually were not in a very good condition. The President had but little influence and things were drifting along in a kind of haphazard kind of way. It was a common saying that if you wanted an enterprise to succeed, get the President to oppose it and if you wanted a measure killed get the President to favor it. This showed very nicely the lack of union among the bretheren.[8]

Although the strength of outside opposition and quality of leadership may have resulted in greater support for church authorities in Apache County, they too had their difficulties. This was true of both temporal and spiritual matters.

Deeply rooted factional discords sometimes divided the leaders themselves. Some schisms were over doctrinal questions; others were social in origin. At Snowflake a deep-rooted split existed between Bishop John Hunt and the Flakes, who hailed originally from Beaver, and Jesse N. Smith and a retinue of followers including Joseph Fish and John R.

---

[7] "Autobiography of Joseph Fish," p. 253.
[8] *Ibid.*, p. 328.

Hulet from Parowan. Rightly claiming that Smith tended to fill important posts with the Parowan clique, which was made the more cohesive by intermarriage, the Hunt-Flake contingent coexisted but carped about favoritism and nepotism until 1885. When Smith led the flight of polygamists from the colony late that year, Hunt took the initiative. Still complaining about nepotism and slights to his authority as bishop, he sought local and Salt Lake City support in a movement to have John Bushman of St. Joseph appointed in Smith's stead. Apprised of the insurgency, Smith gave up his exile and hurried back. After a long and rather petty exchange between the two factions, he finally removed a few of his Parowan friends and relatives from office. Thus patched, relations slowly improved. The cleft, however, was deep and affected many of the functions of the colony. The ACMI directors, for example, divided along the Parowan-Beaver lines. Cross-factional marriages appear to have been less frequent than intra-group unions. The chasm was carried over into the political divisions of the 1890s, the Hunts and Flakes joining the Democratic party and the Smiths the Republican.

A Woman's Life

Perhaps no other function of the church involved its women more fully than did the pioneering process. Called as missionaries along with their husbands, women were partners in a holy undertaking. Without them, colonization could not have succeeded; with their best efforts, the margin of success was still spare. Drab and plagued with inconvenience, theirs was an existence of sacrifice and toil. Families were large and men were often poor providers. Frequently living in the shadow of disaster, women nevertheless found meaning and comfort in the sense of mission that actuated the church and in the associations of their communities.

While by no means silent partners, women were relegated to secondary roles in the church's priesthood-dominated system. Given tasks in the auxiliary organizations, they took little direct part in more important ecclesiastical matters and, with the exception of rare occasions, such as when the brothers of the St. Joseph United Order invited them in to help decide the Order's future, they exerted no influence upon temporal affairs except as they could bring it to bear through their men.

The lines of church practice appear to have been somewhat more flexible than in subsequent times, permitting women to participate in activities since obsolete or impinging upon areas now regarded as the exclusive preserve of male members. For instance, cases of women pronouncing prayers that followed the pattern of the patriarchal blessing in everything but the gender of the person officiating were not unknown, and at least one community's sisters divided themselves priesthood-like into "Quorums of the Mothers of Israel."[9] At Snowflake women met frequently in prayer circles where they comforted and buoyed each other. The solace thus found is apparent in the following from the pen of Lucy Hannah Flake:

I felt depressed in my spirits and after I got my ironing done went up to my Dear sister Wests and we talked and then went up stares and poured out our soles in prair we had a glorious feast of prair and blessings we felt the power resting upon us I put my hands on her head and blessed her and she blest me I tasted and was greatly blest and feel so thankfull for this blessed privelage I always get comfort when we offer our prairs up together.[10]

Women of the Little Colorado were even more narrow in their associations than their men. Indeed, something of a dual standard prevailed. Men who, however reluctantly, had broad associations with Gentiles were determined to shield their wives and daughters from all outside contact. This distinction in standards was especially apparent in the sermons delivered during the polygamy crisis of 1884-85. Typically, Jesse N. Smith told his brethren that if they would "be careful and not lose their faith," he was "willing they should work for outsiders." On the other hand, he would never "consent to have our daughters led away by the wicked," nor "work as hired help in the house of outsiders."[11] Linked to polygamy, the insulation of the "weaker sex" was regarded by Mormon men as a means of maintaining what was essentially theirs. In this vein Smith once told followers:

The only real argument ever brought against it [polygamy] is this, the number of males and females being nearly equal it is an injustice for some men to have more than one wife, as this will probably leave others without any at all. So far as proselyting goes, far more women than men receive the gospel. . . . They will not marry outside the Church and were it not for the revelation restoring the principle of plural marriage they would be compelled to remain unmarried. . . . God does not sanction the giving of a pure woman to a corrupt man. . . . If there are men approved of God above their fellowmen is it not consistent and proper that unto them God should give good and virtuous wives?[12]

Thus guarded, women were, nevertheless, encouraged to join the women's rights movement. Interested in the matter from the time coloni-

---

[9] Customarily given only by designated members of the priesthood, patriarchal blessings approximated for individual members the guiding role played by revelation for the church in general.

[10] "Diary of Lucy Hannah Flake," vol. 3, June 7, 1898.

[11] Smith, *Journal of Jesse N. Smith,* pp. 288, 292.

[12] *Ibid.,* pp. 263-64.

zation began, Little Coloradans welcomed the national and territorial movement as it gathered impetus in the 1890s. Guided by the church's interest, which made women's rights something of a pawn in the polygamy and Utah statehood controversies, there were few radical overtones in the Mormon approach to feminism.[13] One woman who in her church calling became a responsible and committed if not an ardent suffrage worker reflected the general attitude when she wrote:

There is much said of women's rights. I don't beleave in equal rights. I would like the Franchize but feel willing for the men to kill the snakes build the bridges and smoothe down the high places and hold the offices. I would like to see women's rights respected and held sacrid at all times and in all places.[14]

Often couched in Biblical terms, speeches in favor of women's rights sacrificed none of the priesthood's prerogatives. L. H. Hatch struck the dominant chord when he played upon the "history of Esther, Naomi, Ruth and of the creation of Adam and mother Eve, and of the women at the tomb and Rhoda declaring the glad tidings of Peter's deliverance."[15] As handmaidens to the priesthood, the sisters were entitled to the right to vote but, like their men, did not conceive of the movement as freeing them from the system of which they were part.

Characteristically, the suffrage movement was embraced on an institutional rather than individual basis. Stake presidencies became its primary advocates and women's Relief Societies the nucleus around which it formed. Organized in the various wards, suffrage clubs were directed by local Relief Society leaders who used church facilities and meetings to advance their cause. Relatively active between 1895 and 1899, the movement declined after an attempt to give women the franchise failed in the territorial legislature during the latter year.[16]

The Little Colorado women's rights movement was essentially conservative in nature, but a few stirrings of change did accompany it. Some women took note of new developments in hygiene, midwifery, and nursing; a few availed themselves of special courses in these subjects. Their interest, however, was in preparation for service, not in emancipation. Indeed, so foreign were ideas of alterations in the wonted patterns of Mormonism that graduates of these courses were "set apart" or designated by church ordination to act as midwives and nurses in the Mormon villages.[17] In addition to such areas of interest, a very limited number of

---

[13] Thomas G. Alexander, "An Experiment in Progressive Legislation: The Granting of Woman Suffrage in Utah in 1870," *Utah Historical Quarterly* 38 (Winter 1970): 20-30.

[14] "Diary of Lucy Hannah Flake," vol. 2, March 15, 1895.

[15] "Lorenzo Hill Hatch Journal," p. 213.

[16] See Kelly, *Legislative History,* pp. 191-205.

[17] "Lorenzo Hill Hatch Journal," p. 217.

women also concerned themselves with silk culture and with "reform in dress."[18]

Little Colorado women were submissive in polygamy as they were in church matters generally. Those who entered into plural relationships raised no question as to the morality of the practice. Those who did not live in polygamous families appear to have been equally committed to it in principle, rarely objecting or stepping forward to testify against it.

Most plural marriages appear to have grown out of nonromantic circumstances. Often there was considerable disparity in age. Intended brides played a passive role in the courting process, with church authorities making the arrangements or the prospective husband dealing with the parents. Not surprisingly, many of these unions were initiated because of church or business ties or of deep friendship between men. An instance of the latter sort was that of Joseph Fish and Jesse N. Smith. Intimately associated in business and church, they cemented their relationship through marriage when Fish took Smith's daughter Adelaide as his third wife. The bonds were further strengthened later by the polygamous marriage of one of Smith's sons to one of Fish's daughters. In other cases women were chosen because of qualities that seemed to suit them for the particular situation of the bridegroom, with more than one Little Colorado girl being selected because of a sweet and permissive personality that gave good promise of being able to tolerate a first wife who was noted for her sharp tongue and bad temper.

However, feminine initiative and romance were not always lacking. An interesting instance of the former occurred in 1879 when Jesse N. Smith, who was in Utah tying up the loose ends of his business and attending the territorial legislature, "received a letter from a young woman at Cedar City asking the privilege to become a member" of his family. Somewhat taken aback, Smith rose to the occasion as the following excerpt from his diary indicates:

I went to Cedar City and called on Bishop Lunt after first receiving the sanction of my family. The Bishop assured me that girl's character was good. I called on the family and explained the circumstances to the mother of the girl. The father was out with the sheep herd. The mother objected to me on two grounds: first I was poor, and second, I was going to Arizona, but the girl still expressed her preference for me. It was arranged that the girl should go home with me and get acquainted with my family, but when I called in the morning she asked me to give her back her letter as her mother was so much opposed to the arrangement. Thus ended the matter.[19]

It is difficult to say just what emotions accompanied these strange proceedings.

---

[18] *Ibid.*

[19] Smith, *Journal of Jesse N. Smith,* p. 237.

On the other hand, Ida Hunt, daughter of the Snowflake bishop, was filled with delight and also with great sorrow by her deep love for David K. Udall. Combined with a belief that the doctrine of plural marriage was uplifting and divine, her affection for Udall guided her through the difficult decision to marry the husband of a woman for whom she had the highest esteem and for whom she knew the entire process would be most painful. Something of her spirit as well as of the challenges implicit in polygamous marriages in 1882 is apparent in the following from her diary:

Marriage, under ordinary circumstances is a grave and important step, but entering into Plural Marriage, in these perilous times is doubly so. May Heaven help me to keep the vows I have made sacred and pure, and may the deep unchangeable love which I feel for my husband today increase with every coming year, helping me to prove worthy of the love and confidence which he imposes in me, and to always be just and considerate to those the Lord has given unto him.[20]

In the poverty and crisis of the 1880s, the lot of the polygamist woman was particularly harrowing. If nothing else, it meant separation. For Ida Hunt Udall, the wedding march led in less than three years to a lonely exile as she fled Arizona to remove the physical evidence that would indict her husband. For others, polygamy meant separation compounded with the direst need. Twice Joseph Fish found it necessary to move to Mexico. Twice he left his wife Adelaide with small children and little means of support. Impoverished and ill, she and the children survived; any sentimental attachment she entertained for Fish did not. Another of his wives, Eliza, who bore no children, left Arizona during this time of trouble, remaining in Utah for thirteen years before returning.[21]

Pioneering in the area of Savoia, New Mexico, during 1876-77, Catherine Hatch, one of L. H. Hatch's three wives, was left "in a lonely condition among Mexicans, Zuñis and Navajo Indians" for five months during the winter of 1877 while her husband brought another family from Utah's Cache Valley. Terrified by the smallpox epidemic, Catherine quarantined her own cabin, admitting no one, not even stricken members of the church, thus meriting the antagonism of braver but scarcely more brotherly individuals who for the remainder of that terrible winter ostracized her, leaving her in almost complete isolation and destitution.[22]

Nor was the lot of the polygamist wives who accompanied their husbands to Mexico in 1885 any better. Camped in a strange and, as it

---

20 "Journal of Ida Frances Hunt Udall," xerox copy, HDC, May 25, 1882.

21 Silas L. Fish, "Notes of the Life and Writings of Joseph Fish," p. 18. Typed copy in the possession of the writer.

22 "Lorenzo Hill Hatch Journal," pp. 101-2.

— Mrs. S. George Ellsworth

Ida Hunt Udall in 1905.

proved, hostile land, they suffered from illness and malnutrition during the summer, and in a few cases were left behind to agonize under child loss and fear when their husbands felt it necessary to return to the United States.

In all this there was little tendency on the part of the women to reject either polygamy or the system that spawned it. Only one case has come to the attention of the writer in which a Little Colorado wife brought civil suit against her husband under the anti-bigamy laws. Even in this case, action was taken after she had exhausted all recourse within the church and lost touch with the economic reality of her husband's poverty.

Monotony punctuated with crisis and muted by village associations characterized the lives of most women. During early days, life was especially void of social amenities to relieve the sameness of pioneering tasks. In the camps and the villages, faces were eternally the same, or at least, so it seemed. Recurrent difficulty required common action; recurrent failure resulted in recrimination and bad feelings. Routines and social defenses broke, laying bare personalities so that to repetition was added the rawness of inconvenienced and anxious human beings. Differences growing from close living frequently led to disdain and, unless averted by changing circumstances or effective leadership, to persistent bitterness. Restricted to the villages without the outside interests that occupied the attention of men, such pressures fell most heavily upon women. Feeling it keenly, they longed for loved ones and for the richer life of the larger communities in Utah. Pent by a cankered social situation, a young wife in one camp wrote home in 1877:

Dear mother, I can realize how you loved the Society of Saints, for I long for the time to come when there will be some good Latter-day Saints come here to live. Do not think there is none here, but when you mingle with people everyday, you begin to know one another so well that there is nothing new.[23]

To social friction and the longings of a woman's heart were added distress occasioned by the natural elements. Less catastrophic in immediate effect than drought or cloudbursts, the spring wind which blew with a furious monotony cut away at morale until at times it seemed life could scarcely go on. Coming from the southwest, the wind blasted down from the Mogollon Rim, rising in its fury as it broke from the pines and cedars of the upcountry to sweep across the desert, flinging rice-sized pebbles before it, filling the atmosphere with dust, and piling sand in drifts. Beginning as a rule in February, it continued with infrequent letups until late June or early July. Recent immigrants looked hopefully for early letup. Seasoned old-timers accepted it with varying degrees of resignation.

---

[23] "Sketch of Maria Taylor McRae," Roberta Clayton Papers, BYU.

Always bad, the effect of the wind was worse in the dry years of the 1890s after overgrazing had removed the meager foliage and loosened the soil of the hill country below the cedar line.

Men struggled with the wind, cursing it as they pursued their affairs, but its abrasive effects told on women as well. One who wilted before it was Lucy Flake, from whose diary for March, April, and May in 1896 — generally the months of the wind's greatest intensity — the following entries are taken:

Monday, March 2: the wind blows all the time day and part of the time nights and I feel nearly sick.
Tuseday, April 14, the wind it blows night and day, it is just fearful the sand drifts like snow . . . John is herding cows William is reeding it seems lonely and dreary when the wind blows.
Wednesday, April 15, the Wind blew hard all night and all day. . . .
Thursday, April 16, all well but the Wind gets worse and worse night and day.
Saturday, April 18, Brother Flake and John came home this morning the Wind was so bad thirsday they laid up all day and could not travel. The wind blows very little today which is so nice. I cleaned up all the rooms and had a bath and am going to town. . . .
Sunday, April 19, today is fearful the Wind blows so bad. . . .
Thursday, April 30, this ends the month and I dont beleave there has been one day that the wind did not blow it has damaged the crops and covered them with sand filled up the ditches and made it very unpleasant but our Hevenly Father knows what this wind is for.
Monday, May 10, I am on the place all alone it seems like this country was going to all blow away.
Friday, May 15, the wind blows fearful the sand almost blinds one the children cant go out to play.[24]

Filled with despair by the unremitting wind, Mrs. Flake found her lonely life on a farm some two miles from town to be nearly intolerable. That it was not entirely so may have been due in part to the busy life she led. Among the activities she chronicled one spring were gleaning wool from carcasses left along the trail over which sheepmen made a seasonal circuit to and from the Salt River Valley, and picking, washing, and carding it to make a mattress; whitewashing her home; gardening and irrigating; sewing, including making underwear, shirts and carpets; tending her grandchildren; and feeding her husband and growing sons, as well as numerous duties in her church capacity. On one occasion she set down in simple detail her morning chores which were certainly characteristic of her life and likely typical of Little Colorado pioneer women generally:

I will just write my morning chores. Get up turn out my chickens draw a pail of watter, watter hot beds make a fire, put potatoes to cook then brush and sweep half inch of dust off floor and everything, feed three litters of chickens

---

[24] "Diary of Lucy Hannah Flake," vol. 2, May 16, 1896.

then mix bisquits, get breakfast, milk besides work in the house, and this morning had to go half mile after calves. This is the way of life on the farm. . . .[25]

Among the trials in a woman's life was the matter of water supply. Water in the Little Colorado was both muddy and impregnated with minerals. In Silver Creek and other mountain tributaries it was usually much better. For years water was hauled in barrels. This was particularly true of places like Woodruff and St. Joseph where the river was hard to control. Elsewhere ditch systems brought water into town but running through corrals and near privies did nothing to improve its quality. As a result the entire colony was plagued by recurrent and devastating out-breaks of typhoid fever and other waterborne diseases. Water was espe-cially unpalatable immediately after the drought of the early 1890s when tens of thousands of cattle piled up around water holes and along the stream beds and died. Running through and over the carcasses, the water — when the drouth finally slacked — was in the vernacular of the time so "bad you had to bite it off." Women used a variety of techniques in their attempts to make it potable. Ashes and other materials were dumped in it to help it settle, but even when mud and other filth had settled water retained a milky color. Inevitably food and clothing cooked and washed in river water showed the effect. Foods took on a dull brownish color and light-colored clothing was reddened.

Hard-pressed financially, most women improvised and adapted, pro-ducing by their own labor many items that even at that early date were ordinarily purchased ready-made in more established communities. At Mormon Dairy and a few other spots throughout the country, women and older girls joined a man or two in milking hundreds of cows and manufacturing thousands of pounds of cheese and butter under the most primitive conditions. At Sunset and St. Joseph, they produced yarn and yard goods in crude woolen mills. Everywhere in the colony, carding, spinning, and knitting native wool into socks and other items of apparel were ordinary tasks. To many, home manufacty of clothing was a necessity. It was often done by hand from the crudest materials, including burlap and wagon tarps.

On the women of the colony fell the major responsibilities of rearing families and, all too often, of providing the living on which they sub-sisted. One widow, Eliza Rogers, with a large family of young boys, homesteaded at a remote mountain spot called Clay Springs some thirty miles southwest of Snowflake. There, with her sons who became less amenable to work as they became physically able, she eked out the barest

---

[25] *Ibid.*

existence. Shifting for herself, Mrs. Rogers raised the entire family. Late in life, but still determined and independent, she took offense at some neighborly slight and, caring for herself as she had done for years, set out to walk the miles between Snowflake and her own home. Losing her way in a December storm, she failed to strike a fire with flint and steel with which she had equipped herself and, among the cedars of Horse Prairie some miles off course, ended her lonely and stubborn struggle with the Little Colorado's frontier.[26]

Few women paid their price in such solitude. Most found some satisfaction for their social needs in the activities of the church. This, however, was more often the case among those who made their residences in one of the villages than for those who like Eliza Rogers lived much of their lives on isolated ranches. Like church leaders who inveighed repeatedly against scattering, women were deeply aware of the advantages of group living, and some of them took occasion to express their preference. Mrs. Flake, living in town during the late fall and winter and on a nearby ranch during the remainder of the year, was one of them. Buffeted by wind and burdened with farm work, she longed for the company of town during the months on the ranch and feared returning to it while in town. After a round of social and church activities in the winter of 1894, she wistfully revealed to her diary:

This closes the month of March. . . . I have had much pleasure with my Sisters in meetings and invited parties and have had the privelage of visiting my children and Grand children but next month we must move to the Farm then these nice times will end for we will have to stay more at home. I dont care much about going but always try to make duty a plesure.[27]

Although she frequently repeated this lonely lament, even her summers were not unbroken solitude. "Invertations," entertainments, and church duties brought visitors to the ranch and gave her occasional excuses to leave it. Not entirely typical in her needs for society nor in her access to it, Mrs. Flake's yearnings and her success in filling them indicate the importance of village society in the woman's life. Perhaps her attitude and that of most Little Colorado women was not, after all, unlike that of the starving Irish woman told of by Carl Degler. Taken from the city and given a job in the country, she was soon back in her urban haunts, muttering that "Paples is more coompany than Sthumps."[28]

---

26 For an account of Mrs. Rogers' death, see *Snowflake Herald*, February 25, 1965.

27 "Diary of Lucy Hannah Flake," vol. 2, March 31, 1895.

28 Carl N. Degler, *Out of Our Past, The Forces That Shaped Modern America* (New York: Harper & Row, 1959), p. 307.

Housing

Colonists spent their first years in a variety of makeshift houses. For some this was a transitional matter, and well-built comfortable homes were soon provided. For many, however, housing remained crude and totally lacking in comforts and conveniences until after the turn of the century.

The first homes were wagon boxes, usually lifted from running gears and set on blocks. Cooking and living outside or under brush-covered, open-sided sheds, pioneers found minimum privacy and escaped the worst of nature's inclemency in these primitive mobile homes. More permanent but still extremely crude facilities soon replaced or at least supplemented the wagon-boxes. Using convenient materials, dugouts, cabins, forts, and rock huts were hastily put together. "Shingled with mud," these had few windows or none at all, dirt floors, and dangerous flues and fireplaces. Lumber being available in the colony, many homes, but by no means all, appear to have had door jams, doors, and window sashes. Size varied from tiny huts in which no more than two people could camp in cramped quarters to the multiunit forts of the United Order villages. Capacity, however, was more a matter of necessity than comfort, and surprising numbers of people crowded into one-room houses. Samuel H. Rogers, who arrived at Snowflake in January of 1880, related that the entire party with which he immigrated "all lived in one room" except himself and his wife, who in spite of abnormally cold weather preferred to stay in their covered wagon because, as he put it, "all in one room was pretty thick." [29] The Standifird family and others totaling eighteen people made their quarters in an eighteen-by-thirty-foot dugout at Silver Creek Crossing during the same winter.

Built close to the ground, if not partially beneath it, many early homes were bothered with rodents and reptiles. In time women overcame their antipathy for certain snakes, particularly the blow snakes, because of their value as rodent killers, and stories of pet blow snakes twining their way among the poles and willows of dugout roofs are not uncommon. In spite of their filth and the fact that they represented a standing invitation to mice and rats, dirt floors predominated in certain areas for years. Woodruff, for example, had no home with wooden floors until the middle 1880s. One oldtimer, Wilford Hatch, who was born in the Woodruff Fort in 1878, recalled the strangeness of lumber's feel to his bare feet on first entering the town's earliest floored home when he was five or six years of age. [30]

---

[29] See "Diamond Jubilee Gems," n.p.
[30] Interview with Wilford Hatch, Franklin, Idaho, August 20, 1966.

Life in such quarters was also rendered miserable by insects. Returning from a summer in a primitive Arizona camp one man with "a taste for matters pertaining to natural history" displayed a large collection of bugs to his friends in Salt Lake City. Possessed also of a wry sense of humor he referred to his collection, which included "centipedes, black scorpions, tarantulas and poisonous caterpillars," as "Arizona Pickles."[31]

While the regular discomforts of flies and mosquitos were borne in silence, bedbugs, which under frontier conditions proved to be a real problem, occasioned considerable comment. Arriving at Alpine — or Bush Valley, as it was then called in the summer of 1880 — the Coleman family had a skirmish with them in which the bugs not only drew first blood but clearly won the initial encounters, though the final outcome is left indeterminant in the account of the event from which the following is extracted:

The "Parson" [G. C. Williams] had several vacant houses and we moved in rent free. Those were built of cotton wood logs, chinked, and dobed, dirt floor and roof and consisted of from one to three rooms. We moved in immediately and set up house keeping. Next morning we moved all the beds out, set the wagon boxes off the wagons and used them for bed rooms. Say, folks, the bed bugs were so bad that we just couldn't sleep inside those houses. We finally had to take our meals outside. The bed bugs would fall down into the vittles when we were eating.[32]

The Colemans fought back; others resigned to their fate accepted the bugs as unwelcome but permanent guests. Such appears to have been the case at a cabin home on the Lone Pine Crossing of the West Show Low where Joseph Fish and Joseph W. Smith held a church meeting that was "eventful on account of the bedbugs." According to the latter's account:

There was a chicken coop near the house, and there [that] had assisted the natural increase somewhat. We had scarcely started the meeting when they started. I never saw such a swarm of them. After I had taken my turn at speaking, I took a seat on a little box. That box was fairly alive with them. I sat quietly crushing them with my feet as they chased one another across the floor. I kept my fingers busy picking them off of my clothes. My situation was very undesirable, but as others seemed more or less engaged in the same business, I did not think I should be benefitted much by moving. Bro. Fish was speaking, and was really giving us a good sermon, but I was not in a situation to appreciate it. My greatest desire was that he would get to the Amen. But that was a word that it seemed he could not find. I finally got so nervous that I could not stand it any longer. Passing out as quietly as possible, I betook myself to the wood pile, and commenced a still hunt. I found fifty

---

31 *Deseret News,* August 10, 1876.
32 Evans Coleman, "History of the Coleman Family," Coleman Papers, p. 34.

before meeting was out. Bad as it was for the balance of us, I felt to sympathize with the lady of the house. Her mortification was greater than our nervousness.[33]

Though colonists had more than a passing acquaintance with bedbugs, most kept them at arm's length by following the Coleman tactics and other preventative practices.

Earthen coverings were another irritant. In dry periods, life under them was tolerable. During severe storms, dirt-covered homes became veritable bogs as mud-laden water worked its way down. At times the only recourse was to move all perishable items back into covered wagons, leaving the house not only for the duration of the storm but until the "after drip" had subsided. Growing weight, as more dirt was piled on in futile attempts to stop leaks, occasionally combined with the rotting of timbers, to result in cave-ins, the consequences of which were more aggravating than serious. In referring to such eventualities, one pioneer wrote:

After a dirt roof had weatherd one or two wet years it's supports became rotted and it "falls in" when least expected. If the family on such occasions was wrapped in profound and peaceful slumber, the rude and sudden awakening caused considerable excitement. The family immediately commenced to "dig out" emerging in all kinds of evening attire. If the family was outside on such an occasion they immediately commenced to "dig in."[34]

Temporary dwellings of this type had some advantages. In the first place, they were cheap, costing no more than a few dollars and a few days' time to erect. Another factor was that they could be built from materials close at hand anywhere on the Little Colorado. Also the skills needed in construction were at an absolute minimum. Anyone could build them and do it rather quickly. During the early period when manpower and skills were at a premium in the development of water and new agricultural lands, they were of great utility. In the transient upcountry ranches and villages where poverty was most pervasive, they continued to be used well into the twentieth century. Generally, however, Little Coloradans made immediate and persistent efforts to upgrade their homes.

The predominant architectural style in the region when they arrived was the low, flat-topped Mexican mud building. Squat and squalid, such structures had grown from the Indian tradition and were well adapted to the materials and natural conditions of the desert and canyon lands in which they stood. Repelled by their looks, Mormons ignored their practicality and in most cases built along characteristic Utah lines. Establishing their own sawmills and brick kilns, some of the Mormon towns began to

---

[33] "Diary of Joseph West Smith," pp. 37-38.
[34] Coleman, "History of the Coleman Family," p. 28.

— Albert J. Levine, Snowflake, A Pictorial Review, 1878-1964

Jesse N. Smith's log home at Snowflake.

take on an appearance of comfortable permanence by the end of their first decade in the country, and by 1895 a good number of substantial private and public buildings were to be found.

Beset with fewer natural and external problems than any other community, Snowflake's progress was relatively consistent; the buildings that rose there represented the colony's best architectural achievement. The first phase of the town's building development began immediately after Flake bought out Stinson in 1878. Before the year had passed, twenty-five or thirty relatively commodious log cabins and a schoolhouse had been built. Constructed in the main of hewn logs hauled twenty miles from the pine forests at Snowflake Camp, later Pinedale, the cabins had two or more rooms as well as doors, numerous windows, and shingled roofs. From the sawmill near Mormon Lake they brought lumber for sheeting, doors, and window sashes.[35] Shingles and, somewhat later, lath for use in plastering were tediously made by hand.

This first construction appears to have been almost entirely a community effort with crews getting logs out and hewing them, and boys —

---

[35] Lot Smith of Sunset donated 25,000 feet of lumber which otherwise sold for $10 per thousand. See Fish, "History of the Eastern Arizona Stake," p. 49.

— *Albert J. Levine, Snowflake, A Pictorial Review, 1878-1964*

some of them very small boys — driving teams on the long haul from Snowflake Camp, while builders in town concentrated their efforts, evidently rearing only one house at a time. As the seasons progressed, the more skilled carpenters continued construction while others worked on ditches and farmed for them. "Nerved up," as one of them put it, by the "anxiety of getting" homes, they found obvious satisfactions in their progress. Recounting the labors of the winter and spring of 1879, Joseph Fish wrote:

A person sometimes takes as much pleasure in building a home as in occupying it after it is built. The life of a pioneer is a hard one but it is mingled with rays of light and joy in seeing the waste places made to blossom, and houses and gardens take the place of the sage brush that cover the deserts.[36]

---

[36] "Autobiography of Joseph Fish," p. 159.

Snowflake about 1895.

One young man, whose trip to Arizona had been his wedding excursion, took a special delight in moving into his home, commemorating the event with the following journal entry:

This was quite an event in our lives. To move into, and set up house-keeping in *our* home. It was a log house to be sure, but if it had been a brick house I dont think it would have been appreciated more. It was big enough for wife and me, and that was enough. And as to style and finish, why it had a *shingle* roofe! And that was sufficient distinction in those times.[37]

During the first year and a half, William J. Flake's home was apparently used for most of the community's public events. Enlarging and

---

[37] "Diary of Joseph West Smith," p. 35. Some idea of the cash outlay involved in construction may be gained from the fact that Smith earned $116 working on the railroad grade; after paying his debts, including those incurred in construction, he "had some $48 left." See p. 43.

Snowflake stake house, built in 1884.

adapting one of Stinson's original adobe buildings, Flake opened his house to virtually all comers. It was the primary stopping place for travelers, both Mormon and Gentile, as well as the site of the first term of court held in Apache County and of Snowflake's first school and church meetings. In the fall of 1879, a log schoolhouse twenty-three by thirty-three feet in dimension was built by "public subscription." Completed in December, it was used for church affairs and school until 1883 when a large brick church known locally as the Stake House was completed.

With the construction of the Stake House, building at Snowflake passed into a new era of which permanent public buildings and two- and three-story homes were the dominant aspect. While neither large nor elaborate in comparison to buildings in older more populous places, these structures had a simple clean strength that reflected an effort to give dignified and appropriate form to the needs of the community for stability and purpose. Bearing the same strong New England influence that characterized Utah architecture of the same period, they showed no Spanish or southwestern qualities whatever. Of local design, they were frame and brick with the latter predominating. Most were of gabled construction. Some, following straight rectangular lines, were relatively simple. Others somewhat more elaborate and varied had multiple gables, porches, and balconies, and at least one was topped by a balustrade or widow's walk. Architectural emphasis was given by covering entryways with pediments and by spanning the length of the buildings with massive chimneys. The salmon color of the native brick set off by white painted woodwork lent itself admirably to the simple yet stable effect of the architecture.

Influenced by a number of capable and skilled builders, most notably Ralph Ramsey who had played an important role in the construction of Brigham Young's Lion House and designed and built the Eagle Gate at the head of Salt Lake City's State Street, building flourished during the late 1880s and early 1890s. Interrupted by the Panic of 1893, neither the pace nor the aesthetic quality of the earlier work was ever resumed, although in terms of devotion and effort as well as architectural value the finest Little Colorado building achievement came in 1910 when the Stake Academy was completed. Unfortunately, this building which housed a secondary school burned almost immediately after its completion and was replaced by a red sandstone structure which in its ruggedness and durability was also indicative of the colony's spirit but lacked the grace and structural beauty of the earlier school.[38]

---

[38] For a good pictorial history of these buildings as well as other aspects of Snowflake's development see Albert J. Levine, *Snowflake, A Pictorial Review, 1878-1964* (published privately, 1964).

"Scattering" on the Southern Frontier

Although much remains unsaid about the social and cultural life of the Little Colorado colony, we may conclude by calling into focus an element of the colony's character that has been implicit in many of the foregoing pages. Possessed of a core of settlers whose steadfastness lent it essential stability, the community was at the same time part of a profoundly restless frontier population. Characterized by almost incessant motion, its society was doubly circumscribed in the area of its movement — once by the personal relations of the colonists and once by the general confines of the Mormon kingdom. Impelled by various factors, many Little Coloradans joined in a protracted desert odyssey that carried them from place to place and drained their energy and consigned them to deepening poverty. Action was not restricted to what might ordinarily be regarded as unstable elements of the community, and the incidence of people taking leave who had for years been regarded as the very pillars of the colony serves to emphasize the extent of restlessness. Movement within the colony was almost constant, but internal comings and goings do not tell the entire story. It was a restlessness that was common to the entire region of Mormon colonization of which the Little Colorado was part, if indeed it was not church-wide.

In some degree instability was the product of widely accepted Mormon values and of practices consciously employed but not fully controlled in the church's process of expansion. A catalog of centrifugal forces initiated by the church would include: the mission call by which the settler was uprooted from Utah and moved from one site to another on the frontier; the general climate of expansion which in Brigham Young's words required a "cautious and gradual" extension of the kingdom until the entire "country south" should be filled; the ferment of polygamy; and the need for good schools.[39] Each of these was in its own way fostered by the church, and each interrupted life, requiring or suggesting change of location. Furthermore, there was an underlying rootlessness in the Mormon community that grew from the subordination of temporal values to the belief that Christ's Second Coming was imminent and the concomitant conviction that Latter-day Saints had to be ready, their "wicks trimmed" awaiting His command. Anticipating cataclysmic changes, including the church's exodus to Jackson County, Missouri, they bore trial and hardship with patience. Without eschewing the material world they saw economic gain, including the acquisition of land and homes, as ephemeral

---

[39] Letter of Brigham Young to Daniel W. Jones, September 19, 1876, and letter of Brigham Young to Lot Smith, July 20, 1876, Brigham Young Letters, HDC.

and passing achievements. Strongly influenced by such thoughts, Little Colorado pioneers frequently failed to take deep root.

But the restlessness of Mormondom's southern frontier was also the product of economic need. Restricted in their alternatives by the self-sufficient agriculture of the church as well as by natural and geographic limitations, almost none of the region's colonists became wealthy, and only a fortunate few enjoyed what may be termed marginal affluence. Stark want joined the general rootlessness of Mormon society to set thousands of settlers on the roads throughout the church's southern provinces.

The effects of this circumstance are revealed in the doings of Joseph Fish, whose detailed diary enables us to trace his life through at least fourteen moves between 1878 and 1900. After rather promising beginnings, his Arizona prospects were blasted by the polygamy dislocation of the 1880s. Thereafter, he never escaped the consequences of drought, washouts, and general mishap, though he moved repeatedly from Snowflake, Holbrook, and Woodruff and back again, took up two ranches, migrated to Mexico twice, and lived on the Gila River. Initiative and determination were not lacking, but opportunity was. The consequent result was a lifetime of movement and disappointment. In spite of his poverty and his general willingness to embrace change to undo it, Fish neither left the general area designated in his call nor succumbed to the temptation to follow economic pursuits other than those prescribed by the church. Once offered an opportunity to set up a business at Holbrook in conjunction with Gentile interests, Fish rejected it for church reasons, though he subsequently "thought many times" that "he might have done better" had he taken the offer.[40]

Fish's case was not unusual. Peter Nielson made at least five moves between coming to Arizona in 1878 and his death at Juarez in 1886. Though he left no firsthand account, Peter Christofferson can also be traced to five moves. Jacob Hamblin, who had known no rest in a long life of church service, wandered in poverty from Alpine, to Pleasanton, New Mexico, to Mexico and back again to Pleasanton and Alpine before death finally relieved him in 1886. John Bloomfield dragged his large family from Cache Valley to Moenkopi and, after a brief residence there, to Obed which he left for Sunset when Obed folded in 1877. Asking troublesome questions about Lot Smith's administration of the Sunset United Order, he was sent to Savoia in 1882. Barely settled, he was uprooted once again by the polygamy prosecutions which sent him fleeing to Colonia Diaz, Mexico, in 1885. Living there until 1887, he returned

---

[40] "Autobiography of Joseph Fish," p. 246.

to Ramah, as Savoia was called by that time. Finding no opportunity there, he moved to Kirtland on the San Juan River in 1889 where he remained until 1894 when he returned to Ramah.[41]

Perhaps the restlessness of pioneering Mormons is nowhere better revealed than in the diaries and letters of the family of Lewis Barney. Their longings focused upon the church, the father and his children anxiously followed the advances of the frontier, crossing back and forth over most of the vast region lying between Mexico and Wyoming. Nowhere were their economic needs met and nowhere were their inner desires satisfied. "Broken up in Sanpete" by the Indian wars of the 1860s, the Barneys probed about in the Sevier Valley, touching down briefly at Richfield, Marysvale, and Circleville. At the latter spot, they planted crops and for a short time enjoyed fair prospects before, according to Barney's account, a "poison wind" sprang up killing their crops and the forage in the area. Discouraged, the elder Barney decided to look for "some more suitable location." In a notation that betrays how he followed the prompting of the spirit and reflects his strong attachment to his family, he wrote:

I then told them [his sons] that we would do no good here and we would not prosper in this valley and that I had made up my mind to go back. They concluded to try it where they were and remain on their claims. Finding I could not persuade them to go with me I hitched up my team and started down the river, but my mind was worried about my family. I was about three miles . . . turned out the team and went back. If possable to get my family to come away. I went up into the canyon where the boys were getting out logs. There I laid before them my feelings in relation to them staying there, and that I did not believe they would ever do any good or be prospered in that place. But I could not induce them to come away. So I left them with a heavy heart bowed down with sorrow.[42]

After shifting about in southern Utah for the next fifteen years, Lewis Barney and part of his family set out for "Lunis Valley" in New Mexico. Working their way through northern Arizona in the direst poverty, they arrived early in 1882. Trading their guns and other items for food, they maintained life during the spring. Resources exhausted, they were temporarily heartened by a word of a "house to be built" in the village of Montrose some twenty or thirty miles away. After a hard trip during the course of which their oxen gave out requiring them to leave their outfit and make their way on foot, carrying their tools, they arrived only to find

---

[41] For Peter Nielson's travels, see "Diary of Peter Nielson," pp. 216-24. Data on Peter Christofferson is found in the diaries of Jesse N. Smith, Joseph Fish, Levi Savage, and L. H. Hatch. Hamblin's last years are traced in Paul Bailey, *Jacob Hamblin, Buckskin Apostle* (Los Angeles: Westlore Press, 1948).

[42] "Journal of Lewis Barney," typescript BYU, p. 90.

they had missed "the party that wanted the house built." While a son went on to Round Valley looking for work, Barney returned to their new home, arriving "sick, tired and hungry." Demoralized and suffering, they were plunged into deepening gloom when a mid-June frost killed their hopes of a harvest. Moving on to the Gila Valley, the family spread, some about southern Arizona and some back to Utah.[43]

Meantime, another son, Arthur, worked at railroad construction and freighting in central and southeast Utah before locating in the neighborhood of Sam Gilson's ranch in the mouth of Salina Canyon. Following the flow of settlers into Castle Valley, he moved onto the Muddy of eastern Utah where he lived from 1882 until 1885. In the latter year he went to "Joe's Valley . . . between Castle Valley and Sanpete county" on the Wasatch Plateau. Moving to Wellington, Utah, the next year, he stayed until 1889 when, frightened by a diphtheria epidemic, he abandoned his small holdings, taking his family "into the mountains" where he cut ties for a year before going on to Smith's fork near Fort Bridger in 1890.[44]

In 1887 Lewis Barney was back in Utah. By now seventy-nine years of age, he longed to get "a place and settle down for life." But even in his advanced years circumstances led his attention from one spot to another without his ever finding a place to rest. His interest now was usually attracted by one of his numerous family. Writing from Wellington where he was staying with his son, he noted:

My family is scattered all over the country. Betsey, Henry and Joseph at Kanosh, Millard county, Utah, Walter is on the Gila River, Arizona. David is in Texas . . . Elizabeth and Emiline is at Bowie Station, Arizona and Martha Ann is at Miller Creek about fifteen miles from here.[45]

But the family was not static long, and the kind of tidings that had always characterized their lives soon came from Kanosh. Venting his discontent, Lewis's son Henry wrote:

Times get worse here for making a living, we have sustained a heavy loss on our sheep herd and we will come out way behind and have lost several head of horned stock and horses. . . . I have not got much of a crop this season, I have just finished my wheat. I only got eighty [eight?] bushels to the acre, my corn did not do well, and have finished hauling my hay and only had eighteen loads at that. I should like mighty well to find a good place to move to, where I could live without so much hard work, you think of going to Colorado and I am thinking of going there myself and homesteading some land, I should like to look at the country and if you find a good place let me know, it may be

---

43 *Ibid.*, pp. 180-87.

44 "Arthur Barney Journal, Leota, Utah, February 7, 1933," typescript BYU, pp. 40-43.

45 Letter to John Barney copied in "Journal of Lewis Barney," pp. 164-65.

that Joseph and I will come out there to that country, I would like it if we could live together in some good place. . . .[46]

Earlier in the same year, another son, David, had made his way back from Texas as far as Mancos, Colorado. Excited by the prospects of cheap land and southwestern Colorado's farming potential, he had written letters encouraging others of the family to join him. Given the dearth of opportunity in their circumstances, the lure of a new beginning drew at them as it had done before. But without revealing how many of the family removed to Colorado, the account of these nomadic wanderings ended with a letter written to Mr. Barney in September of 1890 informing him that "Albert and Emiline" had moved from Bowie Station to Show Low, Arizona.[47]

Colonists whose economic needs were met, even in a modest way, appear to have been far more stable. Such families as the Smiths, Hunts, and Flakes at Snowflake, and the Udalls, and Platts at St. Johns, moved with infrequency though change of residence was not unknown among them either. After his arrival at Snowflake in 1878, Jesse N. Smith made only two moves — to Mexico and back again — both in 1885. After a short sojourn at Savoia, John Hunt appears to have spent the remainder of his life at Snowflake, enjoying a comfortable living and the perquisites of his office as bishop. Udall, on the other hand, was not only uprooted by his imprisonment in Detroit, but lived at various times in St. Johns, Round Valley, and Hunt. In his case, however, desire to develop economic opportunity for himself and the community, rather than dire need, appears to have been the prime reason for movement. Not only did the original pioneers of these families prove to be relatively stable, but a goodly number of their sons and daughters were able to earn a livelihood and remained in the area.

In many cases, however, settlers who to all appearances did well economically and played prominent and satisfying roles in the church and social life of the colony never really struck root. Some of these returned to Utah; others moved on to the Salt River Valley or elsewhere in Arizona. Apparent in the foregoing is another fact about the Mormon society of these outlying areas. Not only did it frequently fail to provide economic opportunity, but some Mormons were unable to fill their needs for participation in the development of the kingdom. A good deal of economic hardship could be borne and frequently was if the other yearnings of men's souls were satisfied.

---

[46] *Ibid.,* June 29, 1888.
[47] *Ibid.,* letter of David Barney, September 14, 1890.

Levi Savage, for instance, lived for years under very close financial circumstances at Woodruff, but as bishop and stake clerk he was a member of the local leadership group. His opinion was valued and respected and, perhaps most importantly, his determination and qualities of leadership were urgently needed. So vital did his local superiors consider his role that when he was released by the president of the church after twenty-five years as bishop, the stake presidency asked him to stay on for a time to accomplish certain crucial tasks. His was not an easy life nor a prosperous one, but it did fulfill his sense of mission. Many of the permanent settlers shared in the essentials of his experience, living fruitful if humble lives.

Some individuals were less fortunate. We have seen the Barneys' quest. Another who was frustrated in his need for involvement was Allen Frost. A versatile and gifted, if cranky, Englishman, Frost arrived in Snowflake from Nutrioso in 1889. His skills — which included carpentering, school teaching, surveying, architectural designing, brickmaking, masonry, and musical talent — were eagerly sought by the community. During the time of prosperity that characterized Snowflake from 1889 to 1892, Frost was in the forefront of affairs, designing important public and private structures, playing a key role in the movement to establish an academy, and helping divide the land purchase, as well as teaching school and building up his own home. A sense of vitality and progress are clearly felt in Frost's journal, as is his own satisfaction at being able to contribute to the town's development.[48]

But in 1893 a change of attitude was apparent. Discharged from his position as teacher in that year, Frost was increasingly barred from public life in the years that followed. Almost complete by 1898, his exclusion appears to have been in large measure the product of personality conflicts, but it was also a matter of social acceptance. Although previously a member of the High Council in the Kanab Stake, he never penetrated the front ranks of church leadership in Snowflake. Furthermore, he lacked the protection that important marital connections afforded many of the polygamist residents of the interrelated community.

As the doors closed before him, Frost turned increasingly to outside activities. Teaching first in other Mormon villages, he later took up freighting and contracting at Holbrook and Winslow to relieve his financial need and provide gainful family-oriented employment for his sons. No longer taking an active part in community affairs, he continued to live at Snowflake, but his talents and enthusiasm were lost. The tragedy was the greater

---

[48] "Diary of Allen Frost," pp. 551-898, for his Snowflake experience.

because, failing to develop a situation in which Frost and the many others who were virtually unused could function effectively, the community and the church as well as the individuals were losers.

Allen Frost's Snowflake and other villages on the Little Colorado River were well established by 1900. The struggle to acquire land, develop water, and to find a place among Arizona's people had all been solved in some degree. While the community's achievement was less than its founders had hoped, there was no doubt that in its minimum requirements, Mormon expansion onto the Little Colorado was successful. This modest success was the product of loyalty, suffering, and communal effort. Because the passing of the American frontier and the developing Mormon reconciliation to the world rendered them obsolete, many of the processes by which it had been founded were increasingly part of the past. But the community remained. Shaped by the determination of its settlers and the paucity of its natural resources, its character would yield only slowly to the greater society of which it was a part.

BIBLIOGRAPHY

ABBREVIATIONS

The following abbreviations are used in the bibliographic entries and in the footnotes to the text.

ALA   Arizona State Department of Libraries and Archives, Phoenix.

AHS   Arizona Historical Society Library, Tucson.

BYU   Brigham Young University Library, Provo, Utah.

HDC   Historical Department of the Church of Jesus Christ of Latter-day Saints, Salt Lake City.

UA   University of Arizona Library, Tucson.

USHS   Utah State Historical Society, Salt Lake City.

UU   University of Utah Library, Salt Lake City.

GUIDES

"A Union List of Arizona Newspapers in Arizona Libraries." Compiled by the Department of Library and Archives. Phoenix: Mimeographed, 1965.

An Arizona Gathering: A Bibliography of Arizona. Compiled by Donald M. Powell. Tucson: The Arizona Pioneers' Historical Society, 1960.

The Annotated Eberstadt Catalogs of Americana. Introduction by Archibald Hanna, Jr. 4 vols. New York: Argosy Antiquarian Ltd., 1965.

Arizona: A State Guide. Compiled by the Writers' Project of the Works Progress Administration in Arizona. New York: Hastings House, 1940.

Bancroft, Hubert Howe. *History of Arizona and New Mexico, 1530-1888.* San Francisco: The History Company, Publishers, 1890.

————. *History of Utah, 1840-1887.* San Francisco: The History Company, Publishers, 1890.

Barnes, Will C. *Arizona Place Names.* Revised edition by Byrd H. Granger. Tucson: The University of Arizona Press, 1960.

Brandes, Ray. "A Guide to the Collections of the Arizona Pioneers' Historical Society." Tucson: Mimeographed by the Arizona Pioneers' Historical Society, 1961.

Ellsworth, S. George. *A Guide to Utah Manuscripts in the Bancroft Library with an Introduction to Hubert Howe Bancroft and the History of Utah.* Reprint from *Utah Historical Quarterly,* vol. 27 (1954).

Esshom, Frank W. *Pioneers and Prominent Men of Utah*. Salt Lake City: The Utah Pioneer Publishing Co., 1913.

Farish, Thomas Edwin. *History of Arizona*. 8 vols. San Francisco: The Filmer Brothers Electrotype Co., 1915-18.

Goodman, David M. *Arizona Odyssey, Bibliographic Adventures in Nineteenth Century Magazines*. Tempe: Arizona Historical Foundation, 1969.

Jenson, Andrew. *Latter-day Saint Biographical Encyclopedia*. 4 vols. Salt Lake City: Deseret News Press, 1901-36.

Lautrell, Estelle. *Newspapers and Periodicals of Arizona 1859-1911*. University of Arizona Bulletin #15. Tucson: University of Arizona Press, 1949.

Logan, Ida Marie. "Utah, the Mormons, and the West: A Bibliography," *Utah Historical Quarterly*, vols. 25-28 (1954-57).

Morgan, Dale L., and Hammond, George P., eds. *A Guide to the Manuscript Collections of the Bancroft Library*. Vol. 1: *Pacific and Western Manuscripts*. Berkeley: University of California Press, 1963.

National Register of Microfilm Masters 1966. Washington, D.C.: Government Printing Office, 1966.

Powell, Lawrence Clark. *Southwestern Book Trails: A Reader's Guide to the Heartland of New Mexico and Arizona*. Albuquerque: Hara and Wallace Publishers, 1964.

Sloan, Richard A. *History of Arizona*. 4 vols. Phoenix: Record Publishing Company, 1930.

U. S. Library of Congress. *The National Union Catalog of Manuscript Collections, Index, 1959-1962*. Hamden, Connecticut: Shoe String Press, Inc., 1964.

————. *The National Union Catalog of Manuscript Collections, 1959-1961*. Ann Arbor: J. W. Edwards, Publisher, 1962.

————. *The National Union Catalog of Manuscript Collections, 1962*. Hamden: Shoe String Press, Inc., 1964.

Wallace, Andrew, ed. *Sources and Readings in Arizona History*. Tucson: Arizona Pioneers' Historical Society, 1965.

Winther, Oscar Osburn. *The Trans-Mississippi West: A Guide to Its Periodical Literature, 1811-1938*. Bloomington, Indiana: Indiana University Publications, 1942.

DIARIES AND OTHER GENERAL MANUSCRIPT MATERIALS

This work rests in large measure upon diary and other personal records. Little Colorado pioneers took literally the admonition of the church to record their activities. Hundreds of them kept daily accounts. Those that appear here and, hopefully, many others survive. Diaries listed vary widely in quality but taken together represent an achievement that even in the record-conscious Mormon community of the era was unusual if not unique.

The most useful record is that of Joseph Fish. Reworked and added to by Mr. Fish as the years passed, it appears first in the handwritten original, then as his journal, and finally in the "Autobiography of Joseph Fish," which has been used extensively herein. Fish considered himself a historian_ and worked with prodigious energy, producing not only a thorough history of his own doings but a manuscript history of Arizona, a history of the Rocky Mountains, and numerous other writings. He was widely involved in the affairs of the Little Colorado community. Serving as stake clerk (record keeper for the major ecclesiastical subdivision in Arizona) for many years, he knew well the doings of the church. A lawyer by training, businessman by profession, politician by interest, and sometimes fugitive by reason of polygamous marriages, he saw as possibly no other Little Colorado Mormon what took place. This he recorded with self-conscious restraint and with a rare ability to interpret. The result is a rich mine of information — well organized and accurate.

Fortunately a somewhat abbreviated version of Joseph Fish's "Autobiography" has recently been published. Edited by John H. Krenkel of the University of Arizona at Tempe, *The Life and Times of Joseph Fish, Mormon Pioneer* is a boon to all partisans of Arizona and Mormon history but is less useful to the researcher than the more complete "Autobiography."

Only a little less impressive than the writing of Joseph Fish are several other diaries. Outstanding in this group are the daily records of Jesse N. Smith, Frihoff Nielson, Lorenzo Hatch, Levi M. Savage, John Bushman, Allen Frost, and John H. Standifird. Somewhat less illuminating than these, though still of great utility, are the pages kept by Christian L. Christensen, James S. Brown, Wilford Woodruff, Andrew S. Gibbons, and dozens of others.

Unique because they were kept by women and portray a different cross-section of life are the diaries of several women. Outstanding among these are the diaries of Lucy Hannah White Flake and Ida Frances Hunt Udall. These are written with feeling and perception and provide a much-needed window into the lives of Little Colorado women.

Diaries are listed alphabetically according to the writer's name and unlike most of the materials included in this bibliography are briefly annotated.

Amundsen, Andrew. "Journal of a Mission to the San Francisko Mountains, Commenced March 26th 1873."
  The delightfully misspelled original is in the Historical Department of the Church of Jesus Christ of Latter-day Saints. A revealing account of the Arizona Mission of 1873, this little record reflects the company's hyper-negative reaction to northern Arizona as well as the make-up and character of the mission.

Ashcroft, Paris Ira. "Life Sketch."
    This brief reminiscence contains some useful data relative to the move-
ment of frontier families and Indian relations. A mimeographed copy is
in the possession of Ida Galagher, Salt Lake City.

"Arthur Barney Journal, Leota, Utah, February 7, 1933."
    Written late in life, Barney's journal focuses upon the colonization of
eastern Utah and Wyoming. He traces his wanderings over the Colorado
Plateau with considerable detail and conveys the atmosphere of poverty
and the unrequited yearnings that were often the product of the Mormon
church's policy of desert colonization. A typescript copy is at Brigham
Young University Library.

"Journal of Lewis Barney."
    The original diary is in the possession of Ray Woodruff Barney of
Randlett, Utah; a typescript copy is at BYU. The first half of Barney's
diary is devoted to a sketch of his early activities. Beginning in 1881, daily
entries are intermittently made. Containing many letters, it indicates the
mobility of Mormon pioneers.

"Memorandum, Account Book and Diary of Alfred N. Billings, 1855."
    J. Dwight Billings had the original in 1941 and a typescript copy is
presently at BYU. This record of the Elk Mountain Mission to present
Moab in 1855 includes an account of a trading trip to the Navajos across
the San Juan River into Arizona.

"History of John A. Blythe, 1876-1877."
    The original of this account of one missionary's trek to Arizona and the
experiences of the first year at Allen City (later St. Joseph) is found
at the Utah State Historical Society. Recorded with youthful veracity,
this little diary is among the best sources for the earliest period on the
Little Colorado.

Brinkerhoff, Joseph. "A History of Tuba City."
    These random notes in the possession of Hazel M. Brinkerhoff, Mesa,
Arizona, are personal in nature and of sharply limited value.

Bushman, John. "Book of Appraisal."
    The original is owned by George S. Tanner of Salt Lake City: a typed
copy is at BYU. This is a useful source for the study of the Arizona United
Orders, especially the one at St. Joseph.

"John Bushman Diaries, 1871-1923."
    Typed by George S. Tanner from handwritten originals that belong
to M. D. Bushman of Snowflake, Arizona, and A. E. Bushman of Mesa,
Arizona, Bushman's record is especially useful for the call, the trip south,
colonization, and dam building at St. Joseph. A typescript copy is in the
author's possession.

"The Life and Labors of John Bushman."
    Rewritten from his original diaries, this journal is perhaps the most
complete source on early day events at St. Joseph. Numerous copies exist
which vary in some important details; the author found his source at BYU.

"Diary of Christian Lingo Christensen."
    The typescript copy at BYU includes a summary of Christensen's life
to 1883, a day-by-day record to 1887, and miscellaneous entries there-

after. It is a good source on Indian affairs and life at Moenkopi from 1876 to 1886, when Christensen removed to Utah's San Juan.

Christensen, May N. "History of Bendt Nielsen Jr. 1855-1944."

A summary of Nielsen's life, it contains a little valuable material on the trek to Arizona and the colonizing experience. A mimeograph copy is in the author's possession.

Coleman, Evans. Papers.

Located at the Arizona Historical Society Library in Tucson, this vast collection fills thirty-one boxes covering 1886-1950. Including stories by Coleman about St. Johns, Alpine, and other northern Arizona places, many biographic sketches of Little Colorado settlers, and Coleman's diary for 1896 to 1902, this collection is one of the most fruitful sources for Mormon colonization of the Little Colorado.

Coleman, Prime T. Papers.

In the two boxes of this collection are Coleman's diary of 1878 to 1890 and various papers. The diary describes his trips from Lower and Upper Kanab, Silver Reef, and Panguitch, and his Arizona cowboying activities. It is also found in the AHS.

"Diary of Winslow Farr."

Among other things Farr traces his flight from Ogden south to Mexico to avoid apprehension for illegal cohabitation. A typescript copy is at BYU.

"Memoirs of George W. Fawcett."

This typescript copy at USHS was dictated in 1936 in the Utah Historic Records Survey and includes an account of a trip to the Little Colorado evidently taken from notes or a previous diary.

Fish, Joseph. "History of the Eastern Arizona Stake of Zion and of the Establishment of the Snowflake Stake, 1879-1893."

Not an official history, this manuscript exists in typed form in several copies, one of which is in the HDC. It is a valuable and usable sketch of the Little Colorado colony.

Fish, Joseph. "Manuscript History of Arizona."

Probably the first general history of Arizona ever written (completed 1906), this substantial work has never been published. Deposited with the territorial historian at an early date, this manuscript has frequently been used by subsequent historians. Chapters 4 through 9 deal with Mormon colonization. The typed original is at Arizona State Department of Libraries and Archives.

"Autobiography of Joseph Fish."

Covering 1840-1926, the five hundred pages of Fish's autobiography begin and end in Utah but also record the period spent in Arizona, 1878-1916. Ably written by a pioneer historian, it is among the best sources on travel between Utah and Arizona and on church and cultural affairs in the Little Colorado colony. It is also the best single source on pioneer Mormon economic and political affairs in northern Arizona. The typed original is in HDC; various family members and the present writer have xerox copies.

"Diary of Joseph Fish."
    The handwritten original — in the possession of Silas Fish of Phoenix — was used to develop the later journal and autobiography.

"Journal of Joseph Fish."
    Somewhat shorter than the "Autobiography," it was used in compiling the latter. Like the "Autobiography," it represents the Mormon point of view but does it with restraint and justice. The typed original is in the HDC; an earlier handwritten copy is owned by Silas L. Fish of Phoenix.

Fish, Julia Ann Reidhead. "A Sketch of the Lives of John Reidhead, Julia Ann York Reidhead and Julia Ann Reidhead Fish."
    This pioneer account briefly describes the lives of its subjects including the time they lived on the Little Colorado.

Fish, Silas L. "Notes on the Life and Writings of Joseph Fish."
    This summary of the writings of Joseph Fish has value as an index to Joseph Fish's "Autobiography" and "Journal." A typed copy is in the HDC and in the author's possession.

"Autobiography and Diary of Lucy Hannah White Flake."
    Beginning in 1894 and ending with the death of Mrs. Flake in 1900, this record includes pertinent reminiscences on the migration to Arizona and colonization. Original and typed copies are at BYU.

Fox, Ferramorz Young. "A Study of Joseph Smith's Order of Stewardships, and Brigham Young's United Order."
    This typescript copy in HDC is valuable for general study of the United Order.

"Diary of Allen Frost, 1838-1901."
    This faithfully kept account of a versatile settler at Kanab, Nutrioso, and Snowflake is at BYU in a typescript copy; the original diaries belong to Augusta Flake of Snowflake, Arizona.

"Andrew Smith Gibbons Diaries, 1858, 1877 and 1878."
    These diaries include information relative to the first Mormon effort to do missionary work among the Hopis and later efforts to colonize Moenkopi and Tuba City. The originals are owned by Francis Gibbons of Salt Lake City; a xeroxed copy of a typescript is at USHS.

"Diary of Thales H. Haskell 1859-1860."
    The diary covers an expedition to the Hopi Mesas and Haskell's sojourn among the Indians. The original and typed copies are at BYU.

"Thales Hastings Haskell, Pioneer, Scout, Explorer, Indian Missionary 1847-1909."
    Edited and compiled by Albert E. Smith in 1964, this is a compilation of sketches and documents the most useful of which are excerpts from Haskell's "Diary" which contains some information on early day Sunset and considerable on Moenkopi before 1879. A multilithed copy is at BYU.

"Lorenzo Hill Hatch Journal."
    Edited by Ruth S. Hilton from the original handwritten diaries, which are in HDC, the Arizona period of Hatch's journal (1876 to 1901) includes in addition to much data on the Zuñi Indian mission, church matters, and polygamy, an account of nearly a quarter of a century's struggle to dam the Little Colorado River at Woodruff. The best source for early Woodruff, a multilith copy is in the author's possession.

Heywood, J. N., Jr., Collection.
   Located at AHS, this collection includes correspondence, family diaries telling of trips to Kanab, Alpine, and other places, as well as manuscripts on events and personalities of early northern Arizona.

"J. N. Heywood Diary 1872-1880."
   This diary has to do with ranching and stock raising at Kanab, St. George, and Fort Pearce and is only indirectly related to the settlement of northern Arizona. It is among the Prime T. Coleman papers at AHS.

"Oliver B. Huntington Diary."
   A typed copy of this account of the Elk Mountain Mission to "Little Grand Valley" or present Moab in 1855 is found at BYU.

"Anthony Woodward Ivins Journal."
   This journal contains a day-to-day account of two missions to the Little Colorado country, one in 1875, the other in 1878. There is also considerable information on Indian affairs, the Mexican Mission, and northern Arizona's cattle industry. The handwritten original is in HDC; a microfilm copy is at the University of Utah Library.

"The 1882 Journal of Warren Marshall Johnson."
   A typescript copy was made available to the author by P. T. Reilly, Los Angeles. The journal deals primarily with Johnson's mission and travels and only in passing with his role at Lee's Ferry.

Keam, Thomas V. Letters, 1887-1894.
   This material is located in the National Archives; microfilm is found at the Center for Study of the American West, UU.

Ladd, Samuel G. "Settlement of the Little Colorado Country, Arizona."
   The original of this eleven-page resume of the Little Colorado's settlement is in the Bancroft Library; microfilm copies are at BYU and UU.

Le Sueur, James Warren. Papers.
   This collection at the AHS includes manuscripts on various subjects and characters of northern Arizona history, such as Lot Smith, the Hashknife Company, the United Order, and Jacob Hamblin, as well as autobiographical material and numerous letters from Wilford Woodruff to Ammon M. Tenney and others.

"Journal of Platte DeAlton Lyman."
   Several typewritten copies of this journal of Utah's San Juan are available and are on file at USHS, BYU, and HDC. Some of these are copies of copies and contain errors.

"Journal of Daniel H. McAllister, Northern Arizona, 1876-77."
   Beginning in January, 1876, this is a running account of the fourteen months McAllister spent on the Little Colorado. A typescript copy is at the BYU, a photocopy of which is in the possession of the present writer.

McLaws, John. "Account Book."
   This careful account reveals the economic affairs of one St. Joseph settler in day-to-day detail; particularly apparent is the substitution of barter for money. The original is in the possession of George S. Tanner of Salt Lake City.

"Biographical Sketches of John McLaws."
   This collection includes biographical materials on John W. McLaws, Ellen Elsie McLaws, and several other Little Colorado pioneers. Typed copies are at BYU.

"Diary of John McLaws, Jr. 1852-1895."
     This diary recounts the writer's role in dam building, Indian missionary work, and general life at St. Joseph. A typed copy is at BYU.

Michie, R. E. L. "Report on Lot Smith Killing, July 13, 1892."
     This report is found in the National Archives, Records of the War Department, Record Group 98, Department of Arizona.

"Minute Book of the Allen City United Order."
     This careful account of the St. Joseph United Order is the best source of information on the Little Colorado United Order. The original is owned by George S. Tanner of Salt Lake City; typed copies are at BYU and HDC.

"Minutes of Frihoff Nielson for the Sunset Committee."
     This typescript in the possession of the present writer contains sundry notes on the settlement of the Sunset United Order.

"Minutes of the Little Colorado Stake Conferences."
     These are the official minutes of sermons and directives given to the membership of the Little Colorado Stake in the late 1870s and early 1880s. Unlike other official church records, this original is found at University of Arizona. This useful source has recently been typed from the original by George S. Tanner, rendering it much easier to read than the original.

"Minutes of the Woodruff Irrigation Company, 1895-1906."
     This record consists of rather detailed minutes of the Woodruff Irrigation Company. The original minutes are in the possession of Earl Crofford, Woodruff, Arizona; copy is in the author's possession.

"Horatio Morrill's Book."
     This is a record of an 1869 mission to the Hopis and is in typescript form at USHS.

"Diary of Emma W. Mechan Nielson."
     Beginning with 1887 and running with lapses until 1895, Mrs. Nielson's diary reveals much about a woman's life at Ramah, New Mexico. One of the few Little Colorado diaries by a woman, it is a most valuable source on polygamy and the cultural stagnation felt by some Little Colorado pioneers. Typescript copy is at BYU.

"Frihoff G. Nielson Diary 1875-1935."
     Placed in the HDC in 1966 by Frihoff Ellis Nielson, this typescript is probably the best account of life in the Sunset United Order. Also in the HDC are Nielson's "Autobiography and Notes 1851-1933."

"Diary of Peter Nielson."
     This diary has been translated from the Danish by J. F. Nielson and compiled by Frihoff E. Nielson. Only the last few pages deal with the diarist's decade on the Little Colorado frontier but these nevertheless provide useful data on movement within the colony and about the growth of Ramah, New Mexico. A multilith copy is in the possession of Mrs. LaVinta Shiner, Price, Utah.

"Diary of L. John Nuttall, 1834-1905."
Secretary to John Taylor and Wilford Woodruff, Nuttall recorded many of their activities. His diary is consequently most useful for tracing the role of church leaders in the colonizing process including that of the Little Colorado. The handwritten original belongs to Mrs. Clara Nuttall Glass of Provo; a typed copy is at BYU.

Nuttall, L. J. Letter Press Books.
Several letter press books of Nuttall's are at BYU. Though mostly concerned with affairs at Kanab, some of his correspondence overlaps into northern Arizona matters.

"William B. Pace Diary of the Elk Mountain Mission 1855-1856."
Begins April 6, 1855 with Pace's call and ends in February of 1856. Typed copy is at BYU.

Petersen, Joseph L. "Life Sketches of Niels Petersen and Mary Mortensen Petersen."
The sketches are reminiscences of pioneering experiences. A mimeographed copy is in the possession of the author.

Porter, Rulon E. "Joseph City Irrigation Company."
This material is useful for an understanding of water problems. Typescript is in the possession of the author.

————. "The Little Colorado River Valley, Its Description, Its History, Its Settlement by the Mormons."
A manuscript history of the Little Colorado colony, this work is based on numerous early records no longer extant; consequently, it is most useful for the first years of colonization. A typescript copy is in the possession of the author.

"A Journal of the Life and Travels of S. U. Porter."
In two handwritten volumes, Porter's journal is now at the BYU. Dealing with northern Arizona after 1884, it traces Porter's activities at St. Joseph and Heber.

"Diary of John Pulsipher."
While not pertaining directly to the colonization of northern Arizona, Pulsipher's account contains much relevant material on the mission call, polygamy, and colonization. A typescript copy is at Bancroft Library, microfilm at UU.

Reilly, P. T. Personal Collection.
Mr. Reilly of Los Angeles has collected many valuable primary materials dealing with the Colorado River and its environs.

"Diary of Andrew L. Rogers, 1882-1902."
This typescript diary dealing with Roger's pioneering experiences is at USHS.

"Life Sketch of Andrew L. Rogers."
Reminiscences of Andrew L. Rogers are found in this typescript at BYU.

"Journal of Samuel Hollister Rogers."
The journal traces Rogers' move to Arizona and his activities as a colonist there. The original belongs to Sarah Rogers Decker of Snowflake, Arizona; a typescript copy is at BYU.

"Diary of Levi Mathers Savage, 1873."
    This daily account of young Savage's affairs includes a call to Arizona which was not filled until later. Recording several meetings with returning missionaries of 1873 and their unsuccessful attempt to colonize the Little Colorado, the diary throws much light on their reaction to northern Arizona. The original belongs to Joseph Savage of Chandler, Arizona; a typed copy is in the Western History Center at UU.

"Journal of Levi Mathers Savage."
    Chronicling over a half century on Mormon frontiers, most of this diary deals with Savage's experiences at Sunset, in Mexico, and at Woodruff. The original is in the HDC; a multilithed version has been edited by Ruth S. Hilton.

Shoemaker, Samuel E. "Interview with the Navajo, Cat-chose, on the Death of Lot Smith." February 17, 1895.
    This interview is at the Southwest Museum, Los Angeles, California.

"Diary of Charles Smith."
    Basically a diary of southwestern Utah, it sheds some light on Mormon culture, particularly polygamy and the United Order. A typescript copy is at BYU.

"Journal of Jesse N. Smith 1834-1906."
    The handwritten original of this very valuable journal is in the HDC. The Smith Family Association has published it as the *Journal of Jesse N. Smith*. This record by the leading Little Colorado Mormon faithfully portrays Smith's public, church, and private affairs from the time of his first visit to the Little Colorado in 1878 until his death in 1906.

"Diary of Joseph West Smith, 1859-1936."
    Active in business, education, church, and political affairs, Smith provides one of the better accounts of Little Colorado development. A typescript copy in two volumes is at BYU; the original diaries are in the possession of Lenora S. Rogers, Snowflake.

Smith, Lot. Papers.
    This important collection consists of official correspondence between Smith and the Salt Lake City leaders of the church. It is of primary worth for study of colonization of the lower river villages of Sunset, Brigham City, Obed, and Joseph City as well as a rich source on the role of one of northern Arizona's most colorful characters. Originals are at the UA; xerox copies are at the HDC and USHS.

Solomon, William Henry. "Diary of the Arizona Mission 1873-1874."
    The diary is useful primarily for the Arizona Mission of 1873 and missionary activities at Moenkopi in 1873 and 1874. A typescript copy is in the possession of Mrs. Mary Elizabeth Shumway, Taylor, Arizona; also at ALA.

"Journals of John Henry Standifird 1831-1923."
    The record of a ward bishop, Standifird's diary is probably the best account of Taylor's development. It also traces the various roads to Utah with unusual clarity. Microfilms of a typed copy are at the ALA and BYU.

Steele, John. "Report of Exploring Trip South of St. George as Far as the Moquis Nation, November 1862 to January 7, 1863."
This report is in the Jacob Hamblin Papers in the HDC.

"Sketch of the Life of Brigham Stowell."
Compiled in 1966 by Gertrude S. Romney, this sketch includes a copy of the account of the trip to northern Arizona and pioneering experiences. Typescript is in the possession of the author.

Tanner, George S. "United Order."
Part of a forthcoming work on the history of Joseph City, this manuscript reveals a thorough grasp of the Arizona Orders.

"Journal of John W. Tate."
This diary of an 1880 trip to Arizona is of outstanding value for study of trails and the Mormon villages of the Little Colorado. A typescript copy is at USHS.

Tenney, Ammon M. Collection.
Located at the AHS, the Tenney collection consists of four boxes including his diaries beginning in 1866 and various papers relative to his experiences in northern Arizona and Mexico. Mission activities, railroading, Fort Defiance, and matters of church policy are all included.

Tuba City Collection.
This collection located at the Southwest Museum, Los Angeles, consists of many letters from Indian farmers, Indian agents, and non-Mormon missionaries. It throws much light on anti-Mormon sentiment which led to the expulsion of the Mormons from Tuba City.

"Journal of Ida Frances Hunt Udall."
The first part of the diary is a sketch of Mrs. Udall's early life written by herself and a sister. From May 1882 to December 1886, entries are regular. It is a useful source on polygamy and the Arizona prosecutions. The original is in the possession of Maria Ellsworth of Logan; a xerox copy is at the HDC.

Whitaker, John M. Papers.
Deposited at the UU, the Whitaker Papers include personal letters to John W. Young and others and railroading papers that are pertinent to the construction of the Atlantic and Pacific road across northern Arizona.

"Daily Journal of John M. Whitaker."
Photostatic copies of the journal's three volumes are at the UU. While Whitaker spent his life as a business and church man in Salt Lake City, his job as private secretary to John W. Young in the late 1880s led him to make a number of entries that are important to an understanding of Young's role in northern Arizona.

Wiltbank, Milo. Collection.
This collection consists of a number of tape recorded interviews with pioneers of northeastern Arizona and is found at the AHS.

Woodbury, Angus. "The United Order."
A copy of this manuscript is at the Utah State University Library. It is a useful contribution to the United Order literature.

"Wilford Woodruff's Journal, January 1st 1873 to February 7th 1880 (A Synopsis of Wilford Woodruff's Travels and Labors taken from his Journal by Himself.)"

Including the year 1879-1880 Woodruff spent on the Little Colorado in hiding from federal authorities, this handwritten original at the HDC contains most useful insight into polygamy, travel, and Woodruff's role in the development of the mission.

Zulick, Conrad M. Papers.

Letters and official papers of Governor Zulick are located at the AHS.

CHURCH RECORDS AND OFFICIAL LETTERS

By no means exhausting the official church records on the Little Colorado colony, the following histories, minutes, and letters were particularly useful in gathering data for this study. The official histories yielded the general outlines of development. Letters and minute books were indispensible in establishing official policy and in studying the problems of the colony. All entries under this heading are located at the Historical Department of the Church in Salt Lake City. Materials relating to Arizona are scattered at random through the letters and papers enumerated. In some cases, alphabetical indexes speed the work of searching the letterpress books; otherwise, the materials must be worked through piece by piece.

Bleak, James G. "Annals of the Southern Utah Mission," Books A, B, and C.

Haight, Horton D. Personal File.

Hamblin, Jacob. Letters.

Hatch, Lorenzo H. Personal File.

"History of the Saint Johns Ward."

Jenson, Andrew. "History of the Eastern Arizona Stake."

_____. "History of the Little Colorado Stake."

_____. "History of the San Juan Stake."

_____. "History of the Snowflake Stake."

_____. "History of the St. Johns Stake."

_____. "Index for Arizona References in the *Deseret News.*"

_____. "Southwest Indian Mission History."

"Journal History of the Church."

"Minute Book or Record of the Mutual Improvement Association for the Young Men, Sunset Ward."

"Minutes of a Quarterly Conference of the Little Colorado Stake, May 31– June 1, 1884."

"Minutes of the Eastern Arizona Stake Conferences 1879-1882."

"Minutes of the Eastern Arizona Stake Conferences 1883-1885."

"Minutes of the Eastern Arizona Stake Conferences 1886-1889."

"Minutes of the Snowflake Stake Conferences, 1890-1892."

"Minutes of the Snowflake Stake Conferences, 1892-98."

Porter, Rulon. "History of the Joseph City Ward."

"Ramah Ward Record," Books A, B, and C.

Roundy, Lorenzo. Personal File.

Smith, Lot. Personal File.

Snow, Erastus. Letters.

Sunset United Order Papers.

Taylor, John. Letters.

Udall, David K. Personal File.

Woodruff, Wilford. Letters.

Young, Brigham. Letters.

Young, Brigham Jr. Letters and Personal Papers.

Young, John W. Letters, Personal Papers, Personal File, and Railroad File.

BOOKS AND PERIODICALS

Albright, George Leslie. *Official Explorations for Pacific Railroads, 1853-1855.* Berkeley: University of California Press, 1921.

Alexander, Thomas G. "An Experiment in Progressive Legislation: The Granting of Woman Suffrage in Utah in 1870," *Utah Historical Quarterly* 38 (Winter 1970): 20-30.

Allen, Edward J. *The Second United Order Among the Mormons.* New York: Columbia University Press, 1936.

Alter, J. Cecil. *Utah the Storied Domain: A Documentary History of Utah's Eventful Career....* 3 vols. Chicago and New York: American Historical Society, 1932.

Anderson, Joseph F. "Pioneers and Pioneering in Southeastern Utah," *The Improvement Era*, vol. 17 (1915).

Anderson, Nels. *Desert Saints: The Mormon Frontier in Utah.* Chicago: University of Chicago Press, 1966.

Arrington, Leonard J. *Great Basin Kingdom: An Economic History of the Latter-day Saints 1830-1900.* Cambridge: Harvard University Press, 1958.

————. *Orderville, Utah: A Pioneer Mormon Experiment in Economic Organization.* Monograph Series, vol. 2, no. 2. Logan: Utah State University Press, 1954.

Bailey, Lynn R., ed. *The Navajo Reconnaissance: A Military Exploration of the Navajo Country in 1859.* By Captain J. G. Walker and Major O. L. Shepherd. Los Angeles: Westernlore Press, 1964.

Bailey, Paul. *Jacob Hamblin, Buckskin Apostle.* Los Angeles: Westernlore Press, 1948.

Bancroft, Hubert Howe. *History of Arizona and New Mexico, 1530-1888.* San Francisco: The History Company, Publishers, 1890.

Bancroft, Hubert Howe (*cont.*)

————. *History of Utah 1840-1887.* San Francisco: The History Company, Publishers, 1890.

Banta, Albert F. "Albert Franklin Banta: Arizona Pioneer," ed., Frank D. Reeve, *New Mexico Historical Review,* vols. 27-28 (1952-53).

Barnes, William C. "Arizona Place Names," University of Arizona Bulletin 4: 1, *General Bulletin* no. 2 (January 1935). Tucson: University of Arizona Press, 1935.

————. "The Pleasant Valley War of 1887: Its Genesis, History and Necrology," *Arizona Historical Review* 4 (1931-32): 5-40.

————. *Western Grazing Grounds and Forest Ranges: A History of the Livestock Industry as Conducted on the Open Ranges of the Arid West, with Particular Reference to the Use Now Being Made of the Ranges in the National Forests.* Chicago: Breeder's Gazette, 1913.

Bartlett, Richard A. *Great Surveys of the American West.* Norman: University of Oklahoma Press, 1962.

Beadle, J. H. *Western Wilds, and the Men Who Redeem Them: An Authentic Narrative, Embracing an Account of Seven Years Travel and Adventure in the Far West; Wild Life in Arizona; Perils of the Plains; Life in Canon and Death on the Desert; Adventures among the Red and White Savages of the West; the Mountain Meadow Massacre; the Custer Defeat; Life and Death of Brigham Young.* Cincinnati and Chicago: Jones Brothers & Co., 1879.

Beaman, E. O. "The Canyon of the Colorado, and the Moquis Pueblos," *Appleton's Journal* 11 (April-May 1874): 481-82, 513-16, 545-48, 590-93, 623-26, 641-44, 686-88.

Beck, D. Elden. "Mormon Trails to Bluff," *Utah,* vol. 4-5 (1940-41).

Birney, Hoffman. *Zealots of Zion.* Philadelphia: Penn Publishing Co., 1931.

Bliss, Robert S. "Journal of . . . with the Mormon Battalion," *Utah Historical Quarterly* 4 (July and October 1931): 67-96, 110-28.

Bolton, Herbert E. "Escalante in Dixie and the Arizona Strip," *New Mexico Historical Review* 3 (January 1928): 41-72.

————. *Pageant in the Wilderness: The Story of the Escalante Expedition to the Interior Basin, 1776, Including the Diary and Itinerary of Father Escalante Translated and Annotated.* Salt Lake City: Utah State Historical Society, 1950.

Bourke, John G. *On the Border with Crook.* New York: Charles Scribner's Sons, 1891.

Brandes, Ray. *Frontier Military Posts of Arizona.* Globe, Arizona: Dale S. King, 1960.

Brimhall, George W. *The Workers of Utah.* Provo, Utah, 1889.

Brinkerhoff, Sara E., and Brewer, Nina B., comps. "Our Town and People, A Brief History of Woodruff." Multilithed, 1965.

Brooks, Juanita. "Indian Relations on the Mormon Frontier," *Utah Historical Quarterly* 22 (January-April 1944): 1-48.

————. "Jacob Hamblin, Apostle to the Indians," *Arizona Highways* 19 (April 1943): 31-35.

————, ed. "Journal of Thales H. Haskell," *Utah Historical Quarterly* 12 (January-April 1944): 69-98.

————. "Lee's Ferry at Lonely Dell," *Utah Historical Quarterly* 25: 284-95.

————. *Mountain Meadows Massacre.* New ed. Norman: University of Oklahoma Press, 1962.

————, ed. *On the Mormon Frontier: The Diary of Hosea Stout, 1844-1861,* 2 vols. Salt Lake City: University of Utah Press and Utah State Historical Society, 1964.

Brown, James S. *Life of a Pioneer: Autobiography of James S. Brown.* Salt Lake City: George Q. Cannon & Sons, Co., 1900.

Bufkin, Donald. "The Lost County of Pah-Ute," *Journal of Arizona History* 5 (Summer 1964): 1-11.

Carter, Kate B., comp. "Historic Letters of the Past," *Daughters of Utah Pioneers Lessons* (November 1959).

Christensen, Christian Lingo. "Accounts of Experiences among the Navajos, Hopis and Zunis," *Times Independent* (Moab, Utah), February 9, 16, 23, March 9, June 29, 1922, October 9, 1924, and April 25, 1935.

Clayton, Roberta Flake, comp. and ed., "Pioneer Women of Arizona." Mimeographed. Mesa, Arizona, 1968.

Cleland, Robert Glass, and Brooks, Juanita, eds. *A Mormon Chronicle: The Diaries of John D. Lee, 1848-1876.* 2 vols. San Marino: The Huntington Library Press, 1955.

Clyde, George Dewey. "History of Irrigation in Utah," *Utah Historical Quarterly* 27 (January 1959): 27-36.

Corbett, Pearson H. *Jacob Hamblin, Peacemaker.* Salt Lake City: Deseret Book Company, 1952.

Cowley, Matthias F., ed. *Wilford Woodruff, History of His Life and Labors as Recorded in His Daily Journal.* Salt Lake City: The Deseret News Press, 1909.

Cozzens, Samuel Woodworth. *The Marvelous Country or Three Years in Arizona and New Mexico.* Boston: Lee and Shepard Publishers, 1876.

Crampton, C. Gregory. "Mormon Colonization in Southern Utah and Adjacent Parts of Arizona and Nevada, 1851-1900." Mimeographed. U. S. National Park Service, 1965.

————. *Outline History of the Glen Canyon Region, 1876-1922.* Edited by Charles E. Dibble. Glen Canyon Series no. 9. Anthropological Papers no. 42. Salt Lake City: University of Utah Press, 1959.

————. *Standing Up Country, The Canyon Lands of Utah and Arizona.* New York: Alfred A. Knopf, 1964.

————, and Miller, David E., eds. "Journal of Two Campaigns by the Utah Territorial Militia Against the Navajo Indians, 1869," *Utah Historical Quarterly* 29 (April 1961): 149-76.

————, and Rusho, W. L. "A Report on the History of Lee's Ferry, Arizona." Mimeographed. U. S. National Park Service, Santa Fe, 1965.

Creer, Leland Hargrave, ed. *History of Utah 1847 to 1869 by Andrew Love Neff.* Salt Lake City: Deseret News Press, 1940.

Creer, Leland Hargrave (*cont.*)

————. *Mormon Towns in the Region of the Colorado.* Anthropological Papers no. 32. Salt Lake City: University of Utah Press, 1958.

————. "Spanish-American Slave Trade in the Great Basin, 1800-1853," *New Mexico Historical Review* 24 (July 1949): 171-83.

————. *The Activities of Jacob Hamblin in the Region of the Colorado,* Glen Canyon Series no. 4. Anthropological Papers no. 33. Salt Lake City: University of Utah Press, 1958.

Daniels, Howard E. "Mormon Colonization in Northern Arizona." Unpublished Master's thesis, University of Arizona, 1960.

Darrah, William Culp, ed. "Journal of John F. Steward, May 22-November 3, 1871, [with sketches of] Beaman, Fennemore, Hillers, Dellenbaugh, Johnson, and Hattan and Three Letters by Andrew Hall," *Utah Historical Quarterly* 16-17 (1948-1949): 175-251, 491-508.

————. *Powell of the Colorado.* Princeton: Princeton University Press, 1951.

————, ed. "The Exploration of the Colorado River in 1869," [Including the Journals of J. W. Powell, George Y. Bradley, and J. C. Sumner, together with other Original Documents, Including Biographical Sketches and Preparations for a Second Expedition]. *Utah Historical Quarterly* 15 (1947): 1-153.

Degler, Carl N. *Out of Our Past, The Forces That Shaped Modern America.* New York: Harper & Row, 1959.

Dellenbaugh, Frederick S. *A Canyon Voyage: the Narrative of the Second Powell Expedition Down the Green-Colorado River from Wyoming, and the Explorations on Land in the Years 1871 and 1872.* Second ed. New Haven: Yale University Press, 1926.

————. *The Romance of the Colorado River; the Story of its Discovery in 1540, with an Account of the Later Explorations, and with Special Reference to the Voyages of Powell through the Line of Great Canyons.* New York and London: G. P. Putnam's Sons, 1902.

Edwards, Elbert. "Early Mormon Settlements in Southern Nevada," *Nevada Historical Society Quarterly* 8 (Spring 1965): 25-44.

Euler, Robert C. "Southern Paiute Ethnohistory." Mimeographed. Flagstaff, Arizona, 1956.

Farish, Thomas E. *History of Arizona.* 8 vols. San Francisco: The Filmer Brothers Electrotype Co., 1915-18.

Farquhar, Francis P. *The Books of the Colorado River & the Grand Canyon, a Selective Bibliography.* Los Angeles: Glen Dawson, 1953.

Fewkes, Jesse Walter. *Preliminary Report on a Visit to the Navajo National Monument, Arizona.* Bureau of American Ethnology Bulletin 50. Washington, D.C.: Government Printing Office, 1911.

————. "Two Summers' Work in Pueblo Ruins," *Twenty-Second Annual Report of the Bureau of American Ethnology . . . 1900-1901.* Part I. Washington, D.C.: Government Printing Office, 1904.

Flake, David Kay. "A History of Mormon Missionary Work with the Hopi, Navaho and Zuni Indians." Unpublished Master's thesis, Brigham Young University, 1965.

Flake, Osmer D. *William J. Flake, Pioneer-Colonizer.* Published privately, 1954.

Flake, S. Eugene, comp. *James Madison Flake, Pioneer, Leader, Missionary.* Bountiful, Utah: Wasatch Press, 1970.

Foreman, Grant, ed. *A Pathfinder in the Southwest: The Itinerary of Lieutenant A. W. Whipple During his Exploration for a Railway Route from Fort Smith to Los Angeles in the Years 1853 & 1854.* Norman: University of Oklahoma Press, 1941.

Forrest, Earle R. *Arizona's Dark and Bloody Ground.* Rev. ed. Caldwell, Idaho: Caxton Printers, 1952.

_____. "Riding for the Old C O Bar," *Arizoniana, The Journal of Arizona History,* vol. 5 (Spring 1964).

Gannett, Henry. *A Gazetteer of Utah.* U. S. Geological Survey Bulletin 166. Washington, D.C.: Government Printing Office, 1900.

Geary, Elmo G. "A Study of Dramatics in Castle Valley from 1875-1925." Unpublished Master's thesis, University of Utah, 1953.

Geotzman, William H. *Army Exploration in the American West, 1803-1863.* New Haven: Yale University Press, 1959.

Gibbons, Helen B. *Saint and Savage.* Salt Lake City: Deseret Book Company, 1965.

Gillmore, Frances, and Louisa Wade Wetherill. *Trader to the Navajos: The Story of the Wetherills of Kayenta.* Second ed. Albuquerque: University of New Mexico Press, 1953.

Golder, Frank A. *The March of the Mormon Battalion from Council Bluffs to California.* New York: Century Co., 1928.

Gordon, Clarence. "Report of Cattle, Sheep and Swine Supplementary to Enumeration of Live Stock on Farms in 1880," *Report on the Production of Agriculture as Returned at the Tenth Census (June 1, 1880) Embracing General Statistics and Monographs. . . .* U. S. Department of the Interior, Census Office, Tenth Census. Washington, D.C.: Government Printing Office, 1883.

Gottfredson, Peter. *History of Indian Depredations in Utah.* Salt Lake City: Skelton Publishing Company, 1919.

Granger, Byrd H. *Will C. Barnes Arizona Place Names.* Rev. ed. Tucson: University of Arizona Press, 1960.

Greever, William S. *Arid Domain: The Santa Fe Railway and Its Western Land Grant.* Palo Alto: Stanford University Press, 1954.

_____. "Two Arizona Lieu Land Exchanges," *Pacific Historical Review* 19 (1950): 137-50.

Gregory, Herbert E., ed. *The Navajo Country, a Geographic and Hydrographic Reconnaissance of Parts of Arizona, New Mexico, and Utah.* U. S. Geological Survey Water Supply Paper 380. Washington, D.C.: Government Printing Office, 1916.

Hafen, LeRoy R., and Hafen, Ann W., eds. *Old Spanish Trail, Santa Fe to Los Angeles. . . .* Glendale, California: The Arthur H. Clark Company, 1954.

Hansen, Alice et al., comps. "Diamond Jubilee Gems, Snowflake Stake of Zion, 1887-1962." Multilithed. Snowflake LDS Stake, 1962.

Hansen, Klaus J. *Quest for Empire: The Political Kingdom of God and the Council of Fifty in Mormon History*. East Lansing: Michigan State University Press, 1967.

Harris, Llewelyn. "Miraculous Healings Among the Zunis," *The Juvenile Instructor* 14 (1879): 160.

Haskett, Bert. "Early History of the Cattle Industry in Arizona," *Arizona Historical Review* 6 (1935): 3-42.

_____. "History of the Sheep Industry in Arizona," *Arizona Historical Review* 7 (1936): 3-49.

Hatch, Ira. "The Moquis Indians," as narrated to James A. Little, *Millennial Star* 32 (April 1870): 242.

Hunter, Milton R. *Brigham Young the Colonizer*. Salt Lake City: Deseret News Press, 1940.

_____. "The Mormons and the Colorado River," *The American Historical Review* 44 (April 1939): 449-55.

Ives, Joseph C. *Report upon the Colorado River of the West Explored in 1857 and 1858. . . .* U. S., 36th Cong., 1st sess., House Ex. Doc. 90. Washington, D. C.: Government Printing Office, 1861.

Jennings, James R. *The Freight Rolled*. San Antonio: Naylor Company, 1969.

Jones, Daniel W. *Forty Years Among the Indians*. Salt Lake City: Juvenile Instructor's Office, 1890.

Journal of Discourses. 26 vols. Liverpool, England, 1854-1886.

Kane, Elizabeth D. *Pandemonium or Arcadia: Which? Twelve Mormon Homes Visited in Succession on a Journey Through Utah to Arizona*. Philadelphia: privately published, 1874.

Kelley, Charles. "Chief Hoskaninni," *Utah Historical Quarterly* 21 (1953): 219-26.

Kelly, George H. *Legislative History, Arizona 1864-1912*. Phoenix: Manufacturing Stationers, 1926.

Krenkel, John H., ed. *The Life and Times of Joseph Fish, Mormon Pioneer*. Danville, Illinois: The Interstate Printers & Publishers, Inc., 1971.

Lamar, Howard Roberts. "Political Patterns in New Mexico and Utah Territories, 1850-1900," *Utah Historical Quarterly* 23 (October 1961): 362-87.

_____. *The Far Southwest 1846-1912, A Territorial History*. New Haven: Yale University Press, 1966.

Larson, Andrew Karl. *"I Was Called to Dixie," The Virgin River Basin: Unique Experiences in Mormon Pioneering*. Salt Lake City: Deseret News Press, 1961.

_____. *The Red Hills of November, A Pioneer Biography of Utah's Cotton Town*. Salt Lake City: Deseret News Press, 1957.

_____. *Erastus Snow, The Life of a Missionary and Pioneer for the Early Mormon Church*. Salt Lake City: University of Utah Press, 1971.

Larson, Gustive O. *Outline History of Utah and the Mormons.* Salt Lake City: Deseret Book Company, 1958.

Law, Wesley R. "Mormon Indian Mission, 1855." Unpublished Master's thesis, Brigham Young University, 1958.

Layton, Christopher. *Life of Christopher Layton.* Edited by George Q. Cannon and Selina Layton Phillips. Salt Lake City: Deseret News Press, 1911.

Leigh, Rufus Wood. *Five Hundred Utah Place Names, Their Origin and Significance.* Salt Lake City: Deseret News Press, 1961.

Le Rue, E. C. *Colorado River and Its Utilization.* United States Geological Survey Water Supply Paper 395. Washington, D.C.: Government Printing Office, 1910.

Lesley, Lewis Burt. *Uncle Sam's Camels, the Journal of May Humphreys Stacey Supplemented by the Report of Edward Fitzgerald Beale (1857-1858).* Cambridge: Harvard University Press, 1929.

Levine, Albert J. *Snowflake, A Pictorial Review, 1878-1964.* Published privately, 1964.

Little, James A. *Jacob Hamblin: A Narrative of His Personal Experience, as a Frontiersman, Missionary to the Indians and Explorer. . . .* Salt Lake City: Juvenile Instructor's Office, 1881.

Lockwood, Frank C. *Pioneer Days in Arizona from the Spanish Occupation to Statehood.* New York: Macmillan Company, 1932.

Lyman, Albert R. *Biography of Francis Marion Lyman Apostle, 1880-1916.* Delta, Utah: Published privately, 1958.

————. *Indians and Outlaws: Settling of the San Juan Frontier.* Salt Lake City: Bookcraft, 1962.

McClintock, James H. *Mormon Settlement in Arizona: A Record of Peaceful Conquest of the Desert.* Phoenix: Manufacturing Stationers Inc., 1921.

McNitt, Frank. *The Indian Traders.* Norman: University of Oklahoma Press, 1962.

Meyakawa, Scott T. *Protestants and Pioneers: Individualism and Conformity on the American Frontier.* Chicago: University of Chicago Press, 1964.

Miller, David E. *Hole-in-the-Rock: An Epic in the Colonization of the Great American West.* Salt Lake City: University of Utah Press, 1959.

Miner, H. Craig. *The St. Louis-San Francisco Transcontinental Railroad: The Thirty-fifth Parallel Project, 1853-1890.* Lawrence: University of Kansas Press, 1972.

Mosk, Sanford. *Land Tenure Problems in the Santa Fe Railroad Grant Area.* Berkeley: University of California Press, 1944.

Mott, Dorothy Challis, "Don Lorenzo Hubbell of Ganado," *Arizona Historical Review* 4 (April 1931): 45-51.

Nagata, Shachi. "Modern Transformation of Moenkopi Pueblo." Unpublished Ph.D. dissertation, University of Indiana, 1968.

Nelson, Lowry. *The Mormon Village: A Pattern and Technique of Land Settlement.* Salt Lake City: University of Utah Press, 1952.

Nevins, Allan. *Frémont, Pathmarker of the West.* New York: Appleton-Century Company, 1939.

O'Dea, Thomas F. *The Mormons.* Chicago: University of Chicago Press, 1957.

Olsen, Robert W., Jr. "Pipe Spring, Arizona, and Thereabouts," *Journal of Arizona History* 6 (Spring 1965): 11-20.

Palmer, William R. "Further Notes on Paiute Names," *Zion and Bryce Nature Notes* 8 (September 1936): 18-20.

Peplow, Edward H. *History of Arizona.* New York: Lew Historical Publishing Company, 1958.

Peterson, Charles S. " 'A Mighty Man was Brother Lot': A Portrait of Lot Smith, Mormon Pioneer," *Western Historical Quarterly* 1 (1970): 393-414.

————. "Settlement on the Little Colorado 1873-1900: A Study of the Processes and Institutions of Mormon Expansion." Unpublished Ph.D. dissertation, University of Utah, 1967.

————. "The Hopis and the Mormons: 1858-1873," *Utah Historical Quarterly* 39 (1971): 179-94.

Pinchot, Gifford. *Breaking New Ground.* New York: Harcourt, Brace and Company, 1947.

Porter, Kenneth. "Little Colorado River Settlements Brigham City, Joseph City, Obed and Sunset." Unpublished Master's thesis, Arizona State University at Tempe, 1956.

Powell, John Wesley. *Report on the Arid Lands of the United States, With a More Detailed Account of the Lands of Utah.* Washington, D.C.: Government Printing Office, 1878.

————. *Reports of the Exploration in 1873 of the Colorado of the West and Its Tributaries . . . Under the Direction of the Smithsonian Institution.* Washington, D.C.: Government Printing Office, 1874.

————. "The Ancient Province of Tusayan," *Scribner's Monthly* 11 (1875): 193-213.

Rees, Ellen Greer. "The Christian A. Kempe Family History." Multilithed. 1958.

Reese, John Major. "The Indian Problem in Utah, 1849-1868." Unpublished Master's thesis, University of Utah, n.d.

Reilly, P. T. "How Deadly is Big Red?" *Utah Historical Quarterly* 37 (Spring 1969): 244-60.

————. "Warren Marshall Johnson, Forgotten Saint," *Utah Historical Quarterly* 39 (1971): 3-22.

Richards, J. Morris, and Westover, Adele B. *Unflinching Courage, Joseph City, Arizona.* Joseph City, Arizona: John H. Miller, 1963.

Ricks, Joel E. *Forms and Methods of Early Mormon Settlement in Utah and the Surrounding Region, 1847-1877.* Monograph Series, vol. 11, no. 2. Logan: Utah State University Press, 1964.

Roberts, B. H. *A Comprehensive History of the Church of Jesus Christ of Latter-day Saints: Century I.* 6 vols. Salt Lake City: Deseret News Press, 1930.

Roberts, Paul H. *Hoof Prints on Forest Ranges.* San Antonio: The Naylor Company, 1963.

Simpson, James H. *Journal of a Military Reconnaissance from Santa Fe, New Mexico, to the Navajo Country, Made with Troops under the Command of Brevet Lieutenant Colonel John M. Washington, Chief of the 9th Military Department and Governor of New Mexico, in 1849.* U. S., 31st Cong., 1st sess., Senate Ex. Doc. 64. Washington, D.C.: Union Office, 1850.

Sitgreaves, L. *Report of an Expedition Down the Zuni and Colorado Rivers in 1851.* U. S., 32nd Cong., 1st sess., Senate Ex. Doc. 59. Washington, D.C.: Robert Armstrong, 1853.

Sloan, Richard A., ed., *History of Arizona.* 4 vols. Phoenix: Record Publishing Co., 1930.

Smith, Grant Gill, ed., *The Living Words of Alice Ann Richards Smith.* Published privately, 1968.

Smith, Jesse N. *Journal of Jesse N. Smith.* Salt Lake City: Jesse N. Smith Family Association, 1953.

Smith, Joseph. *History of the Church of Jesus Christ of Latter-day Saints.* 7 vols. 2d ed. rev. Salt Lake City: Deseret News, 1948.

Smith, Lot. "The Echo Canyon War," *The Contributor* 3-4: 18, 27-29, 47-50, 167-69, 224-26, 381-83.

Smith, Melvin T. "The Colorado River: Its History in the Lower Canyons Area." Unpublished Ph.D. dissertation, Brigham Young University, 1972.

Smith, Pauline V. *Captain Jefferson Hunt of the Mormon Battalion.* Salt Lake City: Nicholas G. Morgan, Sr., Foundation, 1958.

Smith, Robert II. "Among the Zuni's," *The Juvenile Instructor* 11 (1876): 224.

Sonne, Conway B. *World of Wakara.* San Antonio: The Naylor Company, 1962.

Stegner, Wallace. *Beyond the Hundredth Meridian: John Wesley Powell and the Second Opening of the West.* Sentry ed. Boston: Houghton Mifflin Co., 1962.

_____. *Mormon Country.* New York: Duell, Sloan & Pearce, 1942.

Tanner, Faun McConkie. *A History of Moab, Utah.* Moab: Press of the Times-Independent, 1937.

Tanner, George S. "Henry Martin Tanner, Joseph City Arizona Pioneer." Multilithed. 1964.

Teller, Irving. "Ramah, New Mexico, 1876-1900, An Historical Episode with Some Value Analysis," *Utah Historical Quarterly* 21 (April 1953): 117-36.

Thomas, George. *Early Irrigation in the Western States.* Salt Lake City: University of Utah, 1948.

_____. *The Development of Institutions Under Irrigation with Special Reference to Early Utah Conditions.* New York: Macmillan, 1920.

Tyler, Daniel. *A Concise History of the Mormon Battalion in the Mexican War, 1846-1847.* Privately printed, 1881. Reprinted. Chicago: Rio Grande Press, 1964. Glorietta: Rio Grande Press, 1969.

Udall, David King and Nelson, Pearl Udall. *Arizona Pioneer Mormon, David King Udall, History and His Family, 1851-1938.* Tucson: Arizona Silhouettes, 1959.

Underhill, Ruth M. *The Navajos.* Norman: University of Oklahoma Press, 1956.

U. S., Work Projects Administration, Utah Writers' Project. *Origin of Utah Place Names.* Third ed. Salt Lake City: State Department of Public Instruction, 1941.

Vogt, Evon Z., and Albert, Ethel, eds. *People of Rimrock: A Study of Values in Five Cultures.* New York: Atheneum, 1970.

Vogt, Evon Z., and O'Dea, Thomas F. "A Comparative Study of the Role of Values in Social Action in Two Southwestern Communities," *Sociological Review,* December 1953, pp. 642-54.

Wagoner, Jay J. *Arizona Territory 1863-1912: A Political History.* Tucson: University of Arizona Press, 1970.

Warner, Matt, as told to Murray E. King. *The Last of the Bandit Riders.* New York: Bonanza Books, n.d.

Waters, L. L. *Steel Trails to Santa Fe.* Lawrence: University of Kansas, 1950.

Wayte, Harold C., Jr., "A History of Holbrook and the Little Colorado Country, 1541-1962." Unpublished Master's thesis, University of Arizona, 1962.

Weinberg, Albert K. *Manifest Destiny: A Study of Nationalist Expansionism in American History.* Baltimore: The Johns Hopkins Press, 1935.

Wentworth, Edward Norris. *America's Sheep Trails: History, Personalities.* Ames: Iowa State College Press, 1948.

Wharfield, H. B. *Cooley, Army Scout, Arizona Pioneer, Wayside Host, Apache Friend.* Privately published, 1968.

Wheat, Carl I. *1540-1861: Mapping the Transmississippi West;* I (1957) *The Spanish Entrada to the Lousiana Purchase, 1540-1804;* II (1958) *From Lewis and Clark to Frémont, 1804-1845;* III (1959) *From the Mexican War to the Boundary Surveys, 1846-1854;* IV (1960) *From the Pacific Railroad Surveys to the Onset of the Civil War, 1855-1860;* V (1963) *From the Civil War to the Geological Survey;* Vol. V in two parts. San Francisco: Institute of Historical Cartography, 1957-1963.

Wheeler, George M. *Report upon United States Geographical Surveys West of the One Hundredth Meridian . . . Geology.* Washington, D.C.: Government Printing Office, 1875.

————. *Report Upon United States Geographical Surveys West of the One Hundredth Meridian . . . vol. 1: Geographical Report . . .* Washington, D.C.: Government Printing Office, 1889.

Whipple, A. W. "Report of Explorations for a Railway Route, Near the 35th Parallel of North Latitude, From the Mississippi River to the Pacific Ocean." In *Reports of Exploration and Surveys to Ascertain the Most*

Practical and Economical Route for a Railroad from the Mississippi to the Pacific Ocean. Vol. 3, Washington, D.C.: Beverley Tucker, Printer, 1855.

Whipple, Maurine. "Arizona," *Collier's,* May 24, 1952, pp. 24, 64-66.

————. *The Giant Joshua.* Cambridge, Mass.: Houghton Mifflin, 1941.

Whitney, Orson F. *History of Utah.* 4 vols. Salt Lake City: Cannon and Sons Co., 1892-1904.

Widtsoe, John A. *Dry-Farming, A System of Agriculture for Countries Under a Low Rainfall.* New York: The Macmillan Company, 1911.

Williams, Eugene E. "The Territorial Governors of Arizona," *Arizona Historical Review,* vols. 6 and 7 (1935-36).

Williams, Mattie. "History of the Woman Suffrage in Arizona and the Nation," *Arizona Historical Review* 1 (January 1929): 69-73.

Wilson, Alice Kathleen. "History of the Arizona Strip to 1913." Unpublished Master's thesis, Arizona State Teacher's College, Flagstaff, 1941.

Woodbury, Angus M. *The History of Southern Utah and Its National Parks.* Salt Lake City: Utah State Historical Society, 1950.

Wyllys, Rufus Kay. *Arizona, The History of a Frontier State.* Phoenix: Hobson and Herr, 1950.

Index

Academy, Snowflake, 44, 265
Adamson and Burbage (Company), 144
Agrarianism, 154
Agriculture: evocative of virtue, 157;
  separatism served by, 156; small
  farms, 162; subsistence, 160;
  village pattern, 161, 163
Albuquerque, New Mexico, 130
Albuquerque Morning Journal, 235-36
Allen, Lewis, 230.
  See also Wilford Woodruff
Allen, William C., 17, 71, 100
Allen's Camp, Arizona, 17, 18, 20, 99.
  See also Joseph City and St. Joseph
Allen's Company, 181
Alpine, Arizona: Co-op, 139; described,
  35; home of Jacob Hamblin, 267;
  Indian raids, 209; settled, 35
Alton, Utah, 73
American Colonization Company, 1, 2,
  15. *See also* Boston party
Amity, Arizona, 35, 143.
  See also Eagar and Union
Amundsen, Andrew, 12, 76
Anderson, Lars, 56
Angell, Sanford, 174
Apache County, Arizona: county seat
  controversy, 219-22; created, 222;
  Mormons in, 218; political affairs,
  224; polygamy controversy, 231;
  two-party politics, 239-40
Apache Chief, 228-31
Apache Indians: appeasement of, 210;
  claim Forest Dale, 26, 27; hostilities
  in Arizona, 207; Mormon fear of,
  208; outbreak of 1881, 209-10; raid

Mormon ranches, 210-11; south of
  Mormons, 192. *See also* Indian tribes
Apache Review, 239
Arizona: Brigham Young sends
  colonists to, 10; colonization of and
  God's will, 8; colonization of
  initiated, 1; described, 8-9; explored
  by Elk Mountain Mission, 3;
  explored by Indian missionaries, 6;
  fever, 53; Utah approaches secured, 4
Arizona Cooperative Mercantile
  Institution (ACMI): banking
  functions, 146-48; barter trade,
  140-46; credit, 142-43; dividends, 152;
  financing of, 137, 149; freight
  contracting, 144-46; Holbrook, 138,
  144; organized, 136-37; photos, 139,
  141, 142; stock held by United
  Order, 118; wholesale and retail
  business, 136; Woodruff, 139;
  wool trade, 141
Arizona Exploring Company, 6, 7, 55, 56
Arizona Miner, 208
Arizona Mission: duration of, 60;
  exodus from, 58-59; of 1873, 9,
  12-14, 41; of 1876, 41; promotion of,
  51-52; tours of, 49, 55; volunteerism
  in, 51
Arizona, northern, 2, 3, 8, 16
Arizona Orders, 92-95.
  See also United Order
Arizona Pioneer, 228
Arizona Weekly Journal, 229
Atlantic and Pacific Railroad: *A. and P.
  v. Mingus,* 167; anticipated by
  Mormons, 168; Aztec Land and

organization of, 242-44; stabilized
labor, 131; Twelve Apostles of,
242-43. *See also* Mormons
Clawson, Hiram B., 237, 239
Cleveland, Grover, President, 234, 237
Clifton, Arizona, 220
Cluff, Alfred, 26
Cluff, Moses, 25
Cluff, Oscar, 26
Cluff's Arizona, 25, 208.
See also Show Low
Coleman, Evans: describes Alpine,
35; on attributes of Little Colorado,
15; on dam building, 188-89; on
housing, 259-60; on migration to
Arizona, 87; polygamy influenced
mission call, 47
Coleman family, 35, 259
Colorado River: and Mormon
expansion, 9; crossed by Jacob
Hamblin, 1858, 194; crossed by
the Arizona Exploring Company, 7;
Crossing of the Fathers, 201;
crossings below Grand Canyon, 70;
explored by George W. Brimhall, 42;
explored by Jacob Hamblin, 3;
John Wesley Powell's expedition,
11-12; Lee's Ferry crossing on, 46;
on route to Arizona, 73, 76-81;
recrossed by Mission of 1873, 14
Concho, Arizona, 34, 139, 163
Cooley, Croydon E.: efforts to pacify
Apaches, 208; Indian scout and
rancher, 24; settler at Show Low, 24;
visited by Daniel W. Jones, 210
Cooperation: difficulties of, 124;
preferred to United Orders, 96-98;
replaced United Orders, 123
Cowdery, Oliver, 200
Cozzen, Samuel W., 1, 2
Crookston, William, 27
Crosby, Joseph, 232, 235
Crossing of the Fathers, 201.
See also Colorado River

Dairy operation, 111
Dalton, Heber, 25
Dame, William H., 48, 49, 51
Dams: construction of, 178-79;
described, 18, 19, 178; diversion
dam at Snowflake, 178; Lyman Dam,
179, 186; on Little Colorado, 18, 19;
St. Joseph Dam, 191; Woodruff Dam,
185-91; Woodruff Dam, photo, 186;
Zion's Lake, 182
Day, Henry, 11

Dean, James, 187
"Defense fund," 146
Democratic Party, 238-39
Denver and Rio Grande Railroad,
124, 131
Deseret News: forts described, 20, 21;
missionary letters published, 64, 65,
66; on Arizona land, 163; promoted
Arizona migration, 52, 53
Detroit House of Correction, 232
Dillman, Peter, 150
Ditching, 180. *See also*
water development
Doctrine and Covenants, 52
Doremus, Abraham F., 130-31

Eagar, Arizona, 35, 139, 163.
See also Amity and Omer
Eastern Arizona Stake, subdivision of
church, 137, 243
Eastern Arizona Stake Presidency, 60,
97, 243
Echo Cliffs, Arizona, 14
Edmunds, George F., Senator, 231
Edmunds Act, 232
Education: at United Orders, 107;
friction in St. Johns, 226-27; prepared
Mormons to integrate, 160; role of
Karl G. Maeser in, 44; Stake
Academy erected, 265
Elk Mountain Mission, 2, 3, 201
Endowment House, 68
Escalante, Utah, 45
Everett, Elijah, 55
Expansion: a reason for Mormon
mobility, 266; caused friction, 218;
desired by George Q. Cannon, 9;
in Southern Utah, 4; Mormon
attitudes toward, 4, 8, 9; of the
church, 65; permanent, 158-59;
preemptive, 8; served United Orders,
92-93

Farish, Thomas E., 237
Fences, 101
First Presidency, 45, 59, 242
Fish, Adelaide, 252
Fish, Eliza, 252
Fish, Joseph: buyer for ACMI, 142;
describes conflict between Smith
brothers and William H. Dame, 48;
drafted constitution for ACMI, 137;
follower of Jesse N. Smith, 247-48;
member of land committee, 171;
on attitude toward authorities, 247;
on barter trade, 143-44; on financing

Take Up Your Mission

Mormon Colonizing Along the Little Colorado River 1870-1900

Charles S. Peterson

FORTIFIED with a strong sense of mission and a firm belief in a form of manifest destiny, guided by desert pioneering experience, a group of Mormons trekked from Salt Lake City in the spring of 1876 to begin colonizing along the Little Colorado River in Arizona.

The land along the river was originally chosen by the Latter-day Saints because it appeared to be of so little value that others would not want it. A record-conscious group, they set down in diaries and other personal accounts the hardships they endured — the long, isolated trip to the area, limited access to already muddy water, frequent outbreaks of typhoid, dugouts roofed with mud which collapsed during heavy rains, and constant fear of dislocation for illegal polygamy practices.

But underlying the colonists' awareness of their tribulations was an even greater dedication to working with the Indians in the area and to extending their organized expansion southward to Mexico and eventually to South America.

The colony components — towns, aspirations, and experiences, and, above all, its personalities — appear in the primary records cited with vivid strength: a cross-section of humanity, grained and

textured with man's feelings; a cross-section highlighted by soaring ideals, a sense of mission, and
the heroic.

CHARLES S. PETERSON, Associate Professor of History at Utah State University and Associate Editor
of the *Western Historical Quarterly,* writes from the
vantage point of a descendant of the Mormons who
participated in the migration to Arizona. His biographic sketch of a Mormon pioneer, "A Mighty
Man Was Brother Lot," won the Oscar O. Winther
Award as the best article published in the *Western
Historical Quarterly* in 1970. He is former director
of the Utah State Historical Society.

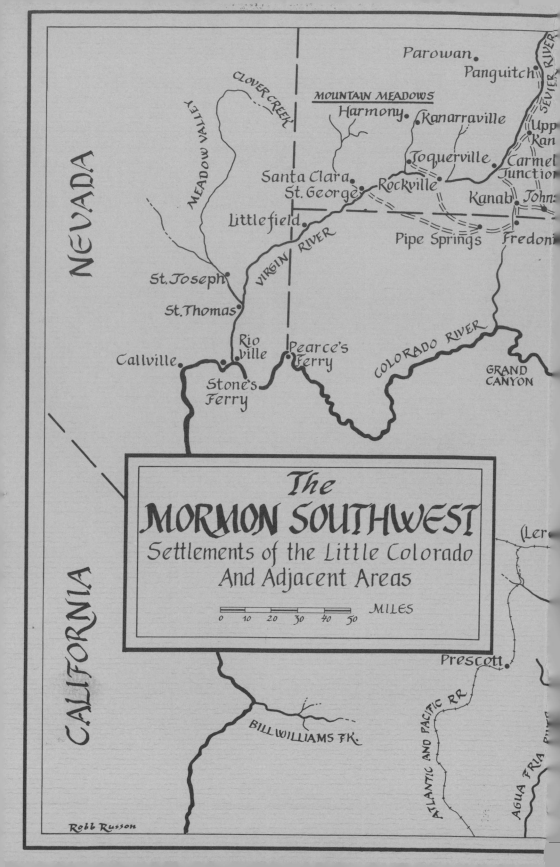